# INDIA'S FIRST DIPLOMAT

V.S. Srinivasa Sastri and the Making of Liberal Internationalism

Vineet Thakur

First published in Great Britain in 2023 by

Bristol University Press
University of Bristol
1-9 Old Park Hill
Bristol
BS2 8BB
UK
t: +44 (0)117 374 6645
e: bup-info@bristol.ac.uk

Details of international sales and distribution partners are available at bristoluniversitypress.co.uk

© Bristol University Press 2023

British Library Cataloguing in Publication Data
A catalogue record for this book is available from the British Library

ISBN 978-1-5292-1766-7 hardcover
ISBN 978-1-5292-1767-4 paperback
ISBN 978-1-5292-1768-1 ePub
ISBN 978-1-5292-1769-8 ePdf

The right of Vineet Thakur to be identified as author of this work has been asserted by him in accordance with the Copyright, Designs and Patents Act 1988.

All rights reserved: no part of this publication may be reproduced, stored in a retrieval system, or transmitted in any form or by any means, electronic, mechanical, photocopying, recording, or otherwise without the prior permission of Bristol University Press.

Every reasonable effort has been made to obtain permission to reproduce copyrighted material. If, however, anyone knows of an oversight, please contact the publisher.

The statements and opinions contained within this publication are solely those of the author and not of the University of Bristol or Bristol University Press. The University of Bristol and Bristol University Press disclaim responsibility for any injury to persons or property resulting from any material published in this publication.

Bristol University Press works to counter discrimination on grounds of gender, race, disability, age and sexuality.

Cover design: blu inc, Bristol
Front cover image: Alamy/Matteo Omied

Louise and Peter

For a life full of love

# Contents

| | | |
|---|---|---|
| List of Photographs | | vi |
| Acknowledgements | | vii |
| 1 | Introduction: The 'Native' Diplomat | 1 |
| 2 | Shirtless Srinivasan | 19 |
| 3 | A Worthy Successor to Gokhale | 37 |
| 4 | The Silver-Tongued Orator | 61 |
| 5 | The Most Picturesque Figure | 85 |
| 6 | A Rather Dangerous Ambassador | 105 |
| 7 | Like the Anger of Rudra | 123 |
| 8 | An Honourable Compromise | 153 |
| 9 | A Trustee of India's Honour | 175 |
| 10 | We Have No Sastri | 195 |
| 11 | Conclusion: An Amiable Usurper | 217 |
| Appendix A: The 1921 Imperial Conference Resolution | | 235 |
| Appendix B: The Cape Town Agreement of 1927 | | 237 |
| List of Archives | | 243 |
| List of Illustration Sources and Acknowledgements | | 245 |
| Notes | | 247 |
| Index | | 289 |

# List of Photographs

| | | |
|---|---|---|
| 1 | 'The Famous Brahmin Visitor': Sastri in the *Victoria Daily Times* | 1 |
| 2 | 'It ain't polite to interrupt' | 3 |
| 3 | 'His big brother' | 3 |
| 4 | Sastri and Bajpai in America | 86 |
| 5 | Sastri at the Conference on Limitation of Armaments, Washington | 96 |
| 6 | Sastri in Australia | 114 |
| 7 | 'Equal in rank but inferior in status' | 140 |
| 8 | The delegates to the Cape Town Conference in 1927 | 172 |
| 9 | Sastri with the Governor General, Lord Athlone | 186 |
| 10 | With the Education Committee | 190 |
| 11 | The Agency | 214 |
| 12 | The family | 218 |

# Acknowledgements

The Phoenix settlement near Durban – established in 1904 but reopened in 2004 after a tragic fire in the 1980s – is where Indians go to pay obeisance to arguably the most revered modern Indian, Mahatma Gandhi. A visitor to the city, however, is also introduced to another local monument, dedicated to an Indian of whose glory only South African Indians are aware. It is an educational institute called Sastri College, named after India's first Agent to South Africa, V.S. Srinivasa Sastri.

When I first visited Durban in 2014, I knew embarrassingly little about Sastri. I had just started working on a journal article on the 1921 Imperial Conference, where Sastri was India's representative, so his name was somewhat familiar. But this was my first encounter with the Indian leader who was probably one of the better-known Indians not only in his country but also in the wider world in the 1920s. I racked my brains over any reference to him in my whole north Indian educational life, but nothing stood out.

What intrigued me about Sastri was not that he wasn't remembered in India, which had been a fate of many in the independence struggle, but that he was memorialized in South Africa. Works by South African historians, in particular by the unfailingly generous Uma Dhupelia-Mesthrie, piqued and encouraged me to follow Sastri's life and work more closely. The project, I knew by now, would be more than a 10,000-word article.

I did not have the skills to write a full-scale biography. So I imagined this project as a series of episodic histories of Sastri's diplomatic work in the 1920s. As a diplomatic historian – or at least trying to be one – I felt more at ease with this format. A few years later, I made fledgling efforts at consolidating and presenting my thoughts on Sastri's work at our research seminar to colleagues in Leiden, where Lindsay Black, Anne-Isabelle Richard, Andy Gawthorpe and Noa Schonmann provided valuable feedback.

Karen Smith, Alanna O'Malley, Nicolas Blarel and Michiel Foulon have been bountiful with their time, intellectual support and warm friendships. How does one even begin to thank Beatrix Futák-Campbell, Maxine David and Simon David who have also thrown the keys to their own houses into this mix? André Gerrits and Isabelle Duyvesteyn have promptly responded to all my requests and queries, including letters of support often written at very short notice. Leiden has come to be my academic home, mostly for the convivial spirit and collegiality of these and other colleagues, several of whom remain unnamed here.

In addition, Akta Kaushal, Kalathmika Natarajan, Avinash Paliwal, Sasikumar Sundaram, Ole Birk Laursen and Ghulam Ali have all read parts of the book and their sharp eyes have saved me intellectual hara-kiri and accordingly several blushes. Fellow diplomatic historians Pallavi Raghavan, Khushi Singh Rahore, Medha, Amit Das Gupta, Sanchi Rai, Alexander Davis and Raphaëlle Khan have measurably enhanced my understanding of this period and its protagonists.

Visits to archives are often opportunities to feast on the magnanimity of friends. Aditya Balasubrahmanian and Cees Heere, brilliant young scholars themselves, have altruistically shared their own archival notes with me. Naresh B.K.'s house in Delhi is my second home, and Nikhil Gupta and Virender Rathore are school friends who never tire of offering me their help and love. I can't think of two people more selfless and giving than Prashant Kumar and Khurshid Mir. Shefali Rawat has been my best friend for as long as I can remember and also a welcoming host in Bangalore. Arani Basu and Amrita Datta have their hearts and homes open for me whether in Chennai or in Berlin. Amya Agarwal's care and unfailing support in Delhi and Duisburg has been a blessing. Ian Patel and I have walked and run together several hours in Goa, London and the Hague and discussed endlessly our respective work, ideas, writing, disappointments and joys. These friendships are life-nurturing.

I was a fellow at the Netherlands Institute for Advanced Study (NIAS) between September 2019 and January 2020. These were easily the most productive months for the book, but also very enriching for my own intellectual growth. Jan Willem Duyvendak and Fenneke Wekker are both inspirational academics, and their humanity and care for the institute and its residents shines through in everything they do. At NIAS, one also has the bliss of experiencing a most wonderful and supportive administrative staff. Furthermore, in the company of an extremely versatile, warm and indulgent cohort of fellows – who obviously can't all be named – my every moment was cherished. But if I could just name three: Susanne Klausen is a star; her comments on my draft as well as on life in general have made both far richer. James Mark and Mirjam Künkler read through and provided very pointed and rich feedback on my proposal and the introduction.

The second big chunk of writing happened at the University of Cambridge, where I arrived as the Smuts Visiting Fellow in February 2020. I am grateful to the Smuts Management Committee, in particular Saul Dubow – whose work has long been an inspiration – and Lucy Gager for making this happen. Barbara Roe and Kevin Greenbank at the Centre for South Asian Studies were warm, welcoming and helpful. Delightful and often reassuring conversations with Harshan Kumarasingham, whose visiting fellowship briefly coincided with mine, provided the much-needed motivation. Paola Velasco Herrejón and Alex Guizar took it upon themselves to provide me with a support system in Cambridge just as the pandemic hit.

In addition to the Smuts Foundation, the archival work for this book was supported by generous funding from the Leiden University Fund (LUF) and Gratama Foundation as well as from Leiden's Institute for History. Stephen Wenham at Bristol University Press has been patient and encouraging at various stages of this project. Stephen and three anonymous reviewers have guarded me from my own biases, helping with producing a book leaner by 30,000 words from the first draft. It took no time for my grudging acceptance to turn into a fawning admiration for their perspectives and comments. Meticulous copy-editing work by Joan Dale Lace has made this a far more readable book. Dilip Menon's erudition has kept me both in awe and inspired to push through a project that he supported right from its inception. All historical work stands on the capable shoulders, thorough minds and – with digitization – nimble fingers of librarians and archivists around the globe. I am particularly indebted to those spread across libraries and archives in South Africa, India, the United Kingdom, Canada and Australia whose work has allowed me to tell this story of Sastri's life.

An email exchange with Sastri's great-great-granddaughter Ragini Tharoor Srinivasan, an accomplished academic herself, reaped rich rewards. Not only did Ragini send me some invaluable pictures, but she also put me in touch with Sastri's extended family. Alamelu Padmanabhan, who is Sastri's granddaughter, Rajeshwari Viajayan and Krishnamurthy Vijayan were exceedingly kind in granting me access to the material in their possession. And so was Nirode Bramdaw, whose father Dhanee Bramdaw had coedited a book on Sastri's speeches in South Africa.

In mid-September 2020 I was offered a contract for this book. That very day, my father, Kabir Thakur, passed away back in India. Last summer as I spent over a month at my home in the hills near Shimla, he would come in during the day and we would chat about my work, of which he knew little. He regretted that he couldn't read what I write. Partly because the difficult academic prose made it boring, but also because it had no relation to his lifeworld. I imagine he would be happy about the book coming out, but the book he wanted me to write would be a political history of our own people, the people in the hills.

While he slowly slid his way towards a certain death, my sister Geetanjali and brother-in-law Paviter never let my pandemic-forced absence matter. As he struggled with a debilitating illness in the last few months, both of them with my mother, Usha, and my uncle Surender nursed him, spending nights on cold hospital floors. But superhumanly, they all also made it a point to constantly give me strength and assurance as I sat far away in Europe.

Mel has heard me talk about Sastri endlessly for a few years now. From Johannesburg, she read and edited the first draft and even made two day-trips to Pretoria with the extremely kind Mihlali Ngxobongwana to help with last bits of archival research. Mel's love, companionship and cheerfulness make academic life, despite the physical distance of continents between us, bearable.

Finally, the book is dedicated to two amazingly benevolent people, Louise Vale and Peter Vale. Married for more than three decades, they give Mel and me inspiration for a life full of love and hope. Louise's own career in the media industry puts her husband's illustrious academic career to shame, for which the latter can only compensate with his cutting wit. It is also generally accepted that she gives him better manners and a kinder heart. Prof. Vale, as I call him, is my 4am friend, my philosopher-in-chief and 24/7 life guide. Alas, he is also an incredibly hard mentor to impress. Since all else has failed, I end with a hope of bribing him with a dedication, meant mostly for Louise, so as to elicit from him the golden words: 'a decent second draft!'

More seriously, this is for Louise and Peter.

# 1

# Introduction: The 'Native' Diplomat

## I

On 12 August 1922, the readers of *The Victoria Daily Times* in Canada awoke to a stolid Indian face on the paper's front page. A sharply dressed man with a receding crop of white hair, a tie knotted around the neck and upper body clad in a coat stared at them with earnest and disarming eyes. Valangaiman Sankaranarayana Srinivasa Sastri, the man in the picture, was 'one of the most interesting and important personages to reach these shores for some time past'. This 'distinguished visitor' had arrived in Canada to plead for the rights of racial equality for Indians. The Canadian Prime Minister had sent his Deputy Foreign Minister, Joseph Pope, who had travelled over four days from Ottawa to receive Sastri in Victoria. Sastri's face radiated the 'magnetism of his eyes' and the 'supreme sincerity' of his intentions, the anonymous correspondent writing for the *Daily Times* gushed.[1]

'Sastri is a Brahmin', who were 'the intellectual leaders of India', the paper emphasized. His caste status was 'the complete answer' to those who questioned his credentials. Added to this, 'his eloquent singleness of mind' made him a 'rare jewel' in a setting

1: 'The Famous Brahmin Visitor': Sastri in the *Victoria Daily Times*

'corroded and discoloured by the baser elements'. Rather than opposing the 'colourless' British, Sastri's preferred term for the whites, his whole life had been dedicated to the upliftment of the 'coloured of India, the poor lethargic untouchable caste'. This made him different from the 'fanatical types' like Gandhi and his associates, whose motivations were ostensibly driven by the hatred of the empire and the white man. Moderate in both temperament and political views, Sastri was 'an exact type to whom the British government thinks India must look for its ultimate liberty'. Indeed, his 'personal accomplishments, provide[d] ... an assurance that there is potential material upon which to build India's case for autonomy'.[2]

Half the country away on the same morning, the *Manitoba Free Press* subscribers in Winnipeg faced a decidedly less assuring visual. Two cartoons appeared under the heading: 'The Turkish Question'. The first cartoon, drawn by the Virginia cartoonist Charles Henry Sykes originally for a Philadelphia newspaper, shows a cigar-smoking, fez-wearing figure whose head and torso jut through a half-open door of, seemingly, an outhouse, presumably in the western world. Wearing a smirk and wielding a scimitar that looks almost alive, as if pulsating with blood, the Turk, mildly irritated at being interrupted in the middle of his defecatory purge, utters in confident Americanese: 'It ain't polite to interrupt'.[3]

The accompanying opinion piece, also an import, this time from *The New York Times*, cast more light on the cartoon. It reported the ghastly mass-killing of Greek and Armenian Christians by Mustapha Kemal's Turkish troops in the ongoing Greco-Turkish War. A horrified observer wrote that although young Christian children had been spared the cull and allowed to escape to the American-financed orphanages, on reaching the age of 12, the boys were forcibly taken away, Islamized and recruited into the Turkish army. The girls were allegedly dispatched to harems. This war had turned into a hideous splurge of racial and religious persecution, but its savagery was set against an even larger canvas. A 'war of civilizations', a war between a 'member of the European family' and a 'central Asian nomad', 'a war of progress against stagnation' was upon the West, concluded the writer.

If the first cartoon worked up a bombast of brazen racism, the second layered itself in allegorical subtleties. Slotted right under the first, this cartoon was by a different artist (borrowed from yet another American paper, *The Los Angeles Times*). The Turk here carries none of the devilish ferocity of the first cartoon. He appears as a scheming gnome, who instead of a cigar between his lips, is mockingly sticking out his tongue to those behind him. A nonchalant swagger in his step is

2: 'It ain't polite to interrupt'

3: 'His big brother'

palpable, as he holds tightly to the trouser-fold of a colossal figure next to him. This giant, captioned 'His Big Brother', wears a turban, a thick beard and a handlebar moustache that swerves upwards as confidently as the man himself. Both his hands are slipped inside his pockets; a large sabre is neatly tucked in his waistband. His eyes are piercing and squinted, suspiciously aware of a group of characters tailing the Turk. Great Britain leads this pack of caricatures, followed closely by France, Greece, Italy – all the interested parties in the Greco-Turkish War. In the first cartoon the Turk warns the Europeans about interrupting; in the second he is showing off his support as Europeans rally together; '300,000,000 Moslems' blares out in large print from the giant's chest.

But who is this giant? The specific style of the turban, the facial hair, the sabre at his waist – reminiscent of the *kirpan*[4] – are unabashedly Sikh, not Muslim, characteristics. The cartoonist, Edmund Waller Gale, had a reputation for drawing ethnic caricatures. In this instance, was he amateurish or deliberate in drawing a Sikh instead of a Muslim? And why '300,000,000 Muslims'? There is no census data for the 1910s or 1920s which gives an estimated figure of 300,000,000 as the global Muslim population.

Why had the *Manitoba Free Press* reprinted the two cartoons, vertically next to each other, several months after their appearance in two different American newspapers?[5] A cryptic, seemingly unrelated, penultimate sentence in the opinion piece is all we get in the form of an explanation: 'Mr. Gandhi in India has definitely turned aside from western culture, judging it had.'[6]

## II

Let us attempt to piece together a plausible explanation.

In 1920, a pan-Islamist movement called Khilafat was started in India by Oxford-educated Mohammad Ali and his brother, Shaukat Ali. Khilafat's purpose was to protest the British policy of the dismemberment of the Ottoman Empire. The Mahatma Gandhi-led Indian National Congress joined forces with Khilafat to turn this agitation into a pan-India non-cooperation movement against British rule. The tremors were also felt along India's frontiers, as the newly Bolshevik government in Russia cosied up to the ruler of Afghanistan. Mohammad Ali announced that if the Amir of Afghanistan were to attack India to free the country of its infidel masters, all Muslims in the country would fight alongside the Amir.[7]

Seeing the united forces of civil resistance in India against Britain's Turkish policy as well as the trouble brewing on the frontiers, Lord Reading, the British Viceroy to India, sent London urgent pleas.[8] In a letter, he requested altering the Treaty of Sevres to reaffirm the Caliph's suzerainty over the Holy Places, and restoring Ottoman Thrace and Smyrna. The Indian government, this former Chief Justice-turned-Viceroy wrote, must 'range itself openly on the side of Moslem India'.[9]

The letter was received by the Secretary of State for India, Edwin Montagu. A radical liberal with a sharp tongue often used masterfully in support of India's concerns, Montagu's views on a range of issues including racial discrimination had already made him unpopular with his Cabinet colleagues. He published Reading's dispatch without consulting either the Cabinet or the Prime Minister. The actions of Reading and Montagu – the second and third Jew, respectively, to ever serve in the British Cabinet – raised a storm of protest from the Tory die-hards and anti-Semitic politicians. Particularly riled was Foreign Secretary Lord Curzon, himself a former Viceroy of India. Curzon wrote Montagu a stinging epistle asking if the Indian government had become 'the final court of Moslem appeal', not just in Thrace and Smyrna, but also in Egypt, Sudan, Palestine, Arabia, Malay Peninsula and any other part of the Muslim world.[10] Montagu was forced to resign.

Incidentally, the second cartoon was first published just two weeks after Montagu's resignation in March 1922; in Canada, it was published five months later on the day of Sastri's arrival to appeal for the rights of Indians. What if – the facts are certainly more suggestive than conclusive – the number 300,000,000 does indeed refer to Indians, as a whole, rather than Muslims only? After all it was India, with its 300,000,000 people (the number generally used to denote the country's population at the time), which had stomped along at Turkey's side. And in that act all Indians were now one with Muslims, or, metaphorically, had become Muslims.

Why does a Sikh represent the Indian? Shipped around the world as soldiers of the empire, the Sikhs were deemed a 'martial race' in the imperial scheme of things. Unlike other dominions, where Indian settlers were considered largely docile, in Canada (and the United States' West Coast), the activities of Indian revolutionaries (the *Ghadar* Party, particularly) and the *Komagata Maru* incident of 1914 had created a radical image of Sikhs.[11] In any case, Sikhs were the predominant Indian community along the Pacific Northwest (although, to complicate matters further, in Canada they were referred to as 'Hindu/East Indian').[12]

Our early detour sums up to this: the Big Brother is a palimpsest, Sikh, Muslim and Indian at the same time, inscribed over each other. With all its deliberate ambiguity, the giant in the second cartoon is the doubly ungrateful Indian. Not only is he an outsider to the geo-body of 'White Canada' and its western culture, but he is also a potent danger to the empire itself. In standing with the barbarian Turk, indeed even providing him safety against the forces of civilization,[13] the Indian was turning away from civilization ('judging it had'); a vicious betrayal, both material and moral, of the British Empire and its civilizing mission.

These two different stories playing out about India in Canada on 12 August 1922 – one in Victoria, another in Winnipeg – are sharply contrasting in their message. Two Indias stalk the empire: a civilizing India and a de-civilizing India, Sastri's India and Gandhi's India. Undeniably, both position India at the cusp of something spectacular. Indians had finally arrived at the gates of civilization, but only the unfolding currents of passing time would reveal whether they came as barbarians eager to raid the citadel, or as pliant pupils ready to take their place in the civilized world.

## III

V.S. Srinivasa Sastri, the protagonist of our story, navigates these contrasts as a diplomat, and this book chronicles and analyses a decade of his life between 1919 and 1929. A leading member of the Indian National Liberal Federation, for much of this period he was also India's most authoritative voice abroad. He played a crucial role in the drafting of the 1919 political reforms, collaborating closely with

Edwin Montagu in his first visit to London. In his second visit two years later, he was India's representative to the Imperial Conference. At this conference, he scripted a historic diplomatic victory on a resolution about racial equality for Indians in the empire. From London, Sastri travelled to Geneva in September 1921 to represent his country at the second session of the League of Nations Assembly. Here, along with the Haitian diplomat Louis-Dantès Bellegarde, he was hailed as the speaker to have made the deepest impression.[14] His voice became 'the very voice of international conscience'.[15]

His performances encouraged the British government to send him to the Washington Conference on Naval and Far Eastern Questions as India's chief representative, where he signed the eventual treaty on the country's behalf. Soon after the conference, in 1922, he sailed to Australia, New Zealand and Canada as part of a public diplomacy effort to appeal for the equality of Indians. In 1923, he led a delegation of Indians on the Kenya question in London. As part of an Indian delegation to South Africa in 1926–27, he was instrumental in the signing of the Cape Town Agreement, the first bilateral agreement within the British Empire without Britain's involvement. Soon thereafter, on Gandhi's request, he agreed to become India's first Agent to South Africa, where he remains, after Gandhi, perhaps the most remembered Indian to travel to that country.

By the end of the 1920s, taking stock of the period since the First World War, an article in the widely respected journal *India Review* argued that Sastri's emergence as India's leading voice ought to be seen in conjunction with the rise of the 'scholar-statesman in modern public life'. The war was thrust upon the world by short-sighted politicians. It was left to the 'scholar-statesman', with 'his high character, his liberal culture, and persuasive force and humane sympathies', to lead the world back to peace. Woodrow Wilson in America, Tomas Garrigue Masaryk in Bohemia, Herbert A.L. Fisher and Arthur Balfour in England, Gustav Stresemann in Germany, Aristide Briand in France, Benedetto Croce in Italy, among others, had furnished 'a lofty direction and a beneficial purpose' to public life. No wonder the scholar was 'raised to exalted positions of power and prestige'. Sastri, with his 'profound knowledge of men and things, a wide experience of public life, a remarkable intellectuality and moral eminence, a rare gift of speech, and above all, a high character, and an inspiring personal example' belonged to the same group of scholar-politicians. He had emerged as one of the most distinguished scholar-statesmen in the world, the author argued.[16]

But history is often forgetful. In the historical rear-view window, some footprints appear larger, others insignificant and most are invisible (a philosopher may remark that all history is a misremembered, brutalized past). Sastri's 150th birth anniversary passed virtually unnoticed on 22 September 2019, just ten days before the Mahatma's. A community hall, named 'Srinivasa Sastri Hall', atop the Ranade Library in Mylapore, Chennai, and the administrative building of the Annamalai University, called 'Sastri Hall', are the only monuments to his legacy.[17] In contrast, South African Indians remember their first Agent more fondly with a famous secondary school named 'Sastri College' in the city of Durban.

## IV

Diplomacy, to paraphrase the French historian-philosopher Michel Foucault, is the negation of the diplomat. A diplomat's skill is vested in the ability to turn first-person singulars into 'small we's' (that is, foreign ministry) and coalesce them into 'large We's' (that is, the government and, thus, the country). So, the small voice of the diplomat is never their voice, it is the voice of their respective government. In a rapidly changing world, the rituals, routines and writings of diplomats, as the Norwegian ethnographer of diplomacy Iver Neumann shows, are choreographed to ensure uniformity and predictability.[18] A successful diplomat's laurels rest on making the first-person singular indistinguishable from their government/country.[19]

The 'native diplomat' in the colonial setting is, perhaps, the exception to this categorization. The native diplomat, like Sastri, is chosen because they are an ode to colonialism, a living tribute to the success of the civilizing mission. The apogee of the civilizing mission cannot be to merely turn the colonized into a sloppily assembled derivative of the colonizer. To be sure, the typical 'mimic-men' make good native bureaucrats. And the colonial order produces an army of them. But colonialism has a higher purpose. It is in producing native leaders, who are manifestly original but sufficiently compliant, that colonialism elevates itself into a moral mission. Nothing shines like a colonial savant who can think on their own and yet chooses the colonial order. Shaping the native into an ideal product of the intermixture of colonial–colonized cultural interface, blending their exotic charm with a hospitable cheeriness, is where colonialism finds its *raison d'être*. The bargain is inevitably hard to strike. Original leaders often cannot remain compliant for long.

Contrastingly, the civilizing mission is also a self-negating idea. The more you civilize, the less the need for the mission itself. Ergo, colonialism's *raison d'être* can, and must, always remain a promise – the eternal promised land, with only a limited few having found access to it. The exceptional few (exceptional to their own people, that is) are the ones who are ready to be paraded globally. They represent the people to the world and, in turn, they also end up legitimizing in some manner the colonial state itself.

For the native diplomat, therefore, diplomacy is not limited to representing interests, but also includes navigating the thin wedge between assertive exceptionalism and disempowering fetishization. As that native diplomat, Sastri had to find his agency while being empowered as well as caged by this image of being someone who marries oriental sagacity with western forbearance.[20] How he manoeuvred this space is the main theme that will run through the course of this book.

Aside from the native diplomat being the representative of a civilization, mediated and modulated by the colonizer, in the Indian case this figure is also imbued with a civilizing mission of their own. Indians abroad, stamped with the odium of being 'coolies', are a perpetual reminder of India's inferior status.[21] Their ill-treatment, as Kalathmika Natarajan's work shows, troubles Indian diplomacy because it accords India a status of a 'coolie' nation, a decidedly *shudra*[22] function in the Indian social–global imaginary.[23] The figure of Sastri – English-speaking, upper caste, scholarly – performs diplomacy as a 'cultured Brahmin', as one who upends the image of India abroad. In fact, what remains of the public memory of Sastri even today is mostly reduced to the epithet of 'the silver tongued orator', which is quite indicative of the tremendous hold of the civilizing narrative accompanying the English language. But in his mission he also speaks to these Indians abroad as a *petit* civilizer, whose attempt is to 'uplift' coolie Indians to the standards of civilization, a process akin to what the Indian sociologist M.N Srinivas calls 'sanskritization'.[24]

So this exceptionalism, like all others, is Janus-faced. On the one hand, their exceptionality allows the native diplomat to punch above the supposed weight of their people and be attentively listened to in the councils of the world. On the other hand, the exceptionalism of the native diplomat also highlights the ordinariness of their countryfolk. The native diplomat is seen more as a standalone individual, 'civilized and cultured', who was 'but all a brilliant exception … [who] must not be taken as a sample of that bulk'.[25]

Sastri's diplomatic endeavours were channelled towards easing racial barriers for Indians across the British Empire. The white settler dominions often suspended their own racial barriers for him on account of his being a 'diplomat' and a Privy Councillor. And when they did, they could easily make the argument that such barriers were never racial, but cultural and economic; in these spaces, individuals like Sastri, from high culture and caste, were always welcome.[26] In a curious way, Sastri's own personality ended up sabotaging his mission and agenda. He argued, often forcefully, that racial barriers were against the spirit of the British Empire. To which his hosts could often use the hospitality shown to him as proof of the non-racial character of such barriers.

Sastri's own approach to diplomacy was shaped by his liberal politics practised in a colonial setting. Liberalism, he reasoned, was not a philosophy of ideal positions. Instead, he saw it as a practice of constant negotiations. The latter did not necessarily imply an abandonment of principles – as we will see, he seldom compromised on these – but finding new ways to articulate ideas which needed constant updating from realities. Instead of committing to an absolute principle, a liberal required complete commitment to the principle's fulfilment in practice. A great difference lay between the two, he was often to emphasize.[27] And thus liberals and diplomats shared the conviction that progress proceeded not through a devotion to the best argument, but a laboured pursuance of the last argument. In diplomacy, as in politics, one had to be satisfied with the second best. A sympathetic writer described his approach thus:

> [Sastri] sets his face steadily against movements for political paralysis, or political revolution, social revivalism or social reaction, against quietism and asceticism in morals, against economic reversion to the garden of Eden type, against obscurantism in thought and all violent excess. He comes very near the definition of a complete personality – a personality in which intellect seizes and holds the truth, love realises it in human relations, and will rest content with nothing less than incarnating the truth in a deed.[28]

## V

All biographies are attempts to retrieve individuals from the clutches of grand narratives; acts of rescuing their voice from the monotony of the myriad. While a historian obsesses over context in the pursuit of a broader narrative, a biographer fetishizes the individual. This book places itself somewhere in the middle between history and biography. It narrates the life of an individual, but its aim is to amplify the context. The personal in this case is, fundamentally, the contextual. Sastri's life, or at least the specific decade this book is interested in, is a conduit through which the story of India's diplomacy and approach to liberal internationalism in the 1920s must be told. Let's turn to these two themes, and set up the rationale for this book before we move to Sastri's life and work from the next chapter.

Liberal internationalism has a chequered history.[29] The specifics of liberal internationalism are hard to pin down; mostly it is a wide tent, but generally understood it implies that the conditions of international peace could be preserved through the spread of liberal democracy and international institutions. However, critical scholarship has convincingly demolished the liberal pretence of this peace, and shown how liberal peace has oftentimes been, and continues to be, 'imperialism by other means'.[30] Its 'birth' is often credited to Woodrow Wilson, who was manifestly duplicitous about his own liberalism. While Wilson dangled self-determination as a promise, he limited its application to East European nations, and actively excluded non-white nations. Although the struggles of several colonial nations were certainly invigorated by the promise of 'Wilsonianism', and even the Indian National Congress included the term 'self-determination' in a 1918 resolution, their disillusionment with his vision was equally swift (some looked towards perhaps the even more emancipatory ideal of the time, Leninism).[31]

In any case, 'self-determination' and 'internationalism', two central ideas at the core of Wilson's liberal internationalism, pulled apart in opposite directions. The former entailed the fragmentation of larger empires at the time, while the latter envisaged developing institutional superstructures and larger federations out of pre-existing states. Self-determination pushed for more sovereignty, internationalism for reducing it. Terms such as self-determination, responsible government, trusteeship, segregation, mandates, the Commonwealth, the League (of Nations/against Imperialism), closer union, federations, dyarchy, internationalism and world federation (and possibly others), which gained political salience in the period between the two world wars, reflected the myriad and often contradictory ways in which the spirit of freedom and the spirit of colonialism entwined in the early decades of liberal internationalism.

The 1920s, as Daniel Gorman argues, was also a decade of vibrant internationalism from below. A rich stream of supra-, sub- and non-state actors,[32] including networks of people, organizations and ideologies, generated a widely diffused sensibility of belonging to the international. The early years of the League of Nations were filled with enthusiasm for greater cooperation and a hectic political and bureaucratic agenda.[33] Outside of the League, the Washington Naval

Conference of 1921–22 was a spectacular success. Three contemporary great powers – the United States, Japan and Britain – had, for the first time, come to an agreement on arms control. The Kellogg–Briand Pact of 1928, which outlawed war, was a result of years of fine-grained legal work and commitment towards peace. It was widely hailed as a significant achievement then, even if retrospective assessments are likely to regard it a naiveté.[34] Even as the world economy slithered towards recession, the political fortunes of international peace never seemed more salubrious than in the early-to-mid 1920s.

However, the always prescient W.E.B. Du Bois noted a contradictory tendency. He saw the further hardening of the colour line; the world was being increasingly divided into worlds of colour.[35] Instead of the widening expanse of freedom and peace, Du Bois saw the enactment of racial barriers which eviscerated any gains that might have accrued from liberal internationalism. Pronouncements of the next war being a 'race war' were not uncommon in the 1920s. Madison Grant, a wealthy New York lawyer and eugenicist, warned of this in his widely influential bestseller *The Passing of the Great Race* that the First World War was actually a 'civil war' among whites. To prevent against committing racial suicide, the white races needed to come together through transnational forms of unity. A young Adolf Hitler wrote to Grant from Germany to tell him that this book was his 'bible'.[36]

The white settler dominions in the British Empire had used the war to raise further their walls of official prejudice and introduced emergency measures targeting Asians, several of which were made permanent soon after.[37] The battle lines were drawn, literally, as shown in one of the chapters, between the whites and the Indians in Kenya on the racial question. Lothrop Stoddard noted in his widely popular racist tract *The Rising Tide of Colour*: 'nothing was more striking than the instinctive and instantaneous solidarity which binds together Australians and Afrikanders [sic], Californians and Canadians, into a "sacred Union" at the mere whisper of Asiatic immigration'.[38] White transnational networks had galvanized to make the 'colour line' an enduring feature of the new international order.

Up until the war, Britain would have opposed any explicitly racial measures and immigration laws, insisting instead on seemingly non-racial criteria, such as 'education tests' or 'Gentlemen's Agreements', which to a large extent achieved the same effect of keeping Asians out of the dominions. But now Britain was considerably reliant on the dominions for military support to protect its vast and spread-out empire. The Pacific dominions, with the United States serving both a model of segregation as well as a potential military protector, dangled the prospect of siding with the United States. In Africa, new white settler colonies, like Kenya, looked towards South Africa for support on racial laws. Post-war, the imperial balance of power measurably shifted in favour of the white dominions, which increasingly dictated imperial policies on racial questions. Their immigration policies specifically made race a criterion of exclusion. In 1923, the British parliament sanctioned, for the first time, racial discrimination against Indians in Kenya.

However, in succumbing to the dominions, Britain could also not disregard the discontent these policies generated in an increasingly restive India, the jewel of imperial crown. So, as Britain abdicated its responsibility towards its Indian subjects, it simultaneously offered India more autonomy in dealing with such questions by placing the onus for negotiating the rights of Indians on the Indian government, its bureaucrats and diplomats. Paradoxically, therefore, the more the dominions became autonomous and restrictive in their immigration policies, the more the Indian government was tasked with calibrating its relations with the dominions on a bilateral basis. India's agency as a *dominion-like* colony, a vicarious form of sovereignty, was asserted in the context of the fateful circumstance of the increasingly racialized nature of sovereignty in the British Empire.

This paradox awards us an opportunity to look at the histories of liberal internationalism in a new light. Despite the rich, diverse and newly available critical histories on the period, we do not yet have many narratives that centre non-western actors as co-creators, or protagonists in their own right, in advancing and reforming the liberal international project. The typical non-western actor in these histories is absent, or petitioning (usually being spoken on behalf of by western interlocutors), or staunchly resistant to the liberal international order.

V.S. Srinivasa Sastri, as India's premier diplomat in this period, this book argues, navigates this world with dexterity, nuance and purpose. In doing so, he helps shape the contours of a more 'liberal' international order. He is a protagonist in his own right who shaped the liberal internationalism of the era, and cannot be reduced to being an appendage or an epigram to Wilson's grand scheme.[39] Indeed, as we will notice throughout the book, it is in the slippages between abstract ideas and practical politics, and through the crafty negotiation of such fractured entanglements by people like Sastri, that liberal internationalism is shaped into a viable project. Reducing the struggle for equality of non-western peoples, and liberalism in general, to specific moments (the Wilsonian Moment) or abandoning them entirely into the realms of ideas is often divorced from the long history of such rights being fought for, through and through. The ideas of equality and self-determination were not abstract ideals handed down from an American president to the anticipant non-western publics, they were fought for at multiple sites by many protagonists; and what this book aims to show is that diplomacy was one such site, and Sastri one such protagonist.

## VI

A good start to saying something about Indian diplomacy in the 1920s would be to acknowledge that there *was* Indian diplomacy *before* independence. The claim appears simplistic but is counterintuitive for students of Indian foreign policy. The literature on pre-independence diplomatic history is so scanty that it needs iteration. India's 'anomalous status' in the inter-war years, as a country represented but not necessarily with a voice of its own, a colonized country with an international representation, a dominion-like colony, certainly limits what all Indian diplomats could achieve. But at the same time, it also delivered narratives of triumphs, manoeuvres and capitulations achieved under enormous constraints that remain either undocumented or undervalued.[40]

There are other important reasons why we must investigate this period of Indian diplomacy more closely. First, as every historian knows, the un-layering of colonial interactions can seldom proceed via binaries. Indian diplomacy in the 1920s, as the book hopes to show, has no outright (British) villains and virtuous (Indian) heroes. They all serve as actors often working together to serve the needs of Indians abroad. British secretaries of state such as Montagu and Peel; viceroys such as Chelmsford, Reading and Irwin; officials, both British and Indian, such as Geoffrey Corbett, Girija Shankar Bajpai and Muhammad Habibullah; liberal leaders such as Tej Bahadur Sapru and Sastri; Congress stalwarts such as Gandhi and his supporters, as among them Charles Andrews and Henry S.L. Polak; and even the princely states, are all arranged on one side, albeit with various degrees of commitment and motivations. Indeed, liberals play a crucial role in bridging the gaps between the officials and the nationalists.

Second, Indian historiography has been generally unkind to liberals. The liberals post-Gokhale have progressively disappeared from the presentist narrative of post-independence history. Liberals are not easily accepted as important actors in their own right, by both the leftist and the nationalist traditions of historical writing. They are often dismissed as Britain's 'advertising agents',[41] and 'a body of sycophants and self-seekers' who had no role in India's independence movement.[42] Their contributions to constitutional politics, from which India has gained immensely in the past 70 years, is wholly underappreciated. Likewise in foreign policy and diplomacy, especially concerning the rights of Indians abroad, their role is deserving of several tomes.

In the early 1920s, as Gandhi dominated the streets and the Congress-aligned Swaraj Party swept the assemblies, the liberals increasingly became marginalized voices in India's internal politics. But, correspondingly, they became the foremost champions of the rights of Indians in the empire. Contrary to the perception, Gandhi's Congress was little interested in discussing issues of overseas Indians in these years, choosing to focus its energies on the widespread ferment within the country. Benarasidas Chaturvedi, Gandhi's disciple and a fervent campaigner for the rights of Indians abroad, had repeatedly failed to get Congress interested in the plight of overseas Indians.[43] In comparison, the Liberal Party discussed such issues with so much fervour that it was about to split in 1923 on the issue of Kenyan Indians. This, as an observer noted caustically, also reflected how divorced the liberals had become from India's domestic politics.

Third, there is the glaring absence of the issue of caste from discussions about Indian diplomacy. Despite the fact that caste is woven intimately into the fabric of the Indian society (not just for Hindus), making any social analysis without it superfluous, studies on Indian diplomacy and diplomats have rarely ventured into asking: what role does caste play in Indian diplomacy?

In fact, independent India and its diplomats have been acutely sensitive to any linkages between caste and race.[44] The story, however, plays out somewhat differently in pre-independence India.

As a Tamil Brahmin, Sastri was more than aware of the social mobility that his caste status allowed him, even internationally. His sagely disposition and enviable mastery of the word, both verbal and written, could easily be reduced to his caste, and often was, by his audiences. Our opening vignette is a case in point. His caste was personified in his virtues, facilitating his access, legitimacy and authority in white spaces. This allowed for a trans-racial empathy, analogous to the 'honorary white' status that the Japanese enjoyed in apartheid South Africa. In turn he used this in-group access to fracture understandings of racial purity. When speaking to his white audiences, he would empathize with the 'race' purity argument, comparing it with Brahmanical purity, but then go on to make a distinction between biological purity and the deprivation of social, political and economic rights. In its benign form, the former implied self-exclusion which was understandable, if not commendable, he would argue. The latter, however, was oppressive and discriminatory towards others, something from which India had suffered for centuries.[45] The lesson that the world, especially the white world, needed to take from India was that caste/race prejudice stifled the growth of societies and nations, and no nation must tread the path of India. Caste is an ever-present reality in Sastri's diplomacy, in his person, personality and polemic.

Fourth, a detailed investigation into this period allows us to think more deeply about what it means to have an international status as a colonized country. Spelling this out: What does it mean when a colonial subject, without full citizenship rights at home, is asked to represent their country to an international audience in order to appeal for equal rights of their compatriots?

The native diplomat is a transversal being; a 'subject' who becomes, momentarily, a 'citizen' of the world. International diplomacy affords a semblance of equality that a colonial subject does not possess at home. India's signatures on the Washington Four Powers' Treaty are in Sastri's name. He has signed for all of India on perhaps one of the most crucial treaties of the inter-war era, and yet within his country, as a colonial subject, he was not seen fit to govern. This mapping of the citizen–subject binary onto the international–domestic binary, however, also allows the native diplomat to politicize the 'international' as an important site for claiming citizenship at home. In this context, Indian diplomacy, beyond just the instrumentality of an immediate goal, also has an intuitive function of claiming and legitimizing native sovereignty. It pushes liberals to call for more reforms in India, as well as strengthen the political struggle within the country. To return to our original point via a technical term often employed in the literature on international relations and foreign policy, diplomacy during the colonial period allows us to see the 'second-image reversed', that is, how the international system shapes domestic politics.[46]

Finally, although one has to be cautious of aligning the past too closely with the present, one cannot help but notice how the story that unfolds in the book is disturbingly opposed to the India of the present. In late 2019 and early 2020, India saw widespread protests against measures which potentially can, and will, if the Union Home Minister is to be taken at his word, identify and disenfranchise citizens on a religious basis. Indian diplomacy has been on an overdrive to justify these measures, and responded trenchantly to any international criticisms. This is quite ironic, sadly so, considering that the origins of Indian diplomacy are in fact in precisely the opposite: in protesting the disenfranchisement of Indians abroad and mounting an often nuanced and laboured diplomatic effort towards securing their rights. Between

Srinivasa Sastri and his nemesis Jan Smuts, as we will discover, it is not difficult to guess who would be more pleased.

However, this is also exactly the reason why this book and Sastri's life assume increased importance. India's diplomatic future is unlikely to be guided by its past, but the story helps us contextualize its present. If nothing else, it shows us a stunningly naked emperor.

## VII

On his 70th birthday, Sastri told his friends that he was opposed to writing an autobiography, and barred anyone else from attempting a biography.[47] A month later, he sent a letter to the person he suspected of being the most likely to write about his life. 'I interdict it', commanded Sastri to his former political secretary, P. Kodanda Rao. But the very next year Sastri wrote a series of autobiographical notes for a Tamil publication, *Swadesamitran*.[48] In the early 1960s, when Kodanda Rao finally set out to write the biography he had been barred from attempting, he reasoned that since Sastri had himself written a series of autobiographical articles and published several other of his lectures and writings, the pupil was absolved from the interdiction. In 1963, Kodanda Rao's 'political biography' of Sastri was published. Hesitant about his own competence to write objectively about his guru, Kodanda Rao called his own attempt a mere 'sketch' and urged future historians to write a full-length biography.[49]

Six years later, on the centenary of Sastri's birth, the scholar and social activist T.N. Jagadisan wrote another biography of Sastri. Written as part of the 'Builders of Modern India' series for the Indian Ministry of Information and Broadcasting, the biography was, once again, not meant to be an elaborate study.[50] Jagadisan was also a disciple of Sastri, so the life-sketch was hardly meant to be a detailed and critical interrogation of his life and work.[51] In the following five decades, only two other books on Sastri have appeared. Both are primarily concerned with elaborating on his ideas rather than his life and work.[52]

This book is not a full-scale biography either. Instead, as hinted, I am primarily interested in exploring Sastri's life as India's representative abroad. In that, I have attempted to be as thorough as possible, but this also means that some of the better known aspects of Sastri's work, such as his contributions to India's constitutional development, Indian philosophy (especially his work on Ramayana) and education, are out of the purview of this book. The task of extracting a slice of Sastri from Sastri himself, in terms of his life as well as his work, will inevitably be a limiting evaluation, although not necessarily of limited value.

# INTRODUCTION

Biographies are, at best, astute approximations of a life lived. Invariably, they are also windows into the minds and skills of the biographers. The typist on the computer, in this case, is a diplomatic historian, whose limitations of craft must drive the selection, ordering and analysis of the content. Evidence is never fully impartial, nor is its presentation. As stalkers-in-chief, intruders into conversations, private or otherwise, all biographers are wont to feel empathy towards their 'subjects'. But, going further, biographies are also mildly autobiographical. The story of one life is seen through the eyes of another; the events of one life are sifted through the values of another; the chronicle of experiences of one life lived is a sequence of choices made by another. The telling of one life could well be a telling statement on another.

With that caveat in mind, dear reader, let us turn the page.

2

# Shirtless Srinivasan

I

V.S. Srinivasa Sastri was born on 22 September 1869 in a small village, Valangaiman, along the banks of the Kudamurutti nearly 300km south-west of Madras (now Chennai). He was fourth child born to his orthodox Brahmin parents, Vaidik Sankaranarayana Iyer Sastri and Balambal Sastri. Srinivasan was preceded by three sisters and, in due course, an equal number of brothers followed. His father had inherited the family profession of teaching and reciting Sanskrit scriptures and, by all accounts, a life of rituals and pecuniary struggle awaited the eldest son. The family was very poor, and Sankaranarayana, in spite of trekking near and far in search of a dedicated clientele, earned little.

Sankaranarayana was exceedingly strict in his observation of rituals and enforced them unfailingly in his own household. He was also emotionally volatile, which meant that fatherly warmth and dramatic outbursts were both par for the course in the household. Srinivasan's mother could not have been temperamentally any more different. Balambal was calm and composed and consequently a stabilizing influence on Srinivasan. He later recalled that his mother had 'a melancholy and pious disposition' and cultivated in him the trait of listening. Her 'street expositions of scriptures' and bountiful resources of mythological lore kept the young Srinivasan enchanted but also grimly terrified of the mystical world of goblins and ghosts.[1] He found his solace in the outside world, playing marbles and digging street pits, and quickly distinguished himself as a marble player of local repute among the neighbourhood children.

Once he hit school-going age, Srinivasan was sent to the Native High School, six miles away in Kumbakonam, where he stayed until matriculation. On most days, 'shirtless Srinivasan' walked to school, too poor to afford one anna for the bullock cart and, as the nickname reveals, sometimes even without a shirt.[2] He was an unusually bright student, however, and the founding headmaster, Rao Bahadur Appu Sastri, nurtured him. While Srinivasan received ample doses of conservative Hinduism at home, Appu Sastri awakened in him a spirit of reform and liberalism. The headmaster introduced him to the wider world through newspapers, history books and magazines, and parliamentary records, and induced in his pupil 'an early subdual of passions'. 'Decency, seamless, propriety, repression of an outward show of anger or joy', Appu Sastri taught him, were characteristics of a 'gentleman'.[3] His father's volatility had generated in him a repulsion which, guided by his mother and teacher, turned into a characteristic trait of emotional restraint for the rest of his life.

On Appu Sastri's call, Srinivasan and his classmates resolved not to get married before the age of 18. This reformist enthusiasm against child marriage was put to the test within a few months when Srinivasan's parents chose him a bride from within the community. They mocked him for his vow, and with expeditious disregard thereof, married him off to the young bride, Parvati. Srinivasan's defiance broke at the first assault. He wrote later that since he was under the protection of his parents he had little freedom of action in the matter. Was a forced vow any different from a forced marriage, he mulled? It was an early lesson in liberalism that even progressive ideas ought not be forced without consent. This marriage lasted 12 years. Parvathi tragically died in 1895, leaving him with a one-and-a-half-year-old child, Sankaran.

In 1883, Srinivasan passed his matriculation. He had done exceedingly well in these exams, securing 13th rank in the whole of Madras presidency. He qualified for a fellowship which enabled him to go to the intermediate college. Two years later, he performed even better in his FA (Fellow of Arts Intermediate) exams. He topped the presidency, earning him free education for his bachelors' degree at the Government Arts College in Kumbakonam. In 1888, Srinivasan completed his BA degree, with a second position in the presidency overall.

Secular education had turned a boy whose fate, as a local astrologer had forecast, was to become a priest and eventually end up like his ancestors in *sanyas*[4] into a youth brimming with aspirations to be a lawyer. He joined the Law College, but his soaring academic future was whipped away by his family's financial condition. Vishwanatha Iyer, his elder sister's husband and benefactor since primary school, passed away. Srinivasan was now compelled not only to stop his education but also earn a wage to sustain his whole family. With his academic record and glowing letters of recommendation it did not take him long to secure a job. Soon, he was called for an interview for a teaching post at Mayavaram Municipal High School (in today's Mayiladuthurai, about 45km north of Kumbakonam). A shy Srinivasan, looking younger than his age, was interviewed by the local sub-registrar and appointed as a teacher on a monthly salary of 50 rupees; so impressed were his employers that he was paid 10 rupees more than the position's budget.

For someone accustomed to poverty this was a princely salary. With it, he provided for his big family of parents, siblings and their children, and financed the education of his brothers and nephews. In subsequent years, he tried twice to enrol for a master's degree, but his family responsibilities prevented him both times.[5]

At Mayavaram, he was in charge of standard four with some additional classes in standards five and six. Sastri enjoyed teaching – contemporary accounts suggest that he was a popular teacher[6] – and the financial stability made him thankful for the job he now had, but Mayavaram also felt claustrophobic. He complained later of being constantly haunted by a sense of underachievement, of being locked into a place and a situation with no exit. His 'cruel circumstances', he wrote, had forced him into a setting which was both 'uncongenial and beneath [him]'.[7] Unless he professionally trained to be a teacher he had little chance of progressing further in his career. After three years at the school, he decided to join the Teachers' Training School in Saidapet, Madras. Seeing their son abandon the advantage of a regular salary and the good fortune of living close to the Cauvery, a river held in great reverence by Brahmins, his parents protested strongly. But the young teacher's mind was made up. Risking the 'serious displeasure' of his parents, Srinivasan moved to Madras. It was 'essential for my soul', he later confessed.[8]

## II

The provincial capital exposed Srinivasa Sastri to a vibrant social life. Alongside studies, he actively participated in extracurricular activities such as debates, drama and sports. Here, he started gaining a reputation for his command over the English language, especially his punctiliousness regarding grammar and diction.[9] He returned to Mayavaram after a year, and subsequently, in 1893, moved to Salem to teach at the local Municipal College. His initial brush with active politics came here through his contact with C. Vijayaraghavachari. Vijayaraghavachari had risen to regional prominence after he successfully defended against the Madras government's attempts to prosecute him for the Hindu–Muslim riots in Salem in 1882. He had been fired by the government from his position at the Salem Municipal Council. He fought back in court and returned to his elected office to much celebration, gaining the titles 'Salem hero' and, later, 'The Lion of South India'. He was a special invitee to the founding of the Indian National Congress (INC) in 1885.

Vijayaraghavachari first noticed Sastri when the latter opposed his motion in a public meeting on the question of holding the Indian Civil Service (ICS) exams in India, which were at that time held in England. Prominent liberals like Pherozeshah Mehta demanded that these exams should be conducted in England and India simultaneously, but conceded to the government's view that those selected in India should go to England for training before the start of their career. Vijayaraghavachari was against the compromise of training in England, and proposed a motion in this regard. In the public meeting, Sastri spoke in favour of Mehta's scheme, and carried the motion against the senior leader's wish. Despite the defeat, Vijayaraghavachari was impressed and began to cultivate Sastri. Soon, Vijayaraghavachari was in another public dispute with the Madras government over the appointment of the municipality chairman. Vijayaraghavachari led the party of non-officials against the government, which Sastri joined. He published several articles in *The Hindu*, for which the Madras government even threatened to remove him from his job as a public official.[10]

He returned to Madras in 1895, this time as English Assistant at Pachayappa's High School with an increased salary of 100 rupees. Parvathi, as we have noted previously, passed away soon after they moved to Madras. His parents insisted that he remarry, which he did in 1897, to Lakshmi. At Pachayappa's, he played a key role in founding the Madras Teacher's Guild.

Another job shift accompanied with promotion came in 1899. Still very young, at the cusp of entering the fourth decade of his life, Sastri was appointed as the headmaster of the Hindu High School. His seven-year tenure at this school as headmaster, even from a distance of nearly two lifetimes, is fondly remembered by this school as a formative period in its 170-year history.[11] Sastri was a disciplinarian inside the class and extremely approachable outside it.[12] His lectures, delivered in faultless and flowing English, were enthusiastically attended by his students.[13] A strong believer in a schoolteacher's role in shaping the national character, he encouraged all sorts of views and ideas among his students.[14] But he was also strongly opposed to his students' participation in political activities outside the class. Among the many students who passed through his classes in these years was the prominent Indian anarchist M.P.T. Acharya.[15] Although polite to a fault, Sastri stood his ground in his run-ins with the management and would occasionally threaten to resign when the latter was unnecessarily intrusive and disrespectful.[16]

In Madras, he fraternized with local intellectual circles. In particular, he formed a deep friendship with V. Krishnaswami Iyer, a sharp legal mind who rose quickly to become a judge of the Madras High Court and eventually a member of the Governor's Executive Council. Iyer also became an institution-builder of repute, playing key roles in establishing Madras Sanskrit College, Venkataramana Ayurveda Dispensary, Ranade Public Library, Mylapore Club and the Indian Bank.[17]

These years were also the beginning of Sastri's life-long friendship with the legendary publisher G.A. Natesan. Natesan was only four years younger than Sastri. He had joined *The Madras Times* as an apprentice to its long-time editor Glyn Barlow in 1894. But racial barriers prevented him from securing a full-time job at the newspaper. He quit to found his own publishing house, eponymously named G.A. Natesan & Company. He was merely 24 years old then. Sastri was one of the few people who encouraged Natesan to start *The Indian Review*, and he became its sponsor. They also shared the same house in Triplicane, Madras. Natesan edited the journal, and in its early years Sastri toiled long nights under candlelight in proofreading and performing other labours. He was, and always remained, scrupulous about the use of grammar and vocabulary, no doubt contributing to the journal's stellar rise in reputation as one of the country's leading intellectual magazines. Sastri once jokingly attributed the early onset of poor sight to the nightly vigils in service of the *Review*.[18] He also edited another journal, *The Education Review*. Later in life, at Gandhi's request, Sastri spent countless hours over four years between 1935 and 1939 correcting English translations of the two volumes of the latter's *Autobiography*. Despite strong opposition in views, as Gandhi's secretary and in this instance the translator Mahadev Desai recorded, Sastri showed tremendous restraint in suggesting changes, limiting his edits to issues of language.[19] In 1915, when Gandhi toured Madras, Sastri acted as his translator, and was unimpressed with the Mahatma's use of pronouns: 'tedious and annoying', the schoolmaster wrote in his diary.[20]

Sastri had begun to fashion a place for himself within the all-male, Brahmin-dominated intellectual space of Madras.[21] He had also become an important voice on education-related issues in the city, especially on improving the quality of the committee-run schools in the presidency, which received little government support.[22] In early 1903, he was the chief organizer of a study group that met weekly at the premises of the Triplicane Literary Society. When the numbers started to dwindle at these dry study meetings, they were transformed into semi-social gatherings at each other's houses.[23]

One evening over a study group dinner at Sastri's house on 17 Sydoji Lane, the idea for a co-operative society was discussed. Ambika Charan Ukil from the Co-operative Union of Calcutta was in town for the INC meeting in 1903. The gathering decided to start the Triplicane Co-operative Society and put together a sum of 139 rupees. It became the first co-operative consumer society in India, and continues to this day. The first day, 9 April 1904, fetched around 90 rupees; 100 years later the society's annual sales were in excess of 900 million rupees.[24]

In Madras, Sastri's life had come to achieve a degree of stability that he surely cherished. A good job, stable family life and considerable social standing within the intellectual community in Madras was gratifying. But an undiagnosed internal ferment grabbed him for the second time. As he confessed later, he was also given to bouts of depression, occasionally even pushing him to actively contemplate suicide.[25] Just as he had gained steadiness in life and finances, he found himself once again reflecting over the course of his life. This was exacerbated when he read one day a 'confidential' paper that Natesan shared with him. This was a pamphlet of the 'Servants of India Society', written by Gopal Krishna Gokhale.[26]

## III

Gokhale (1866–1915) was the shining star of Indian politics at the time and a moderate liberal to boot. Bal Gangadhar Tilak (1856–1920) and Gokhale occupied polar opposite positions on the spectrum of the INC's politics. Both had remarkably similar backgrounds. Born ten years apart, Tilak being the elder, the two *chitpavan* Brahmins from Ratnagiri in Bombay presidency went to the same college, became mathematics professors, associated themselves with the Deccan Education Society and taught in the society's Fergusson College in Pune.[27] Both first became joint secretaries of the INC in 1895 but spent most of the 1890s and 1900s opposing each other. They even squared off in an election for the Bombay Legislative Council in 1899, which Gokhale won. By the mid-1900s, they had become the keystones on their respective ends of the political spectrum, Gokhale the moderate and Tilak the radical.

By 1905, Gokhale was dismayed at the waning influence of the INC, which was not limited to the challenge presented to its leadership by a radical faction. Most leaders and workers of the Congress considered politics an occasional diversion from personal and professional commitments. They went to its annual sessions, debated arguments and policies, but thereafter retreated to their personal and professional lives, treating the Congress organization with apathy for the rest of the year. For Gokhale, who had quit his job as the principal of Fergusson College a couple of years previously, politics was a full-time service, not a part-time engagement. He worried that hundreds of youths graduating from Indian universities were disillusioned with this expedient, even opportunist, approach to politics. The energy, verve and idealism of the youth needed to be channelled towards a purer and elevated form of politics, which was cleansed of personal ambitions and pursued the task of nation building with staunch devotion; a patriotism that was rooted in the soul rather than sporadically whipped up by circumstances.[28]

He envisioned an organization meant for training educated and dedicated youth committed to political and social reform.[29] In the Indian tradition of *sanyas*, an individual subjected themselves to rigorous self-discipline, self-negation and renunciation of the material world in the pursuit of the enlightenment, or *moksha*. Gokhale wondered if the same rigour and techniques could be used to prepare youth with a single-minded focus on nation building; *sanyas* for creating political missionaries. The idea had first germinated in the mind of his political guru, M.G. Ranade.[30] But Gokhale also took direct inspiration from the Society of Jesus of the Jesuits. On similar lines, he planned a Servants of India Society.[31] Although he had first expressed a desire to start such a society in 1897, only in early 1905 did he finally sit down to write the creed of the organization.

'Public life must be spiritualized', he exhorted in this pamphlet which had made its way to Sastri. The Society would train 'men prepared to devote their lives to the cause of the country in a religious spirit'.[32] Gokhale listed six primary objects of the Society: (a) creating a deep love for the motherland through self-example, service and sacrifice; (b) strengthening the public life of the country through political education and agitation; (c) promoting inter-community harmony; (d) helping advance industrial and scientific education particularly among women and the depressed classes; (e) assisting in the industrial development of the country; and finally (g) uplifting the depressed classes. The ascetic discipline of the Society required young men to give up their profession, and instead depend on the meagre salary of the organization, barely enough to make ends meet.[33] Each recruit would spend the first five years in a form of apprenticeship, where they were disallowed from expressing their personal opinions publicly.

Gokhale wrote seven vows that every member must take, which included an absolute surrender to the Gokhale's will.[34] The brutal irony, not lost on Gokhale, was that, as the liberal exemplar, he had an absolutist hold on its membership, functioning and observance of its creed.[35] Any Russian Secret Society would be proud, chimed a critic.[36] Gokhale reasoned that without this stifling of individual liberty for a brief period 'there was but small chance, with our disorganized and undisciplined public life, and the want of self-restraint which characterizes most of our young men, of any real useful work being done by the Society'.[37] The Society was more of a monastery and less of a public institution.

At sunrise on 12 June 1905, Gokhale trudged up a hill behind his former place of work, Fergusson College. He sat at a suitable place and administered to himself the seven vows as the first member. Three more disciples, G.K. Devadhar, A. V. Patwardhan and N.A. Dravid, all in their thirties, also took oaths of membership that morning. Not much later in Madras, Natesan, looking for someone to write a profile of the incoming Congress president for the *Review*, gave Sastri a bunch of papers related to Gokhale. The Society's creed was in the pile. Its language, the sentiments and the noble ideals stirred the ferment that put Sastri on a train to Benaras, where the 1905 annual Congress session was scheduled to be held.

## IV

From a guesthouse in Benaras on 27 December 1905, Sastri wrote perhaps the most important letter of his life. Addressed to Gokhale, he introduced himself as a 'schoolmaster in Triplicane with about 17 years' service', and asked to become a member of the Society. Conveying interest and conviction, he wrote: 'I don't write this letter under an impulse of the moment; but the idea has long been in my mind, and I know it was for this purpose chiefly that I made up my mind to come here as a delegate'. At 37 years of age, Sastri was too old for the type of young university graduates Gokhale primarily intended to recruit (although Gokhale's first three recruits were also well into their thirties). Sastri understood that Gokhale may have reservations, but nevertheless asked him to inquire from his Madras connections, particularly his friends Iyer and Natesan, about Sastri's character. The applicant added that if Gokhale did indeed accept him, he would require six months to settle his 'not particularly prosperous' affairs.[38]

Gokhale had more important matters on his mind that day than responding to a Society enthusiast. He was ordained as the president of the INC for the first time. This Congress session was being held in the immediate aftermath of the Bengal partition. Through an administrative fiat, the conservative imperialist and Indian Viceroy, Lord Curzon, had partitioned the province of Bengal. The official reason was that a divided Bengal was administratively more convenient to govern. A thinly concealed fact was Curzon's contemptuous regard for the nationalist movement then dominated by the *bhadralok*, or the Bengali Hindu upper-class elite. He wished to break the strength of the Bengali language- and culture-based nationalist movement. The newly created Muslim majority province of East Bengal was meant to weaken the hold of the land-owning high-caste Bengali Hindus; while in West Bengal, the people of Bihar and Orissa would overtake Bengalis in population.[39]

The Benaras Congress session was expected to be explosive. An emerging faction of extremists, led by Tilak and Lala Lajpat Rai, was advocating boycotts and agitation, while the dominant faction of moderates like Pherozeshah Mehta (who did not come to Benaras) and Dinshaw Wacha opposed such measures, limiting their protestations to assemblies. Gokhale however, himself a moderate, managed to keep the peace between the two factions in Benaras.

Meanwhile, Sastri waited anxiously for a reply. Weeks passed in anticipation. He now sought Iyer's help. Iyer wrote to Gokhale in support of his younger friend from Madras.[40] This time, the first member responded and asked Sastri to come to Pune for a few days. Over Easter in 1906, Sastri spent four days with Gokhale in his house, discussing politics and ideas of service. Gokhale introduced him to other Society members and the literati in Poona.[41] For Sastri these days spent with Gokhale 'opened a vista about the outside world'. If he had any lingering doubts about joining the Society, they were swept away. Gokhale advised him against any haste. Appropriately so, because Sastri returned to a storm of protest from his family, specifically his mother and Lakshmi.

Most of his friends, including Natesan, dissuaded him from joining. Even Iyer was lukewarm.[42] But Sastri had made up his mind and placated Lakshmi by agreeing to take her with him to Poona. After a teary-eyed farewell at the school in mid-December 1906, he journeyed to Calcutta to join Gokhale, who was there for the annual session of the Congress.

The embers of the previous year's session had turned into full-scale fireballs in Calcutta. Even moderates like Surendranath Banerjea had advocated *swadeshi* and boycott in Bengal, but Bipin Chandra Pal, accompanied by another fiery radical, Aurobindo Ghose, went even further and held protest meetings defying bans. Pal's blistering rhetoric in Bengal had a particular appeal among the youth. Tilak toured Bengal in May 1906 to a rousing welcome. The triumvirate of Lal-Bal-Pal – Lala Lajpat Rai, Bal Gangadhar Tilak and Bipin Chandra Pal – now led the extremist faction within the Congress, with a dedicated band of supporters in their respective provinces of Punjab, Bombay and Bengal. Ghose, Rai and Pal proposed Tilak's name for the Congress presidency in its Calcutta session. In order to prevent extremists from gaining the leadership, the moderates unscrupulously sent an invitation to Dadabhai Naoroji, the 82-year-old 'grand old man of India', presenting the extremists with a fait accompli. Naoroji, decidedly moderate in his politics but someone who had the distinction of being the first non-European ever to be elected to the British parliament as well as being a member of the Second International, was respected across the board. Although Pal sheepishly cabled Naoroji to stay away, few, including Tilak, had the gumption to openly oppose the revered statesman. In Calcutta, the extremists demanded the extension of boycotts and *swadeshi* to the whole country, while the moderates supported limiting it to Bengal. An eventual compromise was reached through the adoption of *swadeshi* as the aim of Congress, although the term was appropriately ambivalent: moderates insisting on dominion status while extremists suggested independence. Nevertheless, Naoroji's presidency staved off the crisis, for another year at least.

Soon after the conference, Gokhale took Sastri and other members of the Society to meet Naoroji. The grand old man confessed to Gokhale that he had desired similarly to organize a band of young men and blessed his initiative. On the early morning of 6 January 1907, in the upper storey of a house on Rowland Road, Ballygunge, in Calcutta, Sastri was formally admitted to the Society upon the recitation of the seven vows.[43] His life had come around in a spiral; the *sanyas* he had been astrologically foretold turned out to be political, rather than spiritual. The new addition to 'Gokhale's Young Men', as Naoroji called them, was only three years younger than the first member.

## V

Sastri's next few years were spent in training, touring, studying and preparing for public work. He started immediately; a few days after joining he was dispatched further east on a month-long tour of East Bengal, Assam and Manipur. East Bengal was still caught in the throes of the agitation. Barred by the Society's rules from making public speeches in his period of apprenticeship, Sastri observed quietly. He witnessed the success of the *swadeshi* campaign, but also a troubling, deep rift developing between Hindus and Muslims.[44]

When in Poona, all members carried out a schedule of activities, including long and rigorous hours of independent study. Gokhale had paid special attention to building a library at the headquarters where the trainees were expected to immerse themselves in careful and detached study of political questions. Gokhale's creed was that patriotism and public spirit when bereft of knowledge were productive of harm and mischief. Well-meaning intentions were no substitute for the conscientious use of knowledge, and indeed often served the same ends as ill-intentioned actions.[45] The profession of politics, just like any other, required the development of knowledge and skills.

If dedicated learning was one element of political education, clear and forceful articulation was another. At the Poona House, two common meetings were usually organized every week; in one a paper was read and discussed, and the other was meant for debate. In these timed debates, members sparred over propositions, and then took the opposite sides and sparred again. Sastri developed an oratorical style, which remained unchanged throughout his life. He would make a sequence of arguments in his mind and rehearse them. Only in exceptional situations did he write his speeches down; most often his notes consisted of some key words written on a piece of paper. His argumentative jousts were woven with sober and clinical answers, but also effectively peppered with clever and biting jests. Smart and teasing one-liners were often the sharpest arrows in his oratorical quiver.[46]

On 12 June 1910, Gokhale's first three disciples and Sastri were raised to become ordinary members. Unlike the other three, who had completed five years, Sastri had only completed three and a half years.[47] He had closely assisted Gokhale in his work as member of the Imperial Legislative Council, as secretary of the INC, and in his proposals for the Morley–Minto Reforms. The five-year moratorium on public speech was also at times relaxed for Sastri by Gokhale, especially on occasions when he needed Sastri to speak about the Society and solicit donations for Ranade Memorial in Pune. The Society also brought out *Dnyanaprakash*, and soon acquired two publications, *Hitaeveda* and *Hindustan*. The members helped in famine relief, the campaign against the plague, the education of women through the *Seva Sadan* of Poona, the education of workers through its Social Service League, fund collections for patriotic initiatives such as the British Indian National Congress' publication *India* and Gandhi's South African fund, and even went on tours to mobilize support for Gokhale's Education Bill.[48]

By dint of his association with Gokhale, Sastri was also pulled into the infamous 'Surat split' of the INC in 1907. The extremists and moderates came to blows, literally, at Surat. The rivalry, however, was scarcely over just ideology. The aims of the two factions were tactical – about who would take the presidency. Six weeks before the actual conference, the venue for the 1907 Congress had been hastily moved from Nagpur, a Tilak stronghold, to Surat, after factional fights among the Nagpur reception committee.

At Surat, Rash Bihari Ghose, Gokhale's choice for the presidency, was expectedly opposed by Tilak and his faction. After the president's speech, Tilak approached the dais and was refused permission to speak out of turn. He declined to move, and a shoe was hurled at him from the audience. Soon, *lathi*-bearing men lunged onto the stage. In the ensuing pandemonium, blows were exchanged, chairs thrown around, the pandal vandalized. Sastri too went up to the stage, where a young man was ready to strike him with a chair.[49] It was Sastri's own former pupil from the Hindu High School, M.P.T. Acharya, later a prominent anarchist. Acharya retreated on seeing his former headmaster.[50] The very next day liberals like Mehta, Gokhale and Iyer, among others from the moderate section, met and formed a new convention. This convention organized the 1908 Congress session in Madras, where Iyer took on most of the work, and 'like a practiced general conducted its affairs with thorough dexterity'. Sastri assisted him as 'a small lieutenant'.[51]

Sastri had a ringside view of this tumultuous phase of national politics. In many ways, he was expected to fulfil the functions of being an insider as well as an outsider, a contradiction that lay at the core of the Society's mode of functioning. The political views of Gokhale, a man Sastri almost revered, were obviously much closer to his own. But as someone who was only meant to 'study' politics with a militantly dispassionate sense of enquiry in this phase of training, how much distance in politics could there really be from his mentor? However, this did not prevent ambiguities from arising. This is perhaps best illustrated in his own views on the methods of struggle, as well as on Gokhale's *bête noire* Tilak.

Gokhale and Tilak shared a difficult relationship. Keir Hardie's description that Congress moderates were 'extreme in moderation', while the extremists were 'moderate in extremism',[52] perhaps applied best to this duo. They were more sympathetic towards each other's views compared to their fellow factionalists. Gokhale was more likely to compromise with the extremists, and vice versa for Tilak with the moderates. Their rivalry had also been very personal, even bitter at times; although moments of tender concern also shone through. At the Surat session, when Congress volunteers came to the stage to physically remove Tilak, Gokhale threw his arms around his fellow Maratha to protect him.[53]

Sastri had a deeper and emotional admiration for Tilak, perhaps also a mild fascination for his methods ('an extremist in disguise' is how Sastri once characterized himself).[54] When Tilak was sentenced to a six-year exile in Mandalay in July 1908, Sastri spoke of how this came as a crushing 'catastrophe' to him personally. Tilak's exile was 'a great gap left in the ranks of public men' with a sobering realization that 'few hope[d] to see him alive at the end of his exile'.[55] A few days later, on reading a book on Russian anarchists, he lauded their 'daring aspiration, ceaseless endeavor and delirious uncertainty'.[56] For the homegrown revolutionaries, he had similar and, in hindsight, prophetic words:

> [M]y honest opinion is that on every occasion the manifestation of [extremist] virulence will leave the forward movement in India outwardly discredited, but inwardly stronger and more firm based. ... succeeding generations of [extremists] will contribute more character, virility, and persistence to the party; and though their hold on the country may never become very strong, impartial history will perhaps record that every onward step in our liberation was rendered possible by their seeming reckless bravado.[57]

## VI

Gokhale passed away in late evening on 19 February 1915. His diabetes had steadily worsened his cardiac asthma. On hearing of this news, Sastri, who was on his way to Madurai, turned back to Madras, and from there to Poona. Another Gokhale disciple hastened westward from Shantiniketan near Calcutta; this was Mohandas Gandhi. Both Gandhi and Sastri arrived in Pune the same evening: Sastri's carriage passed Gandhi, who was quite characteristically walking all the way from the station to the Society home.[58] Sastri and Gandhi were born only ten days apart; both were only three years younger than Gokhale but saw themselves as his pupils. Gandhi considered Gokhale his *rajya guru* (political guru).[59] Sastri called him 'Bada Sahib' ('Chief', which combines the dry warmth of pupillage with the reverence for authority, would be a faithful translation).

Three concerns had consumed Gokhale's thoughts at the time of his death. The first was the succession of the Servants of India Society. As early as 1909, even though he was still in his early forties, Gokhale had worried about the consequences of his early death for the Society.[60]

Its affairs were teetering even while Gokhale was alive. Gokhale himself had not devoted enough time to it, and its finances were in an abysmal state. He was consumed by his political work, which involved travelling abroad, mostly to England, almost on a yearly basis. At the time of Gokhale's death in 1915, the Society had only 27 members, despite opening four other branches in Madras, Nagpur, Bombay and Allahabad.[61] Several young men had left the Society because of its strict rules, while others like C.Y. Chintamani (later chief editor of *The Leader*), M.R. Jayakar (the prominent inter-war Indian liberal leader) and Rajendra Prasad (independent India's first president) had decided not to join because of such rules.[62] In a moment of despair, Gokhale wondered if he had been too bold to start it, and asked Sastri: 'I will do all I can while I live; but you will get Krishnaswami [Iyer] to take it up after me, will you?'[63]

However, diabetes took Iyer's life three years before Gokhale. He passed away on 28 December 1911, at the relatively young age of 48. Iyer was in many ways Sastri's other mentor. Sastri, the shy, polite, teacher-turned-political ascetic, and Iyer, the volatile, sometimes boisterous, lawyer-turned-government minister, were poles apart as personalities. But there was a commonality of sincerity, a communion of earnestness on which they connected. On his deathbed, Iyer had called Sastri separately and in addition to handing over his private papers, imparted his last words of wisdom: 'flattery of officials, knee-crooking, fawning of the powers that be, tale-bearing, etc., are unnecessary for a man's rise even to the top'.[64]

But Iyer was also partly the reason why Gokhale did not consider Sastri his natural successor, even though the latter had informally served as the second member since 1909 and led the Society when Gokhale was abroad.[65] Iyer had told Gokhale that Sastri lacked 'strength of will and purpose' and 'the quality of leadership'.[66] This made Sastri unsuitable to take the Society forward. Iyer had revealed this himself to Sastri, who accepted it without rancour as a fair characterization.[67]

Gokhale then considered his other disciple: Gandhi. Gandhi's *ashrams* in Durban and Johannesburg (Phoenix and Tolstoy respectively) and Gokhale's own Society were similar, as they both focused on ascetic living. However, the differences between them were also considerable. The Society placed more emphasis on intellectual learning while Gandhi's ashram revolved around notions of personal asceticism. As a witness and part sufferer of Gandhi's idiosyncratic living philosophy during his South African tour of 1912, Gokhale was sceptical of Gandhi's obsession with personal suffering, which included severe dietary restrictions, an almost luddite aversion to technology and a disavowal of western civilization.⁶⁸ Despite the hardships of a disciplined life, Gokhale's disciples lived and worked in decent living conditions in the Society's house in urban Poona, with servants providing for their daily needs. Gandhi's ashrams, in contrast, were rural farms with a focus on the dignity of physical labour. Furthermore, Gandhi's political methods, such as passive resistance, would be anathema to Gokhale and the moderates in India, although Gokhale accepted them as necessities of special circumstances in South Africa.⁶⁹

Gandhi's unmitigated idealism and romanticism, however, also had an impassioned attraction for the liberal leader. Was this focus on service not exactly what he was trying to inculcate in the Indian youth through the Society? With his monastic simplicity and unbending conviction, Gandhi, a known leader of mass movements as well as small ashrams, could be just the right political missionary to inspire the youth. He could advance Gokhale's plan of opening a branch in every district. Gokhale felt confident that once Gandhi had a closer understanding of the realities of his own country, his personal and political methods would undergo a change. As soon as Gandhi returned to India in early 1915, Gokhale counselled him to tour India for a year without expressing any opinion, at the end of which he should join the Society.

In the last week of February, with Gokhale's death forcing the issue of leadership, Gandhi sat down to discuss his plans with other members of the Society. A wide gulf existed between them. Gandhi wanted to start a rural community with an emphasis on the dignity of manual labour. The Society instead viewed itself primarily as a vehicle of political education whose members were expected to take part in 'every movement of modern life, educational, political and economic'.⁷⁰ Gandhi detested the fact that the Society's members took a detached, elitist, and even casteist view of the poor. In a testy meeting, he was rather blunt and told them, as Sastri recalled:

> You pride yourselves in being Servants of India. You don't go amongst the poor Harijans and labourers. I wonder what you do, you who live this sort of life here. You don't live amongst them. You don't know the language they speak. You don't eat their food. You don't suffer their sufferings. And what good it is?⁷¹

It was left to Sastri to defend the Society. He was irritated by Gandhi's deprecatory tone. More than a month prior, when he had first seen Gandhi, the Mahatma was dressed 'quite like a *bania*', with 'a big sandal mark on his forehead and a *kumkum* dot besides'. Out of fear of being caste ostracized, Gandhi had refused to stop at a Parsi's house, so this virtuous belittling was mildly disingenuous.[72] Sastri retorted that Gandhi's view of social service was itself western; that in order to do true service one had to 'to strip [oneself] bare, to be the poorest among the poor' was the ideal of a Christian life. The *Bhagavat Gita* instead offered the principle of '*yuktahara vihara*' where the key was regulation, not denial. To suffer so that others do not suffer was a noble pursuit, but that was different from extolling suffering itself as a primary form of service. It leaned towards the idea 'I suffer thus let others suffer too', an entirely counterproductive notion of service.[73] Sastri noted that it had only been two or three years since Gandhi had started to travel third class. The Society's members should be given a chance to learn rather than be deprecated.[74]

Gandhi apologized to Sastri for his harshness. Their disagreements were however irreconcilable. Both sides mutually decided that Gandhi would withdraw his plea to join the Society.[75] Four months later, Sastri was elected as Gokhale's successor.

## VII

The second of Gokhale's dying worries was the split between the extremists and the moderates. The moderates had won in Surat, but the victory had come at a great cost. They were firmly in command of the INC, but were fast losing the pulse of the Indian nation. The vigour that the Congress had gained following Curzon's contemptuous Bengal Partition evaporated; the subsequent Congress sessions haemorrhaged numbers.[76] The extremists temporarily bowed out of national politics, as several leaders and younger revolutionaries were either arrested or left the country. Lajpat Rai, first deported to Mandalay in early 1907, moved his base to the United States (and briefly Japan) during the war. Pal toned down his rhetoric, spending the 1910s pushing pliant ideas about India's unity under the 'Empire ideal', while Aurobindo Ghose retired from politics altogether and turned to spirituality. Tilak was imprisoned in Mandalay for half a decade. After his return on the eve of the war, he followed the example of the Irish-origin theosophist and socialist Annie Besant in starting a Home Rule League which envisioned self-government in India on the lines of Ireland.[77] For the extremists, *swaraj* (self-rule) was no longer complete independence, but a dominion-like status.

Gokhale was keen to reconcile the two factions, and so was Tilak when he emerged from prison. Besant, who had plunged headlong into the Indian national struggle in 1913, after 20 years of social work in India, had based herself in Madras to start a magazine, *Commonweal*, and a newspaper, *New India*. She attempted a compromise between the two leaders. Early signs were hopeful, but illusory. Although both sides agreed on a common aim, that of self-government within the British Empire, they differed significantly on the methods of struggle. The moderate creed was cooperation with the government where possible and opposition when needed. The extremists insisted on continuous opposition to the government through constitutional means. The moderates looked to progressively enlarge the Indian share in the affairs of the government, while the extremists insisted on complete opposition to the government until the final goal was conceded.[78] The talks to rehabilitate the extremists between Gokhale and Tilak brokered by Besant broke down a few days before Gokhale's death. Gokhale breathed his last, more bitter than ever about his adversary, and heartbroken about the failure of his efforts to unite the Congress.[79]

Consequently, the first task that Sastri prioritized for himself was working towards unity. Pherozeshah Mehta, the tallest moderate leader but also the most obdurate to reconciliation, passed away in late 1915, opening a way for compromise. With a general desire for unity and expectations of impending reforms after the war, the extremists and the moderates came together in 1916. Sastri played a role in this reconciliation, chairing a session in Bombay where the two factions met. Tilak and his faction were reinstated, and the united Congress even achieved a compromise with the Muslim League in 1916. However, the moderate–extremist peace lasted for no more than two years. In 1918, 'a reverse Surat' was orchestrated, and this time the moderates were at the receiving end.

## VIII

Sastri's journey into constitutional politics had been jump-started, ironically yet again, by the untimely demise of Iyer which left a vacancy in the Governor's Council in Madras. The Governor flirted with the idea of nominating Sastri, but upon consultation decided it was better for him to first gain experience of the Legislative Council. But soon even that idea was shelved because the Society had then been under government suspicion. Sastri was followed by intelligence department men, and in the princely state of Mysore his scheduled talks had been banned. Things eased in a year when the new Viceroy, Lord Hardinge, took oath in Delhi, and Lord Pentland in Madras. Pentland had been briefed by the liberal leader and one of the INC's founders, William Wedderburn, about Sastri. Within a year of the first proposal, Sastri was nominated to the Madras Legislative Council by the new Governor. The council functioned more as a debating club, and less as a legislative chamber. Between 1913 and 1916, a total of 103 resolutions were introduced by Indian members, not even one was accepted by the government.[80]

In his four-year term from 1913 to 1916, Sastri quickly established himself as a fine speaker and a sharp critic of the government. He could lighten a tense situation with his playful oratory and bring mature sobriety to issues which needed attention. Although he spoke on several issues, much of his focus remained on issues relating to education. His successful tenure helped him in 1916 when he contested an election for the Indian Legislative Council. He was elected, along with B.N. Sarma. One of the two people he had defeated was his first political companion, the Salem hero, C. Vijayaraghavachari. The other was T.M. Nair. This little-known election in many ways changed the course of political history in south India. Nair blamed his defeat on the Brahmins, who held a python-like hold on the INC. He quit the party, and launched the South Indian Liberal Federation in November 1916, also known by the name of its journal, *Justice*, as the Justice Party, which spearheaded the Non-Brahmin Movement in the Madras presidency.

Gokhale's third major worry was about the political future of the country. Gokhale himself was one of the first people to sketch a scheme of reforms which was released after his death as his 'political testament'. In 1916, as Sastri entered the Indian Legislative Council, he joined a stream of politicians calling for political reforms, and as will be shown in the next chapter, played a significant part in the most extensive set of political reforms of British India's history until then.

3

# A Worthy Successor to Gokhale

I

'Already feel the monotony of life', Sastri scrawled in his diary on 30 April 1919.[1] The Arabian Sea was calm; the SS *Manora* travelled at a leisurely pace of about 12 knots per hour on its journey towards England. This was his first trip abroad. On earlier occasions he had pointedly refused to go overseas because of his mother's illness. Now when he had grudgingly given in, Balambal fell ill and never recovered. She passed away soon after he arrived in England.[2]

Anxiety about his mother's health and recurring bouts of back pain chained him to his cabin for long periods on the ship; the motionlessness of time snoozing in sync with his body. The cabin that he shared with three other people had a porthole and a fan, making it barely tolerable. The proverbial silver lining was that he spent his days feasting on books and writing letters to family and friends. Of all of the ship's passengers from Bombay only nine were Indians. Six of them were Indian political leaders travelling to London to present evidence on the historic Montagu–Chelmsford Reforms. Sastri and H.N. Kunzru, both from the Servants of India Society, were representing the moderates. Kunzru, younger than Sastri by 17 years, was the more experienced traveller of the two, having studied at the London School of Economics. In views as in temperament, Sastri and Kunzru were quite alike.

The other four politicians were going to join the veteran radical Bal Gangadhar Tilak to represent the Congress' point of view; although it was not clear if Tilak, who was in London to fight a defamation case against the journalist Valentine Chirol, would be the leader of this delegation. Vithalbhai Patel, a firebrand lawyer and member of the Indian Legislative Council, had recently introduced a bill to legalize inter-caste Hindu marriages, for which he faced the scorching ire of Tilak's papers, *Mahratta* and *Kesari*, ostensibly for the crime of polluting Hindu culture. With no love lost between the two, Patel, now on his way to London, was clear that Tilak could not be the delegation leader. It turned out, as we'll see later in the chapter, that the Maratha radical had retreated into a moderate shell in London.

Other congressmen were V.P. Madhava Rao, the former dewan of Mysore and Baroda; S. Satyamurti, then a 32-year-old activist who after arriving in London would function as the London correspondence of *The Hindu*; and N.C. Kelkar, a close confidant of Tilak.

On the ship, Sastri noticed that racial protocols maintained on the mainland were notched up a shade. Food and tea were served separately to the Indians; there was no social mixing. Only some of the missionaries seemed to be interested in speaking to the Indians, albeit in patronizing tones. Madhava Rao resented the missionary behaviour. 'They have given us the character of savages we bear in Europe and America. Don't trust them', he warned his colleagues.[3] Madhava Rao's ideas about politics were even more radical. Indians should bluntly tell Montagu, he suggested, that if the English could not give Indians self-government, they should hand over the country to the Americans.[4]

The ferment of ideas stoked on this ship, even as impossible as those of Madhava Rao, as well as the England-ward march of these six gentlemen, were a result of an ongoing political churning that India was witnessing in early 1919. A landscape of politics in the second half of the second decade of the twentieth century is a good place to begin, before we return to the SS *Manora*.

## II

In the course of the 'Great War', Ireland saw a full-scale mutiny against Britain, South Africa came perilously close to it, and the Bolshevik Revolution fanned the flames of self-determination across the empire. Yet remarkably, India, which had seen a growing unrest against colonial rule just before the war, remained by and large peaceful. This was despite the depleted strength of British and Indian troops in the country. Indian revolutionaries and their activities operated primarily from abroad, mostly in America and Germany.[5] The sole effort at mutiny by the returning *Ghadrites* had been smothered in its early days.

In fact, the two Indias – British as well as princely – had enthusiastically marched their men, money and materiel on the side of the empire. Even the likes of Besant, Tilak and Gandhi, otherwise radically opposed to the government, had appealed for wartime recruitment into the army. Gandhi made the only known exception to his abhorrence for violence and urged Indian men to take up arms to protect the empire. The fiery poetess-politician Sarojini Naidu appealed to 'give the very flower of our manhood' so that 'England's need may be served incidentally and India's need ultimately'.[6]

India's popular leadership endorsing Britain's war effort, however, also signalled a giant shift in the mode of politicking in colonial India. In the moderate phase of Congress, popular politics was seen as anathema to politics, a pandering to the lowest common denominator, a crippling subjection to the whims of the unenlightened and conservative masses, a rule by anarchy even. For the moderates, education, both political and otherwise, was a prerequisite for doing politics. However, the Home Rule Movement had taken politics out of the annual pandal pageantry of the Congress and into people's homes. Besant, Tilak and Gandhi were cut in the mould of agitational politics, the first stream of popular politicians who could amass numbers behind their politics. Their aims may have been the same as the moderates, but their methods imbued a sense of urgency.

The war itself had brought a radical new hope for people's power. Britain's former Prime Minister, Arthur Balfour, had worried that the war had taught that 'organised forces of men' either by industrial devices or by united action of their numerical superiority could enforce their views. A lesson that if the East were to learn and act upon would bring the British rule in India to an abrupt end.[7] Consequently, what the political reform movement had not achieved in the past three decades through appeals to the British sense of justice had now gathered a sense of inevitability, even for the British.

On another front, the broader question of the constitution of the British Empire had haunted imperial enthusiasts on the eve of the war. The surge of Japan, Germany and the United States from the late nineteenth century onwards increasingly chipped at the British hegemony of the seas. By the first decade of the twentieth century they were no more distant challengers but serious contenders. Britain could no longer foot the military bill alone, and needed the empire's constituents to pull their military weight to defend its vast territorial and naval expanse. In the war, the dominions and India had come to the empire's aid, temporarily deferring the crisis. But the question remained: could the instrumentality of purpose ever be a guarantee of a longer-term commitment? The war was an exceptional event of an unimaginable scale; would this support also be forthcoming when the empire was forced to retreat by nudges and pokes? Further, with every ounce of imperial defence required for guarding the empire's borders, Britain could ill afford the luxury of continuous coercion against assertive nationalisms in the colonial empire, especially in Ireland, India and Egypt. The empire needed a new empire ideal, an Empire 2.0.

An empire-wide community of imperial enthusiasts, self-identifying as the Round Table Movement, was perhaps the most committed to heralding such a new vision. While the Victorians had flirted with notions of imperial federation to little avail, the Edwardians of the Round Table had now resuscitated them, but with a much stronger focus on a spiritual, not merely physical, unity of the empire. More than all others associated with this group, the life's work of one particular member had the greatest impact in developing the ideas and work of the Round Table. This was 'its globe-trotting doctrinaire with a positive mania for constitution mongering',[8] Lionel Curtis.

Curtis cut his political teeth in southern Africa playing a self-propagandized crucial role in the formation of the Union of South Africa in 1910. Subsequently, he was instrumental in starting the Round Table movement of which he became the roving ambassador, or 'the prophet'.

The historian Arnold Toynbee once said that Curtis had the ability to '[ferret] out an old name from the historians' store-cupboard and [make] this name do new work by giving it new application'. The 'Commonwealth of Nations' was one such '[feat] of analogical imagination'.[9] Indeed, in the 1910s, Curtis proposed a British 'Commonwealth of Nations', a sort of de-centred federation constituting an imperial parliament representing Britain and the white dominions. His Commonwealth was an 'Organic Union' of the empire where Britain and the white dominions would be jointly responsible for policies governing the empire, including its 370,000,000 people in the colonies. Consequently, they would also pool their resources for the defence of the empire, although, as he would emphasize, the purpose of this great Commonwealth was more than just the instrumentality of self-preservation.

This Commonwealth, Curtis argued, was founded on the notion of a sacramental duty towards others; a political community joined not by a transactional social contract between its constituents and the sovereign, as political philosophers such as Thomas Hobbes, John Locke and Jean Jacques Rousseau would argue, but rather a sacramental bond, an innate sense of duty towards each other, represented in the sovereign. Each political constituent cared for the other, and took on concomitant responsibilities. Consequently, the political institutions within the Commonwealth were designed to uphold values of justice and welfare. Hence, the basis of the autonomous political units coming together was not a matter of just expedience, but an evolutionary fulfilment of the ideal of a Commonwealth. In other words, the British Empire had an inward purpose driven by its history of evolution rather than an outward motive presented by the contingency of the times.

Having placed the Commonwealth on this evolutionary scale, he would argue that its eventual purpose, or *telos*, was twofold: to raise those who were yet unable to share this duty within the Commonwealth, and to continuously expand its reach outwards to bind the whole of humanity. The latter idea, of creating a world state, was fleshed out in Curtis' three-volume study *Civitas Dei* in the 1930s. The former was emphasized strongly in his 1916 study, *The Commonwealth of Nations*. '[P]reparing for freedom the vast multitude of human beings who have yet to realise what freedom means', he wrote in this book.[10] In other words, Britain and the co-heirs of the empire, the dominions, were to govern its 370,000,000 non-whites until they could be taught to self-govern. The defence of the empire, its preservation, was important for the sake of its noble aims: of preserving and spreading peace and civilization.

How do you raise those who were incapable of governing on the principles of other-regarding duty to becoming so? To answer this, Curtis argued it was first important to understand that Britain's vast empire was not a binary between whites and non-whites. The empire had broadly three sets of people at three different levels of political evolution: Europeans, Asians and Africans. In Africa, primitive and pre-rational humans were 'scarcely capable of forming any valid opinion'. India, in contrast, had a small class of Indians who were capable of rational, dispassionate political judgement, although their numbers were not yet big enough to be given the 'responsibility' of discharging and enforcing their opinions for they would be 'overpowered' by the overwhelming majority. Hence: 'Indian opinion cannot rule India … until the Indians capable of forming such opinion are united, organized, and numerous enough to exact regular, willing and continuous obedience from their fellow countrymen who have not as yet acquired the faculty of political judgement.' The responsibility of the government in India was to improve both the quantity and quality of that opinion until a sufficiently large section of Indians were ready to be transferred power.[11]

The sum of his argument was that, despite what the Indian nationalists demanded, India was not yet ready for self-government to be granted in one stroke. The Indian electorate, 'disinterested and capable of sound political judgement', had to be trained and created. The essence of the problem, he argued, was 'how to create them'.[12] His suggestion was a system called Dyarchy, another old term summoned to modern usage by Curtis, although he credited the term itself to the Indian civil servant William Meyer.[13]

Dyarchy, or two governments, implied that in a slow, measured and phased manner Indians had to take the responsibility of governing themselves. To begin with, certain provincial subjects could be transferred to legislatures and ministers elected through popular vote, leaving others as 'reserves' in the hands of governors and their nominated executives. Effectively, a provincial government would be two governments composed of elected ministers and appointed councillors, the former answerable to Indian opinion and the latter to the British parliament.[14] This would serve a pedagogical function of training Indian electorates, legislatures and executives for exercising responsibility, but also progressively lead to the transfer of more subjects from the part of government responsible to British electorates to the one responsible to Indian electorates. Another implication of the dyarchy in the provinces was that at some future date such reforms could also be introduced at the central level.

Having identified the principle of rule, Curtis then requested William Duke, a former Lieutenant Governor of Bengal, to brainstorm the idea with the Round Table group in Oxford and prepare a blueprint for a scheme like this in Bengal. Armed with a more fleshed out plan prepared by Duke, Curtis travelled to India in November 1916, staying until February 1918, to devise a scheme of constitutional change.

### III

Sastri was alarmed at Curtis' proposals: 'a new humiliation' was facing Indians, where constitutional schemes devised by imperialist thinkers would make India a 'household drudge' of the empire.[15] White dominions with an impenitent record of treating Indians as an 'inferior race' were being urged to administer India's affairs for the 'purpose of teaching [Indians] how to govern yourself'.[16] Could Indians be expected to take such suggestions patiently, he asked? Unless Indians fleshed out ideas of their own, initiated schemes which reflected the demands and desires of Indians, the dangers of being out-thought by imperial enthusiasts had become horrifyingly real.

His guru, Gokhale, had taken a preliminary stab at sketching Indian demands. Gokhale's last notes, released as his political testament, laid out an outline for a potential post-war scheme. Its core demands were full provincial autonomy with an Indian elective majority, and somewhat enlarged legislative powers at the centre, albeit with a European majority.[17] However, a more concrete set of Indian proposals was published in late 1916, when 19 non-official members of the Imperial Legislative Council submitted a 13-point programme of post-war reforms to the Viceroy. The memorandum asserted that such reforms were due 'not as a reward to India's loyalty' but as 'a right' to occupy 'a position of comradeship', not subordination within the empire.[18] The very next month, in November 1916, the leaders of the two main parties, the Congress and the Muslim League, finalized a joint document proposing extensive reforms. It was called the Congress–League (CL) Scheme. Sastri was a key participant in finalizing both these proposals.

The CL scheme was the most extensive set of demands for reforms presented until that time, as well as the most widely agreed among Indian leaders. The scheme had brought together not only the Muslim League and the Congress, but also the extremists and the moderates within the Congress. Consequently, the scheme is most remembered for proposing a system of communal franchise for Muslims in provincial legislatures and ensuring adequate representation of other minorities in a system of territorial franchise. However, its more far-reaching proposals with regard to constitutional change focused on four underlying principles: elective majority in the legislative assemblies at both provincial and central level; dominance of elective councils over executive councils; financial control by the legislatures; and absolute equality with respect to the status and rights of citizenship with other British subjects throughout the empire. The tone of this document was moderate and conciliatory, yet ambitious, and it set off a wide debate within India.

Sastri wrote two pamphlets in quick succession where he explained the proposals in arduous detail, as well as strongly defending their political philosophy and principles against Curtis' proposals. The first of these, 'Self-Government under the British Flag', appeared a week before the CL scheme was placed for endorsement before the Congress annual session in December 1916. The other, 'The Congress–League Scheme – An Exposition', was published in November 1917. From February 1918, he also founded and edited the *Servant of India Newsletter*, whose pages were repeatedly put to good use in defending against contemporary critiques of the CL scheme. In this period, he became the most authoritative voice on the CL reforms as well as the most resolute critic of Curtis' scheme.

Indeed, *Self-Government* was mostly a riposte to Curtis (and another imperial thinker, Richard Jebb). Robert Brand, Curtis' Round Table colleague, once famously said that the key to unravelling Curtis' schemes was to hit at their first principle, usually the weakest point of his scheme, on which the rest of his ideas were mounted like a deck of cards. Sastri went for the jugular, that is, the measure of 'fitness'.

Was fitness to rule a precondition or a result of self-government, Sastri asked? Going over in great detail the socioeconomic and political condition of each of the dominions, and indeed England before 1832 when self-governing institutions were granted, Sastri showed that none of the white polities could fulfil the fitness criterion. Education was scarce, political disorder was rife, crude ideas dominated political discourse, poverty was ubiquitous and in cases such as Australia, which was 'a large gaol' until a few decades before parliamentary institutions were introduced, the character of the people was anything but salutary. All of them were much worse than India was. In each of these cases, however, the introduction of self-government considerably improved their status and general condition.[19] The chief lesson from this experience was that self-government was not a consequence but 'the only sure remedy' for ending internal strife.[20]

India's case for political autonomy was far stronger than that of the dominions or even England when they were granted self-governing institutions. The record of provincial legislative councils was testimony to the admirable conduct of Indians in parliamentary institutions. Indian members had participated in deliberative institutions with moderation and self-restraint, despite the impotence of the legislative chambers. This resentment had 'on no occasion broken out in any of those disorderly or violent forms which disfigures the annals of the legislatures of England and the Dominions'.[21]

The strength of the self-governing institutions, Curtis would argue, depended not on a country's elite but the education of its electorate. It was the uneducated millions in India who required tutelage. Sastri retorted: is there any self-governing country in the world which had universal education before being granted franchise? Furthermore, how could representatives and apologists of the Indian government make the lack of education a disabling criterion when they had done precious little towards making elementary education universal? A few years ago, Sastri had campaigned vociferously for universalizing elementary education on behalf of Gokhale, a proposal that the government shot down. The Indian government had themselves denied Indians education, and its apologists now used the prevailing illiteracy as a reason for denying Indians a right to choose their own representatives. It was 'a double wrong'.[22]

Sastri scoffed at Curtis' idea of dyarchy.[23] Where in the world had people acquired 'autonomy in compartments'?[24] Barring issues such as defence, police and communications, on which it was important that the central government retained control, what was the necessity of keeping several issues reserved? If the people could be trusted to handle the bulk of provincial affairs, why could they not be trusted in central affairs, he asked?[25] Dyarchy's only intention was to conciliate the bureaucracy, which had 'persuaded itself that it is going to teach what it does not believe and foster what it does not approve'.[26]

Underlying Curtis' liberal façade, Sastri concluded, was a clear racial underbelly of arguments.[27] His counsel for Indians to 'wait, wait in patience' emerged from the belief that Asians were not fit to rule because they were made by God to obey, just as Europeans were designed to rule. The two races were '*shudras* and *kshatriyas*' of creation. Curtis took a social-Darwinist line that racial unfitness was not 'incurable'; rather, over time, 'under careful and benevolent political education such as our slowly-broadening institutions afford', it was possible that the people of India might become fit for self-rule.[28] The wait was indeterminate and unending. Sastri countered with the prevailing scientific opinion on the falsity of the racial line, and reminded Curtis that the 'best training was obtained by grappling with your difficulties by yourself', as the dominions and England had themselves realized. It was by practising self-rule that Indians would become fit for self-rule; there was no other way.[29]

## IV

On 12 July 1917, Edwin Montagu, Under-Secretary of State for India from 1910 to 1914, rose up in the House of Commons and flayed the government of India for being 'too wooden, too inelastic, too antediluvian' to be able to govern. It was a medieval political machinery running on twentieth century fuel. The Viceroy himself was four people rolled into one: the King, the Prime Minister, the Foreign Secretary and the Speaker of the House of Commons. The government required a major overhaul. Unless a new system of government, more responsible to the people of India, was introduced, he warned, 'you will lose your right to control the destinies of the Indian Empire'.[30] Five days later, as a begrudging acknowledgement, India-agnostic Prime

Minister David Lloyd George handed him the reins of this very political machinery. Although Montagu would have preferred to become the Viceroy, Lloyd George gave him the keys to the India Office. The new Secretary of State took less than five weeks to make one of the most significant announcements of the entire British rule in India. On 20 August 1917, Montagu declared that the goal of British policy in India was the 'gradual development of self-governing institutions' with a view towards 'responsible government'.[31] The statement was greeted with much applause.

Importantly, for India-watchers, Montagu had implicitly accepted both of Curtis' assumptions: that Indians were not yet fit to govern, and that they ought to serve an indeterminate period of tutelage. Furthermore, the phrase 'responsible government' was infinitely more laboured than a mere semantic preference. Indians had demanded 'self-government' (albeit under British rule), like the dominions. And it appears that Montagu's original draft had carried the term 'self-government'. But Curzon, now a War Cabinet member, inserted 'responsible government'. This innocuous-seeming change was meant to prevent the 'lawyer-class' and a 'Brahmin oligarchy', who controlled the Indian Home Rule Movement, from gaining political office. Self-government envisioned a transfer of power to Indians, while responsible government implied greater accountability to a wider Indian electorate.[32] Indians could be kept in the waiting room for as long as it took to make the electorates responsible enough for a robust democracy.

In *Congress–League Scheme: An Exposition*, Sastri questioned making 'responsible government' the pillar of reforms. Its underlying principle – the subservience of the executive to the legislature – worked most efficiently in two-party parliaments. In a diverse country like India with a multi-party set-up, responsible government would be perversely counterproductive, he argued. It encouraged corruption of money and of public morals; it incentivized the government to dole out favours to sectional interests in order to keep enjoying their confidence. The executive focused more on preserving itself than on the task of governing. The CL scheme, in contrast, had strengthened the legislature by increasing its influence over the executive, giving it better control over finances and making it more representative. But it had placed 'responsibility' solely with the executive, as in the case of America and Switzerland, which allowed a democracy to be both representative and stable. A five-year tyranny was still preferable to anarchy forever, he wrote. Hence, to argue that in Indian conditions responsible government was an advance over the CL scheme was not only an untested but also an outdated view.[33]

Meanwhile, the reforms were staunchly opposed by the British bureaucrats and commercial interests in India. In October 1917, under the leadership of Lord Sydenham, a highly unpopular former Governor of Bombay, the Indo-European Association representing these interests was formed in London. The association issued calumnious warnings about any weakening of British authority which would jeopardize British interests and its civilizing mission in India. Reforms would unleash a state of anarchy, destroy industries and railways, they warned.[34] In pamphlet after pamphlet, the association, before folding in 1922, ranted against the uneducated and uncivilized Indians who were ruled by a tiny Brahmanical minority which was intent on throwing out the British and enslaving the depressed classes.[35] Sydenham and the ultra-conservative *Morning Post* made the responsibility towards depressed classes their main propaganda point against reforms. The Justice Party, led by T.M. Nair, joined forces with this group, arguing that unless the non-Brahmins in Madras had a communal franchise, these reforms would merely entrench the Brahmin oligarchy.

Sastri argued that while the Justice Party's demands were reasonable, a plural vote rather than a communal vote was a more appropriate addressal of their concerns.[36] But the Indo-European Association's fear-mongering was merely 'a grotesque survival of primitive tribal distrust'.[37] He accused the Indo-Europeans of behaving like the Ulsterites, intent on forcefully preventing the move towards self-government in India, and warned that by listening to them the British government would be repeating its mistakes in Ireland.[38]

## V

Edwin Montagu and his 11-member delegation arrived in Bombay on 10 November 1917 in official secrecy, Indian-style. Word had got out and Indian crowds flocked to see the first British minister ever to visit India. Montagu's party was treated to a lavish display of pomp, a reception that he noted was deserving of a King or a Viceroy. A special train, decked in supreme luxury, took the visiting party straight to Delhi, halting at several stations along the 973-mile journey, where sahibs and soldiers of local administrations turned up in full gear to greet and salute the visitors.[39]

If Indians and their colonial government were trying to play up the occasion for their minister-in-charge in London, they could not have wished for a man more converted to faith. Montagu was evangelical in his conviction that the visit would be engraved in the annals of history. He pencilled in his diary: 'My visit to India means that we are going to do something, and something big. I cannot go home and produce a little thing or nothing; it must be epoch making, or it is a failure; it must be the keystone of the future history of India.'[40]

His high idealism immediately encountered the steely recalcitrance of the behemoth he had set out to tame, the government of India. Lord Chelmsford and his government were considerably less enthusiastic about wide-ranging reforms. Montagu's ambition and Chelmsford's caution were locked in a battle of attrition, which left the former often frustrated and short-tempered. However, after multiple rounds of discussions with several stakeholders for about six months, the two arrived at a set of proposals which Montagu was happy to carry back to London.

Montagu first met Sastri on 20 December 1917 and both took an immediate liking to each other. Although Sastri argued for the CL scheme, he laid four minimum conditions for any other proposals: (a) an element of progress and a guarantee of progress in the scheme; (b) substantial, not cosmetic steps, without any humiliating stipulations about fitness; (c) fiscal liberty; and (d) absolute racial equality between Europeans and Indians.[41] On 1 February 1918, Montagu shared the broad contours of his scheme with Sastri, but the latter showed little enthusiasm. Montagu was convinced that if a moderate like Sastri was unappreciative of the scheme, the 'remedies will fall short of the circumstances of the country'.[42]

The Montford scheme (short for Montagu–Chelmsford) was announced on 8 July 1918. It adopted dyarchy at the provincial level and in general proposed a scaled-up form of autonomy. Local governments were to become completely autonomous; provincial governments would have two executives, elected and nominated, handling subjects which were reserved and transferred, respectively; and the central government was to retain its authoritarian character, albeit with an increased Indian representation in the Viceroy's Executive Council. The demands for democratizing and Indianizing the central government were mostly ignored. The Montford scheme granted a four-fifths elective majority to a new central Legislative Assembly and a more representative Council of State.[43] But these organs were given no teeth. They would continue to be glorified debating societies.

At first brush, the proposals satisfied almost no one. The more extremist factions in Congress ridiculed them. Tilak called it 'a good report but a useless scheme'; his newspaper *Kesari* wryly commented: 'it has dawned but where is the sun?'[44] In *New India*, Besant called the scheme a 'profound disappointment', 'a foolscap bluebook of 185 pages' whose 'spirit was petty and grudging'. Its content was 'not only inadequate but also reactionary', thus 'undiscussable'.⁴⁵ Sixteen Madras leaders including Vijayaraghavachari and S. Kasturi Ranga Aiyangar, the editor of *The Hindu*, issued a manifesto declaring that the scheme radiated an 'unqualified distrust' of Indians and was 'so radically wrong alike in principle and in detail' that it was impossible to discuss any improvement.⁴⁶

Moderate leaders were willing to accept the report with some modifications, however. The veteran leader Surendranath Banerjea called the proposals a 'distinct and definite stage towards the progressive realization of responsible government', and so did Dinshaw Wacha and Ramachandra Rao.⁴⁷ Gandhi called for a 'sympathetic handling rather than summary rejection', and Jinnah likewise.⁴⁸ Among publications, radical newspapers such as *New India, Hindu, Swadeshamitran, Indian Patriot, Hindustan* and *Kesari* as well as European-inclined papers such as *Statesman* and *Empire* rejected the scheme. More moderate papers, such as *Tribune, Servant of India, Leader, Bengalee* and *Panjabee* as well as the English-moderate *Times of India, Pioneer* and *Times* (Madras) took a reform-with-changes stance.⁴⁹ European officials and local governments predictably criticized the report.⁵⁰

Even before the proposals were made public, Sastri had counselled that Indians must get ready to negotiate. 'Compromise was the soul of negotiation', he wrote; and a delegation of Indians must proceed to England with 'precise ideas about what to press and what to yield'.⁵¹ The future course of action was a subtle question of strategy: negotiations will necessarily involve sacrificing some specific points on the CL scheme, but the quest should be to uphold its principles, he reasoned.⁵² After the Montford proposals were announced, he repeated his earlier criticisms on responsible government, dyarchy, progress in stages and lack of financial autonomy. But he noted that the authors had called the scheme 'transitional'.

The liberal negotiating credo was to take what you get and fight for more, he argued.⁵³ An outright rejection of reforms by the Indian leadership would only bolster the conservatives in Britain, especially the likes of Sydenham, and help them to convince the executive and the parliament to reject the reforms. A rejection would be disastrous, even 'madness': it would lead to disorderly agitations, in turn evoking strong repressive measures from the government. The ensuing disorder might seem 'to an abnormal type of mind' a necessary prelude to self-government, but 'if we throw everything into chaos, God will only know how to bring cosmos out of it!' By choosing to discard negotiations, 'a comparatively easy solution in our time', 'we shall hopelessly thicken the problems of our children'.⁵⁴ In general, the

Montford scheme validated or accepted the three broad principles of the CL scheme, even as it differed in the specifics: elective majority, dominance of the elected over the executive and fiscal autonomy. This allowed for a healthy negotiating ground.

Sastri's seeming about-turn, from being one of the architects and most forceful supporters in public of the CL scheme to appealing for compromise with the Montford reforms, invited the wrath of the extremist press, particularly *Mahratta* and *Kesari*. He was accused of having sold his soul and country for profit of office, and becoming a stooge of Montagu. What amused him about the criticism from Tilak's papers was that the only leader who had publicly agreed to support Montagu's scheme in full was Tilak's close associate B.S. Moonje. In an interview with the chief commissioner of the Central Provinces, Moonje, later a major Hindu Mahasabha leader, had accepted Montagu's proposals, provided India was given self-government within 50 years.[55]

## VI

A special session of the Congress Party was scheduled for late August 1918 to discuss the Montford reforms. The party was split between those who counselled acceptance with modifications and those who outright rejected the scheme. Unlike in the past, however, moderates no longer dominated the party.

Anticipating certain defeat, old Congress leaders Banerjea and Wacha canvassed moderates to boycott the Congress session. They suspected not only a defeat but also a campaign of sustained slander and abuse by young radicals in the party. Engineering a 'reverse Surat', they proposed an alternative meeting of Congress moderates. While many moderates endorsed Banerjea and Wacha's call, Sastri was ambivalent. He was required to decide not just about his own political future but also about the Society that he until then led in trust for his guru.[56]

Could the Society sever its association with the INC, a party whose first two decades carried Gokhale's stamp, but had now decidedly turned away from his 'lifelong associates', the moderates?[57] Initially Sastri appealed for a middle way. In a joint statement issued with his Society colleague R.P. Paranjpe, Sastri urged the moderates to attend and make a bold opposition in Bombay. 'We may fail, but even failure may justify our policy to the future', the two urged.[58]

Things quickly became worse. The opposition to reforms from the Indo-European Association in London was fierce, and reports suggested a surge in sympathy for the vile propaganda campaign in

England at their behest. In the House of Lords, Sydenham warned of the reforms throwing the empire off the cliff and in wild rhetorical flourishes painted 'a tragic vision of India's future unless the *status quo* was maintained'.[59]

The British public and politicians were notoriously ignorant about India, but the empire sentiment when steamed in hot rhetoric could park them on the side of the Conservatives. Newspapers like the *Morning Post* did Sydenham's bidding. *New India* and *Hindu* were now counselled by their own respective London correspondents not to wreck the reforms. To go into 'hysterics of denunciation of the scheme' was 'to play into the hands of the Sydenhamites', warned the *Hindu* correspondent.[60] Sydenham had, in fact, quoted Tilak's denunciation of the reforms to make his own point. Besant attempted to moderate her own view, now calling for 'non-acceptance with modifications'. This was neither rejection nor acceptance with modifications but a knotted formulation implying that the Montford scheme, although unacceptable, could be made less objectionable through modifications. Her subtle turnaround, however, made her unpopular among her own followers in Madras, who accused her of pandering to Montagu. In a stormy meeting of the Madras Provincial Congress Committee in early August, the high priestess of radicalism was shouted down and not allowed to address the conference as the chairperson of the reception committee.[61]

'The rubicon is crossed' announced the 27th issue of *Servant of India*. Sastri asked the members of the Society to abstain from attending the Congress special session in Bombay. It was obvious that the Congress would pass resolutions which would express disappointment with the reforms and demand such drastic changes as would amount to their abandonment. Rather than fight a losing battle it was better for the moderates to preserve their energies and morale and come together to provide a constructive roadmap at an alternative meeting, he wrote.[62]

## VII

With about 5,000 delegates in attendance, the organization's largest gathering to date, the Bombay Special Session of the Indian National Congress in late August passed several significant resolutions. It repudiated the assumption in the Montford proposals that Indians were not yet fit for responsible government, but kept the door for conciliation with the moderates open by not outright rejecting the scheme, primarily due to the efforts of Madan Mohan Malaviya.[63]

Instead, the Congress Party proposed significant revisions, a great many of them about granting greater power to Indians at the centre.

Among other things, the special session also asked for the democratization of foreign policy. India's representatives must come from among elected representatives, and the Congress asked the government to send Tilak, Gandhi and Syed Hasan Imam as India's delegates to the Paris Peace Conference. The Congress also tapped into Woodrow Wilson's endorsement of self-determination, and proclaimed that the principles of self-determination should be applied to India as 'a progressive nation'; accordingly the session issued a Declaration of Rights.[64] The Congress' claim to self-determination rested on a firm resolve that India was civilized enough to be considered ready for self-determination, and in the process also implicitly endorsed the scale of civilization argument. In fact, Vithalbhai Patel was to later tell the Joint Select Committee on reforms quite bluntly that the right to self-determination could not be granted to 'barbaric or semi-civilized peoples or races', but since India was the oldest civilization in the world with a history longer than the British in cultivating political institutions it could not be excluded from Wilson's proclamations.[65] This was not a call for solidarity of the oppressed under the term self-determination, but rather a claim to the high table.

Sastri had questioned the use of the term 'self-determination', although for entirely different reasons. It was fine to use self-determination as a politically expedient term, to bandwagon with a resounding appeal made by an American leader, but to celebrate as if this was a new revelation, as the Congress did, was moonshine. Congress extremists were using this term to push for abandoning the Montford reforms. So, Sastri asked, stripped of its momentary fame, how was the term any different from 'self-government', around which Indians had converged their claims for the longest time? Demands for self-government had been in currency in India since 1867, when W.C. Bonnerjee asked for self-government, before any 'modern prophet' attempted to own it.[66] It was useless, as Sastri's colleague Tej Bahadur Sapru had said, to base their hopes on Wilson. Would Wilson break with the British if they did not award self-determination? A direct reference to America, the newspaper *Tribune* wrote, was incompatible with India's self-respect. It was alright for the Irish, with a large influential diaspora, to appeal to America, but what would India gain by doing so?[67]

The moderates followed up with their own convention in Bombay two months later. Almost 500 people turned up on 1–2 November, one-tenth the number at the Congress session, conclusively indicating on which side public opinion rested. In the session, the Montford reforms were broadly accepted. The conference also decided to send a delegation to London to push for modifications in India's favour.[68]

Madan Mohan Malaviya, the conciliator-in-chief at the special session, was the Congress president for the 1918 annual session, held in the last week of December in Delhi. Quite characteristically, Malaviya appealed for unity, which was promptly supported by Sastri through *Servant of India*.[69] He allowed the Society's members to participate in the December 1918 Congress, insisting that the earlier embargo was only meant for the special session.[70] Sastri himself attended the Delhi session, where he made a failed attempt to remove the words 'disappointing and unsatisfactory' from the Congress' resolution on the Montford proposals in the special session. However, instead of any conciliation, the Delhi Conference went one step further and demanded an immediate grant of full provincial autonomy and full responsible government at the centre within a maximum of 15 years. Both of these proposals were stricter than the special session resolutions. The Congress Party also decided to send a delegation to London, but bound it strictly to the mandate of the Delhi resolutions, leaving little leeway for negotiations.

These conditionalities alienated two Congress leaders of note, Annie Besant and Jinnah. Both felt that the Bombay resolutions were passed in a spirit of conciliation with moderates, but the Delhi resolution had sabotaged any hopes of a compromise. Moreover, since the Congress had tied its London-bound delegation to the Delhi resolutions which wholly rejected the principle and substance of these reforms, there was nothing left to negotiate. 'To gain the shadow', Besant wrote, 'the Congress majority has surrendered the substance.'[71] Accordingly, Besant and Jinnah decided that they could not be part of any Congress delegation, and proceeded separately to London.

While different delegations prepared to go to London, the Indian government introduced two bills in the Imperial Legislative Council: the Indian Criminal Law Amendment Bill and the Criminal Law (Emergency Powers) Bill. Based on the recommendations of the Report of the Sedition Committee, headed by Sydney Rowlatt, the bills proposed strong repressive measures, such as preventive and indefinite detention without judicial recourse. They served the exact opposite purpose of the reforms and were partly a nod to the British bureaucracy in India, who had actively campaigned for these repressive acts and curtailing reforms. With these, Montagu also hoped to placate the Tories, especially in the House of Lords, in favour of the reforms.

In an unusual display of solidarity in the Legislative Council, all Indian members, elected as well as nominated, vehemently opposed the bills. These bills evidenced the government's distrust and its eagerness to repress and indeed signalled a lack of intent to actually go ahead with meaningful reforms. Sastri made one of the most memorable speeches in the debate. On 7 February, with Gandhi sitting in the audience chamber for the only time in his life, Sastri reminded the British that Indians had been 'hourly on trial' during the war. Indians met with every demand of the British, every test thrown India's way to show its loyalty to the empire had been 'cheerfully submitted'. When 'bidden to bring the milk of a beast of prey', Indians had 'brought a jugful of the milk of the tigress', only now to be asked to 'bring the milk of the male tiger'.[72]

The government's plea was that these repressive laws were only meant to be used against a handful of anarchists and revolutionaries. Sastri argued that the good intentions of lawmakers laid the pavements for petty bureaucrats to stomp through using every limb of the state. These laws – the history provided many illustrations – would always be misused by the securocrats in the Central Investigation Department (CID), whose job was to distrust the people. Even a moderate like him had been regularly followed and hounded by the CID in the past.[73] However, more importantly, he underlined that the rule of law cannot be suspended even for the anarchists. Sound statesmanship required offering them 'satisfying methods of political emancipation', and curing the general atmosphere which led to chaos. Reforms, not repression, was the way to end anarchy.

The speech was a masterclass in the expression of measured rage. Gandhi noticed the Viceroy being 'spell-bound' as Sastri 'poured forth the hot stream of his eloquence'.[74] But disregarding the opposition, the government still passed the bills, although their provisions were never actually implemented. Nonetheless, their passing led to Gandhi's protest movement against them, ominously culminating in the massacre at Jallianwala Bagh in Amritsar on 13 April and aerial bombings in Gujranwala two days later.

In addition to the draconian bills and the ruthless oppression in Punjab, the government of India did something evidently more damaging to undercut the Montford reforms. It sent an official dispatch to Montagu with recommendations on specific aspects of the reforms. Among the government's proposals were reducing the transferred departments in the provinces to the minimum, limiting financial autonomy and retaining as far as possible bureaucratic supremacy in the government's functioning. This was a blatant effort to whittle down the reforms in the specifics, a rear-guard action by the bureaucracy to kill the principles of reform via a thousand cuts.[75]

The high tide of 1917–18 – paeans to Indian bravery by British politicians and the announcement of the Montford reforms – had quickly descended into a low ebb of 1919 with the Rowlatt bills, Punjab repression and the government of India's despatch. It was in such circumstances that Sastri and Kunzru found themselves with four congressmen boarding the SS *Manora* on 28 April 1919.

## VIII

The SS *Manora* dropped anchor at Tilbury in the late evening on 23 May 1919, although the passengers could only be disembarked the next morning. A train carried the six Indian leaders to St Pancras in London, where Tilak's men were waiting for the Congress members. Henry S.L. Polak, Gandhi's old friend, was expected to receive the two moderates, Sastri and Kunzru. Polak did not show up. They waited for a long time before taking a taxi to nearby Russell Square; it took them even longer to find lodging for the night. When they finally booked into a hotel room after being declined by several hotels, they were beyond caring that it was small and dirty. The rituals of state surveillance in post-war London required them to fill elaborate forms with personal details twice over, on arrival as well as on exit. It was a 'nuisance', wrote a peeved Sastri.[76] His first day in the imperial capital was utterly forgettable.

Hoping the next morning would turn out better, they went with their luggage to Polak's father's house on a hunch they would find Polak. The culprit was luckily there, and after stern reprimands from Kunzru, took them to a lodging that he had pre-arranged for the two visitors.[77]

Now that they had a place to settle, Sastri and Kunzru started their work; and indeed their schedule over the next few days and months was quite busy. The moderates had sent a rather large group, which included Banerjea, Krishna Gupta, N.M. Samarth, Benode Mitter, D. Gupte, P.C. Roy, B.S. Kamat, C.Y. Chintamani and Ramachandra Rao.[78] Sastri and Kunzru would leave in the morning for meetings with English politicians and publicists, or to attend public and social gatherings at the India Office, and return only by dinner-time. For both, frugal living was an article of faith as part of the Servants of India Society,[79] and they survived with help from the Society and friends. Sastri's letters from London reveal a grudging fondness for the city's mad hustle, even as he shuttled between various meetings, spoke at gatherings across the city and the countryside, and complained profusely about the sky-high living costs. London's lifeline, the Tube, transported him to 'the enchanted land of the Arabian nights'.[80]

His public speeches had started to gain him a following. He made his first public speech on 2 June at Essex Hall in London, which had an immediate impact. Four weeks later, he spoke in Leeds, where he made a powerful appeal for partial self-government. Michael Sadler, the Vice Chancellor of the University of Leeds, wrote: 'I have no hesitation in saying that his addresses have won the respectful and cordial sympathy and support of the leading citizens – men and women. But far more than his spoken words, his personality has charmed and impressed those who have had the privilege of meeting him.'[81] On 3 September, Sastri attended an official lunch where the veteran journalist Stanley Reed called him the 'silver tongued orator', an appellation that stuck with him for the rest of his life.[82]

Meanwhile, on the reform bill, Sastri collaborated closely with Montagu.[83] Montagu presented the Government of India Bill to the parliament, from where it was referred to a Joint Select Committee.[84] The committee was headed by Lord Selborne, the former High Commissioner to South Africa. Sydenham was also included in the committee, which included among others Montagu and his under-secretary, the recently ennobled Satyendra Prasanno Sinha. Lord Sinha had added being the first Indian peer to his growing list of accomplishments, which included becoming the first Indian to sit in the Viceroy's Executive Council and the first Indian to hold a ministerial position in Britain.

In July and August 1919, Indian visitors were called to present evidence before the select committee. Banerjea, Besant, Tilak, Jinnah, Kurma Venkata Reddi, Patel, Madhava Rao and Sastri were among the many who presented evidence. Banerjea presented the moderate case; Besant's evidence and cross-examination also solidified the moderate position. Tilak presented evidence but was not cross-examined on account of his near-deaf condition.[85] He had been in London since October 1919 and seemed to have endorsed the Montford reform scheme in large part. The radical nationalist had turned, Sastri wrote, 'moderate with a vengeance'.[86] The Congress view was officially presented by Patel, whose evidence and cross-examination were confrontational. The Indian government's position was represented by James Meston. In cross-examination Montagu and Sinha were able to blunt the effect of the government's despatch and pushed Meston to concede on several points.

Sastri was called on the afternoon of 13 August. In the morning, Jinnah had brought fire to the proceedings. He attacked the bill for being 'timid and prejudiced', leading to an extended back-and-forth exchange with a seething Montagu.[87] Sastri thought that Jinnah had antagonized committee members with his 'strong language and slippery generalities'. His own evidence instead was presented with characteristic moderation; in it he warned against any whittling down of the proposed scheme.[88] Montagu was impressed with Sastri's presentation, noting that it was 'characterized by phenomenal mastery, independence, outspokenness and dignity'.[89] Among others, in Sastri's estimation, N.M. Samarth 'marred his evidence by an incautious phrase' (he had said that there would be a widespread agitation if central government was not liberalized[90]), C.Y. Chitnamani did 'exceedingly well', Rama Rayaningar 'proved an ass' and K. Venkata Reddi gave 'most damaging evidence', indulging in 'lies & distortions & innuendos'.[91]

Sastri's negative comments about Reddi and Rayaninger, two men from his own province, Madras, need elaboration. Reddi represented the Justice Party in the absence of Nair, who had just passed away. Comparing the INC to an *agraharam*, a Brahmin-exclusive residential enclave, the Justice Party saw no hopes in its politics, and nor indeed in the politics of the newly-formed moderate convention which was also dominated by Brahmins.[92] Earlier, the Justice Party had refused to appear before the Franchise Committee, which heard petitions on communal representation, because the two Indians it included were both Brahmins, Sastri and Banerjea. Sastri was, thus, a symptom and a symbol of the monopolistic hold of Brahmins over politics, especially in the Madras presidency. Reddi argued that the only demand of the non-Brahmins of Madras, a constituency he represented, was to secure communal representation, with or without reforms. On the whole, he was not enamoured by the idea of reforms, because the demand for political reforms was foisted upon India by Brahmins, who had also put such ideas into the minds of gullible non-Brahmins. However, Reddi and his party's politics were far from inclusive. When asked about whether the *panchamas*, the outcastes, were included in the non-Brahmin fold, Reddi included them as voters but not as elective candidates. He insisted that they had not yet become eligible to be elected on account of the low development of their minds. Although they were considered 'slaves of the nation', non-Brahmins treated them more humanely 'as children'. So, while claiming to represent the *panchamas*, he refused to grant them political and social equality with the upper-caste non-Brahmins. Rayaningar, representing the interests of Madras landlords, who were also predominantly non-Brahmins, then argued for non-Brahmin communal representation as well as for an upper chamber in the provinces to preserve landlords' interests. These were contradictory testimonies for they tended to be anti-Brahmin yet casteist, pro-poor and anti-poor, anti-elite and pro-elite, anti-government and pro-government, all at the same time.[93]

Montagu met Sastri on the evening of his testimony, and asked to assist in incorporating the amendments to the bill. Over the next few months, Sastri worked closely with Montagu in inserting amendments and drafting rules and the instruments of accession. Sastri saw Montagu's work from close proximity and was convinced that India had no better friend. The latter stood resolutely against the government of India's repeated attempts to undercut the bill. Working tirelessly on the bill, Montagu even stopped attending Cabinet meetings, to the displeasure of his colleagues and the Prime Minister. Sastri felt that Montagu had risked his whole career for the bill and was sure to be fired sooner or later.[94] Montagu was equally appreciative of Sastri's work, referring to him, ironically, as the 'Lionel Curtis of India'. When asked in an interview about who he thought was the ablest Indian supporter on the reforms, Montagu had replied 'Sastri'.[95]

While Sastri got along well with Montagu, his relations with some of his moderate colleagues were increasingly unpleasant.[96] Sastri had pushed for working jointly with other Indian deputations, especially on seeking amnesty for political prisoners in Punjab and on the South African question (which we will discuss in the next chapter). But he was opposed particularly by the secretary of the moderate delegation, N.M. Samarth, who accused Sastri of causing 'mischief and fissiparous tendencies'.[97]

The Joint Committee's final recommendations which were incorporated into the bill improved considerably upon the original Montford proposals. Broadly, the financial powers to the provincial legislatures were expanded, fiscal control from England was relaxed, the numbers of elected members in the upper chamber were increased and its remit was reduced to acting only as a second chamber and not a blocking chamber, and legislatures were relatively cushioned from control by the executive by making provisions for their leadership coming from elected members after four years. Education as a subject was transferred in the provinces to Indian ministers, a significant step to improve the access and quality of education in the country.

One major setback was the announcement that the scheme of reserved and transferred subjects would be reassessed at the end of ten years. The Montford proposals had suggested five. But considering the Indian government's reactionary dispatch of 5 March, the Joint Committee's final suggestions brought much relief. The Government

Amritsar tragedy, and its sneaky dispatch on the reform bill, the Indian government could not afford to be seen as doing nothing to secure the rights of Indians abroad. This was a question of the country's prestige, or *izzat*, an issue which generated robust solidarity across the Indian political spectrum. A joint delegation of leaders of the Congress, the moderates and the Indian government, led by Surendranath Banerjea, met Montagu in London and demanded, in implacable terms, a repeal of the Act. The Indian government, through its recently appointed High Commissioner in London, William Meyer, also registered a strong protest to the imperial government. Meyer told the gathering that the Indian government was considering retaliatory measures.[6] Tej Bahadur Sapru, then a member of the Viceroy's Executive Council, doubted the efficacy of any retaliatory steps since there were hardly any South Africans in India. Instead, he demanded a royal veto.[7] Writing in *Young India*, Gandhi supported Sapru's call. At worst, the Mahatma wrote, South Africa would secede from the empire in response to a royal veto. This was 'a thousand times better than it should corrupt and undermine the whole of the imperial fabric'.[8]

Montagu was equally determined not to let this pass. He wrote to the Colonial Office, who would pass his message to the South African government, that the Act could not be interpreted solely as South Africa's internal matter. India was now an 'equal member of the British Commonwealth', and the welfare of its people resident in the dominions was a 'growing rather than a diminishing factor in imperial politics'.[9] The South African Act was imperial in its ramifications, and accordingly the Indian government should be allowed to make a representation to the proposed commission in South Africa. The South African government, while disputing Montagu's take on the Act's external ramifications, agreed to allow the Indian government to make a representation to the commission.

Who should India send as its representatives? Both the Indian government and the India Office knew that any delegation to South Africa without an Indian member would carry little legitimacy with Indians in both countries. The South African government strongly resisted sending someone like Gandhi, who would fuel the South African Indian agitation. Montagu had Gokhale's other disciple in mind. He was convinced that Sastri would make the same impression as his guru Gokhale who had visited South Africa in 1912. Chelmsford agreed. The other member of the delegation would be Benjamin Robertson, a senior ICS officer.

Quite characteristically, while 'Slim Jannie', as Smuts was called under hushed breaths for being two-faced, celebrated imperial brotherhood in Durban, he resorted to an underhand game once he became the Prime Minister. Intervening in these ongoing discussions between the two governments about Indian representation, he disapproved of any Indian, in this case Sastri, being part of the delegation. He argued that an Indian could not be given the same treatment as a European diplomat because of local compulsions. Even if the government were to treat Sastri on a par with Robertson, Sastri would face racial discrimination at private gatherings. So, for instance, no European hotel would accommodate Sastri. South Africa asked that Sastri be sent in a junior capacity with Robertson.

Sastri responded that how could he be expected to plead for the equality of Indians with whites in South Africa, if he himself accepted an inferior position to his white colleague. And, accordingly, refused to join the delegation.[10] Geoffrey L. Corbett, a British civil servant, replaced Sastri on the commission. Smuts may have prevented Sastri from visiting South Africa by offering demeaning terms, but little did he suspect that that not only would he have to face Sastri soon, but that Sastri would hand Smuts his first diplomatic embarrassment.

## II

Exactly two years after his first arrival in London, Sastri was back in the imperial metropolis in May 1921. This time, he attended officially as a member of the Indian Railway Committee, led by W. Ackworth, which had finished taking evidence in India. But he was to stay behind afterwards for the Imperial Conference, to which the outgoing Viceroy, Chelmsford, had appointed him as India's representative. Chelmsford's selection had raised some concern among his officials. Sastri was at that moment practising a non-cooperation of sorts with the government. Chelmsford had disallowed him from moving a resolution condemning the government's atrocities in Punjab, and in retaliation he was refusing to move any other resolutions listed in his name. But Chelmsford responded to his officials' concern about Sastri's recent anti-government stance: 'Mr. Sastry [sic] is the most competent person. If he opens his mouth, and speaks two sentences in the conference, everybody would have the surprise of their lives and listen to him with wonder'.[11] The other Indian representative was the Maharao of Kutch, Khengarji III. Montagu, as the Secretary of State, was to lead the Indian delegation.

Aboard the SS *Kaiser-e-Hind*, Sastri had departed from Bombay on 16 April with two civil servants, Geoffrey Corbett and Girija Shankar Bajpai. Corbett had returned from South Africa after presenting evidence to the commission, so had first-hand knowledge of the of India Bill of 1919 was generally acknowledged as a sufficient advance over the Montford proposals.

## IX

In the last week of November, Sastri was on a ship back to India. Terribly homesick by now, he was eager to see his family after seven months. They journeyed to Bombay, where upon landing Sastri made several speeches about the reform scheme, endorsing it in full. He paid tribute to Montagu who in his estimation stood among everyone else as the truest friend of India. But Sastri's own role was not small. Polak wrote in *The Leader*:

> [S]o much of [Sastri's] work had been of the quiet and unobtrusive kind that is not advertised and does not come under the direct observation of more than a dozen people. But it is no exaggeration to say that no member of any deputation has done as much as he did to give the Bill its present shape. In so many respects, he has shown that he is a worthy successor to his great leader, Mr. Gokhale. ... Mr. Gokhale's mantle seems to have fallen upon his shoulders, and he has worn that majestic garment with an ease that would have delighted his master.[98]

From Bombay, Sastri journeyed north to Amritsar to attend the annual session of the INC. Sastri had earlier appealed to his moderate colleagues that they should go to the Congress session in Amritsar with a well-defined moderate programme. In response, Samarth had threatened him with expulsion. Sastri could not care less.[99] While he was on the train, an unnamed member of the Viceroy's executive council asked him to oppose a resolution calling for Chelmsford's censure. Sastri declined point blank, costing him, if one believes Natesan, a seat in the Viceroy's Executive Council.[100]

The year which had begun with much agony for the city of Amritsar, the country and the Congress finally appeared to be ending on a happy note. On the very first day of the Congress conference, Tilak, Gandhi, Besant, Jinnah, Malaviya, Madhava Rao and Sastri, covering a spectrum of political beliefs on the reforms, sat next to each other on the main platform.[101] Along with giving his assent to the reform bill, the king had also announced a general amnesty for all political prisoners. 'The heart of India', Sastri had declared, had received 'a much-needed balm'.[102] Special cheers were reserved for the political leaders from Punjab, just released from prison.¹⁰³ In his presidential speech, Motilal Nehru counselled accepting the reforms while continuing to agitate for more, a suggestion that found acceptance in a resolution.¹⁰⁴ Sastri was pleased.

Midway through the conference he dashed off from Amritsar to Calcutta, where the moderates were holding their own session. Arriving a day late, Sastri brought the good news that the Congress had accepted the reforms. But if he had hoped for any reconciliation between the two factions, it was not to be. At Calcutta, the gathering formally established the National Liberal Federation. The name 'National Liberals' was suggested by the incoming president, P. Sivaswamy Iyer, after Surendreanath Banerjea had complained the previous year that the term 'moderate' was too mild.¹⁰⁵ The moderates, now calling themselves liberals, had officially seceded.

The Montford reforms had been a victory of the liberal creed Sastri had championed for most of his adult life. As Polak noted, he had proven to be the ideal successor of Gokhale and had played a role akin to that of his guru in the Morley-Minto reforms of 1909. Sastri had well and truly taken the liberal baton from Gokhale, and had been catapulted into the top rungs of the Indian leadership. His strong critique of liberal imperialists like Curtis combined intellectual and moral force. But at the same time, as a politician, he navigated the often wide gulf between policy and critique by first assisting in framing, and then becoming the most articulate defender of, the CL scheme and subsequently the Montford reforms.

These reforms should have ideally strengthened the kind of liberal constitutionalist politics Gokhale embodied. But it was the rise of another Gokhale disciple that took national politics into an entirely opposite direction. In 1919, with Tilak in London, Gandhi had taken the baton of a more popular, radical politics and turned it into a mass movement. When Tilak died in mid-1920, Gandhi became the face of the Congress.

If the two decades from the mid-1890s to the mid-1900s were the high tide of the Gokhale–Tilak encounter in the Indian freedom struggle, the 1920s pushed Gandhi and Sastri onto the frontlines of their respective ideologies. The battle over ideology was fierce, but was also fortunately less acrimonious and spectacularly devoid of any personal antimony between its two protagonists. In 1919, both had just turned 50.

4

# The Silver-Tongued Orator

I

On 26 August 1919, the South African Minister of Defence, Jan Smuts, was in the coastal town of Durban in the Natal province. Informally referred to as 'the largest Indian city outside India', it was, as it is now, a place abundant with South Africans of Indian descent.[1] They had first arrived as indentured labour in the colony of Natal in 1860, followed a few decades later by traders, or 'passenger Indians'. The Union of South Africa, a state formed in 1910 out of the four colonies of the Transvaal, Natal, the Cape Colony and the Orange Free State, treated its non-white subjects as second-class citizens, although the degree of discrimination differed from province to province; the Orange Free State being the most racist and the Cape Colony the most liberal.

In his address to local Indians that day, Smuts assured them of 'fair treatment in all parts of the Union'. A frisson of excitement ran among the crowd, as Smuts summoned empire sentiment to appeal for conciliation between whites and Indians. He announced: 'We have to live side by side in conciliation … so that we may live together and grow together. We are members of one family … the same Empire.'[2]

For an Afrikaner leader, let alone a former Boer War general who had fought a brutal war against the British Empire, this could seem an odd choice of words. However, Smuts was the most empire-loving of all Afrikaner leaders, and the empire loved him back. In fact, he had just returned from England after two and half years. There, his former Boer War opponents had feted him publicly for leading troops against Germans in South West Africa and East Africa in the First World War. Several cities, including London, Plymouth, Cardiff, Manchester and Bristol, bestowed on him their freedoms. The parliament gave a banquet in his honour. David Lloyd George made him a member of the War Cabinet, and used him as his trouble-shooter, whether it was sending him to speak with the striking miners in Wales or offering him the command of Palestine (which he turned down). He played an instrumental role in the founding of the League of Nations as well as the Royal Air Force. The journalist-politician C.P. Scott called him in 1917 'the most popular man in the country'.[3] He even nearly got a country of his own, when the British considered renaming German East Africa. 'Smutsland', like Rhodesia, was a strong contender before being discarded in favour of Tanganyika.[4]

The context of the newly crowned imperial statesman's assurance to South African Indians was the passing of the Asiatics Land and Trading Amendments (Transvaal) Act by the South African parliament, another piece of legislation in the long history of laws of segregation and discrimination passed against Indians (and Africans). The Act barred the issuing of new trade licences to Indians outside of their designated spaces in the Transvaal province. This legislation also ended a brief wartime lull in enacting discriminatory laws against Indians. On the eve of the First World War, Gandhi and Smuts had signed an agreement which ensured the 'vested rights' (a phrase full of legal ambiguities) of Indians in South Africa. But in 1919, a parliamentary select committee prohibited the granting of any new trading licences, although it allowed Indians to retain all licences issued until then. South African Indians protested that 'vested rights' could not be limited to a time period, while the anti-Indian white group, the South African League, lashed out at the Act for being too favourable to Indians. In response to these criticisms and demonstrations, the South African government set up a commission to reconsider the whole question of Indians in the Transvaal. With Smuts back from London after a long absence, Indian hopes were raised. In 1917, he had announced at the Imperial War Conference that white 'intolerance' was a response to the 'fear of swamping' from incoming Indian immigrants. But since Indian immigration had stopped in 1913, he fully expected the relations between whites and resident South African Indians to normalize. His Durban speech assured Indians of his commitment to their betterment.

Later that evening, Smuts was urgently summoned back to Pretoria. His 'best friend' and Prime Minister, Louis Botha, was seriously ill and died in the night of heart failure.[5] Smuts was his obvious successor. South African Indians anticipated a more sympathetic commission under the new premier.

Meanwhile, across the Indian Ocean, the South African Act could not have come at a worse time for the British Indian government. Facing backlash for the Rowlatt Acts, the general repression in the wake of the conditions. The 29-year-old Bajpai was something of a young prodigy, having topped almost every exam from primary school to Oxford. In the supremely competitive ICS exams, he had a 100-mark lead over the next rank holder. His rise within the ICS was equally spectacular. Within 12 years of service, he would go on to become the youngest secretary ever in the ICS and, in another few years, a member of the Viceroy's Executive Council. He eventually became independent India's first Secretary General of External Affairs.[12]

The young bureaucrat had been suddenly plucked from United Provinces and deputed to go with Sastri to London as the latter's private secretary, most likely on the recommendation of Tej Bahadur Sapru. Bajpai witnessed Sastri deliver a speech at the Deccan Sabha in Poona just before their departure and was wonderstruck at the 'mastery of diction, beauty of manner, mellifluousness and charm of utterance'. In a private letter to Sapru, Bajpai commented that Sastri's style of 'restrained phrase and invincible logic' was far superior to the ornate and impassioned manner of delivering speeches. Oratorical performances were key to any diplomatic success, but as Bajpai observed, the logic of what made a great speech in diplomacy had measurably changed. The stirring of passions, the signature move of all great orators of the pre-World War era, was slowly disappearing. In the new scientific age, where matters of war and peace were resolved over arguments held to public accountability, rather than privately arrived through cunning, reason triumphed over passion. The arguments and speeches, reproduced in newspapers across the world and thus affecting public perceptions and mood, required reasoned, rational arguments which could slip past early excitement into long memory. Consequently, public discourse was increasingly framed by an appeal to logic, rather than flirtations with passion. Sastri, Bajpai surmised, appealed to the new age of public speaking and was 'destined to triumph' at the Imperial Conference.[13] What worried Bajpai, however, was Sastri's reticence and shyness, his introverted inclination to avoid social occasions, for '[i]n the circles in which he will soon have to mingle social charm counts for as much as intellectual power or political sagacity'.[14] From the ship, Bajpai happily reported his successful efforts at 'humanizing' Sastri by teaching him to play bridge.

Sastri's arrival in London this time was quite different from his last visit. For one thing, unlike last time, Polak was present at Victoria Station, along with Bajpai's younger brother, and a luxurious flat at St James Court, a short walk away from Buckingham Palace and Westminster Abbey on either side, was prearranged. For another thing, he was relatively well-paid; and his accommodation, food and travel were taken care of. This contrasted starkly with his grim pecuniary state on the previous visit, when he depended mostly on the generosity of friends to sustain himself. As a member of the Servants of India Society, he denied himself more expenditure than was strictly required. Bajpai, who had a taste for the finer accoutrements of life in dress, food and art, was a hit on his savings, he complained, but enriched his experiences. Sastri's letters to his brothers reveal his mischievous amusement at the perks of luxurious living. When in early June he was moved to the nearby Carlton Hotel, he wrote to Suryanarayana Rao:

> Tell Venkatasubbaiya,[15] the chief of this place [Carlton Hotel] gets £1000 a year, and he is inquiring, with bated breath and whispering humbleness, whether I am to be addressed as His Excellency or His Highness. [This hotel] is meant for princes and noblemen. ... I tread on the carpets with reverence and sit on the edges of the chairs as though I was afraid of being seen in them.[16]

The two Indian delegates to the conference were a study in contrast. The Maharao of Kutch, decked in expensive silks and colourful jewels, travelled with an entourage, while soberly dressed Sastri, retiring in disposition, could be found reading a book in a secluded corner of his hotel.[17] Given to periods of melancholy, his letters from London reveal a joyous, mildly vain Sastri who enjoyed his time, and took pleasure in luxury as well as the spotlight.[18]

On the work front, Sastri, Corbett and Bajpai conducted a series of discussions with the India Office. Sastri had identified securing the rights of overseas Indians as his main mission and accordingly prepared a resolution for the Imperial Conference. Smuts would mostly likely endeavour to brush the issue aside as an unimportant matter at the conference. India Office mandarins, whom Bajpai described 'as an extra-cautious body of men who are apologetic even when claiming what is no more than due to India', insisted on toning down the language of the resolution.[19] Sastri was equally determined not to allow the issue to be shoved aside by Smuts or diluted by bureaucrats. He did a series of interviews and speeches on the issue of overseas Indians to create enough noise to make it harder for the dominions as well as the agenda drafters to ignore.[20] In one instance, Sastri was invited to speak at the Colonial Institute. He sat listening to others discuss colonial problems without a word on India. Exasperated, in a 'short but sharp speech' he reminded the audience that without India there was no empire. He wrote later: 'they were annoyed, and I enjoyed it'.[21]

On another occasion, at a dinner given in the honour of dominion and Indian representatives Winston Churchill made one of his characteristic speeches, speaking of 'our race', 'English speaking peoples' and 'four great dominions'. Sastri delivered, wrote Neville Chamberlain who sat in the audience, 'one of the most scathing rebukes [of Churchill] I have heard'.[22]

Bajpai pushed Sastri to attend several social functions which offered opportunities for 'making informal but very useful political discussions'.[23] Against someone of Smuts' stature, the Indian delegation needed every opportunity to cajole and persuade other delegations and the London political elite.

## III

Back in India, the passing of the 1919 reforms had brought in progressive changes at the level of government. For the first time, half of the Viceroy's Executive Council was Indian. Lord Sinha was appointed as the first Indian Governor, to Bihar and Orissa. A new Legislative Assembly and a Council of State with a substantial Indian majority were inaugurated in 1921. Sastri himself was elected to the Council of State. Despite these changes, however, the public mood regarding the reforms had moved in the opposite direction, for several reasons.

In March 1920, the Congress issued its report on the Punjab tragedy by a sub-committee that included Gandhi. The report blamed the Governor Michael O'Dwyer, General Reginald Dyer ('the Butcher of Amritsar') and a few other government officials for the 'acts of atrocious injustice on a wholescale scale' and demanded that they be brought to justice and the Viceroy recalled.[24] However, the government-appointed Hunter Committee exonerated O'Dwyer and Chelmsford while censuring Reginald Dyer. Meanwhile, on 15 May 1920, Britain and France announced their peace terms imposed on Turkey, which dismembered the Turkish empire, the seat of the Muslim caliphate. The 'malicious and humiliating' terms were seen as a betrayal of the 'unbounded and loyal help which the Indian Muslims had rendered into the war'.[25] In conjunction with the Khilafat Committee, formed to oppose the Turkish settlement, Gandhi started a non-cooperation movement in 1920. After accepting them in Amritsar, it now repudiated the 1919 reforms and declared progressive non-cooperation as the Congress' method for achieving Swaraj in one year. By early 1921, the country was fully in the grip of the non-cooperation movement, which had progressively expanded its methods from *hartals* to the boycotting of councils, government services, schools, universities and colleges.

A constitutionalist through and through, Sastri had an innate dislike for the politics of non-cooperation. He was critical of the explosive potential of mass movements for their susceptibility to violence. It was one thing to conduct non-cooperation through trained workers in Gandhian tactics, but quite another to expect everyone in a mass movement to behave responsibly. Even though Gandhi repeatedly insisted on strict discipline, a few reckless and violent passive resisters were enough to scupper the whole movement, and in turn legitimize the government's harsh and violent response. Even if the government were eventually to yield, it would do so only 'after exacting terrible suffering and trial'.[26] The victory would be pyrrhic.

Relatedly, he cautioned against underestimating the warping and twisting effects of a deep communal divide among Indians. Mass movements tended to fan rather than contain communal prejudices. The Moplah rebellion, which started as a response to the crackdown on the Khilafat movement in mid-1921 in Madras province and turned into communal violence against Hindus and Christians, was for Sastri a proof of such tendencies.

Finally, for him, Gandhi's non-cooperation sought a breakdown of administrative machinery. When there was a grave possibility of violence, an administrative breakdown was a recipe for disaster.[27] Anarchy bred more anarchy. Only in truly exceptional circumstances, when all constitutional measures had been exploited, could non-cooperation be contemplated. Sastri, as with other liberals, did not believe that constitutional methods had been fully utilized. If at all, the 1919 reforms had vindicated their belief in constitutional methods.

In the September 1920 session of the Congress, organized in Calcutta, Gandhi appealed for the adoption of non-cooperation. Although liberals had been specially invited to this special conference by the president Lala Lajpat Rai, they were deliberately excluded from the Congress committees. Annie Besant, who three years prior would have been called an 'extremist', rose to speak and was immediately howled down with cries of 'spy' and 'a woman in the pay of the government'. Besant returned from Calcutta convinced that the 'old Congress is dead'.[28] Refusing to accept non-cooperation and resign from the council, Sastri finally broke off his relationship with the party. In fact, not only was he elected to the council, he had also accepted the official position of India's representative to the Imperial Conference. For this, he was routinely pilloried in the nationalist press.

Sastri's political troubles at home however were quite different from those of his main opponent at the conference, Jan Smuts. In

May 1921, on Smuts' orders, 163 Africans belonging to a sect were gunned down in a place called Bullhoek in the Cape province. The sight of 800 soldiers shooting randomly at a peaceful bunch of cult members picketing on a piece of land was reminiscent of the Jallianwala massacre. A writer called Smuts 'the Butcher of Bullhoek'.[29] As critics in South Africa demanded his resignation, he arrived in London to an unsurprisingly warm reception. Back in his stomping grounds where Bullhoek was only mentioned in whispers, Smuts wore his international statesman garb with poise. In London, he facilitated a dialogue between the British government and Eamon de Valera's Irish administration. His recommendations were key to the declaration on Ireland on 22 June, when the king appealed for reconciliation.[30] He recommended dominion status for (southern) Ireland, and authored a memorandum on the constitution of the British Commonwealth, insisting that the term British Empire be replaced with the British Commonwealth.[31] His 'good work', he was confident, would be 'felt throughout world politics – in Asia, America and Ireland'.[32]

## IV

The term 'British Commonwealth', although an old one, had come into vogue recently. In the previous chapter, we noted how the Round Table, and in particular Lionel Curtis, had recently theorized the idea of the British Commonwealth as a political form based on sacramental conceptions of citizenship. In 1917, Smuts had taken the same term, and appealed for understanding it as the specific way in which the British Empire had turned into a partly cloistered but organically evolving system of states, where its constituents were joined by their allegiance to the common sovereign, the traditions of freedom, and a firm belief in the fullest development of its constituent parts towards self-government. On his 1921 visit, however, he described the British Commonwealth as 'a federation of white races'. This contrasted with several of Smuts' own earlier pronouncements about the new ideals of a more equal Commonwealth.

Sastri and Smuts, two beleaguered liberals, met for the first time on the afternoon of 15 June 1921 for an hour and a half at the Savoy Hotel. He told the South African leader that to argue for a racial Commonwealth was unworthy of a statesman of his stature and placed the empire in great peril. On the issue of South African Indians, Sastri 'poured out [his] soul', alternately 'cajoling and threatening' Smuts. Smuts first showed sympathy, then 'pulled himself together' and pointed to his domestic difficulties. Sastri tried to trap Smuts in his own words by pushing him to acknowledge the equality of races, but 'the rogue got out of it by disowning it'.[33] Smuts prevaricated by promising to continue discussions in further meetings (and subsequently ignored all of Sastri's requests for a follow-up meeting).[34]

Later that evening, Sastri relayed the conversation to a disappointed Montagu. The latter cabled the Prime Minister's secretary, Edward Grigg. Grigg was born in India to an ICS father, Henry B. Grigg, with known pro-Indian proclivities. Expecting him to be sympathetic, Montagu asked Grigg to insert a statement about the empire being a multi-racial Commonwealth in his boss' opening address to the conference to counter Smuts' white Commonwealth.[35] Meanwhile, Sastri met with other dominion prime ministers to canvas support. The New Zealand Prime Minister, William Massey, was 'generally favourable' to India's case. Arthur Meighen, the Canadian Prime Minister, also assured Sastri of his full support. However, he raised a practical difficulty. In Canada, any amendment to electoral laws could only be made by provincial legislatures, and hence Meighen's assistance could go no further than a recommendation to the provinces. In response, Sastri asked how Meighen would feel if India sent a delegation to help with convincing provincial legislatures. Meighen welcomed the suggestion.

William Hughes, the Australian premier, was sympathetic, but did not fully commit a vote. Slightly intimidated by the Australian initially, 'an able downright chap, very deaf and full of mannerisms, but dogged and full of fights',[36] Sastri came out of the meeting assured of Hughes' goodwill for India's resolution.[37]

These meetings, however, also convinced Sastri that it would be difficult to compel the dominions to enact pro-Indian policies on their own. Imperial Conference resolutions in any case did not have any enforcement mechanism. So he proposed to Montagu what he had mentioned to Meighen. If Sastri could get the dominion leaders to agree to some general resolution on the rights of Indians, it would be fruitful to send an Indian delegation to the dominions to influence their publics and parliaments. Dominion leaders were more likely to accept a resolution if the task of actually convincing their domestic publics, largely hostile to propositions of racial equality, was shared by India. Montagu readily agreed.[38]

On 20 June, Lloyd George's inaugural speech to the Imperial Conference called the British Empire a 'co-federation of races'. '[N]o greater calamity could overtake the world than any further accentuation of its divisions on the lines of race',[39] and indeed the principles of the empire were 'incongruous with the inequality of races', he added, to the joy of Indian delegates.[40] Montagu's nudge to Grigg seems to have worked. In his opening speech the next day, Smuts avoided his 'white Commonwealth' pitch. He limited himself to discussing the glowing ideals of the League of Nations instead, an organization which he had done much to bring into existence, as embodying 'the most deeply-felt longings of the human race for a better life' and for a lasting peace. He called upon the British Empire to back the League's ideals as the 'the foundation of the new international system'.[41]

Sastri cleverly dovetailed his own remarks with those of Smuts. Peace, he reminded his audience, particularly Smuts, could only be founded on 'a stable and unalterable relationship between communities – based on honourable equality and recognition of equality of justice'.[42] India's note to the conference had mentioned in strong terms that Indians could no longer acquiesce in a state of 'permanent inferiority' in the dominions. Indians had fought shoulder to shoulder with other members of the empire, yet they were treated better in Portuguese East Africa than in South Africa. Were Indians to face such disabilities outside of the empire, they would be protected by treaty rights or by active intervention of His Majesty's Government. But not within the empire. Why, asked Sastri, must Indian representatives carry different weight with foreign governments than within the British Commonwealth of Nations?

Such disabilities not only compromised India's self-respect as a country, but also raised questions about it remaining within the Commonwealth. India must be treated as an absolute equal and its people given full citizenship rights in whatever part of the empire they were domiciled. India had addressed the concerns of the dominions: it had stopped indentured emigration and accepted their right to maintain the composition of their population. It was essential now that the dominions treat the Indians domiciled in their territories as they would treat any British subject.[43] Accordingly, Sastri's resolution recommended 'the adoption of a policy of removing any disabilities under which such Indians are placed, and … merging them into the general body of citizens in whatever part of the Empire they may be lawfully domiciled'.[44] Sastri made a good impression, although he himself was not satisfied with his speech. 'Was not in good form. Rather in a funk', he penciled in his diary.[45]

Rhetoric was important, but so was the agenda of the conference, where the Indian question was given low priority. The main issue at the conference was the Anglo-Japanese alliance, which was due to expire in July 1921 (discussed in the next chapter). It was followed by a long list of other issues. The Indian delegates had after considerable difficulty succeeded in listing their resolution on the agenda, but it was pushed so far down in the pecking order that a detailed discussion was unlikely.[46]

To make matters worse, the conference progressed at a glacial pace. The Prime Minister's sickness had delayed the opening by three days, and the opening speeches consumed several more days. As the days passed, the Indian delegation grew increasingly anxious. Sastri intervened a few times to request a discussion on his resolution, to which Smuts would immediately intervene that the issue could wait. Worryingly for India, Meighen was leaving the conference early. Meighen and Sastri had developed a good friendship, and his support was guaranteed.

On 5 July, Smuts was away in Dublin, incognito as Mr Smith, to convince Eamon de Valera into talks with the British government. Sastri utilized his absence to urge Lloyd George to make time for discussion on his resolution. Lloyd George agreed to schedule it for 8 July, provided Smuts was back in time to attend the discussions. Sastri was elated to be sitting next to Smuts at a dinner in the latter's honour the next evening, less for the company and more for the assurance that Smuts would no longer be able to prevent discussions on the Indian resolution.

The South African leader had more tricks up his sleeve, however. On 7 July, Smuts suggested that since the Indian issue was a matter of deep contention, it should be first discussed in a sub-committee. This approach of death by sub-committee – the issue would be buried in specifics and never reappear at the main conference – received quick and sympathetic support from the Colonial Secretary, Winston Churchill. Sastri was dumbfounded at Smuts' duplicity and Churchill's enthusiastic cheerleading. Sastri, Montagu and the Maharao appealed directly to the British Prime Minister later that evening not to let that happen. The next morning, Lloyd George took the middle course. He agreed to send the matter to the sub-committee but only after allowing Sastri to make his speech at the plenary. A lot depended on Sastri's speech.

This speech had consumed Sastri's thoughts for many days. He could not merely rely on an emotional pitch; the speech had to make a rational case for the equality of rights of Indians against the established principle of each dominion's internal autonomy. His speech had to persuade rather than harangue; it ought to cut through the rationality of the dominions' response, engage them rather than strum an idealistic tune.

On a quest for clarity of ideas, he had gone to Shakespeare Hut a few days earlier, and attended a lecture by the philosopher-politician

Richard Haldane. In the lecture on university ideals, Haldane wandered off to discuss Einstein and relativity and, much like the rest of the audience, Sastri understood little and nodded profusely. However, after the talk, Sastri asked for his advice on the Indian resolution. Haldane agreed with Sastri that while the British Empire was based on allegiance to the same sovereign (as Smuts had argued in his 1917 lecture on the British Commonwealth), its larger principle was the sense of community fashioned through the recognition of equality of rights for all its subjects.[47] But going further, Haldane – 'calm, human, persuasive, benevolent, yet shrewd and practical minded'[48] – argued that dominion citizenship, which allowed for immigration restrictions, was a deduction from the larger principle of imperial citizenship, and not a creed of its own. During this meeting, which took place in Haldane's car as they drove towards his home, the liberal imperialist asked Sastri to consider Smuts' position more sympathetically. Smuts would not survive for a week in power if he accepted India's resolution. For better or worse, Smuts was the best option Indians had in South Africa. Even within Smuts' own party, there were calls for repatriating all South African Indians; his colleagues as well as opponents were far more racist. So it was important not to isolate him completely, but to engage him. 'Try the prime minister … he is the only man in England who could get Smuts to do something', Haldane said to Sastri before the two parted.[49]

## V

For two hours on the morning of 8 July, Sastri presented the Indian case on the rights of Indians overseas. He referred to the 1918 reciprocity resolution of the Imperial War Conference, which had accepted two principles: the dominion right to manage their populations and the Indian right to be treated equally within the empire. But the two principles emerged from two different motivations. The first was based on a principle of dominion self-preservation, the latter on a principle of justice. Self-preservation was an inferior principle to justice and equality. What made the British Empire a beacon of hope for people across the world was its endorsement of justice and equality, not the instrumentality of self-preservation. Sastri had teased out a relationship between the dominion right and the equality principle, a point he drew from his discussion with Haldane. But he had also made a fundamentally different argument. He had argued that the relationship was not a deduction of the dominion right from the equality principle, but that the two were different ideas of the new Commonwealth, one manifestly inferior to the other. In subsequent years, he would emphasize this further by calling them the principles of a Boer Commonwealth and a British Commonwealth, respectively.

The transformation of the empire into the Commonwealth, he acknowledged, could not solely rest on finding a higher ideal of the unity of empire. Even from the point of view of the preservation of the empire, however, the continuing discrimination against Indians across the dominions had fuelled the agitation of those who saw no hope of equality within a white man's empire.[50] Gesturing towards the threat posed by Gandhi's movement to the British Raj, he asserted that racial equality had to be the absolute cornerstone for the sake of the empire's continuance. A 'white Commonwealth' was a dead commonwealth, Lloyd George's 'co-federation of races' was the best way to define and sustain the empire in its new clothes, that is, the Commonwealth.

Acting on Haldane's second piece of advice, Sastri acknowledged Smuts' domestic limitations. He added that he understood that the principle and the practice could differ, the latter invariably lagged behind the former. But it was important to proclaim an ideal or a principle which would direct the practice. He urged the dominions to accept the principle of racial equality, and 'at the earliest opportunity begin the process of conforming to this principle'.[51] He gave Smuts and other dominion leaders a way out. They did not have to immediately institute measures to abolish racial inequality, but only commit to it in principle. Suggesting this as a fair compromise, he concluded: 'Let me be enabled ... to go and tell my countrymen that there are still hopes for us within this British Empire, in this Empire where we wish to live in confraternity with other peoples, that there is room, and honourable room for us.'[52] Sastri's rational appeal was elevated by his 'magnificent flow of oratory'. Lloyd George listened in rapt attention and cancelled his other morning appointments. He relished the way Sastri 'arraigned General Smuts, who used on every occasion to preach the Sermon on the Mount with a sanctimonious air'.[53] An Australian journalist later noted that the delegates were unanimous that it was a speech of 'the greatest elegance'.[54] Bajpai was certain that it created a 'great and abiding impression' on his listeners.[55] The issue was now sent to the sub-committee consisting of dominion prime ministers, headed by Churchill.

Smuts' response, made at the sub-committee, was blunt. He shed his liberal garb and asserted that racial inequality was 'the very bedrock of our constitution'.[56] South Africa's political system was fundamentally based on differences in colour, and no South Africa government could go against it and grant political equality to Indians. South African

Indians were economically better off compared to their compatriots in India. Economic prosperity without political rights, to him, was the best compromise to the Indian question.[57]

Let us recall that Smuts had earlier assured that his government had no wish to discriminate against Indians once the immigration stopped. Sastri protested that Smuts' statement was 'of enormous danger to the Empire, and to the principles on which the Empire is built'. Smuts had effectively told India and Indians that they are 'never to be the equal of any white community'.[58]

Smuts responded in anguish: '[n]o one had done more for India in this Conference for her position in the Dominion than I have done'.[59] The Maharao of Kutch intervened to ask if Smuts were to speak as an individual, not as South Africa's Prime Minister, would he accept the principle of racial equality? The Maharao had touched an important nerve in calling upon Smuts the liberal, rather than Smuts the white South African. Smuts' politics was ambivalent on both. Liberalism often provided him a convenient conceptual veneer to mask his racism (through terms such as 'separate development'). But on some occasions, such as Smuts was now faced with, liberalism did not yet summon a convenient vocabulary. Smuts realized that this was not an occasion to preach from the pulpit and weaselled in response: 'there is no point exploring a road which I am sure will take us nowhere'.[60]

The Indian delegation's exchanges with Smuts had pleased at least one dominion Prime Minister, William Hughes. At the Paris Peace Conference two years earlier, when the Japanese proposal for racial equality was turned down, Hughes had become the 'fall guy' while Smuts played 'the suave international statesman'.[61] At this point in the discussion, the Australian chimed in: 'The position of South Africa cannot be supported from the standpoint of justice. ... I cannot for the life of me see how it is compatible with our frequent declaration of the principle which governs this Empire.'[62] Since Smuts had recently invoked the 'ideals of freedom and co-operation' for Ireland,[63] Hughes suggested that Smuts should follow his own advice on Ireland and apply it to India.[64] William Massey, the New Zealand Prime Minister, argued that South Africa was making a 'mistake'.[65] The Canadian Minister of Defence, Charles Ballantyne, who had replaced Meighen, also supported the Indian position.

Just as Smuts looked certain to be outvoted, Churchill intervened on his side. As the committee chairman, he declined to make any revisions to the resolution. Churchill's support to Smuts suddenly made Hughes hesitate; he now refused to vote for the resolution unless it was voted unanimously. He may have enjoyed fingering Smuts, but the shrewd

Australian was aware that the resolution's language would be used by his domestic opponents as an attack on the country's sacrosanct 'White Australia' policy. Since unanimity was out of question as South Africa would obviously oppose, Churchill reported to the conference that the sub-committee had failed to reach a conclusion.[66] The resolution was effectively staring at its death. On returning to his hotel that evening, a dejected Sastri wrote in his diary: 'Had a most bitter and disheartening experience. Smuts showed all his slimness. Churchill went clear over; at last Hughes himself wavered. Came home to all but cried.'[67]

With some days to go for the plenary, the Indian delegation worked through back-channels. Montagu, related to Churchill by marriage, opened a line of communication with him to arrive at a mutually agreeable solution with Smuts. Sastri was tasked with placating Hughes over dinner.[68] Montagu sent Churchill a revised draft from the Indian side which deleted the mention of South Africa in the resolution. Churchill conferred with Smuts, re-drafted the resolution even more in South Africa's favour and added 'East Africa' to the resolution. This equation of East Africa, a crown colony, with other white dominions and India was meant to strengthen the case of Kenyan whites against Indian residents and prevent the immigration of Indians to the colony (more on this in Chapter 6). This 'mischievous and positively wicked move' infuriated Sastri and Montagu. Sastri 'most disliked Churchill', 'the *enfant terrible* among politicians', for using Smuts' troubles to stab Indians in the back on East Africa and wreck the Indian resolution.[69] Montagu threatened to resign, forcing Churchill to back off and remove the mention of 'East Africa'.[70]

Two weeks of backroom negotiations finally yielded results. Smuts accepted that he would let the resolution pass on the condition that South Africa would in the view of its 'exceptional circumstances' indicate its reservations. The Indian delegation first insisted that he replace 'exceptional' with 'present' circumstances to show that in the future things may change. When he refused, Indian representatives added their own note to South Africa's dissent, expressing 'profound concern' at the conditions of Indians in South Africa and hoping for bilateral negotiations between the two countries. Smuts agreed.

On 2 August, the resolution was finally tabled with Smuts onboard. Things looked propitious until Hughes 'ratted' again. He now argued that even if Smuts agreed to the resolution, he could not because it would embarrass him domestically. In Australia, accepting the equality of Indians in principle would cause resentment among other Asian populations such as the Japanese and the Chinese. Lloyd George intervened at this point, making a personal appeal to Hughes. He said:

> [D]o not let Mr. Sastri go back to the scores, and the Maharao to the hundreds of millions of Indians and say – 'The British Empire have refused us justice'. It will be an appalling thing to say to a people who sent a million and a quarter volunteers to aid us in a quarrel they had not the slightest concern with.[71]

Hughes yielded. He would place the resolution before his parliament, he said, and let Sastri himself present the Indian case to the Australian parliament. Ballantyne was also initially reluctant to accept the resolution, fearing that it would commit the Canadian government to something that it was not legally empowered to enact. However, when it was made clear that the resolution was only an expression of the opinion of the conference, he agreed. Massey, as expected, supported the resolution.[72] The resolution was passed with South Africa's note of dissent and India's counter-note (see Appendix).

As the drama ended, the Indians heaved a sigh of relief.[73] Sastri was, surprisingly, not too enthusiastic about the resolution. He felt the result was 'not anything to be proud of' as it was not 'by any means satisfactory'. South Africa, the main culprit when it came to discrimination against Indians, had opted out. However, for the first time, the Imperial Conference had made an exception to its custom of passing resolutions by unanimity. Three dominions had broken the ranks of white solidarity and voted with India. The resolution acknowledged the principle of the equality of Indians as British subjects in the empire – another first. Against all odds, Montagu and Sastri were able to keep East Africa out and the dominions were generally 'bound to give their franchise to Indians'. These were significant victories, and it was the best India could get under the circumstances.[74]

The resolution was actually a landmark in the history of the British Empire. A common imperial citizenship straddling the colour line was now encrypted in a resolution by the highest body of imperial decision-making. At the same time, it affirmed India to be 'an equal member of the Empire': as *The Times* reported, 'the first explicit recognition … in an authoritative document of India's equal status as a member of the Empire'.[75]

Two further aspects of this resolution need more attention. Despite the fact that Sastri couched his arguments in universalist terms, using words such as racial equality and justice, what he implied was not the racial equality or equality of *everyone* in the empire but only the equality of Indians with other members of the empire. Indians are deemed equal, not because of the innate equality of human beings, but because of the equal status of India as a political entity in the Commonwealth. Racial distinctions still remain. However, notionally, they no longer apply to Indians. In other words, equality here is not an assertion of human rights, but of sovereign equality. The principle is therefore a principle of law rather than of abstract justice. In a way, then, the exception here is India and Indians to racial inequality in general. This is important to understand why, as we will see later, Sastri is not really arguing for the equality of Africans as a natural corollary of universalist equality. In fact, his own vision of Africans, as civilizationally inferior people, is quite racist. The *Bombay Chronicle* was on point to argue that Sastri's racial equality argument was flawed considering that 'the whole constitution and practice of the Empire has been to exalt a white oligarchy at the expense of races whose inexplicable sin it has been to lack a particular chromatic distinction'.[76]

Second, South Africa's dissent note was interestingly framed. 'Slim Jannie' had indeed responded to the Maharao's question about his personal opinion: it implied that while Smuts was personally in sympathy with the resolution, South Africa's circumstances were too 'exceptional' for him to accept it as its premier. He did not torpedo the resolution by insisting on unanimity, which he easily could have. He let it pass, with a dissent from his country. Whether it was a genuine act of liberal belief or a manipulative nod to his self-image was, as was always with Smuts, difficult to tell. This vexing ambivalence was best captured by Montagu. In a letter to Churchill, he wrote that Smuts being the most favourable South African leader for Indians was 'one of the axioms of the situation … one of the reasons of our dismay'.[77] Two years later, Smuts would come to the Imperial Conference much better prepared, armed with a memorandum suited up in elegant liberal vocabulary on why all subjects were not equal. But for now, he agreed he was out-reasoned.

## VI

In and outside the conference, Sastri's reputation as the silver-tongued orator continued to grow. Over these months in London, the more he spoke, the more he was admired. One such instance was his short speech at the Empire Parliamentary Dinner on 24 June. An eyewitness described:

> Few who were present will forget the impromptu speech ... All the speakers had erred in the matter of length and relevancy, some had even been extremely tedious, and the hour was late. Mr. Sastri had the toast of 'The Chairman' to propose, and, doubtless, had prepared a speech of some political or imperial significance. Diagnosing the temper of his audience, he put his well-considered oration into his mental pocket, and in a few minutes, he had that bored assembly galvanized into life with his delicate humour and his rapier thrusts of irony. The stately chamber rang with laughter, and more than half the pleasure of the evening was condensed into seven minutes of masterly mischief.[78]

Lord Birkenhead, Lord Chancellor and the host, commented that it was worth one's while to travel miles just to hear Sastri speak.[79] Another attendee wrote for a Canadian newspaper: 'so far as sparkle and quality were concerned, this speech was certainly the good wine left until the last'.[80]

On 27 July, both Sastri and the Maharao of Kutch were awarded the Freedom of the City of London at Guildhall. In a cleverly worded speech, he feted the British Empire as 'the greatest Temple of Freedom on the planet', and immediately proceeded to remind his audience that freedoms could only be 'fully appreciated by those who have had the misfortune to lose them for a time'.[81] His cutting indictment of the empire masqueraded as soaring praise in this instance.

On other occasions, his speeches produced spectacles of another kind. A meeting in Shakespeare Hut, the YMCA's hostel in Bloomsbury, London, on 25 May turned into a hothouse when Sastri spoke on the 'Present Political Situation in India'. He spoke last in the gathering of nearly 1,000 people, largely comprising students,[82] and in his usual, measured tone expressed Indian grievances against British rule. As he spoke, some Indian students started aggressively heckling him, with epithets such as 'traitor', 'hireling', 'liar', 'government man', 'flunkey', among others.[83] Sastri's remarks were followed by an unscheduled speech from Syed Hussain, an Oxford-educated firebrand journalist who had just resigned from the editorship of Motilal Nehru's paper *Independent*. Hussain made, according to Sastri, a 'nasty and ill-natured reply'.[84] Bajpai seated in the audience seethed in rage, but also wondered how Sastri withstood 'these shocks as a granite rock'.[85] The small mutinies against him continued as he lectured in Oxford and Cambridge in the following weeks. Syed Hussain, his tormentor at Shakespeare Hut, followed him to these meetings.[86]

## VII

At the end of the Imperial Conference, Montagu asked Sastri and the Maharao to proceed to Geneva as India's delegates to the second assembly of the League of Nations.[87] The delegation was to be led by the High Commissioner in London, William Meyer. Travelling through Paris and Brussels, Sastri arrived in Geneva, with Bajpai in tow, in early September.

The League of Nations Assembly was by its very nature, as an observer wrote, 'an unspectacular body'.[88] Much of its actual work was done by the secretariat and the council, while the first assembly of the League in 1920 had turned into a talk-shop with long and frequent speeches. The one in 1921 promised to be the same. With 48 states in attendance, the second assembly started on 5 September at the Hall of the Reformation: 'an ugly looking place … very ill-adopted for public speaking', is how Sastri described it.[89] Arthur Balfour, the former premier and head of the British delegation, characterized it as the worst place in which he had ever spoken.[90]

The assembly's proceedings were dull and slow. Treated as a dispensable chamber by the council, the assembly sought its revenge by treating council members with equal disdain. Members from the great powers were barely tolerated.[91] In a truly democratic fashion, they were hemmed in with everyone else rather than being given a special voice. A half-deaf Balfour seated in the middle of the hall could barely hear most things, so would stand near the dais to listen to the speeches. Long speeches, often uninspiring and filled with propagandist generalities with a wink at home newspapers, tested the audience's patience.[92] The little that could be savoured through spontaneity and animation was sucked out by speech translators. Each speech was translated into English and French. An interpreter would stand beside the speaker, note down the speech in shorthand, and rush to the rostrum as soon as the speech was done to reproduce it in a monotonous, breathless fashion. Most spoke in French and Sastri concluded that 'a man without French here is like a man who has only half a life'.[93] The opening speeches alone took more than ten days.

The work of the assembly was divided into six committees; Sastri was deputed to two of those: the committee on constitutional and legal questions and the committee on humanitarian questions. A big part of the latter dealt with the opium trade, where India and China were to face off. Meyer, who for all his qualities as an efficient civil servant lacked 'tact and smooth speaking',[94] asked Sastri to speak to the assembly on India's behalf.

Sastri's turn to speak came on 12 September. He awoke that day to sharp pain in his chest, which left him barely able to move and walk. Speaking in 'slow sentences with their faultless phrasing',[95] Sastri started his speech with an arresting call to his 'Brother and Sister delegates': 'I come from India, separated from you by many thousands of miles, but I trust you will recognize akin to you, alike in loyalty to the League, in the spirit of humanity, and in zeal for the welfare of our kind.'[96] He acknowledged that the League was not a perfect institution, but it was more useful to partake in this work, both inside and outside the assembly, than to merely criticize it. He called upon the assembly to take more initiative; it must not thrust everything on the council. 'We, representing the different peoples of the world, are in a measure custodians of the peace of the world. We, I dare say, are the authentic voice by means of which the conscience of the world will speak', he said.[97] Unlike the council, which was a gathering of stronger powers, the assembly was 'bound to act in the interests of all of the others; that we are cosmopolitan reality, that we are the citizens of the world, and not merely the limited countries which we happen to represent'.[98] The assembly, in short, was a parliament of the world.

Having provided the assembly with a cosmopolitan purpose, Sastri now presented India's grievances. The first was regarding India's contribution to the League. India paid nearly 5 per cent to the League's expenses, and yet had only 1 representative in its secretariat. This contrasted sharply with 138 from Britain, 73 from France and 13 from America, which was not even part of the League. He appealed for democratizing the League's own secretariat.

The second grievance was the League's mandate policy with regard to the South African claims on the former German colony of South West Africa. Reminding that even Germans did not introduce a colour bar in South West Africa, he cautioned South African delegates against introducing it. Speaking on behalf of the non-white people of the world, he said that a South African colour policy in the mandate would mean that 'we are worse off under the trustees of the League than we were under the Germans'.[99] South Africa's delegates – the British politician Robert Cecil and the liberal academic Gilbert Murray, whom Smuts had asked to represent his country – writhed in their seats. Cecil and Murray immediately cabled Smuts for an appropriate response. The British delegation was also peeved, as Sastri had raised an internal issue at an international platform. But Sastri held that at the League, the Indian delegation was not subordinate to the British delegation and the criticism of South Africa was justified.[100] Bajpai thought it to be a 'frank and courageous protest' which would make it plain to the dominions that India would never accept the extension of the colour bar to the mandates under their control.[101]

The speech was a sensation. H. Wilson Harris, the president of the International Association of Journalists, identified Sastri and the Haitian diplomat, Louis-Dantès Bellegarde, as the two speakers to have made the deepest impression.[102] Sastri's voice, according to another commentator, became 'the very voice of international conscience'.[103] *The Times* correspondent wrote that his was the rare speech in which 'no attempt was made to avoid "making people jump"'.[104]

After the speech, Sastri's main role was in the humanitarianism sub-committee. The sub-committee was to discuss a council resolution based on an advisory committee report on opium. The resolution asked for prohibiting the illicit production, manufacture and trade in opium, except for medicinal and scientific purposes.[105] However, the council had set aside an important recommendation of the advisory report which counselled the League to appeal to the Chinese authorities to do more to curtail opium production. This was done at the behest of the council's president at the time and also the Chinese representative, Wellington Koo. As Bajpai put it, Koo's resolution wanted the world to shut its eyes to the irregularities in the production of opium in China, while embarking on a 'holy and humanitarian crusade against its use' in every other country.[106]

In his interventions in the sub-committee, Sastri objected to the resolution. He argued that in India dispensaries and medicinal facilities were scarce and people had for generations relied on opium to numb pain. This use was not strictly 'medicinal', but essential. He proposed an amendment to the phrase 'medicinal and scientific', and suggested replacing it with 'legitimate', which was accepted.

Further, hinting at Koo, he added that the council's outright dismissal of the advisory report's recommendation on China, a country that produced four-fifths of the world's opium, was an unsavoury sidestepping of rules. While he did not mind altering the wording of the advisory committee's report to make it more palatable to the Chinese authorities, the substance of that recommendation – urging Chinese authorities to do more – must be maintained. China was the crux of the opium problem, and if the League of Nations failed to take cognizance of China's failure to live up to its own declared policy, the League would be subverting its obligations under the covenant.[107]

For his attack on Koo, a French delegate noted that Sastri was 'a great orator, with knives'.[108]

Koo's initial approach was conciliatory. He assured Sastri that it was the council's, not his personal, stand that the League could not be seen as interfering in China's internal affairs.[109] But as he was increasingly cornered, Koo 'negotiated, bullied and threatened us with constitutional difficulties', wrote Sastri.[110] Koo warned that the sub-committee was contemplating 'a most dangerous precedent' by altering a council resolution; it had no right to do so.[111] Sastri made a strong rejoinder and Koo was thoroughly isolated. The final report asked the Chinese government to take appropriate measures to combat the smuggling of opium.[112] This was, as the internal report of the Indian delegation claimed, a total victory for the Indian position. Much credit was due to Sastri's sharp skills in legal jousting.

A few months earlier, seeing Smuts participate in every discussion at the Imperial Conference, Bajpai had lamented that Indians only spoke on issues that concerned them. Precisely because Smuts held a view on everything, even if the view was often couched in abstract phrases to the extent that he had an active aversion to specifics and a dubious record of supporting exactly opposite things, his, and with him his country's, stature grew internationally. Now at the League, Bajpai rejoiced that India's constant interventions, in particular from Sastri, in general as well as on specific debates, had helped elevate India's position in the international community. Sastri's own reputation grew with every speech, but the League also served as 'a valuable field for international advertisement' that India must make full use of, Bajpai wrote. The more Indians spoke on international platforms and the more issues they spoke on, the more the country's stature would rise.[113]

Sastri had high hopes from the League in 1921 but his views changed on it over the years as he grew critical of the great power machinations. He wrote in his reflections: 'I was foolish enough to believe that all over the world among the people a feeling of unity had come about. Was I not misguided and was not my hope misplaced?'[114]

Sastri and Bajpai had been away from home for seven months now. They had formed a close bond. Sastri found Bajpai to be 'excellent' and indispensable for his work, while Bajpai had inculcated a fond regard for his 'chief'. Bajpai confessed that he had 'learnt more in these few months than … in my whole life'.[115] In early October, Sastri and Bajpai were back in London, where they were asked to pack their bags again to prepare for their next journey. Washington was their next stop.

5

# The Most Picturesque Figure

### I

Aboard the White Star Line's magisterial ship the SS *Olympic*, Sastri and his team of advisers, Girija Shankar Bajpai (secretary), Geoffrey Corbett (civil adviser) and Colonel K. Wigram (military adviser), left Southampton on 26 October 1921. The Washington Conference was convened by America's President Warren G. Harding to discuss two sets of issues: disarmament and affairs concerning the Pacific. Harding had originally invited a combined delegation of the British Empire, aware that his predecessor, Woodrow Wilson, had been criticized by the republicans for granting the units of the British Empire separate votes at the League. Three dominions – Canada, Australia and New Zealand – had direct interest in Pacific affairs and feared Japan. The dominions were more likely to be supportive of America's plans in the Pacific so Harding wanted them to attend.[1] But as we will note, they also had different interests and positions and insisted that they would sign separately on each of the agreements reached, so that each could withhold their signatures in case of specific disagreements.[2] Lloyd George and Harding had to agree, and since India had a status equal to the dominions, Montagu and Sastri insisted on India's separate representation.[3]

Sastri, who had impressed the Prime Minister at the Imperial Conference, and even more so with his work in Geneva, was the automatic choice for India's representative. India's interest in Pacific affairs may have been marginal except for the issues relating to China, but a conference like Washington was a legitimacy-enshrining platform. India's claim to dominion status would be bolstered by its equal representation at what promised to be a defining international conference.[4]

**4: Sastri and Bajpai in America**

Between April 1921 and November 1922, Sastri and Bajpai travelled together as India's diplomatic representatives to London, Geneva, Washington, Australia, New Zealand and Canada. The young Bajpai and his 'chief' developed a loving bond that was to remain strong for the rest of their lives.

The five-day journey to New York was spent in relative luxury, Sastri's cabin was 'a commodious little house'.[5] But his mind was uneasy. On the very day Sastri took the ship westwards, the Prince of Wales had travelled eastwards to India as part of his empire-wide tour to show the king's appreciation of his subjects' contribution to the war.[6] Sastri had strongly advised against the prince's visit.[7] Gandhi had announced a boycott. The visit, Sastri reasoned, would provide new momentum to the otherwise declining non-cooperation movement.[8]

Before leaving, Sastri also debated whether his own political skills were required in India at the moment, rather than in another country. Over the next few months, as we will later discuss, he was anxious to return at the earliest opportunity for the country's, and perhaps his own, political future. He had been away for far too long while political agitation in India had grown. But a seat at the main table in Washington was striking proof of India's elevated status. No other non-self-governing country was a member at the League of Nations, and now India was invited as an equal participant to a major international conference. The occasion was of unparalleled significance for India's political future, he wrote to his brother, even though he was sure to receive opprobrium back home for attending it.[9] His anxieties were also familial. His daughter Savitri had been terribly sick in the preceding few months. He worried about her and about how Lakshmi, his wife, must be coping.[10] The conference was expected to run anything between two to six months. 'Six months is a big slice of what remains of my life, and I grudge it, bitterly grudge it, even to the service of my country.'[11]

Arriving in New York on 1 November, the city of skyscrapers left the two Indians, Sastri and Bajpai, unimpressed. Bajpai lamented 'the most unaesthetic disarray' of huge and small buildings that made up New York.[12] Sastri complimented the 'lavish outlay' of the city's awe-inspiring architecture and its culture of omnipresent advertisements, meant to draw the beholder's undivided attention. But it was no Paris. New York was resolutely devoid of any 'beauty or art', he lamented. He returned disappointed from a play, *Twelfth Night*, for neither the play nor the theatre it played in had a soul.[13] Compared to London's tubes and trains, New York's subway, criss-crossing the city, was an 'offence to the eye'.[14] The American accent failed to please Bajpai: 'English is spoken with the most cacophonic accent and is not at all pleasing from American mouths.'[15]

Washington, in contrast, was more tolerable for Sastri. Well-laid-out streets intersecting at right angles with an easily identifiable grid pattern, east–west streets named with letters and north–south with numbers, evoked a disarming sense of ease. Bajpai found new excuses to remain unimpressed though; his hotel furniture fell 'just a bit below his standard'.[16] They had little time to reflect on the American capital, however. Their official engagements started immediately, and included official dinners and a visit to the White House.

The conference had stimulated varying reactions. Harding's initiative was partly inspired by the desire to reinsert America into global affairs after the disastrous League of Nations policy of Wilson, which had been voted down in the Senate, Harding being one of the voters against it. Harding's approach was disarmament rather than collective security. The conference also suggested a geopolitical shift from the Atlantic to the Pacific, with America and Japan as the two powers to emerge relatively unscathed from the rubble of the First World War.

The *Washington Times* sought comments from three leading minds of the time on the prospects of the conference: the writers H.G. Wells and George Bernard Shaw and the inventor-cum-businessman Thomas Edison. Shaw was the most pessimistic. Refusing an invitation to come to Washington, he declared the conference a sham with little hope of any lasting peace. The American inventor, Edison, concurred that permanent and complete disarmament, as the conference aimed at, was hardly a possibility. Wells was more optimistic, and had travelled to Washington to report on the conference. It would either be 'a turning point in human affairs', or would be 'one of the last failures' before the 'disasters and destruction that gather our race', he wrote.[17]

## II

Washington DC snuck out of bed before sunrise on 11 November 1921. The occasion was the entombing of 'The Unknown Soldier' on the third anniversary of Armistice Day. An overflowing crowd of residents gathered along Pennsylvania Avenue. At 8:27am, President Warren G. Harding arrived at the Capitol to lead a mourning procession. The clatter of horse hooves, the briskly moving batteries of soldiers, the creaking of wheeled guns, and the sober faces of the country's who's who – living presidents, supreme court judges, senators, congress members, decorated generals, church leaders – all joined in a collective outpouring of grief. Other Americans across the country congregated in their own cities and hamlets; Times Square in New York alone hosted upwards of 25,000 people.

The remains of this soldier had been chosen from among the 2,079 that had perished in France who were so badly mutilated that they could not be identified. The Unknown Soldier now stood in for the 124,000 Americans who had died in the war. Harding walked behind the bier as the chief mourner from the Capitol Hill rotunda to the White House. Closely following him was the former President, now Chief Justice, William Taft. Woodrow

Wilson arrived in an open carriage, too sick to walk. This was his first public appearance in eight months. The last time he was seen was when he had motored with his successor along the same route to pass on the presidential baton. The politicians climbed on to the wheels after the procession passed the White House. General Pershing, the army chief-of-staff, walked all the way to Arlington Cemetery, about six miles via Georgetown.

The procession reached the Arlington Memorial Amphitheater across the Potomac after midday. About 5,000 people took their seats in this newly constructed marble building, including the delegates to the conference. Sastri and Bajpai were seated among their colleagues from the British delegation. Sastri had laid a wreath at the coffin the day before, which Bajpai had marked with the motto: 'They never die who die to make life worth living.'[18] They witnessed the President declare to his listeners, his voice aided by a wall of amplifiers around the tombstone: 'the dead shall not have died in vain'. '[T]here must be, there shall be, the commanding voice of the conscious civilization against armed warfare', he added.[19] Wells added to this touch of idealism in his special column for the *Baltimore Sun* the next morning. He hoped that just as the soldiers of the Confederate South lay beside the federal soldiers in Arlington, the unknown soldier would eventually also represent those who fought against him – the Germans – and the new enemies of America – the Russians. The tomb would then embody the 20,000,000 bodies lost and mutilated in the war as the 'Unknown Soldier of the Great War'.[20] Sastri wrote in his diary: 'a most solemn and impressive ceremony'.[21]

### III

The sombreness of the occasion, inspiring a yearning for idealism, carried on to the Memorial Continental Hall the next day as the conference opened. The delegates arrived at this conference venue, and a journalist could not help but contrast its spartan, 'homely simplicity', the white-panelled walls with barely any touches of colour, against the gaudily ornamental clock-room of the Quai d'Orsay in Paris. The 'red and gold' walls of the venue of the Paris Peace Conference, dripping with imperial symbols and insignia, oozed a sense of grandeur.[22] A turn from the elaborate deceptions of European diplomacy to the stark countenance of the American order. The Americans meant business, which very soon became clear.

The opening speech from Harding was strewn with the usual rhetoric; he appealed for 'a better order which will tranquillize the world'. The tranquillizer was delivered with great force by the speaker after him, Charles Evans Hughes. Secretary of State Hughes was a former Governor of New York and the Republican nominee for the hard-fought 1916 election, which he lost by a narrow margin to Wilson.

Hughes' speech had been zealously guarded against leaks; only nine people were shown its content before the Secretary of State rose to speak that morning.[23] Soon it became clear why. Hughes called for real action on disarmament, and proposed a suspension of the construction of all capital ships for the next ten years. The United States, he said, would scrap 30 of its capital ships, amounting to a total tonnage of 845,740. The audience was stunned; no power had ever willingly committed to a naval downsizing of this magnitude. Hughes was not yet finished. He went on to demand that other naval powers, Great Britain and Japan in particular, also inflict punishing cuts on their naval capacity. He even named the specific ships from the two navies that needed to be destroyed. Overall, based on the proportion of current naval strength, he proposed a ratio of 5:5:3 for the US, Britain and Japan in terms of total tonnage of capital ships. In other words, the US and Britain were allowed to retain a capital fleet of 500,000 tonnes each, while Japan was authorized 300,000 tonnes. As secondary naval powers, Italy and France were permitted a quota of 175,000 tonnes.

Everyone in the hall looked dazed after Hughes finished his bull-in-a-china-shop speech. The British soldier-turned-correspondent Charles Repington, who coined the term First World War, noted the enormity of this move in his conference diary. In little over half an hour Hughes had consigned a total of 1,874,043 tonnes to scrap, considerably more than 'all the admirals of the world have destroyed in a cycle of centuries'.[24] Naval armaments were 'beckoned towards the cell of the condemned'; America had led the way through 'a great renunciation', 'the most magnificent gesture in all history', Repington wrote, even as his enthusiasm at what had happened struggled to find an appropriate lexicon.[25] A humourist complained: 'I'm going home. This is going to be a bum show. They've let the hero kill the villain in the first act.'[26] In a flush of words, Hughes had radically redefined the meaning of diplomacy.

The propriety-conscious European diplomats were in for another rude shock, although not as devastating as Hughes' speech. Loud cheers rang from the galleries to encourage speakers. The boorish Americans had seemingly mistaken a crucial diplomatic conference for a Republican convention. The first speaker to be cheered like this was French Prime Minister Aristide Briand. A celebrated public orator, Briand delivered a fine speech, although some of his rhetorical flourishes were lost in translation, literally. The French premier's speech was interspersed with the translator's voice. Another radical shift in diplomatic etiquette was apparent: English, not French, was now the *lingua franca* of diplomacy. The delegates from Japan, China, Portugal, Italy, Belgium, Holland followed with pleasant words, each called forth by cheering crowds. They cautiously guarded their responses to Hughes' proposals. At least some things were going to remain the same.

Sastri, observing from the main table sitting diagonally across from Hughes, was highly impressed with the approach taken by the American delegation. He called Hughes' speech a 'capital stroke' which presented a 'cut and dried proposal'. With the image of the Unknown Soldier in the background, public opinion had been worked up in such a manner that any opposition to American proposals was sure to invite the opprobrium of the masses. The negotiating parties had been caught by surprise and pushed into a corner. The main question had been 'decided beyond recall' and only the details were left to be debated, Sastri wrote to his brother.[27] With this, the old diplomacy of 'euphemisms and concealments … periphrasis and indirectness, its mystifications and long-drawn delays' was dead, 'long live the new', wrote Sastri.[28]

The British Empire delegation retreated to the British embassy to discuss their response. Over the course of the two and half months of the conference, they would meet regularly as a group, 26 times in all.[29] On what approach the delegation should take towards Hughes' proposals opinions varied internally. However, it was agreed that the delegation must push for 'the greatest possible limitation of armaments consistent with the safety of the British Empire'.[30] Despite differences, the British Empire delegation was able to present a united face to the public, so much so that *The Times* editor William Steed applauded them for behaving like 'a band of brothers'.[31]

When the conference resumed on 15 November, the British and the Japanese, two of the most important participants, excluding the Americans, came up with measured responses. Arthur Balfour spoke on behalf of the British delegation. A consummate diplomat, Balfour was a pessimist by design. Britain, it was said in closed circles, had only two men to use alternatively: 'Mr. Lloyd George to act, Mr. Balfour to negate'.[32] An English author once remarked: '[Balfour] never once has felt the call of future nor experienced a genuine desire to leave the world better than he found it'.[33] But on this occasion the American journalist Mark Sullivan noted that Balfour showed 'an unmistakable and most engaging warmth of feeling for this adventure in altruism'.³⁴ Speaking haltingly, stuttering at times, he expressed Britain's support for the American proposal. Lloyd George had cabled the delegation not to commit to anything concrete yet, so he expressed his agreement only 'in spirit and in principle'. Japan's representative, Vice Admiral Kato, also 'gladly accept[ed]' the plan in principle.³⁵

The *enfant terrible* for the conference was France. The French delegation bulldozed one proposal after another. Briand doggedly refused to accept any limits on the size of the French army or its armaments with a one-word rationale: Germany. The fiery orator pushed Britain and America to either commit militarily to France's help if Germany ever attacked the country, or to let France arm itself sufficiently.³⁶ In response, a commentator noted satirically that America and Britain were assured to come to France's rescue with 'five hundred thousand words'.³⁷ With no guarantees forthcoming, any prospects of reduction in land armaments were expeditiously consigned to the land of no hope.

Naval downsizing therefore remained the only negotiable disarmament matter.³⁸ Japan raised issues about the specifics of the 5:5:3 ratio, and pushed for the acceptance of 10:10:7. Anything less than 70 per cent of the US and Britain quota was injurious to Japan's sense of dignity. Hughes refused to relent, and eventually Japan agreed to a 5:5:3 ratio on the condition that all concerned powers must stop any further fortifications of their Pacific naval bases.³⁹

The French *amour propre* militated against consigning France to being a second-rate naval power, along with Italy, without even consulting its delegates. The French delegate and future Prime Minister, Albert Sarraut, retorted: '*Nous ne sommes pas le domestique*' (We are not the servant to be ordered about).⁴⁰ Until 1914, France had the third largest navy. But as it sunk its resources into building a large army to fight Germany, its navy became both inadequate and technologically outdated. Thus, France demanded 350,000 tonnes for its capital ships and stonewalled any efforts at persuasion. Hughes grew increasingly tired of the French demands, shooting off a strongly worded telegram to Briand, who had left for Paris midway through the conference, to convince his delegation to moderate its demands.⁴¹ Privately, Hughes disclosed to Balfour that if everything else failed, America could use France's war debt to America as a weapon.⁴² After considerable dallying France relented, but not before it had sabotaged another of the conference aims.

France made the limits on its capital ship tonnage conditional on the satisfactory acceptance of France's demands on submarines and smaller craft. Hughes had proposed to limit the submarine tonnage proportionally in line with the current status, with Britain and America allowed a maximum of 90,000. In the US, there was a moral outcry against the submarines. After all it was the sinking of the *Lusitania* by a German submarine which had officially brought the US into the war. During the war, German submarines had sunk a total of 12,000,000 tonnes with a value of $1.1 billion, costing 20,000 non-combatant lives.[43] American newspapers had run sustained campaigns for outlawing the 'viper of the sea'.[44]

The strongest voice for scrapping the submarines was Balfour's.[45] The British delegation had planned to raise the issue of submarines in a public rather than a closed session. This way, American public opinion would overwhelm any technical objections that countries like France might raise.[46] However, Hughes dissuaded Balfour from raising the moral stakes through public pressure. He reasoned that submarines protected smaller countries against attacks by bigger navies, and also provided them with a strong incentive to forgo building more capital ships.[47]

Nevertheless, Lord Lee, Britain's Minister for Navy, and Balfour made the case for the abolition of submarines, albeit in the committee rather than publicly. But France refused to give up, arguing that as 'weapons of the weak' submarines and smaller craft were essential for maintaining France's imperial interests against other colonial powers. Admiral De Bon of France in fact insisted on building 90 submarines of 1,000 tonnes each, that is, a total of 90,000 tonnes (almost three times its existing tonnage). Since France would not budge, Britain too refused to set any limits to its own vessels, as the French naval armament was primarily against Britain. With no solution forthcoming, Hughes proposed keeping the ship size of all non-capital ships to a maximum of 10,000 tonnes with an upper limit of 8 inches for the calibre of the gun employed. The total tonnage of the large aircraft carriers was fixed at a maximum of 27,000. In his report, Sastri blamed the French for the failure to come to an agreement on banning submarines. Would it not be in the interest of humanity, he wrote, 'if this insidious weapon of destruction, so helpless against armed ships but so formidable a menace to unarmed craft, had finally disappeared'?[48]

The final result of these efforts was the Five Powers Treaty, signed between America, the British Empire, France, Italy and Japan, which incorporated the provisions discussed.

## IV

The second important set of questions were broadly placed under the rubric of 'Far Eastern Questions'. By far the most important was the issue of the Anglo-Japanese Treaty. Signed in 1902 and renewed in 1905 and 1911, the treaty provided Japan a buffer against potential rivals in the Pacific. But it was signed primarily to forestall Germany and Russia's meddling in China, which were no longer salient threats. Instead, America and Japan had emerged from the First World War as primary strategic adversaries in the Pacific. Student mass meetings in Japan were discussing methods of fighting the US, the 'hypothetical enemy number one',[49] while books such as Frederick McCormick's *The Menace of Japan*, Walter Pitkin's *Must We Fight Japan?*, Sidney Osborne's *The New Japanese Peril* and Jesse F. Steiner's *Japanese Invasion* fuelled Japanophobia in America.[50] The chief propagandist of Japan's 'yellow peril' was William Hearst, owner of the powerful Hearst Press, whose arsenal of nationwide newspapers ratcheted up anti-Japanese hysteria.[51]

The British dominions had differing views of the alliance. Canada with its Atlanticist aspirations was staunchly opposed; Australia and New Zealand had mixed feelings. The alliance protected them against possible misadventures from Japan, but their racial immigration policies also always kept the threat alive. An alliance with America was preferable, but how much it could be trusted to come to their aid was questionable. So, while Canada wanted the Anglo-Japan alliance terminated, Australia and New Zealand favoured a tripartite engagement involving the British Empire, Japan and America. India had little or no strategic interest in the alliance.[52]

Britain was keen to discontinue the treaty to address American and dominion sensibilities without invoking Japan's opprobrium. The conference provided a good opportunity. On the journey to America, Balfour had prepared a tentative draft of a potential tripartite agreement between the US, Japan and the British Empire. America suggested including France, which claimed to be a Pacific power because of its colonial possessions. Its inclusion would also massage the French ego, while making the passing of such a treaty possible in the Senate. Accordingly, a Four Powers Agreement was signed in early December 1921, where each of the parties agreed to retain the status quo in the Pacific. Any dispute was to be referred to a joint conference of the contracting parties. Sastri signed the agreement as India's plenipotentiary. The Four Powers Treaty made the Anglo-Japan alliance redundant, and was consequently officially terminated in 1923 soon after the American Senate passed it.

Other issues discussed in the conference related to issues regarding China, and only one of them affected India directly: the 'open door policy'. The conference discarded the old policy of 'spheres of influence' practised by the western powers in China, and adopted the policy of 'open door'. Hence, preferential trade access to China was abandoned in favour of equal access. The principal beneficiaries of preferential access had been countries like British India that carried trade with China through land borders. India exported yarn to the value of £15 million sterling per year to China. At the conference, China demanded a 7.5 per cent surcharge on all imports. On India's behalf, Sastri took the position that whatever the disadvantages to India, China had full right to assert its sovereignty. India, which had only recently exercised its fiscal autonomy to impose tariffs on goods imported from the rest of the empire, could not oppose it. The best that could be done was to negotiate a graduated increase for trade to adjust to altered conditions.[53] After negotiations, the rate was brought down to 2.5 per cent.

Overall, the conference had exceeded expectations. In many ways, it had presented an alternative model of post-war diplomacy. The League had proved to be a failure to resolve issues of great power confrontations. America's refusal to endorse collective security had condemned it to irrelevance as far as key issues of security were concerned. The Washington Conference showed that intergovernmentalism was alive and well, and America was still willing to invest in it. Interestingly, the Four Powers Treaty was read to the conference by the wrecker of Paris, Senator Henry Lodge. His fellow opponent to the Paris Peace Treaty in the Senate had been the then-senator Harding. In his presidential election campaign in 1920, Harding had called the League 'as dead as slavery', but then proposed an 'Association of Nations', the details of which were so cryptic that both the supporters and opponents of the League among the Republicans signed letters of support for him. The Washington Conference had provided one possible avenue through which such an initiative could be channelled. However, like several other inter-war initiatives, the Washington Conference was also eventually a failure. Japan pulled out of all the Agreements signed at Washington in 1936.

## V

Where was Sastri in all this? He hardly spoke at the conference; or almost as much as he has appeared in our narrative on the conference thus far.[54] A reporter commented: 'Content with looking the part, Mr.

**5: Sastri at the Conference on Limitation of Armaments, Washington**

Sastri (in white turban) admired Hughes' (signing the document) approach at the conference. Through his audacious and blunt proposals, Hughes had buried the old diplomacy of 'euphemisms and concealments … periphrasis and indirectness, its mystifications and long-drawn delays'.

Sastri sits quietly, never opening his mouth.'[55] His turban, rather than his voice, drew more ink from the reporters. He was routinely billed as the 'most picturesque figure' at the conference. His white turban draped in perfect folds provided ocular relief from the drab black surtouts of almost every participant.[56] It also invited jocular jabs: 'A Hindu named Sastri who had just been getting a shampoo and the barber forgot to take the towel off his head', one humourist wrote. He also rarely spoke in the meetings of the British Empire delegations. The minutes of these 26 meetings mention him making an intervention only once.

Was he merely a 'prop of the Empire'? A commentator explained that India was riddled with religious and racial tensions; 'anything might happen if a fool happened to drop a match'. Hence, the British Empire depended upon native leaders like Sastri to 'preserve their rule'.[57] However, the significance of his presence was not merely contextual, but also historical. What would Robert Clive and Warren Hastings, two of India's early colonizers, think of Sastri participating in the conference, asked an observer? '[Clive] would open his eyes in amazement to see the Right Honourable V.S. Srinivasi [sic] Sastri elbow to elbow with Balfour of old England in representing the weal of the empire. Warren Hastings ... would think probably that Englishmen have gone crazy.'[58] Sastri's representation of India was crucial for navigating the tides of the emerging world order. The American journalist Arthur S. Draper wrote that 300 million Indians could no longer be ignored at any future conference. Indians were rapidly rising in opposition to the British rule. As and when they looked for alternative world visions, whether it was America or Japan would become an important consideration.[59] Wells dismissed Draper's view. In his column, he questioned the very idea that India was a nation capable of singular views or being represented by a single voice. Sastri was merely a British nominee not an Indian representative, he wrote. How could he 'represent' Indians when India had no democratic institutions? For Wells, India was a hotchpotch of assembled polities, and scarcely a nation worthy of representation.

The conference, Wells argued, also served as an opportunity for the British Empire to reflect on India. For him, the Washington Conference had laid bare the liberal pretence of the League of Nations. The League's idea of mandates was 'Pecksniff Imperialism': 'the thinnest, cheapest camouflage for annexation; it was a hopeless attempt to continue the worst territory-seizing traditions of the nineteenth century, while seeming to abandon them'. Washington, however, provided a different way to find a solution to imperialism. He was impressed how the China question was dealt with; 'the method of abstinence and withdrawal': a binding agreement signed among all imperial powers 'to come out of, and to keep out of, that country while it consolidates itself and develops upon its own lines'. He hoped that a similar solution could be thought of for India. The British Empire ought to be ashamed not of its past conduct in India but of its disregard for India's future. (In the former, Wells wrote, there was much to be proud of.) Now that the fear of Russian aggression on the Indian subcontinent was over, India must be 'allowed to develop on its own lines'.[60]

Sastri himself saw his role more as a symbolic nod to India's equal status. His representation at Washington was proof, he wrote, of the recognition of India as a dominion. His status was exactly the same as every other dominion leader; dominion status was 'fully secured' for external purposes.[61] He told reporters that the war had come at enormous economic cost to the country. Taxes had become intolerable and the government was in a high deficit. Hence, any step that led to the reduction of armaments was most welcome to all Indians.[62] But he acknowledged that there was little in terms of direct work that he was expected to do. India had no naval armaments of its own on which he could give his opinion, or direct the empire's policy. The conference was mostly an unmissable opportunity for India to register itself as an international actor, to be seated at the high table of diplomacy, even if the main issues were of only tangential concern.

But he added that he also represented 'the special viewpoint of India', a country whose nature was 'decidedly pacific'. India had never waged a 'war of aggression' beyond its borders. 'Peace, peace, peace intoned three times is part of the daily prayer of our most numerous community', he stated on his arrival in New York. This was to become in later years India's stump speech in international diplomacy, according to which India was a therapeutic power, with a claim to a continuous existence of a pacifist civilization which had resolved societal conflicts through non-violent means.

The British, however, were also somewhat anxious about Sastri's presence in Washington. They suspected that Japan could raise the issue of racial equality. While it had been possible to brush aside Japan's concerns about racial equality at the League of Nations where it was a lesser power, Japan and the racial issue were impossible to evade in a conference specifically about the Pacific. There was 'no issue more fundamental in the ultimate settlement' of the rivalries between the United States, the British Dominions and Japan than racial equality, an internal British memo noted. However, it also argued that Japan was only likely to raise it as a tactic of last resort. Ordinarily, any race-inspired resolution would unite the British dominions and America, which Japan would not want. But if Japan felt that its interests in China were being severely undermined or its armaments reduced below what would be essential to retain its influence in Asia, it would bring up the racial issue. In which case the British Empire might have a problem since India, especially Sastri, given his sharp criticisms of racial discrimination, was more likely to side with Japan than with the British dominions.[63]

Giving plenipotentiary powers to Sastri was thus potentially dangerous. He was the first Indian ever to be invested in such powers. What if Sastri refused to sign on a common British Empire position as well as any other agreement that went against Indian public opinion? If Japan raised the race issue, his refusal was almost a certainty. To prevent embarrassment to the British government, Sastri was asked to consult Montagu before signing any agreement as well as keep him informed about the progress of events. Even the Foreign Office acknowledged that this was 'an unusual and unnecessary whittling down of the powers of the plenipotentiary' but argued for a buffer since 'the whole position [was] peculiar'.[64]

## VI

Inside the conference Sastri may not have had much role to play, but outside of it his presence was adequately noted. His arrival on American shores had evinced some interest from curious reporters, who wrote stories on him, often getting the details wrong. He was variously hailed as a 'Prince', 'Viscount', 'a prominent Lawyer', 'a Hindu chieftain'.[65] News items with his statements appeared with pictures of either Bajpai or the Maharao of Kutch, all seemingly interchangeable faces. Others, while praising his excellent command over the English language, reported enthusiastically, in what would now be called fake news, that Sastri had gone over to England in his twenties to learn English at Oxford and played cricket. The idea of an oriental, brown diplomat moderate in views and speaking in fine English without having gone to English institutions was an assumed impossibility. The author wondered how Kipling of the 'East is East' stories would reconcile such a man with 'the most perfect, the most musical and the most cadenced English'.[66] Sastri had, another reporter wrote, 'won the hearts of the correspondents in Washington' with his honest and endearing manner and his ecclesiastic dignity.[67]

When it came to discussing issues internal to India, he refused to toe the British line. He was consistent in his position when asked to speak about the Indian question. 'There is discontent – much discontent – among my people', he stated in a speech. India's economic condition was 'terrible' and excessive taxes by the government were 'burdensome'. Muslims were greatly displeased by the British government's decision on Turkey. Indians were also considerably aggrieved at the British refusal to punish sufficiently the officers who were engaged in inflicting racial injustice in Punjab. These were genuine issues which he identified with. However, Gandhi's solution of a complete boycott was both 'unwise and futile'. A revolution in India was unlikely.[68] His presence in Washington, Sastri was convinced, was proof that in external affairs India had all but achieved equality and that India was on the path to dominion status. The Anglo-Irish Treaty, which envisioned establishing an Irish Free State in a year, had been signed on 6 December 1921. For Sastri, this implied that in internal affairs too, India's path towards full equality would be hastened. He envisioned dominion status for India within a decade, unless Britain wanted India to turn into the 'Ireland of the East'.[69]

Repeatedly asked to speak on Gandhi, who was gaining popularity in America, with several pastors comparing him to Jesus Christ,[70] Sastri was both effusive in praise and relentless in critique. The Mahatma was 'a character of the purest idealism and saintliness',[71] whose final objective was 'a radical reform of mankind'.[72] But his political tactics promoted anarchism and were 'worse than the disease', he reasoned.[73]

The Indian nationalist press, as well as the Indian revolutionaries in the United States, predictably lambasted him.[74] Syed Hussain had followed Sastri from the UK to Washington and given speeches opposing his participation as India's representative.[75] America had been a major centre of Indian revolutionary activity, before and during the war. However, once America turned to Britain's side during the war, Indian revolutionaries were caught in the grip of British and American intelligence agencies and their activities subsided. After the war, Wilson's Fourteen Points had spurred them to campaign for India's self-determination, but once America retreated into isolationism, their campaign against British rule found much less support.[76]

The Washington Conference, however, provided another opportunity, because of the Anglo-Japanese alliance. Taraknath Das, a 37-year-old Indian revolutionary migrant to America, wrote that the alliance was a 'menace' to America. Japan was likely to come to Britain's aid if hostilities emerged between Britain and America. A war between the two Anglo-Saxon powers was a possibility, because of 'Britain's plan of world domination'. A republican India would be opposed to any such British scheme.[77] The Indian revolutionaries mined the American hatred of Japan further by declaring that Gandhi's non-cooperation movement was also considering boycotting Japanese goods, alongside boycotting British goods, in order to break off the Anglo-Japanese alliance. This was a remarkable turnaround for Das himself, who not too long before had self-published a book titled *Is Japan a Menace to Asia?* and had praised Japan in no uncertain terms, even justifying the country's imperialistic actions in Korea and China by arguing that these actions warded off western imperialists.[78] In the book, his only criticism of Japan was for maintaining the Anglo-Japanese alliance, for acting as a 'watch-dog of Great Britain against the cause of Independent India'.[79] He had counselled the East Asian power to rise up to its historic mission of being the 'true leader of Asia'.[80]

Salindranath Ghose, another Bengali revolutionary who had fled India in 1916, led the Friends for Freedom of India (FFI) in America. Das was his collaborator, and also the secretary of the organization.

Seeing Gandhi's struggle take off in India, they had also formed the American Commission to Promote Self-Government in India, ostensibly to promote Gandhi's movement in America.

Declaring themselves to be the true representatives of nationalist India, Ghose declared that Indians would not accept any limitations on armaments achieved by the British delegates. In the British delegation, Sastri was merely a stooge of the government. Unless India was free, its voice could not be heard. Further, Ghose warned that if Gandhi's peaceful means failed, 'we shall arm as George Washington did'. India had 73 million men of military age, he declared, including tens of thousands who fought in the war, who can respond to such a call.[81] Das proposed sending a 'delegation of Indian and American advisers who stand for a Republic of the United States of India'.[82]

The delegation obviously could not make it to the conference, but their petition did. A letter addressed to the delegates of the conference, jointly by Sailendranath Ghose, Taraknath Das, Sarat Mukherji, Nani Gopal Bose and Haridas Gayadeen, appealed for attention to the torture of Moplah captives in British prisons in South India. Recent reports had provided details about an incident in which more than 100 Moplah prisoners were packed in a closed box car. By the time the train reached its destination, 64 were dead from suffocation and thirst. They were deliberately denied water. The British Raj in India had repeatedly used the practice of 'letting men slowly die of thirst'. Another practice used was 'baking': making prisoners face the full glare of the midday sun without any shade. It was thus supremely ludicrous that the same British delegates who were appealing to the public conscience to abolish submarines because of their barbarous effects were also upholding 'grossly inhuman practices' against 'captives of war'. It showed that the British still valued merchandise, the prime target of submarines, over human life. According to the revolutionaries, consideration thus had to be given to framing rules about treatment of prisoners of war, for the Moplah captives were indeed prisoners of a war against British imperialism.[83]

Sastri was an obvious target of verbal attacks from the Indian revolutionaries, but sometimes matters became somewhat more serious. Sastri even received a death threat through a letter. It is not clear who sent it to him. Bajpai asked him to alert security, but Sastri let it go. Auckland Geddes, the British ambassador, suspected the FFI, which was 'an annexe of the Sinn Finn'.[84] However, one incident became a cause for concern.

On 28 January 1922, Sastri was due to deliver a talk in New York's recently opened Town Hall. Organized under the League for Political

Education, an organization working for women's suffrage, Sastri spoke on 'The Political Situation in India'. As soon as Sastri finished his talk, and started responding to queries, he was heckled by some Indians, who first called him a British agent and then shouted insults. The meeting eventually ended in disorder and Sastri had to depart under a police escort.[85]

## VII

For exactly the period that Sastri was in the United States, India was in the throes of a political movement whose sharp end was as anti-climactic as its rise was stupendous. The arrival of the Prince of Wales had reinvigorated the non-cooperation movement as Gandhi announced the boycott of the visit. On 17 November 1921, as the prince landed in Bombay, the boycott turned into a riot after congressmen started attacking members of the Parsi community, who had welcomed the visit. For five days, the riots in Bombay continued unabated. There were also clashes in Calcutta. Reading, a liberal in politics, had until then responded to Gandhi's non-cooperation movement with considerable restraint. But, keen to make the prince's visit a success, his government now unleashed its repressive apparatus, and among several other measures jailed key Congress leaders. The movement intensified, and so did the government's harsh response. The country was caught in a spiral of violence, and several moderates, who had opposed the non-cooperation movement, criticized the government's repressive measures. Their attempts to mediate between Reading and Gandhi, appealing for a round table conference, eventually came to naught.[86] Instead, the Congress under Gandhi hardened its position further in its December 1921 session at Ahmedabad, giving a free hand to Gandhi. The Mahatma was now, as his biographer called him, 'the generalissimo of the party'.[87] He launched a localized civil disobedience movement in Bardoli on 29 January 1922 and sent Reading an ultimatum that it would be extended across the whole country. While non-cooperation called upon Indians to completely boycott British products, services and institutions, civil disobedience entailed refusal to surrender to every single state law. It was, as Gandhi put it, 'a state of peaceful rebellion'. However, soon after he had sent Reading an ultimatum, on 4 February a procession in Chauri Chaura, a village in the United Provinces, turned violent. A few constables had harassed some protestors and eventually opened fire, killing three of them. A mob later returned to the police station and set it on fire, burning 22 constables alive. Gandhi, both shocked and dismayed, suspended the non-cooperation movement and offered himself for arrest in penance.

Sastri watched these events unfold from afar and was impatient to return. Perhaps, as Corbett wrote to the India Office, he was also worried for his own political relevance.[88] In the year that he had been away, liberals had been further pushed into a corner. In late November 1921, he had also received the tragic news of his daughter's passing. For some days, he remained cloistered in his room and his health also deteriorated. Nevertheless, since he was the country's representative, he decided to remain until the conference was over. In a composed, rather stony manner, he wrote: 'We have to live and get on.'[89]

In the US, his public oratory received copious praise, and while speaking as a representative of the British Empire, he did not shy away from critiquing the same empire in his public utterances. His colleague from the British delegation in the League, H.A.L. Fisher, memorably stated after Sastri's return from Washington: '[N]o Indian in the long annals of Anglo-Indian history had had such richness and variety of experience on international and Imperial discussions as Mr. Sastri, and his work in this connection had raised the reputation of Great Britain all over the world.'[90]

Alongside Sastri, another man was being schooled in the politics of foreign policy. Bajpai noted the pedagogical value of the conference for him. 'I am gathering experience in Washington. I meet interesting people every day and see how foreign policy is fashioned. ... Our presence here is more valuable as affording a training in diplomatic methods and as constituting a recognition of India's right to participate in important international conferences.'[91] The more Bajpai travelled, the more he was convinced that India ought to have a consular, if not diplomatic, representation in important world capitals, especially in Washington. The dominions already had them, and so should India. But this was not just a matter of 'sentimental rivalry' or symbolic claim. Hundreds of Indian students came to the US, and almost all of them were:

> in the clutches of Irish Americans. Their political outlook is distorted. They magnify India's grievances in their own minds and then paint them in the most lurid colours before Americans where the prejudice against Great Britain is as intense as their ignorance of India is profound. Without any effective counter-propaganda, anything that these young 'patriots' say is easily swallowed and rapidly digested.[92]

Two decades later, Bajpai would return to Washington as India's first Agent General to the United States where one of his primary duties was to counter the nationalist view against British rule in India. He wrote articles in the American press criticizing the nationalists. In one of the articles, he cryptically called his future boss Nehru 'the Hamlet of Indian politics'.[93]

# 6

# A Rather Dangerous Ambassador

## I

Sastri and Bajpai arrived in London in mid-February 1922 to a hostile, anti-India public and political mood.[1] Montagu and Reading were up against a wall of opposition for their supposedly soft treatment of Gandhi's non-cooperation movement. The boycott of the Prince of Wales' visit by Indian nationalists inflated this resentment into a full-blown rage. Reading was accused of dithering for far too long over arresting Gandhi, while Montagu faced a motion of censure in the parliament, where he was openly slammed for a 'criminal betrayal of every white man and white woman in India'.[2] The criticism directed at the two Jews came laced with undercurrents of anti-Semitic vitriol. Meanwhile, as will be seen in the next chapter, Churchill had made one of his regular about-turns on the Kenya policy and announced that the Kenyan Highlands would remain reserved for whites, effectively ruining the work done over the several months of Montagu's negotiations with him. This prompted Charles Andrews, Gandhi's friend and a champion of the rights of overseas Indians, to call for Reading's and Montagu's resignations. Montagu, who always appeared eager to step under the guillotine, had also been vocal against Lloyd George's Turkey policy, much to the Prime Minister's annoyance. Sastri found Montagu 'annoyed, weary and querulous'.[3]

Amid all this, Sastri had a moment of personal glory; he was sworn into the Privy Council on 5 March, the third Indian to be given the honour, after Syeed Amir Ali and Lord Sinha.[4] Sastri and Bajpai left for India soon afterwards, and while they were en route two events of history-shaping importance took place. Montagu, perhaps the most liberal, if controversial, Secretary of State for India, resigned from the Cabinet on 9 March. But the news barely registered in India because of a political storm of an even greater magnitude the next day: Gandhi was arrested. On 18 March, after a quick trial, he was sentenced to six years in prison. The exit from the political centre stage of both of these incorrigible idealists saddened Sastri on a personal level, although he was not surprised. Gandhi's exile was temporary, Montagu's permanent. The latter passed away two and half years later; he was just 45 years old.[5]

Disembarking in Bombay on 24 March, Sastri and Bajpai arrived in a country shell-shocked by Gandhi's incarceration and the suspension of the non-cooperation movement. Gandhi had promised *swaraj* within a year; the dream was now off. Sastri and Bajpai were given a two-month reprieve before they were expected to venture out on another tour, to the dominions, which, if we may recall, had been suggested by Sastri to dominion prime ministers at the Imperial Conference.

Upon their return, Sastri made several speeches where he criticized both the government for its high-handedness and the non-cooperation movement for its anarchic methods. In an extempore presidential speech at the Bombay provincial congress of the Liberal Party on 7 May, he declared that people had developed a 'profound distrust' of the government's motives. He demanded that the government immediately carry out internal reforms, allowing Indians into the higher ranks of the civil services and army, and release those prisoners who had been jailed on merely technical grounds. The non-cooperation movement, despite its 'evils' of anarchy, had shown that Indians were impatient for dominion status, and he called upon his own party to agitate constitutionally for that status.[6]

Sastri's criticisms of the government in Bombay riled Reading. The Viceroy had organized a banquet in Sastri's honour at Shimla before his departure for the dominions, and he worried that Sastri would use the opportunity to criticize the government. To prevent this, he sent Sastri a terse message not to venture beyond the imperial question in his speech.[7] Sastri's pitch, as usual, floated between celebrating the British Commonwealth and critiquing the government, particularly the highhandedness of its bureaucracy. Speaking as if 'endowed with prophetic fire',[8] he said: '[w]e have never seen in the country such a wreck of hope and faith in the Government of the day. ... It rests with you to rebuild this hope by constantly remembering that you are but the front wheels of the future'.[9] Reading was not pleased. He was not the only one.

Nationalists were even more riled than Reading over Sastri's continuing participation in the government's delegations. A sympathetic writer noted 'a miasma of hatred, bigotry, suspicion and slander' against Sastri in the nationalist press. He was called 'the Esau of Indian politics ... who sold his birthright for a mess of pottage'.[10] His recent international fame was belittled as 'the accident of an accident', while another author parodied him as 'an adult prodigy'.[11] Indian radicals declared him 'a self-seeking unjust agent of a tyrannical alien government',[12] who basked in the glory of a 'pretentious diplomatic coup'.[13] The *Bombay Chronicle* editorialized that Sastri pleaded for the just and humane treatment of the nationals of every other country except his own.[14]

Troubled by the continuous criticism he received in the domestic press, Sastri had hoped that his dominion tour would keep him out of public attention in India: 'the fugitive is cursed for a day or two and then forgotten!', he wrote to Natesan.[15] His critics had asked exactly the opposite of him. With several leaders including Gandhi in jail, many argued that in this crucial phase of India's struggle a leader of his stature was needed in the country.[16] Thus, the stakes on the success of his mission were even higher. His secretary, Bajpai, was anxious for him: 'I ... hope [Sastri] would achieve some measure of success in his mission. Soft words alone will not satisfy our people or silence his critics. ... We ought not to return empty handed.'[17]

## II

Soon after the Imperial Conference, Sastri had followed up the dominion tour idea with the dominion leaders. Meighen and Massey readily agreed to send an invitation. Hughes, sensing domestic trouble, initially insisted that this was his personal invitation to Sastri, and not an official invitation on behalf of the Australian government. But later agreed to make it official. Smuts, expectedly, declined.[18]

For such a tour to be effective, timing was of crucial importance. It was necessary, Montagu told Reading, 'to strike while the iron is hot'.[19] Bajpai insisted that Sastri had made a huge personal impression on the dominion statesmen, who were all favourably disposed towards him and India's concerns. 'Personal memories', he wrote, 'have their value, but they are not everlasting, hence steps must be taken soon.'[20]

Given Sastri's busy schedule, a tour could only be organized after Washington.[21] He had briefly considered going to Canada first, but Canadian elections were scheduled for December 1921; Meighen was widely expected to lose, and he did.[22] Although various other names were discussed to go as part of the delegation, none materialized. In the end, Sastri wrote to Montagu that it was better he went alone with

Bajpai as his secretary than take along someone 'who may fail to win respect in the dominions'.[23]

But while Sastri was in Washington, Reading had second thoughts. The Viceroy decided that the visit was a waste of precious financial resources, especially as matters with the dominions did not require urgent handling. Indians in the three dominions were very few in number and relatively better off than those in South and East Africa. Montagu warned that calling off the tour would be 'a most tremendous mistake' and would unalterably diminish prospects of realizing the 1921 resolution. Corbett, who had just returned from Canada, concurred with Montagu. He stated that in order to secure franchise for Indians, the dominion governments wanted Sastri's help 'in carrying a measure which will be instinctively opposed by great masses of the white electorates'. This would not be 'insuperably difficult', but it was 'of the utmost importance that Sastri should tour the Dominions immediately'.[24] A reluctant Viceroy finally greenlit the tour. And perhaps, as we have noted, almost immediately regretted it after Sastri's banquet speech.

## III

Sastri and Bajpai boarded the SS *Ormonde*, a former troopship recently converted into a passenger liner, at Colombo; it docked at Fremantle, near Perth, in Western Australia on 1 June 1922.[25] Although officially mandated to 'assist respective Governments to give practical effect to the resolution of the Imperial Conference of 1921', Sastri's mission was more than just canvassing for support among the lawmakers for pro-Indian legislation in local parliaments. He was also expected to educate the dominion publics about India and create a broader sympathy for the rights of Indians.[26] Writing to his daughter, he argued that since the dominions had come to play a greater role in imperial affairs, India's move towards dominion status would be bolstered by sympathetic sentiment in the dominions.[27] However, in these frontiers of empire, there was nothing more sacrosanct than what Marilyn Lake and Henry Reynolds call the 'religion of whiteness'.[28] And any diplomat, especially a non-white one, would have to carefully measure their words and deeds in the face of the wall of racial prejudice.

However, the problems of Indians in these countries were also specific to various provinces. In Australia, Indians in the provinces of Queensland and Western Australia were barred from state franchise, which also deprived them of federal franchise. In Canada, British Columbia, where most Indians lived, prevented Indians from voting at provincial level. In New Zealand, Indians had exactly the same political rights as Europeans. In the Antipodes, Indians had problems in securing old age pensions and gaining employment. Sastri's visit was also an occasion to discuss and, if possible, settle other administrative and economic questions, such as immigration regulations relating to the dominions, the mandated territories of New Guinea and Samoa, and the treatment of Indians in the banana and sugar industries in Queensland.[29]

Expectations had been raised by Sastri's recent performances in London, Geneva and Washington and his arrival in Australia was greatly anticipated. One journalist, A.D. Ellis, hailed Sastri as 'our first great racial ambassador', who 'moves in an orbit that transcends the conventional limits of international diplomacy'.[30] Sastri's visit, Ellis continued, would 'interpret the aspirations of his fellow-countrymen, to seek our understanding and cooperation' in order to 'forge some tangible and material links in the bonds which ... will ultimately unite in amity the Eastern and Western civilisations'.[31] Tasked with 'increasing the understanding and cooperation existing between diverse racial elements of the Empire', Sastri's mission was of greatest significance to the British peoples.[32] The *Chronicle* called Sastri 'one of the most remarkable personalities in India and in the wider sphere of world politics'.[33] A correspondent in Adelaide, who interviewed Sastri, wrote that 'it [was] impossible not to recognize his wonderful intellectual power'.[34]

Between 2 June and 6 July, Sastri visited all of Australia's provinces, except Tasmania. This month-long packed schedule took him to Perth, Adelaide, Brisbane, Melbourne and Sydney. He made several speeches to the provincial and Federal parliamentarians, elite clubs and the general public, gave interviews to the press, and met politicians from different political parties as well as Indian residents. This pattern was repeated in New Zealand, where he spent two weeks on the north island: a week in Wellington, two days in Rotorua and the rest of his time in Auckland.[35]

His speeches broadly iterated two points: first, he emphasized the existence of a new doctrine of the British Commonwealth of Nations. This post-war Commonwealth was 'no longer based on domination, on conquest or on exploitation, but ... on ideas of brotherhood, of equality and of absolute and even-handed justice all around', he emphasized.[36] Second, in this new Commonwealth, India had 'acquired a place of undisputed equality ... which has not been won by force of arms exerted by brother against brother, but ... by honourable participation in the risks, perils and sacrifices of the Great War'.[37] Consequently, the indignities and disabilities that Indians faced in various parts of the empire, 'sometimes by law, sometimes by rules and regulations having the force of law but very often by prejudices',[38] contravened this new Commonwealth spirit. They emboldened Indian nationalists to demand India's separation from an empire which treated them as 'bearers of burdens; never, never sharers of privilege'.[39] In the 'kinship of spirit', he appealed for granting equal rights to Indians.[40]

He also met local Indians and listened to their grievances, such as their exclusion from government positions, trade unions, mining rights and old age pensions, among other things. His counsel to them was to principally focus on political franchise. Once their franchise was secured, other grievances would be automatically addressed, he argued.[41]

Sastri's reception in the Antipodes was a mix of patronizing amazement and stupefying awe. Hailed for his 'memorable eloquence',[42] one *West Australian* reader called him the 'Lloyd George of India',[43] while another listener in Adelaide noted that '[h]e asks very little, simply for his countrymen to be allowed a vote. Why should we not grant it? No just objection can exist'.[44] His performances were applauded even by the Australian Prime Minister, William Hughes, noting that India's case had 'gained in weight by the eloquence and reasonableness with which it had been urged'.[45] In the New Zealand parliament, his speech was hailed as 'the most perfect example of public speaking heard for many years in the Parliament building'.[46] Prime Minister William Massey enthusiastically cheered Sastri as 'our fellow citizen'. To emphasize what he meant, he added: 'don't forget, our fellow citizen'.[47]

Sastri's critics, however, saw these praises as special allowances for his skin colour. A writer, A.G. Stephens, argued that Sastri's allure was enhanced not by his speech (which 'did not rise to Cobbett's standard of eloquence') but by the fact that his speech comes 'a surprise to plain citizens not accustomed (mildly to phrase it) to pay high respect to a brown skin and a turban'.[48] When they see 'suddenly a power of mind, a command of language, and a fluency of utterance, rarely met among English public speakers, and exhibit the traditional perplexity regarding the pearl in the oyster – "they wonder how the dickens it got there"'.[49] An Australian correspondent in the *New Zealand Herald* attributed Sastri's appeal to his 'oriental impassiveness'.[50]

His white publics anxiously waited to see how Sastri would navigate the vexed question of the 'White Australia' policy.[51] He had arrived in Australia amid a raging debate in the country about the policy's feasibility, especially in the tropical parts of northern Australia. Henry Barwell, South Australia's premier, had publicly advocated bringing 'coloured' labour into tropical Australia. Supporters of Barwell pointed to the failure of 'White Australia' to develop the north, while the opponents, especially the Labour Party, warned about the dangers of turning Australia into Natal in South Africa.[52] One Barwell supporter, Matthew Cranston, argued that India could provide Australia with not only labour, but also, as evidenced by Sastri's own bearing, 'men of the highest culture'.[53]

Mindful that an overwhelming majority of Australians considered White Australia 'sacrosanct', Sastri daintily avoided raising the matter in his speeches.[54] However, in Melbourne, when an interviewer asked him directly, he was forthright that White Australia went against the integrity and ethos of the Commonwealth/empire. A citizen of the empire should be able to travel freely within it and be able to develop themselves to the best of their capability. But although he was personally opposed to it, his mission was not meant to question White Australia. According to the dominion's wishes, India had legislated to stop emigration through an act in 1918. It was now incumbent upon the dominions, including Australia, to provide equal rights to the Indians already resident in their countries.[55] He put this forcefully in another speech: 'We ... ask you for nothing but equality. You dare not, you cannot, and I know, you will not, deny it.'[56]

Sastri addressed a Labour Party meeting in Melbourne's Trade Hall Council and also met Labour leaders informally. They had suspected him of attempting to 'white ant' the principle of White Australia.[57] Labour leaders showed public solidarity with the Indian workers in their struggle for home rule, but effectively turned it into a stick with which to beat Sastri. Why was Sastri concerned over the rights of a few Indians in Australia, when he could devote his energies to doing the much more important work of speaking for the rights of Indian peasants and workers and raising the level of abject poverty in India?[58] A Labour sympathizer berated the 'lengthy capitalist press notices' for loudly heralding Sastri's visit which was 'out of proportions to the really minor nature of the issue'.[59]

The purpose of this visit, or the real 'Sastri move', the critics argued, was the assault against transnational white solidarity. Australia and New Zealand were only a hedge; Sastri's real target was South Africa (and to some extent Canada), where Indians were in larger numbers.[60] An *Evening Star* writer cautioned against Sastri's 'stirring appeals to abstract justice', arguing that New Zealand may be able to afford to take a lenient stance on Indians, but in situations such as in Natal in South Africa, where Indians outnumbered whites by 36 per cent, equal rights was a dangerous plea. Urging New Zealanders not to fall 'under the spell of the charmer', the writer noted that Sastri, a man of high culture and impeccable standards, was in fact an exception to Indians in general, in particular to those who emigrated to other parts of the empire.[61]

An anonymous writer in Adelaide opined that the claim for India as a constituent part of the 'British Commonwealth of Nations' was 'manifestly ridiculous'. India was not a nation, but a country of divided people on the basis of religion, culture, foods, class and caste, and thus did not deserve equal consideration within the empire. Under these platitudes, Sastri, whose 'religious faith has biased and warped his character', had a concealed motive of inducing Australia to abandon its 'White Australia' policy.[62] A.G. Stephens urged: 'High policy counsels us to keep European blood pure. Rightly we may dread the extension of Eurasian life in Australia. After electoral rights come human rights; and it is good to block the smallest leaks in our racial dyke against the tide of overwhelming Asia.'[63] Another op-ed writer warned Australians that Sastri's soft-spoken, ascetic image was a ruse to sheath his claws from the Australian people; he was in fact a 'table-thumping politician', a tiger pretending to be a lamb, who had in the past declared that if Japan threatened Australia, India would not lift a finger to help Australia unless the White Australia principle was sacrificed. In India, Sastri was doing secretly what Gandhi did openly, attempting to get rid of British rule.[64]

These criticisms also perhaps indicate how effective Sastri's 'rhetoric' had been. Their sharpness was a response to a generally enthusiastic reception. Sastri's public meetings were well attended and zealously reported. G.S. Bajpai cabled the India Office that 'by his eloquence, sanity and moderation' Sastri had created a great impression.[65] In private, even Labour leaders seemed more sympathetic. But this was in large part because, he acknowledged in his report to the Indian government, he was seen as some sort of an exception to Indians in general. His eloquence, his scholarly manner, his disregard for a life of consumption and embrace of poverty evoked the image of a man of high culture and caste. He himself recommended in his report that unless average white people in the dominions met Indians of 'refinement and culture', it was 'impossible to dissipate the phantom of superiority born of an imperial appreciation of Indian capacity'.[66]

At the end of his tour, Prime Minister Hughes told him: 'You have achieved wonders, and in my opinion have removed for all time those prejudices which formerly prevented the administration of your countrymen resident in Australia to the enjoyment of full rights of citizenship.'⁶⁷ A generous dose of hyperbole aside, he had deferred the question of franchise and gave no commitment. Hughes, Sastri wrote in his report, had become deeply unpopular; Labour had not forgiven him for jumping ship in the previous elections. But his consideration of the Indian issue more sympathetically demonstrated to Sastri that there was a wider acceptance across the political spectrum of the need to enfranchise Indians. A follow-up letter from Hughes was more believable: 'You have brought within the range of practical politics a reform but for your visit would have been most improbable, if not impossible, of achievement.'⁶⁸

Two years later, Indians were granted the franchise at the dominion level, although by then Hughes was already out of power. Queensland granted the franchise to Indians in 1930 and Western Australia in 1934.⁶⁹ In other concessions to Sastri, the Labour government in Queensland removed restrictions on Indians in the banana industry in Queensland. Hughes also promised to extend invalid and old-age pensions to Indians (the amendment was only passed in 1926).

In New Zealand, Indians, around 550–600 in number, had only two specific complaints: they were excluded from receiving old-age pensions and they had difficulty in securing employment. In the case of the former, no Indian resident was expected for many years to become eligible for the old-age pension. The New Zealand government informed Sastri that since this was not a pressing matter it could wait. Discriminations against Indians on social security were eventually removed in the late 1930s.⁷⁰ With regard to employment, Sastri observed that while there was societal prejudice against Indians (although much less prevalent than in Australia), the government as such took a stronger stance against discrimination faced by Indians in employment schemes.⁷¹ The New Zealand government also agreed to relax two specific provisions on the New Zealand Immigration Restrictions Act of 1920, which were restrictive towards Indians.

Another key issue was the mandate question. Earlier in the book we noted that Sastri had objected at the League of Nations to the extension of South Africa's laws to its mandate in South West Africa. Australia and New Zealand had done the same in their mandates in New Guinea and Samoa respectively. Consequently, the laws that barred the entry of Indians into Australia and New Zealand also applied to these mandates. Although there were no Indians in these mandates, and nor was there any likelihood of Indians emigrating to these lands, it was a question of both principle and expediency for India. What if the UK followed the same principle and excluded

Indians from other tropical mandates such as Tanganyika, or South Africa in South West Africa?[72]

Sastri asserted India's position that, as a member of the League, no laws which did not exist before these were mandates could be applied to Indians. Both Australia and New Zealand were stubbornly reluctant to discuss the issue, however. Hughes was 'most unbending'. Sastri wrote in his confidential report that 'no one in Australia regards the mandate as anything but camouflaged annexation'. Hughes, 'obsessed with fear of Japan', was worried that Japan would seek the same privileges, if they were granted to India. Sastri tried to impress upon Hughes that there would be no mandates if not for India's massive contribution to the war effort. But this did not impress Hughes. Massey in New Zealand justified the mandate policy on the basis of protecting the interests of the indigenous people. Sastri reasoned that if the immigration restrictions were meant to exclude all foreigners this policy could be justified, but not if only Asians were excluded. The white population was economically more advanced and hence provided more formidable economic competition to the Samoans than Indians. However, he did not get far in light of the steely opposition to discussing mandates. Sastri proposed to the Indian government to take up the issue at the next Imperial Conference.[73]

**6: Sastri in Australia**

When the by-now famous white turban gave way to a hat, an Australian journalist wrote: 'he is probably not as picturesque a figure as when clothed in the dress of his country, but it is impossible not to recognize his wonderful intellectual power and mental alertness. He has a quick smile, which suggests a kindly heart. He speaks seldom and then only a few words at a time, but he leaves no room for misunderstanding his meaning. There is nothing offensive about him'.

## IV

Pleased with their efforts so far, Sastri and Bajpai left for Canada. After a brief halt in Suva, where they were given a reception by Fiji Indians, they arrived on the SS *Makura* in Victoria on 12 August 1922. The mood was completely different from the Antipodes. The Pacific Coast of the United States and Canada had been a hotbed of anti-Asian immigration sentiment since the late nineteenth century. While in Australia and New Zealand the public atmosphere on Asians was mostly against the Japanese and the Chinese, the anti-immigrant sentiment in Canada was equally strong against Indians, particularly in British Columbia where almost 90 per cent of Indians lived. Canada had about 1,200 Indians in total, a substantial decrease from the pre-war strength of about 6,000 achieved mostly because of the severe restrictions on bringing wives and children.[74] The Asian Exclusion League, a notorious white supremacist organization (which had caused the 1907 anti-Asian Vancouver riots), had recently brought together several church leaders, trade unions, businesspeople and veterans of the war to issue a call for the abolition of all Asian immigration. Among the Indian diasporic communities in the white settler dominions, the Indians in Canada were also the most radical. As on the American west coast, the Ghadar Party had a dedicated following, and the *Komagata Maru* incident was still fresh in memory.[75]

W.L. Mackenzie King, the new premier, was also considerably less sympathetic to Indians than his predecessor, Arthur Meighen. King had written his doctoral degree at Harvard on 'Oriental Immigration to Canada'. As a junior minister, he had visited India and China in 1908 and authored a report that made a case for White Canada and strongly opposed Asian immigration.[76] Even if he could be persuaded to change his views, his government was running on a bare majority (118 out of 235). It was improbable that he would antagonize the League and the strongly anti-immigration parliamentarians of British Columbia.[77]

King sent his Deputy Foreign Minister, Joseph Pope, to receive Sastri in Victoria. On MacKenzie's behalf, Sastri was given a 'mere suggestion', but in reality 'a grave hint', that he should not make any public speeches. Sastri was displeased at this gagging order.[78] His mission was primarily about generating public sympathy for the rights of Indians. To desist from public speaking would constitute a dereliction of duty as well as an affront to the Indian government. He preferred to return than to censor himself, he told Pope.[79] As a way out, he proposed to consult the premier of British Columbia, John

Oliver, on the matter, since it was British Columbia where any trouble was expected.

Oliver confided in Pope that there was little chance of him agreeing to Sastri's request. However, this is not how things turned out when Sastri and Oliver met on 18 August. Not only did Oliver agree to Sastri speaking publicly about his mission, but he also admitted that Sastri's case was unanswerable on ethical and logical grounds. Only an unreasonable prejudice among Canadian whites prevented it, Oliver told Sastri; a bemused Pope reported Oliver's sudden change of heart to his Prime Minister.[80] Subsequently, Sastri also addressed Oliver's Cabinet, who heard Sastri 'with astonishment and pleasure' and readily consented to him speaking in public.[81]

However, despite Oliver and his Cabinet's support, Sastri's chances of seeking relief from a strongly anti-Asian Legislative Assembly in British Columbia were practically nil. Just recently, in 1921, a measure introduced in the Legislative Assembly to confer votes on those Asians who had served with the Canadian forces during the First World War was defeated on account of strong racial prejudice. Sastri's hope was that the federal parliament could be pushed to take the initiative. He soon declared that he had abandoned any hopes for a legislative action enfranchising Indians in the province,[82] and travelled east to the dominion capital Ottawa, via Winnipeg, where the Prime Minister hosted a dinner in his honour.

While the Indian community in the Antipodes had been enthusiastically welcoming of Sastri, the situation was starkly different in Canada. His only address to Indians was at a gurudwara in Victoria, where for over two and a half hours he was heckled, 'lectured on the error of [his] ways' and asked to return to India.[83] He returned 'a sadder and wiser man'[84] and blamed this on the 'protracted and bitter struggle' of the Sikhs with emigration in Canada, especially the bitter memories of the *Komagata Maru*.[85] Furthermore, Sikh leaders passed a resolution in Vancouver that Sastri should not be approached by any member in Canada. Eventually, however, Sastri was able to secure information from them on an undertaking that he would not make any representation to the Canadian government in their name, but only in the name of the government of India.[86]

Sastri addressed several public gatherings and discussed the franchise question with the representatives from labour organizations. The *Vancouver Sun* noted his 'world fame as an able statesman'.[87] More resistance to his efforts by the government and the Indians alike meant that his speeches were distinctly shriller than those in the Antipodes. At the Reform Club in Montreal, Sastri started his remarks in an unusually combative manner, indicative, as Dorothy Walker claims, of 'a certain loss of faith':[88]

> Neither Britain nor any Dominion can afford to play bully with India any longer, and we in India, let me tell you once for all, are determined to be bullied no longer. If we are going to be equal partners with the rest of the Empire in the maintenance of peace, we will contribute what we can to its might, strength and majesty, for we have a contribution to make to the world, and we are prepared and willing to make it under the Union Jack, if the Union Jack is going to bring us the maintenance of self-respect, and our own sense of honour. Otherwise, much as we should regret it we must seek our political salvation outside of this great political organization.[89]

The *Vancouver Sun* called his speech 'captivating in its boldness, disarming in its consummate tact', which evoked 'a storm of approval'. His appeal to the duty of 'higher imperialism' was 'one of the loftiest that has been made' and 'humanity demand[ed] that the East Indians in British Columbia be given the franchise'.[90] The *Montreal Gazette* noted that Sastri was 'nothing if not frank and blunt in telling of the terms under which India is willing to remain within the Empire'.[91] Leon Ladner, the Conservative Party representative from Vancouver, wrote that the speech had an important effect on public opinion in British Columbia. The success of the speech could be gauged from the fact, he wrote, that none of the anti-Asian organizations and complainants had criticized Sastri, even though his speech was published verbatim in most of the newspapers.[92]

Sastri's friend Arthur Meighen, now the leader of opposition, told him that King, with a bare majority in parliament, was afraid of losing votes in British Columbia. The government would not therefore bring a bill in the parliament to enfranchise Indians. Meighen's counsel was to seek informal support from crucial members in the parliament across parties, and persuade a private member to initiate the bill. Meighen promised to urge his own followers, especially those from British Columbia, not to oppose the measure. On this advice, Sastri met several influential members separately, including Lomer Gouin, King's Justice Minister, to canvas for more support. Gouin promised to influence opinion within the Liberal Party. He also met other influential members from the Liberal Party and businesspeople who had a strong influence on the government, several of whom promised support for the Indian franchise. One prominent unnamed liberal and member of the franchise committee 'even going so far as to say that he would bring in a bill next session and force King's hand'.[93]

But these promises remained just promises. Even within the Conservative Party in British Columbia, despite Meighen's strong support for Sastri's efforts, little was achieved. To be sure, upon Meighen's request, some readily agreed to support the Indian franchise for the sake of imperial unity. For instance, John A. MacKelvie from Vernon wrote that after hearing Sastri's address in Vancouver he 'could find no logical reply to his arguments'. However, others expressed strong reservations. One conservative politician argued that 90 per cent of Indians in Canada were 'low caste Hindus, filthy morally and physically, and extremely ignorant with respect to our political ideals'. He had personally not known a single Indian of 'the Sastri type who obviously are truly British'. Hence, Indians as citizens would pollute Canada's political culture. Furthermore, if Indians were granted political rights as British subjects, this would then have to be extended to the naturalized British subjects of Japanese origin. The granting of the franchise to Indians would result in 'a thin edge of the wedge' in that it might seem unimportant in itself but would make political rights inevitable for other Asian immigrants.[94] Broadly, Meighen's party members from British Columbia advised him to let King take the blame for handling the poisoned chalice.

Sastri's meeting with King was rather combative. The premier argued that the government had a majority in only one house of parliament and thus could not ensure the success of a measure to enfranchise Indians. Sastri pointed out that from the opposition, the United Farmer's Party had voted with the government on all progressive measures, so they were quite unlikely to oppose the move, especially since the party did not have a big presence in British Columbia. King then took refuge under the policy and tradition of the Liberal Party not to go against provincial governments in the matters of franchise. Again, Sastri pointed to precedents which went against King's argument.[95] Finally, King attempted to disassociate Canada from the 1921 resolution by saying that Meighen's support for the 1921 resolution was made in his personal capacity and did not bind the Canadian government or parliament to it.[96]

In his farewell speech in Canada, Sastri argued one final time that the British Empire must craft its new form of the Commonwealth on the principle of equality. He added, bitterly: 'it will teach the people of Canada, who require that little education, that they have no right to take away the rights of citizenship from fellow-citizens within the Empire'.[97]

## V

On his 53rd birthday, 22 September 1922, Sastri and Bajpai departed Canada, bringing an end to his dominion tour, and arrived in India on 24 November. Although Canada had proven to be much more difficult than Australia and New Zealand, Sastri was satisfied overall. The Australian and New Zealand governments had granted some legislative concessions, and even in Canada there was hope of bipartisan support in the Dominion Assembly. Seeing his primary task to be of 'political education', he stated: '[i]n British Columbia, I am not hopeful of immediate results; but of the ultimate success of continued endeavours I have no doubt'.[98]

Although Bajpai was also of the view that they had been 'successful beyond expectation' in Canada, these were rather hopeful assessments.[99] Indians in British Columbia were only able to gain the franchise in Canada in 1947. Indeed, at the Imperial Conference of 1923, King blamed Sastri's speeches for a counter-effect of organizing 'the forces that were opposed to granting the franchise to Indians'.[100] He told Peel, the Secretary of State, privately that Sastri was 'sullen, arrogant and false'.[101]

The Indian nationalist press was expectedly critical of the whole tour. Sastri was, quite unjustly, accused of sacrificing Indians at the altar of White Australia,[102] and humiliating Indians by 'wiping the Australian ground with his knees'. Unless India had the power to retaliate, pleading with the dominions would not serve any purpose, the *Catholic Herald of India* claimed.[103] Motilal Nehru chided him for representing the views of neither the Liberals nor the Nationalists.[104] His son, Jawaharlal Nehru, in his *Autobiography*, also made several unkind references to Sastri, particularly for acting as an 'Imperial Envoy' when his own countryfolk were being subjected to the worst forms of oppression. Remarkably, it was left to Gandhi and his close followers like Banarasi Das Chaturvedi and Henry Polak to defend Sastri publicly.[105] Gandhi stated that his and Sastri's love for each other was not lessened at all, even though the latter thought Gandhi was 'leading India down to the abyss'.[106] Chaturvedi wrote in the Lucknow paper *Leader* that it was a pity that no Indian leader of prominence went to the dominions to see the condition of Indians overseas, and those who did go were weakened by ill-informed critiques of intolerant friends.[107] Polak criticized those who argued that India could only help overseas Indians if the country had *swaraj*. He reminded them that Japan was an independent country and yet could not ensure the equal treatment of its citizens.[108]

Even the more sympathetic avenues like the *Indian Social Reformer* questioned Sastri's 'political reverie' in assuming that a tour to the dominions would affect any change.[109] It is obviously unreasonable to expect one visit to bring fundamental changes to policies, especially when they concern existential identity questions as in the case of White Australia, White New Zealand and White Canada. The hopes of the 1921 resolution, and Sastri's initial faith, from one tour were manifestly exaggerated. When, at the end of the tour, Sastri insisted on the educative aspects of the tour, that is of creating a broad public sympathy for the Indian cause, the *Reformer* taunted: 'Failures are often of more educative value than success.'[110]

Educative or not, the tour certainly had a symbolic value. It was the first instance of India's public diplomacy, an instance where India had sent an accredited representative to directly negotiate with the dominions on matters of mutual interest as well as address wider publics to create a more conducive environment for change. As Sastri would insist, each such moment of international recognition and equality was an enormous jump in the direction of constitutional autonomy for India.[111]

In his articulation, Sastri was relentless in basing the new Commonwealth on the ideal of equality. As we have seen in previous chapters, he provided not merely a moral but also a rational case for how India's equality was the very basis of the new Commonwealth, one that, as we have seen in the chapter, even his detractors found enormously difficult to argue against.

The responses to his arguments are interesting. While Sastri's diplomatic endeavours were channelled towards easing racial barriers for Indians across the British Empire, the politics of race intersects invariably with culture, civilization and, indeed, caste. Sastri as a 'cultured, Brahmin' and India's plenipotentiary was able to transgress racial barriers. He became the 'model Indian' who by his very exception proved the rule about 'uncultured and low-caste Indians' in the dominions. He endorsed this view of himself as an exception: it showed India's higher culture to the dominion publics, he would argue, a side they had not previously seen. But the argument had strong casteist connotations: the immigrants to the dominions, most of whom were engaged in either trade or labour, came from allegedly lower castes in India. By implication, more visits by highly cultured and high-caste Indians would give a better impression of Indians to the dominions.

The response of his detractors mostly turned this point on its head. Precisely the fact that Sastri was an exception should be sufficient indication of why more Indians, 'low caste, filthy Hindus', as one characterization went, could not be allowed in. The third set of reactions acknowledged Sastri's logic in support of imperial unity, but placed the question of the Indian in the dominions within the larger context of immigration politics. If Indians were granted political rights as British subjects, this would then have to be extended to other naturalized British subjects of East Asian origin in these dominions, such as the Japanese and the Chinese. The tension and strain of relations at this crucial moment in the post-war empire were negotiated at the floating intersections of the questions of race, culture/caste, immigration, equality and individual agency.

Finally, his excellent command over English made him acceptable to the white audiences, but what established his authority was his being able to master the language while looking and acting authentically Indian. He was neither a closet Englishman nor the fanged native. The former embodies the promise of colonialism, the latter its fear. Sastri, in being neither of the two, was the acceptable exception: the 'authentic Indian' whose sepia-toned authenticity was palatable because it was deviant but not dangerous.

Let us remember then our opening vignette in this book: the two images from Sastri's arrival in Canada. That image was to change now because in a public speech in Canada Sastri, like Gandhi, blamed the British government, and Lloyd George in particular, for failing to keep its promise to the Turks. He added that this had quite justifiably caused strong grievances among Indian Muslims, who then had become anti-British.[112] This angered many. Neville Chamberlain, then touring Canada, sent Peel a letter calling Sastri 'a treacherous, untrustworthy creature'.[113] Reading lamented to Peel that Sastri was proving to be a 'rather dangerous ambassador of the Empire'.[114] Indeed, so riled was Reading with Sastri's criticisms – and he expected more of them – that he recommended taking Sastri's name off of the list of honourees for the year. Reading was sly but prophetic.

In the summer of 1923, incensed at the British settlement in Kenya and the great injustice done to Indians in the country, Sastri was 'roused to incandescent indignation' which 'drove him for once in his life to advocate retaliation and non-cooperation, irrespective of consequences'.[115] We discuss this in the next chapter.

7

# Like the Anger of Rudra

I

In the first weeks of 1923, Nairobi was pregnant with ominous rumours. Local Portuguese settlers, it was rumoured, had been instructed to wear badges on their arms to differentiate themselves from Indians. Up-country white settlers were spotted in town recruiting their racial kin for a militia.[1] While the chatter spread in urban Nairobi, the countryside simmered with rage. The local European associations were 'blowing upon the ambers of revolt' against the Crown Colony government,[2] as E. Powys Cobb, a legislative councillor, and Phillip Wheatley, a veteran artillery officer, toured the country, urging local associations to 'set [the country] alight'. A second Ireland was in the offing, or so some local associations threatened. In Nakuru, a town situated in the Rift Valley, the largest meeting of a local settler community was held, in the presence of key settler leaders including Lord Delamere, who had been secretly designated as the first president of the future provisional government.[3] Here, the crass messaging of the other local European associations was jettisoned for a more polished, yet very targeted, resolution that promised to 'take such action as [the settlers] may consider proper and necessary'.[4]

Stirrings of a coup whirled around the country. Wheatley was appointed as the military leader of the proposed rebellion. With the slogan of 'For King and Kenya', recruiters for local vigilance committees emphasized that rebelling against the local government would be the highest form of duty to the crown. Kenyan Indians, feeling gravely under threat, appealed to the colonial government. But the Kenyan government, under the South African-born Governor, Robert Coryndon, watched passively from the side-lines, dismissing their fears of violence as 'much exaggerated'.[5] In the first week of

February, once the preparations for the alleged coup were practically complete,⁶ Coryndon finally cabled the Colonial Office that plans were afoot to 'paralyse the functions of government'.⁷ The imperial government sprang into action and docked three battleships at the harbour in Zanzibar.⁸

This hoped-for rebellion was astonishingly bold in its aims. After raiding Government House, the insurrectionists planned to install a new de facto government of the settlers. The treasury, armoury, railways, customs and telegraphs offices would be seized and the Governor, if unwilling to cooperate, would be detained and swiftly despatched to a distant farm for 'some amusement' such as trout fishing.⁹ A similar fate awaited other senior officials. European officials in the police and the King's African Rifles were likely to turn out in support of the rebellion. The overwhelming population of Africans was expected to remain loyal to the new government.¹⁰

The main targets of the putsch were the Indians in Kenya. They were to be loaded onto the very railroad they had built, the Uganda Railway, and transported to the coast.¹¹ Wheatley, a veteran of the British Indian Army, was confident that 'a dozen determined men could drive the 20,000 Indians like a flock of sheep'.¹² The *East African Standard*, the premier organ of white settlers, assured Indians in a strangely macabre fashion that 'the extinction of every Indian in the Colony would be hardly necessary'.¹³

By all visible indicators, Kenya sat on a powder keg about to explode. Alarmed at the developing situation, the Aga Khan, the leader of the transnational Ismaili community, cabled to his followers to 'not do anything illegal or unconstitutional',¹⁴ and shot off another to Reading asking for his government's 'timely intervention'.¹⁵ In yet another letter to the *Times of India*, he pleaded that the Indian government send 'two or three universally respected individuals, men like Mr. Sastri, who knows the colonial better than anyone I can think of … as bearers of a message of expostulation and reconciliation to the settlers in East Africa'.¹⁶

## II

In September 1888, when the queen had granted a royal charter to the Imperial British East Africa Company (IBEIC) to administer the area under the British sphere of influence in East Africa, a key reason cited was the protection of Indian traders.¹⁷ Unlike other white settler colonies, Indians had pre-dated white settlers by almost three centuries in East Africa, cultivating trade networks from the coast to the interior. Subsequently, Indians also dominated white settlers in numbers, largely due to their employment in building and maintaining the Uganda Railway. Completed in a record time of five years between 1896 and 1901, the Ugandan Railway was built and subsequently maintained almost entirely by over 40,000 Indians, one third of whom stayed. When originally conceived, the railway was expected to foster circuits of trade along its 600-mile run from the Mombasa coast to Lake Victoria.[18] In addition, it would allow for quick transportation of troops in order to preserve the mouth of the Nile, and consequently the Suez, against any sudden German trespass into Britain's sphere of influence. Finally, Britain spent a considerable fortune guarding the coastal waters against the slave trade. A railway line would discourage slavery by making 'carriage by men' economically unviable.[19]

At nearly £5 million, the railway ended up costing nearly double the expected amount in construction and bequeathed almost none of the economic benefits.[20] African communities which were either pastoral or generated very little agricultural product for export belied the image of 'a teeming population waiting to exchange their raw materials for British manufacture'.[21] The railway ended up being a white elephant, provoking the romantic raconteur of the Kenyan whites, Elspeth Huxley, to comment that 'never before or since has such an impracticable, extravagant and uneconomic railway been planned'.[22]

The ready option was to utilize and promote the existing social and commercial networks of the Indian population. Indeed, Harry Johnston, the special commissioner for Uganda, famously characterized East Africa as 'the America of the Hindu', a region where the Indian entrepreneurial spirit would help to develop the East African peninsula. But the commissioner for East Africa between 1900 and 1904, Charles Eliot, had other plans. A Balliol product with serious scholarly accomplishments, Eliot came to East Africa with set beliefs in social Darwinism, and a firm commitment to the civilizing mission. He proposed granting large tracts of the more fertile, temperate Highlands in the Rift Valley, 300 miles into the interior, to European settlers to produce enough crops for the railways to carry and become economically viable. He preferred Indians to settle along the humid and tropical coast and in the lowlands. His plans, approved by the Foreign Office, sought to turn Kenya into a 'white man's country' – incidentally, another Harry Johnston phrase.

However, as Dane Kennedy shows, the proposed settler colony already had access to large supplies of indigenous labour, hence it offered limited opportunities for working-class white settlers. Instead, from an industrializing and democratizing Britain, new settler colonies like Kenya were more likely to attract a feudal class whose fortunes in Britain were on the wane.[23] Hence, Kenya was specifically advertised as a 'public school boy's colony', an idyllic place for those looking 'to replicate, in a somewhat crude form, some of the attributes of their class which had ceased to exist in contemporaneous Europe'. The 'luring Alpine climate of the Highlands' coupled with 'opportunities for sport, recreation and game-hunting' invited the British barons to enjoy the idealized versions of their high Victorian lives at the frontiers of empire.[24] As the historian A.P.J. Taylor noted: 'Englishmen escaped democracy and high taxation by establishing themselves in Kenya as territorial aristocrats in the old model.'[25]

To attract this specific class of settlers, Eliot granted them land on remarkably generous terms in the fertile Highlands. For instance, in 1903, the government offered freehold grants of 640 acres to any white settler who applied, and soon raised it to 5,000 acres. A number of British aristocrats ended up amassing vast land holdings. The most prominent of these was Hugh Cholmondeley, or Lord Delamere, who remained the unofficial leader of the white settlers until his death in 1931. Born to Baron Delamere and his second wife August Seymour in Vale Royal, Cheshire, in 1870, young Hugh exhibited no talent except for game hunting, of which he did plenty. Between 1891 and 1897, he went on five hunting trips through Somaliland, and in the last of these he entered the Kenyan Highlands through the north. Already poor by aristocratic standards of wealth, he whittled away the little money he had on his exorbitant hunting expeditions, and eventually decided to settle in Kenya. He received 100,000 acres on a 99-year lease at a halfpenny an acre per annum.[26]

Recruitment efforts were also carried out in South Africa and other dominions. English settlers from South Africa flocked to create an even better version of South Africa: a white man's country 'like the Cape without its liberalism, and like Natal without its Indians'.[27] The defeat of the Boers in the war in South Africa led several Afrikaner families to trek up north, where they found the land laws 'to be [the] most liberal in the world' for white settlers.[28] After the war, the Governor, Edward Northey, announced a soldier settlement scheme and allotted 2 million acres of land to mostly elite white settlers of 'pure European origin'.[29]

The land so generously being farmed out to whites was obviously, as in all colonial situations, expropriated from the original inhabitants, who were pushed to the conveniently termed 'reserves'. The success of the new settlement depended upon the ability to command and exploit native resources, in both land and labour. It necessitated an elaborate structure of rules aimed at regulating and channelling

African bodies towards an economy of extraction. The political, economic, social and cultural life of the white settler community as the managerial elite was devoted to preserving the inflated but always tenuous nature of white power. Indeed, their numerical inferiority made the white settler society overtly vigilant regarding anything that questioned their privilege. They were, as Kennedy argues, permanently in a state of siege.[30]

So while the landowning elite and the upper echelons of bureaucracy were entirely white, and the toiling agricultural labour almost entirely African, the petty bourgeoisie and the lower rungs of the Kenyan administration were overwhelmingly Indians. The protectorate's civil and criminal law as well as its currency were Indian. It was 'as if it was governed from India'.[31] In 1921, there were 9,651 whites, 22,822 Indians and nearly 2.5 million Africans in Kenya.[32]

The more the white settlers entrenched themselves in East Africa, the more scandalized they were to be governed by Indian laws and to be treated the same way as Indians. They increasingly called for pro-white policies, hoping to turn the protectorate into a 'self-governing dominion' on the lines of South Africa. They used the First World War to consolidate their political hold over the protectorate. In 1915, first steps were taken in this direction when white settlers were allowed to elect two representatives to the War Council. They were promised a new constitution at the end of the war, a promise fulfilled in February 1919. The new constitution gave Europeans the right to elect 11 members on the Legislative Council, and two seats in the Executive Council.

The story could not be any more different for Indians. During the war, Indian interests received several setbacks. A few key Indian leaders were arrested under martial law. Further, a bill was passed which barred the sale or lease of Highlands by Europeans to Indians and Africans. Racial segregation was introduced at the municipal level in Nairobi and envisaged a gradual separation of residential and commercial compounds on the basis of race.[33]

To top it, a key document, the East Africa Economic Commission report, prepared by a committee dominated by white settlers, was issued in January 1919. The report was less a statement of fact, and more of a jaundiced invective against Kenyan Indians who, among other things, had allegedly an 'incurable repugnance to sanitation and hygiene'. The 'crafty race' of Indians was accused of keeping Africans in servitude by taking up all the jobs that would otherwise go to Africans and inciting the 'innocent' African to 'crime as well as vice'. The admission of Indians into the colony 'was a cardinal error of policy' which had led to the 'retardation of [the] progress [of the native]'. The broader point the report was trying to make was that Africans suffered the most from the presence of Indians, and hence the choice lay between the 'vital interests of the African and the ambition of India'.[34] The report demanded that the Kenyan policy of the British government be based upon 'the principle of self-determination' which considered 'only the interests of the indigenous native and Arab population and of the race responsible for their control [that is, the whites]'.[35]

Showing tactical awareness of the winds of change, with the doctrine of trusteeship emerging as a key principle of rule, Kenyan whites mounted their claims for autonomy on the backs of Africans. However, the report also held out against the creeping influence of what were seen as 'West Coast' ideas of colonization. The Dual Policy, associated with the West African colonies, granted Africans limited forms of self-government, with the promise of eventually transferring sovereignty. In contrast, the settlers in the east embraced the South African ideals of white rule, where 'civilizing' the native never meant the transfer of political power.[36]

## III

Admittedly, the report was also perhaps responding to several assertions made during (and just after) the war, calling for an Indian colony in East Africa. Such demands had been made since 1912 when Alibhoy Mulla Jeevanjee, a rich Indian trader with a business empire in East Africa, had called for the 'annexation of this [British East] African territory for the Indian Empire'.[37] The idea gained traction during the war, as Indian troops did the empire's bidding across the world, but in particular in East Africa. Several public commentators suggested that German East Africa, where Indian troops had fought against Germans, should be reserved for the settlement of the Indian population. The demand gained the attention of the imperial government when Theodore Morison, a former principal of the Aligarh Muslim University and most recently senior political officer in German East Africa, sent a memorandum titled 'A Colony for Africa', which Montagu presented to the War Cabinet.[38] Three months before Morison wrote the memorandum, Aga Khan III, the Karachi-born Imam of Ismaili Shias, had sent a book to the press, entitled *India in Transition* that had also made the case for an Indian colony. In the book, which he wrote during a long health retreat in Switzerland, he had gone further than Morison, insisting that the whole of East Africa, including German as well as British spheres, should be handed over to India to rule.[39]

For both Morison and Aga Khan, however, India's own colonizing claims in East Africa were not merely about rewarding the pioneering efforts of Indians in bringing trade and civilization to the region. Instead, they argued that an East Africa colony would also resolve the issues between the dominions and India regarding immigration. Granting a colony to India, Morison argued, would be an 'honourable bargain', after which India would give up its demand for unfettered access to the dominions.[40] Likewise for Aga Khan, allowing India 'an outlet for colonial expansion' will overcome a major obstacle that 'stood in the way of the growth of Imperial solidarity'.[41] When a mere 65 million whites in the empire had exclusively laid claims to the UK, Canada, Australia, New Zealand and South Africa, 315 million Indians deserved their own colony.[42]

Furthermore, East Africa was also a perfect laboratory to see the success of empire ideals and to test India's claims to equality. The true test of a mature civilization was its ability to be a good colonizer. If Indians 'accept the test they must abide by the result; if they fail to justify themselves they cannot afterwards claim for India a higher status in the Commonwealth than she enjoys today', Morison wrote.[43] Aga Khan went on to justify why Indians in particular would be best suited for this job.

European civilization, he wrote, was too complex and mechanized for the African to learn from and cope with. Africans were at the same stage of development as 'the *Bhils* and other wild tribes' in India. Civilization could only be cultivated in small doses: 'Indians would teach the natives to plough, to weave, and to carpenter; the rough Indian tools are within the comprehension of the African mind'. The methods of the European, in contrast, are 'so far above [the African's] head; they belong to another world which has no suggestions for him'.[44] Indeed, India's 'immigrant sons must feel stronger sympathy and toleration for the Africans than the white settler'.[45]

Hence, East Africa was 'the most appropriate field for Indian colonization and settlement'; it will be for India 'a shop window open to the West [of Africa]'. The growth of civilizations, Aga Khan underscored, was dependent on expansionism; the cultivation and display of knowledge and skills in contexts other than one's own. East Africa was a natural territory for Indians. Traders and merchants had opened vast swathes of territory for markets; Indian subalterns had preserved them for the empire. But now Indian doctors, geologists, foresters, engineers and other specialized professionals would be needed to develop the country.[46] East Africa would not just be a playground for India's new vitality; it would also be a testimony to the success of British colonialism in India.

Both Morison and Aga Khan had wrapped the Indian colonization proposal in the broader need for intra-imperial coordination and solidarity, and, most importantly, in the ongoing discussions around what the Commonwealth meant. As we have discussed, the prevalent Lionel Curtis-inspired understanding of the Commonwealth emphasized it as a sacramental community rather than a contractual one. In other words, while the basis of the contractual state was individual consent to be governed for one's own benefit; a sacramental community was based on the idea of duty towards others. Indeed, it is only through the fulfilment of this duty towards others that one can become a full member of the community. But this sense of duty can only be cultivated through practice, and in order to cultivate it one had to be entrusted with the responsibility. Responsibility could only be nurtured by its exercise. India's elevation to being an equal member of the community could be proof of the success of the Commonwealth. However, it could not be adequately proven until India actually took on such a responsibility.

In any case, the Indian colony scheme found little acceptance among Indian nationalists. Aga Khan published a statement from Gokhale two years after the latter's death which suggested that East Africa should be reserved for Indian administration. However, he later clarified in his autobiography that this was his own shrewd addition to Gokhale's 'political testament'.[47] The demand fit awkwardly with the pleas for Indians' equality in all parts of the empire. How could the rights of Indians in all the settler dominions be sacrificed for a colony in East Africa? Some East African Indians continued to impress the need for colonization upon the Indian National Congress. But after the First World War, as the Indian nationalist movement gained strength, such views were in a significant minority and the focus shifted towards the righteous demands of Kenyan Indians for equality with white settlers, rather than a separate colony for Indians.

As a response to the European efforts to disempower them and turn Kenya into a white colony, the demands of Kenyan Indians centred around four main issues: more representation in the Legislative Assembly, the introduction of elective franchise for Indians, the abolition of municipal and commercial segregation, and allowing Indians to purchase land in the Highlands. The whites demanded the opposite, and in addition they wanted stricter immigration controls on Indians.[48]

## IV

As Robert Blyth points out, the issue of Indians in Kenya emerged at a crucial moment. The Montagu–Chelmsford reforms had just been announced, promising to put India on the path to becoming a self-governing dominion. India had been given an international status on a par with the dominions. The Indian nationalist movement, galvanized under the new leadership of Gandhi, was intent on pushing the government harder for more concessions. Thus, East Africa became a test case for asserting India's new status and resolve, at both the official and the nationalist levels.[49] It was repeatedly couched as an 'acid test' for the British Empire.[50] The discrimination against Indians in South Africa could be blamed on the Boers, but in British East Africa the majority of settlers were British and policy was in the hands of the British government. The newly minted doctrine of the British Commonwealth which claimed India as an equal member put the empire itself in the dock.[51]

The Colonial Office, however, was unsympathetic, if not tetchily opposed, to such concerns. In February 1921, Winston Churchill took over as the Colonial Secretary. The previous incumbent, Alfred Milner, had published a policy dispatch on 21 May 1920 which discarded an elective franchise for Indians and advocated segregation. In July 1920, Kenya was also turned from a protectorate into a colony, which was a crucial advance for the white settlers, who interpreted this as a step towards self-government. Milner's dispatch evoked strong protests from the Indian government as well the Indian leaderships in both India and Kenya. The East African Indian National Congress passed a resolution calling for non-cooperation.[52] Both Chelmsford and Montagu strongly opposed the dispatch, the latter noting with deep concern that 'race-segregation' was a doctrine entirely 'at variance with the established policy of the Imperial Government'.[53]

Churchill's previous utterances on the issue had been sympathetic to Indians. Back in 1909, lauding the contribution of Indians in making the Kenya colony, he had stated:

> Is it possible for any Government with a scrap of respect for honest dealing between man and man, to embark upon a policy of deliberately squeezing out the native of India from regions in which he has established himself under every security of public faith? Most of all must we ask, is such a policy possible to the Government which bears sway over three hundred millions of our Indian Empire?[54]

But he was, as Lionel Curtis once pithily observed, 'as great as a politician can be without principles'.[55] At the imperial conference, as we have noted, Churchill first unscrupulously tried to equate the white dominions and the Kenya colony by inserting 'East Africa' into a resolution meant for the dominions and India, and then refused to grant Sastri a meeting on the Kenyan issue, despite repeated requests from Sastri and Montagu.[56] At the conference, Montagu and Churchill, two fairly eccentric men related by marriage, worked together on a resolution to the Kenyan question, to each other's frustration at times. Eventually, they laid aside Milner's policy and pushed for a compromise formula which accepted the Indian demand for a common roll and a franchise based on educational and income criteria but reserved the Highlands for Europeans. The Kenyan whites opposed these proposals, and started arming themselves for a rebellion. They demanded a pledge towards what they called 'irreducible minimums', that is, strict immigration control, segregation in residential and, where practicable, in commercial areas, no elected representation for Indians and reserving the Highlands exclusively for whites.[57]

Expectedly, it did not take long for Churchill to do another about-turn. In a speech on 28 January 1922 delivered at the Kenya and Uganda Dinner in London, he announced that 'all future immigration of Indians will be strictly regulated'. Kenya was to become 'a characteristically and distinctively British colony', on the path to eventually achieving 'responsible self-government'.[58]

Churchill's statement aroused the strongest of denunciations from India. Resolutions of protest were passed in the Indian Legislative Assembly and the Council of State. Charles Andrews demanded that either Reading or Montagu, or both, should resign; and Kenyan Indians who had suspended their non-cooperation to consider Churchill's previous proposals, renewed their agitation. Indian officials discussed whether India should retaliate by stopping emigration to Ceylon, Malaya and Mauritius.[59]

Sastri had always been wary of Churchill's double-speak: the latter's high polemic often either served or distracted from his schemes. Sastri believed him to be 'a scheming fellow' who played 'an anti-India game' as part of his intrigues to usurp the premier's chair in the Conservative government. It was always India that '[had] to play the price of [his] genius'.[60]

Sastri was in Washington when the news of Churchill's speech reached him. He immediately cabled Montagu, trusting that the Cabinet would discard Churchill's pronouncements.[61] After he arrived in London from Washington, Sastri gave interviews condemning Churchill's speech, and together with Polak canvassed for the rights of the Kenyan Indians.[62] But Montagu's weight in the Cabinet was considerably less than Churchill's at this point and culminated in the former's tragic resignation a few weeks later.[63]

As the pressure mounted on Churchill, he attempted to wriggle out of the situation. He asked the two under-secretaries, Lord Wood from the Colonial Office and Lord Winterton from the India Office, to thrash out a proposal. The Wood–Winterton Agreement, as these proposals were called, gave Indians a common electoral roll and enfranchised approximately 10 per cent of the Indian population. It reserved four seats for Indians in the Legislative Assembly and one nominated member in the Executive Council. It recommended no change in the immigration policy, while continuing with the policy of keeping the Highlands as white reserves. Churchill and Peel, the new Secretary of State for India, made some additions on keeping open the matter of restrictions on immigrants and the Highlands issue for future policy changes. The proposals were offered to the Indian government and the Kenyan Governor in September 1922.[64]

The Indian government cabled a broadly positive response. It protested against the Highlands clause and asked for five instead of four representatives, but largely agreed with the proposals. In contrast, Coryndon cabled back that the proposals were entirely unacceptable and could not be imposed without the use of force on white settlers. Before any response could be drafted, however, Lloyd George's government fell. Churchill not only lost the ministry but also his own seat. The new conservative administration of Stephen Baldwin appointed Victor C.W. Cavendish, the Duke of Devonshire, as the new Colonial Secretary. Devonshire, a former Governor General of Canada, thought it prudent to continue with the Wood–Winterton scheme initially. The Kenyan whites, however, rejected the scheme in its entirety and prepared for 'direct action' in response.

Kenya was ready for a rebellion. Or not just yet.

## V

On 14 February 1923, Devonshire advised the British Cabinet against any military or economic action in Kenya. White troops sent to combat almost 9,000 armed white settlers would be a 'costly enterprise' with severe denunciations from people in the UK and the dominions, he reasoned. Using local African troops of the King's African Rifles was even more 'unthinkable'. It would be 'disastrous for the discipline of the troops ... [and] fatal to British prestige throughout Africa'. African troops reigning on whites would break the bedrock of white supremacy and imperil the lives of Europeans throughout Africa.[65] An economic blockade would affect the large body of officials, the entire Indian community and Uganda, and so was equally inconceivable. Devonshire's only option was to give in. He offered the Kenyan whites the Wood–Winterton proposals with strict immigration control. But if the rebellious white settlers were to reject even this, he was willing to concede more. To discuss these matters, he invited Coryndon and a delegation of white settlers to London, albeit on the condition that the latter undertake to suspend their plans for violence while the discussions were ongoing.

Astonishingly, a band of retired men armed with rudimentary rifles and limited ammunition, and supported by a few thousand settlers, had forced the mighty British Empire to capitulate. This would be a romantic tale of courage and resolve worthy of the rapt attention of future generations, except that the only feature that made all the difference between being slaughtered out of stupidity and a glorious victory was 'whiteness'. Even the settlers knew that.[66]

Despite hysterical ultimatums of a second America and a second Ireland, the settler leaders themselves had expected the situation to resemble a second India, a repeat of an episode in 1884. Against Lord Ripon's Ilbert Bill that year, Europeans had planned to raid Government House in Calcutta, and send the Viceroy packing to Britain. The imperial government's response was to recall the Viceroy. Even Wheatley had imagined the situation would become a 'second Curragh', confident that British forces would refuse to fight against fellow whites. The settlers also dangled the prospect of a Kenya–South Africa Union, and actively courted Smuts, as an effective bargaining chip against the imperial government. With a sympathetic Governor and civil service officers at home and a Conservative government in England, the chances of the empire's might coming down heavily on them were negligible.

As Governor Coryndon and a settler delegation prepared to leave for London on Devonshire's invitation, Sastri marched into the centre of the political agitation on Kenya in India. Troubled by the hypocrisy of the British government's response, he moved a resolution in the Council of State on 5 March. He noted that while Britain capitulated to empty threats of violence by whites, it had used force and repression against a non-violent movement in India. Four years ago, over a thousand people had been massacred in Amritsar for merely gathering in a peaceful meeting. The contrast could not be more telling.

Sastri noted that Indians everywhere had shown remarkable humility, patience and respect for order. In the face of the gravest provocations, they had agitated with forbearance and humility for their right to equality. Despite the justness of their claims, they had also been understanding and patient enough to 'proceed by stages'. Although Indians were the first settlers in Kenya and contributed more than 50 per cent of the colony's public revenue,[67] their demands were already limited. They had asked neither for universal suffrage nor for proportional representation; they only claimed 'very partial fulfilment of the right to equality'. In contrast, Kenyan whites were afflicted with the white supremacist 'spirit of South Africa'. Their desire was to eventually merge with South Africa, to create a future African Confederation in the service of white interests, Sastri alleged.[68]

His resolution at the council was carried, although customarily the government did not accept it, citing the ongoing discussions between the Colonial Governor and the British government.[69] However, bowing to the strong Indian sentiment, the government agreed to send an Indian delegation, nominated by the Indian legislature, to London. Sastri was asked to lead the delegation. He accepted it, although these long tours had now started to take a toll on his health.[70] The two other members of the delegation were Jamnadas Dwarkadas and Balkrishna Sitaram Kamat. Sastri and Dwarkadas sailed for London on 14 April; Kamat joined them a few weeks later.

## VI

Coryndon and the settler delegation led by Delamere arrived in Britain in early April. The delegation also included a protestant missionary, Reverend J.W. Arthur of the Scottish church, ostensibly to represent 'native interests'. In addition, the bishop of Kampala, H.G. Jones, although not officially part of the delegation, offered his own sacerdotal authority to speak for the native in London. Interestingly, the 'military leader' Wheatley was not part of the delegation; the spectre of the rebellion was to be kept dangling in case things did not turn out as expected in London.

Delamere and his delegation received great support from the Conservative press and the die-hards in the Conservative Party.[71] Their deep connections with the British elite afforded them an easy audience and strong press. Even the usually centrist *The Times* published a series of articles broadly sympathetic to the settler viewpoint.[72] Innumerable lunches and dinners at Delamere's lavish Grosvenor Place house helped the cause immensely.[73] The emphatic appeals of the two clergymen, Jones and Arthur, for the continuation of white rule as trustees of native interests added considerable weight to the delegation's propaganda.[74] They demonized the Kenyan Indian as a scheming, degenerate colonist, intent on depriving the natives of their only chance of progress. A pamphlet from the Kenyan White

Women Committee expressed horror at the prospect of English children sharing classes with Indian children, 'who in all probability are trained and initiated into the mysteries of sex'.[75] Africans, domesticated inside white houses and farms, were under 'the rule of [the] white woman', a friend who the African turned to in the times of trouble and sickness.[76] The Indian was a calamity in this paradise, the pamphlet insisted. The conservative magazine *The Outlook* warned of 'An African 1776', stating:

> No sturdy pioneers of our own stock would ever submit, excepting at the point of the bayonet, to control by a mob of brown men, mostly at that of the lower caste, or of no caste. One white Englishman in India is accustomed to govern a thousand natives: is there a reason to suppose that in East Africa the same white man would consent to be ruled by four Indians?[77]

Consequently, the Indian delegation arrived to a hostile public sentiment. Sastri and his colleagues noted that white settler propaganda 'had gained ground to an alarming effect'. London's air was thick with conspiracy theories and evil plots by Indians to snatch power from the white settlers. Indians sought 'to annex the Colony to India and to defraud the natives and whites alike in their just rights'.[78]

As the Indian delegation busied themselves in canvassing on behalf of the Kenyan Indians, they were joined by a delegation of Kenyan Indians, which included the editor of the *East African Chronicle*, Manilal Ambalal Desai, the Nairobi-based politician B.S. Varma, and prominent merchant-politicians Alibhai Mulla Jeevanjee and Hussinbhai S. Virjee. The Kenyan delegation had taken a detour through Bombay, where they had hoped to meet Gandhi. Although they were prevented by the Bombay government from seeing Gandhi, who was in prison,[79] they were successful in bringing Gandhi's trusted aide, Charles Andrews, with them to London. In Britain, the Indian Overseas Association, now led by the former Viceroy, Lord Hardinge, and its able secretary, H.S.L. Polak, supported them in securing connections. Newspapers such as the *Daily Herald*, *Daily News*, the *Observer* and the *Nation* carried appeals on behalf of the Indian deputation.[80]

The Indian and Kenyan Indian delegations also discussed a campaign strategy among themselves. Kenyan Indians were to push for maximal gains, while Sastri, as the leader of the Indian delegation, would eventually 'accept the compromise' of Wood–Winterton proposals, following which the others 'should acquiesce reluctantly'.[81] He expected vicious criticism from the Indian nationalist press for the role that came to him. He wrote to Natesan:

> You would regret, I am sure that the part of compromising has fallen on me. I regret it too. But I have nothing to lose by way of popularity and the press cannot abuse me worse. So, it does not matter so very much after all. Somebody has to bear the odium, why not I?[82]

Sastri gave several well-publicized interviews, including to *Reuters* and the *Manchester Guardian*. In these, he emphasized the limited nature of Indian demands, the role of Indians in developing the colony, and the importance of the principle of equality in the British Commonwealth. The native interest argument of the white settler, he added, was laughable. The Kenyan government had passed ordinances which forced Africans to labour on white-owned lands, and implemented measures such as the hut and poll taxes, which followed the South African template of not only uprooting Africans from their lands but also coercing them to live a life of perpetual bondage.[83] As an anonymous article in the *Guardian* noted, desertion from employment and work strike had both been made criminal offences for Africans. Their wages had recently been reduced by one third, and they had no right to own land. The white settlers owned 11,375 square miles of land, the Indians 22 miles and the Africans nil.[84] The Europeans in Kenya, the Africanist Norman Leys wrote in the same paper, had 'in half a generation reduced the [African] population by a quarter, crushed out native industries, and reduced the surveyors to serfdom in order to make them labour for their profit'.[85]

Roundly dismissing the idea that India was seeking a colony for itself, Sastri asked 'is it possible for serious-minded Indian statesmen, occupied every moment of their lives in removing the humiliation under which they live in their own country, to entertain the idea of annexing territory in a far-off continent?'[86] Neither of the two settler communities had the right to govern Africans, he stressed. The administration of Kenya was entirely the responsibility of the imperial government, and no efforts should be made to tilt Kenya in the direction of a white settler 'self-government'.

## VII

For any outsider, the corridors of power in London could seem impregnable. Navigating the maze of ideology, class and, indeed, race in British political circles was, and remains, daunting. In these circles, networks of influential societies carried considerable weight; perhaps the most important of them was the Round Table, whose roving ambassador, as noted in Chapter 2, was Lionel Curtis. Lloyd George had once termed the Round Table as the most powerful group in Britain. Two of his own political secretaries, Philip Kerr and Edward Grigg, were Round Tablers.

To canvass support for the Indian position, Sastri met Curtis. It is not clear what support Curtis gave Sastri, but a few months later Tej Bahadur Sapru credited him with opening several avenues of propaganda for the Indian question. The political position of the Round Table, however, became clearer in an article published in the society's journal, *The Round Table*, in June 1923.

Philip Kerr, the first editor of the journal, had suggested back in 1917 that the best argument against Indian immigration was 'the case of the Kaffir'.[87] In a co-authored June 1923 article, the journal's editor John Dove now made a strong case for immigration control, for that was 'the mute appeal of the African masses' who like children were 'unable to absorb conflicting ideas [of whites and Indians] without harm'.[88] Consequently, for the medium term, the article suggested the American quota system of immigration control, regulating immigration by allotting quotas to each immigrant group, based on existing numbers.[89] After his meeting with Curtis, Sastri wrote to Natesan that he was not entirely opposed to the American quota suggestion, and that he would yield if white settlers first accepted it.[90]

In general, the British liberal circles and well as India Office pushed Sastri and the other delegates towards more compromises. Indians demanded common franchise, but the Colonial Office pushed for a communal franchise. This was most contentious, and Sastri and his colleagues were repeatedly told that to break off negotiations on the communal franchise issue, especially when Indians had accepted communal franchise in the CL scheme, would lose them sympathy.[91] Back in 1916, Sastri had originally opposed the communal franchise but relented for the sake of compromise in the CL scheme. He now maintained that this comparison was inapt. In India, communal representation was enshrined to preserve against the underrepresentation of the minority community. In Kenya, the case was quite the opposite: it was being pushed to deprive Indians of their elective rights.

The Indian delegates were treated with official apathy by the Colonial Office. Devonshire and his under-secretary, James Masterson-Smith, met Sastri and his colleagues once in early May, but refused to grant them another meeting until after the decision was finalized.[92] Meetings with Peel, Winterton and Louis Kershaw at the India Office were, however, relatively long affairs. Sastri was notably blunt – 'more blunt than my nature'[93] – in expressing his opposition to the India Office's handling of the Kenya situation. Peel and Winterton displayed 'a horror of first principles', namely equality and equal citizenship, and asked the Indian delegation to avoid expressions of hard principle. The Indian delegation, while agreeing to avoid rhetoric where necessary, remained firm that 'if it came to losing a point by losing sight of the equality idea we should not shrink from enunciating it'.[94]

What irked Sastri the most was the India Office's acceptance of the Kenyan white assertion that the 1921 resolution also applied to the Crown Colony. Interpreted this way, the resolution allowed the Crown Colony to decide its own immigration policies. As its author, Sastri insisted that the 1921 resolution of the Imperial Conference did not concern crown colonies, and reminded them of his and Montagu's strong pushback against Churchill's efforts to include East Africa in that resolution. He argued that the conference had no jurisdiction in the affairs of a crown colony, only the British government did. Peel, Montagu's successor, was making a strategic blunder by using the 1921 resolution, Sastri contended. This placed Kenyan whites at a par with white settlers in other dominions, and consequently bolstered their claims for self-government. Opening Kenya for discussions to other self-governing dominions would also place the future of Kenyan Indians in the hands of the white settler dominions. It would give a platform to someone like Jan Smuts to campaign on behalf of the Kenyan white settlers.[95]

With odds climbing against the Indian case, Sastri's tone and tenor became increasingly prickly. In his interview with *Manchester Guardian*, he made it plain: 'if the Indian claims were rejected, India would begin to think of going out of the Empire'.[96] In the face of the treasonous actions of Kenyan whites, if the Imperial Cabinet 'confessed [their] inability to do the right', few Indians would have any faith left in the ideals of the Commonwealth or in the professions of Britain's leaders.[97] In fact, by rewarding an upstart white insurrection, the Imperial Cabinet would also suffocate liberal or moderate politics in India.

## VIII

Back in Kenya, three African leaders, representing the Kikuyu, the Kavirondo and the Nandi, petitioned the acting Governor, Charles

7: 'Equal in rank but inferior in status'

Bowering, to allow an African delegation to proceed to London. They asked how a white missionary, Arthur, could speak for them. Bowering refused to grant them permission.[98] From the Indian side, Andrews, a man of God himself and several church societies from India, including the bishops of Calcutta and Madras, repudiated the views of Arthur and Jones.[99] The Indian cause was also helped by support from J.H. Oldham, secretary to the International Missionary Council, and John Harris, from the Anti-Slavery Aborigines Protection Society (or the Anti-Slavery Society).[100] Harris and the Anti-Slavery Society had played a key role the previous year in pushing Churchill to moderate his stance on the Indian issue after his disastrous dinner speech.

The Anti-Slavery Society organized a key annual dinner event on the Kenya question in the Central Hall of Parliament on 5 June. The list of speakers for the dinner meeting included members of Delamere's delegation, among them Jones and Arthur. Sastri, the lone Indian voice, was the main speaker of the evening.[101]

The gathering passed a resolution against racial discrimination in Kenya. Its mood could be judged by the loud cries of 'no' which interrupted one speaker's assertion that Indians were 'taking the bread out of the mouths of the natives'.[102] Jones, in a rather ineffectual speech, suggested that Indians in Kenya had considerable political rights already, and pleaded patience against introducing a common electoral roll.[103] The other reverend, Arthur, was more fervently anti-Indian in his intervention, holding Indians solely responsible for the lack of African progress.[104] Francis Scott, a settler leader and a former soldier from the British Indian Army, blamed the Congress Party in India for cooking up an agitation and flatly denied that any problems existed between the two settler communities.[105]

Sastri began his speech stating 'without reservation' that African interests should be paramount, and the African 'must be protected from the planter, the capitalist, the exploiter' whether white or Indian.[106] If the franchise was to be given, it should be given without any racial barrier. He stated: '[m]ake your qualifications high enough to ensure that you'll have a qualified electorate, but having made these qualifications, stick to them and admit thereto not Indians only, not Arabs only, but even the natives'.[107] The white settlers would never contemplate giving such rights to Africans and were not interested in African interests but just their own, he surmised. He turned then to his English audience and agonized over their double-speak, which was no less damaging than that of the settlers:

> During the war, when your dangers were truly imperiled and the fortunes of the British Empire seemed now and then to sink, in those trying and difficult hours you rose to sympathize with the smaller nationalities of the world, but the rebound of success has brought confidence and during this visit to mine I have been pained every now and then to come into contact with people in the highest ranks of Society, in the loftiest positions of responsibility, who say now and again, 'Oh yes, those were the ideals that we enunciated then, but there seems no need to pursue them anymore'. Let me tell you, then, you put your flag high, and I beg on my knees, do not take that flag down. That was the flag of freedom for all the nations of the world, whether or not they came under the Union Jack, but especially in this League of Nations, which we often call the British Commonwealth, I pray you dishonor not the Union Jack, but let all who salute it share with you your full privileges and your full rights.[108]

## IX

Sastri's punishing schedule was taking a huge toll on his health. In late June, doctors informed him that his heart condition was serious and strongly advised full rest for at least three months.[109] But he could not leave the Kenya work midway. He believed that his political campaign effort was crucial to countering the white settler narrative.[110] He had at least one big meeting left.

The Theosophical Society in London and the British auxiliary of the National Conference in Delhi had arranged for the gathering at Queen's Hall on 26 June, which, with 2,400 people present, according to one estimate, was the largest meeting on Indian politics in London for several decades. Ramsay MacDonald, the leader of the opposition, was in the chair. Against the advice of his doctors as well as Andrews and Polak, Sastri went to the meeting and launched a blistering attack on the Kenyan whites and Jan Smuts.[111]

MacDonald spoke first, and made things inappropriately confusing when he claimed that all great national elements of the empire must be given dominion status.[112] His audience wondered if he was referring to India or Kenya, and booed him.[113] Unlike MacDonald, Sastri's thoughts were both perspicuous and largely in sync with his audience. He lambasted those who asked Indians 'to be patient'. 'Have you won your famous rights and privileges, your immunities, by the exercise of patience? Are our white friends in Kenya now giving us a model of patience?'[114] Indians still hoped to provide the world an example of achieving dominion status and equality abroad through peaceful methods, but Indians may be learning a thing or two from the Kenyans. What was clearly evident now was that there were two Commonwealth ideals guiding the ongoing transformation of the empire. One was the ideal of equality and the other was the ideal of white supremacy. The former enjoined all races and component parts of the empire to come together in the spirit of fraternity and mutual respect, while the latter suggested that 'the general privileges and profits are largely to belong to the white population'.[115] The Kenyan settlers were chasing the second ideal, and, Sastri alleged, were being personally helped and dictated by Smuts.[116]

As the *Servant of India* editorialized, Kenya lay at the north end of the British protectorates between the Union of South Africa and the Anglo-Egyptian Sudan. If Kenya were 'Africanderised', Smutsian visions of a Greater South Africa, a Boer Africa under British suzerainty, would be closer to reality. With the front and rear secured, the middle territories could be organically incorporated. An area as large as India, fully controlled by the population of merely 8 per cent whites, 'a continent of serfs on the one hand and of plantation and mine owners on the other', would become the great white Commonwealth of the south; the dream of all white supremacists.[117]

Had Smuts really come to the aid of Kenyans? The record is mixed. Undeniably, on a number of occasions, the white settlers had appealed to Smuts to intercede on their behalf. In July 1920, Governor Northey sent an appeal to Smuts on behalf of the white community. In a vaguely framed letter, he asked Smuts for advice. Smuts avoided taking a direct position.[118] The next year, in August 1921, a deputation had travelled to South Africa to plead with Smuts to intervene, just as the Indian government was doing on the behalf of Indians. Smuts declined to meet them officially, but counselled them in an informal meeting they should undertake only constitutional methods to achieve their aims. Smuts also assured the Indian government that he would not intervene.[119] But at the same time Smuts had also secretly agreed to explore a Kenyan proposal which envisioned replacing Kenyan Indians in various trades with unemployed South Africans.[120]

In May 1923, a few weeks before Sastri's Queen Hall address, South African settlers in Kenya made another appeal to Smuts. This time he replied that he was watching with 'sympathetic interest' but would not be able to respond unless the whole white community in Kenya appealed to him.[121] The Indian Viceroy immediately cabled the Colonial Office to protest Smuts' intentions. The Colonial Office was internally divided on how to interpret Smuts' statement. Malcolm Seton, deputy under-secretary, scribbled on the side of the Viceroy's telegram that Smuts had as much right to intervene as the Viceroy since many settlers came from South Africa. Winterton, the under-secretary, thought otherwise.[122] Devonshire was unable to decide, but noted that Smuts had not committed himself to 'the party of defiance'.[123]

While Smuts had been evasive and non-committal until now, Sastri's speeches, particularly the one at Queen's Hall, made him intervene directly. He sent Devonshire a cable on 10 July. Sastri's speeches, he claimed, had exasperated public opinion in South Africa. If the ideal of full civic equality was enshrined in the imperial government's decision on Kenya, it would 'create a dangerous situation for South Africa'. Advising 'extreme caution', he argued that the principle of equality was a ruse for further Indian penetration into other parts of the empire which would 'lead to an intolerable situation'.[124] Four days later, Devonshire replied that he had 'borne continuously in mind the points mentioned in your message and I will impress them upon my colleagues in the Cabinet'.[125] The timing of this exchange is crucial, for it was in these few days that the final decision seems to have been made.

Indeed, on 12 July Sastri wrote to Natesan that the Indian delegation had been informally told that the decision would be in favour of Indians. He wrote: 'The Whites have lost heart. Time has told on the side of justice. Tho' the decision will not be wholly satisfactory – it will not be wholly unsatisfactory either.'[126] Delamere's delegation was similarly given to believe that the decision, while upholding African interests, would be against the white settlers. Delamere quickly cabled Devonshire that he would appeal to South Africa to take up their case in the imperial conference.[127] But on 17 July, possibly after considering Smuts' response, Sastri and the Indian delegation were called into the Colonial Office and told verbally that the decision was favourable towards Indians on segregation and immigration, but accepted the white demands on the Highlands and the franchise. When they asked to see the final written draft, they were refused.

Sastri and Dwarkadas wrote a last appeal to the Cabinet. On the Highlands, which had now been presented as a fait accompli, they wrote: '[s]urely the custodians of the honour and high principles of the Commonwealth cannot afford to make public confession of their impotence to reverse so flagrant a violation of equity as between His Majesty's equal subjects'.[128] They urged the government to at least keep the matter open for discussion. Furthermore, through the communal franchise, the Indian community would be 'reduced to a position of chronic impotence and unredeemed humiliation'.[129] Kenya's example might further lead to the extension of communal franchise to other parts of the Commonwealth. This would make racial citizenship 'the distinguishing feature of the British Constitution, a distinction inimical to the destiny of the Commonwealth, the ideal of democracy and the hopes of humanity'.[130]

The Cabinet did not consider their appeal. It approved the White Paper on 23 July. Indians were given communal franchise with four elected seats in the Legislative Council. Europeans had eleven elected seats, and the Highlands were formally reserved solely for them. Indians were granted the possibility of exclusive reserves in the Lowlands. The only reprieve for Indians in the White Paper was that segregation in commercial and residential areas was declined. But commercial segregation was in any case impracticable in Kenya and residential segregation already existed in practice. The very next day, in a speech in Pietermaritzburg, Smuts announced a policy which embraced segregation in trade and residence for Indians in his country.[131]

Crucially, the White Paper emphatically declared the interests of the Africans to be paramount in any policy on Kenya. The Commonwealth historian Keith Hancock was to note wryly several years later that the White Paper 'had rediscovered the vast majority of Kenya's population'.[132] In this way, it effectively closed off any possibility of a white self-governing colony, but found disingenuous ways to mask white rule as 'native interest'. On the policy on immigration, for instance, it proposed to impose restrictions only under 'extreme circumstances', seemingly a positive nod to the Indian demand. But then it added underhandedly, that 'it is immediately necessary to restrict the immigration of those from whom the African native stands in risk of economic competition'. Such 'undesirable' economic competitors were 'small traders, subordinate clerks in Government and private employ, and mechanical labourers', all professions predominantly occupied by Indians.[133] In fact, a day after the Cabinet's approval, Delamere tactfully exploited a miscommunication that gave the false impression that the settlers, unhappy with the decision, were looking to rebel, to force the Colonial Office to give an undertaking that restrictions on immigration would be implemented as soon as possible.[134]

This prompted one commentator to note that Indians had 'lost all along the line'.[135] Even the Viceroy accepted the proposals, officially, 'under protest'.[136]

## X

The White Paper left Sastri utterly disappointed. He termed it 'a profound humiliation and the deepest affront to India'. In permanently reserving the Highlands for whites and refusing a common roll franchise to Indians, the Imperial Cabinet had effectively sanctioned a colour bar in which 'the people of India are no longer equal partners in the British Commonwealth, but unredeemed helots in a Boer Empire'.[137] An ideal he had placed all his personal capital on had vanished before his eyes. It was the first time, as Charles Andrews commented later, 'the British Parliament had set its seal to racial discrimination in favour of the white race'.[138] The compensation of the offer of Lowlands was a 'trap', which sought to substitute a call for equality of privilege with an equality of disability.[139] Indians had been 'used in peril and thrown aside in security' by the British government.[140] In rewarding the rebellious white settlers, the British Cabinet had also told Indians that '[h]ard words never lost an empire'. Indians may have talked of 'secession, paralysis of the administration, chronic deadlocks' for some years, but these had just been empty threats. 'This cry of "Wolf" has been overdone'.[141] It was time for concrete action, Sastri announced.

His next response shocked his opponents and supporters in equal measure. In several speeches, Sastri asserted that polite appeals had outlived their value. The Kenya settlement 'shakes the foundations of our public life', and the Indian heart must be: '[h]ard as flint, dry as the Sahara ... [and] survey without emotion the long tale of wrongs and indignities to which our people have been subjected within an

Empire that talks all the time of human brotherhood and even handed justice'.[142] The arch-liberal counselled:

> When one is in the grip of a big bully, patient and philosophical submission is no remedy. To hit out with all one's strength may not be effective either, but it is at least a vindication of one's manhood ... the imprisoned cobra strikes not so much to punish the tormentor, as out of wounded pride.[143]

Now was the time for assertive and retaliatory action. As a committed moderate, he could only go so far as constitutional methods sanctioned. But within the fold of this constitutional remit, he demanded that the Indian government must now withdraw from all voluntary and semi-voluntary imperial gatherings, such as the forthcoming Empire Exhibition and the Imperial Political and Economic Conference. He himself resigned from the organizing committee of the exhibition, and so did Jamnadas Dwarkadas.[144] In the League of Nations, Indian non-officials should refuse to participate unless they were allowed to vote on India's interests alone, and not as members of the British group. The leaders of the Indian delegations had so far been only Englishmen, which was 'no longer compatible with the status of India, as a member of her own right'.[145] The Indian representatives must refuse the 'second-class citizenship' offered to them.[146] His gaze was directed at his close friend Tej Bahadur Sapru, who had arrived in London to participate in the Imperial Conference scheduled to start in the month of October. He also asked the Indian legislature to demand that the services of India, such as deployment of its army officers, provided to other colonies be stopped. More steps restricting domicile, legal and trading rights of dominion citizens in India could also be taken 'with the object of showing that the more respectable folk in India resent bitterly being told that they are inferior and will be treated as such in the Empire'.[147]

Although he appreciated the Indian government's support on the Kenyan issue, he wrote that a government that looked to Whitehall for orders even in matters of secondary importance could scarcely be expected to do anything more than 'dispatch-writing'.[148] If India had its own government, it was inconceivable that it would not take any action against the Kenya judgement.

Sastri's relentless attack, calls for boycotts and assertion that Indians had lost because they had not threatened concrete action, drew equally sharp reactions. The conservative daily, *Morning Post*, demanded his removal from the Privy Council. He had gone 'farther than most Privy

Councillors', Reading noted to the India Office.[149] When Sastri went to meet Peel before his departure, his deputy Winterton denied him an appointment.[150]

A leading article in *The Times of India* accused Sastri of taking the unnecessary and vague moral high ground of equality.[151] The veteran journalist Valentine Chirol wrote that 'swaraj has now scarcely a more vigorous supporter than Mr. Sastri'.[152] Some of the pro-India British liberals, Sapru wrote in a private mail to the Viceroy, had also stiffened their opinion, believing that Indians had got better than they had before, and Sastri's radical outbursts were unreasonable.[153] In general, the London correspondent of *The Servant of India* conceded that the White Paper had received an 'excellent press'; even the left-liberal *Manchester Guardian* commended the government for its 'liberality and fairness' in deciding the issue,[154] and liberal supporters such as Charles Roberts, Thomas Bennett and Lord Hardinge advised acceptance.[155] Peel commented that the deal was not unfair to Indians.[156] The only relief was that the Labour Party's Josiah Wedgwood announced in parliament that a future Labour government would reverse this policy.[157]

Some of his own colleagues and friends among Indian liberals disagreed with Sastri. Sapru, then the president of the Liberal Party, declined Sastri's request to withdraw from the Imperial Conference, considering the politics of boycott as a 'fatal legacy of the non-cooperation movement'.[158] P. Sivaswamy Aiyer, while agreeing with Sastri's criticism, differed strongly on whether Sastri's suggested policy of retaliation would bring substantive results.[159] Rather, he argued that it would be 'suicidal' for India's trade.[160]

However, in other quarters, Sastri's call for retaliation was positively received. Bajpai sent him a letter strongly criticizing those Indians like Sapru who advised caution, comparing them to 'the faithful Hindu wife who always ends up blessing the hand that strikes'.[161] He supported Sastri's advocacy of retaliation, even proposing to bar all emigration to the colonies. A policy of caution, he warned, 'will brand us unredeemable cowards'.[162] Benarasidas Chaturvedi announced through his new journal *Indian Overseas* that in the '90 year history of Greater India' – ostensibly beginning with the first ship transporting indentured Indians to Mauritius in 1836 – this was the first occasion when a problem of overseas Indians was regarded with so much concern.[163]

The Indian Legislative Assembly passed a bill, subsequently shot down by the government, that proposed discrimination on immigration against dominion citizens and colonials as a retaliatory measure.[164] There were loud calls for the resignation of the Indian government, most especially of B.N. Sarma, the Indian member-in-charge. *Hartals*[165] were organized in many cities, and numerous organizations passed resolutions in favour of Sastri's Empire Exhibition boycott appeal.[166] The Indian National Congress passed a resolution on 18 September to boycott goods from the British Empire by a vote of 640 to 221; an attendant resolution calling for independence as a national goal in light of the Kenya decision was rejected by 264 to 207.[167] However, Sastri's appeal could not gain enough momentum to close the Indian Pavilion when the exhibition opened in April 1924 at Wembley Stadium.

## XI

Broken in body and spirit, Sastri arrived back in India in late August 1923. His health had deteriorated considerably. He proceeded straight to Poona, where he had summoned a special session of the Servants of India Society from 28 to 31 August. During his talk on the first day, he felt an excruciating pain in his heart. A doctor was immediately summoned, who barred him from any further activity for three months. He retreated to Bangalore, cancelling all his other appointments, but not before issuing an appeal to the public, recommending a 'policy of vigorous action'.

For now, Sapru took centre stage, as he prepared to counter Jan Smuts at the Imperial Conference. Smuts arrived at the conference with the intention of squashing the 1921 resolution, armed with what he believed was a new doctrine of the Commonwealth. In 1921, Smuts had been too evasive on the question of equality in the empire, and when cornered by Sastri, he had to make an uncomfortable acknowledgement that inequality was the very foundation of South Africa. This had allowed Sastri to walk away with both arguments as well as honours. By now, Smuts had appropriately coated racial inequality in political philosophy. The 1921 conception of the British Commonwealth under which all constituents were required to hold on to a singular conception of British subjecthood was a 'profound mistake', Smuts argued. Different people enjoyed different forms of rights within the empire, and hence the arguments for equal rights had no logical basis.[168] Each dominion operated as a de facto sovereign entirety when it came to determining the rights and duties of its constituent populations. There was a unity of purpose in securing peace throughout the Commonwealth that required commitments related to external sovereignty, but internally the constituent parts of the Commonwealth were free to impose their own citizenship ideals.

Sapru's long, 117-minute rejoinder to Smuts was surgical.[169] Smuts was effectively asking the Imperial Conference to treat its own resolution as a 'scrap of paper', Sapru stated.[170] In the end, the 1923 conference upheld the 1921 resolution, but also, importantly, approved setting up an Imperial Committee of Enquiry to look into the steps taken to implement the 1921 resolution in all the dominions and Kenya. With this, Sapru had managed a small opening into the Kenya issue by way of which India could still push for the equality of Indians in Kenya, although he had also accepted the India Office line that the 1921 resolution applied to the Kenya colony.

Sastri, still recovering, followed these events closely. Despite his opposition to Sapru's participation, he had approved of the course of action at the Imperial Conference. And when Sapru succeeded, he not only sent in his congratulations,[171] but also considered giving up his insistence on the boycott of British goods and the Empire Exhibition. Annie Besant strongly advised Sastri against changing his stance. With these creeping doubts nipped in the bud, he wrote confidently to S.G. Vaze: '[w]e can't, for mere confabulations of committee, suspend our action. It is giving away something for nothing'.[172]

At the year-end Liberal Party conference, the big showdown was between the two party stalwarts, Sastri and Sapru. Sastri sponsored a resolution on the boycott of British goods in the Subjects Committee. Sapru, as the president of the party, opposed it. Sastri gave a rousing speech, following which the resolution was passed. A split in the party seemed a strong possibility. But, in deference to his personal regard for Sapru and reluctance to undermine the latter's authority, Sastri withdrew his resolution.

Between December 1923 and February 1924, Sastri made two other crucial speeches on the Kenya question, one in Bangalore and another at St Stephen's College in Delhi. Both of these have turned out to be his better-known speeches on the Kenya issue, the first for the famous expression 'Kenya Lost, Everything Lost'. At St Stephens in February 1924, in a talk titled 'Africa or India', he contended that the Europeans in the dominions and East Africa were the actual 'wreckers' of the empire; those who 'will not tolerate another people in [their] household, except they be serfs and slaves and helots'. Indians were its 'preservers'.[173] At the 1923 Imperial Conference, Smuts had asked Indians why they deserved any more rights than the Chinese or the Japanese. Sastri responded:

> is it right that we, who fought for the Empire and saved these very white people from extinction ... we should be told that we have no more right to demand equality than the Chinese or the Japanese people? What then is the

inducement to remain within this Empire, if there is no difference between who belongs to the Empire and one who is outside the Empire?[174]

The Kenya decision was a personal blow to Sastri; it was a betrayal of his faith in the empire. With the British parliament for the first time approving a specifically racial clause, something the British liberals berated the dominions for, the decision tumbled the last bastion of the pretence of racial equality within the empire. When questioned if his view of the empire had changed, Sastri responded: whose wouldn't?[175]

The former ambiguity with regard to racial classification was gone. The colour line was firmly in place. Andrews was quick to emphasize its transnational ramifications:[176]

> This defeat ... will reverberate around the world. It will immediately redouble the energies of the anti-Asiatic party in South Africa, of which General Smuts himself has assumed the leadership. The Indian community there now is doomed to perpetual racial segregation. It has already reacted on Fiji [imposed £1 poll tax] and brought such a racial conflict there that even the mildest Indian nominee of Government, the Hon. Badri Maharaj, has resigned. ... In Canada we have just had a blunt refusal to give the vote to a tiny band of some 1,500 punjabis who are still lingering in that country. The United States which was regarded as free and impartial in its ideals has just taken away the citizenship from Indians domiciled there. All over the world, the white domination of the coloured races is proving harder and harder.[177]

He added that India, whether willing or not, now stood as the 'champion of the weaker races'. He saw the emergence of a global colour line between the south and the north, and hoped that:

> In the end, in spite of all the ties of blood and race ... just as Northern States [had] decided at last to abolish slavery in America and resisted the Southern States with this object in view ... the 'Northern States' of the British Empire, in Ireland and England and Scotland, and perhaps Canada as well, will stand out against the 'Southern States' of the British Empire in Africa, and insist on the 'Abolition of the Colour Bar'.[178]

## XII

While Sastri rested and recovered in Bangalore, Millie Polak, Henry Polak's wife, sent him a letter. She narrated an incident from *Alice in Wonderland* where Alice is made to run fast and even faster on an empty stretch to eventually realize that she was still at the same place. On expressing surprise, her companion replies: 'that is the game, you have to run fast to retain your position'. Sastri had done more than two years of running for securing the rights of Indians. He had travelled the world, becoming the fiercest voice on the rights of Indians. It had exhausted him physically, but now he found himself in the same position at which he had started. The equality of Indians as part of the British Empire had turned out to be a pipe dream. But, as Millie reminded him, the world around him had actually paced in the opposite direction. The empire was becoming even more racialist in its outlook. He might think that he was at the same place, but one had to run hard to even be there. Was it a nugget of philosophy, or pure nonsense, Millie wondered?[179] On the Kenya question, Sastri had burst out 'like the anger of Rudra'. Millie's letter helped him calm down, and he was thankful for this affectionate appreciation. One also imagines and hopes that it lifted his mood.

8

# An Honourable Compromise

### I

Sastri returned to public life in early 1924 after a few months' rest. The Kenya decision had broken his faith in the British parliament, but only temporarily. In December 1923, the Conservatives were handed a major drubbing in the elections. The Ramsay MacDonald-led Labour Party formed a minority government with the support of the Liberal Party. Sydney Olivier, one of the famed 'three musketeers' of the Fabian Society along with Sidney Webb and George Bernard Shaw, took over as the Secretary of State for India.

The Labour Party had been historically supportive of the Indian cause, and in February 1924, Oliver released Gandhi from prison after having served only one third of his prison term. Given the state of unrest in the country, all Indian political parties agreed that the country could not wait for ten years (from 1919) to pass before the next set of reforms. A major group from within the Congress, the *Swarijists* led by Chitranjan Das, who had entered the assemblies to wreck them from within, demanded an immediate round table conference to discuss dominion status. Annie Besant appealed for a national convention of Indian leaders to draft a new constitution in order to present it to the British government.[1]

Sastri welcomed these winds of change and appealed to the Indian leaders to give the Labour government a chance. He led the dominion status demand from within the liberals, but preferred a new election, instead of a National Convention, to precede the framing of India's demands. He argued that in a democratic set-up, however rudimentary, an altogether new demand must only come from the people. The public representatives elected in the 1921 elections were picked on the basis of the Montford reforms. The people must first express a desire, as he thought they unquestionably would, which should then be duly executed by their chosen representatives. India could not jettison the democratic method, he argued, for the desire of a fully fledged democracy.[2]

To appeal for an urgent change of course in British policy towards reforms, Besant and Sastri went to London between May and July 1924. They were largely disappointed by the Labour government's approach. Barely surviving on a minority, MacDonald's government was reluctant to undertake any significant steps. He noted with dismay that MacDonald, Haldane (who was the Chancellor of the Exchequer) and Olivier had turned into 'ten-yearwallahs', that is, those who believed that the Royal Commission should go to India in 1929, as originally proposed in the 1919 reforms.[3] Olivier advised Indians to stick to the Fabian tactics of an incremental, step-by-step strategy of reforms. Hoping to shake the government out of its Fabian stupor and realize the political urgency of change, Sastri and others submitted a memorandum asserting India's right to self-determination and the right to draw its own constitution.

MacDonald's minority government collapsed after just nine months in power. The Conservatives stormed back into parliament with an enlarged majority in the general elections. Lord Birkenhead, the new Secretary of State for India, agreed to send a royal commission without waiting for 1929, but conditioned it on cooperation from all political parties. However, the appeals for a united political front in India were collapsing by this time. Das, the more conciliatory of the Congress leaders, passed away in June 1925 and under Gandhi's influence the Congress strengthened its own resolve towards non-cooperation. Even when Gandhi called all-party meetings, he insisted on things like 'spinning franchise' and the continuation of non-cooperation. Sastri disliked such conditions. As he wrote to Sarojini Naidu, forcing people to wear *khadi* was not just an 'an innocent fad of a great man' but it did 'violence to the fundamental liberty of the individual'.[4] In any case, such conditions emphasized aspects which were often irrelevant to the more pressing need for devising a constructive political programme.

Meanwhile, Reading's government implemented repressive measures in Bengal to curb revolutionary violence. Sastri called the government's Bengal Ordinance worse than the Rowlatt Act in some respects. On this, he crossed swords with Besant, who had approved of the ordinance.[5] Indian political parties seemed more fragmented than ever.

All this while, Sastri kept to a punishing pace of travel, writing, council work and public speaking engagements which ruined any recovery he had made. His health deteriorated steadily. He was again forced to go on extended rest in the second half of 1924. Early in 1925, he resigned his council seat on account of ill health.

## II

Frail in health, Sastri delivered a series of public lectures in Calcutta in February 1926. The lectures were instituted by the famed Bengali educationist Ashutosh Mukherjee, in remembrance of his daughter, Kamala, who had died, aged 28, in 1923. A set of three lectures, titled Kamala Lectures, were to be given by a leading figure, in Bengali or English, on some aspect of Indian life. After Annie Besant had delivered the first lectures on the 'Indian Ideals on Education', Mukherjee had wanted Sastri to deliver the second set of lectures. But before he could ask Sastri, Mukherjee passed away. Sastri could not refuse when Mukherjee's sons, Shyama Prasad and Rama Prasad, conveyed their deceased father's request. So, against the advice of his doctor, he travelled to Calcutta. Sastri's condition was so critical that on the eve of his first lecture, Calcutta's leading physician, Nilratan Sircar, urged him to cancel his lecture. Bidhan C. Roy, a heart specialist and later West Bengal's Chief Minister, examined him again on the morning of the lecture, and warned that he could collapse during the lecture. Sastri took his medicines, and politely ignored the advice.[6]

Just ten minutes before the lecture on 23 February, his heart was convulsed by sharp pain. He had to be physically carried up the stairs and into the university Convocation Hall on a chair. Robert Greaves, the Vice Chancellor, appealed to the audience to squat on the floor around the speaker to lessen his strain of speaking. Each word from Sastri's mouth took longer to surface and was harder to hear; an hour-long lecture was stretched by another 15 minutes. By the end he was so exhausted that he was carried to Greaves' office. Greaves, Roy and Sastri's secretary, Kodanda Rao, waited anxiously for his breathing to normalize. Eventually, his three lectures were covered over four days; with each day came new anxieties over his failing health. Two weeks later, as was required by the deed of the lectures, he repeated them at Madras University, between 12 and 15 March.[7]

Choosing to speak on the 'Rights and Duties of Indian Citizens', Sastri used the opportunity of a scholarly discourse to put forward in clear terms his own political philosophy of liberalism.[8] His heart condition had made it hard for him to prepare for the lecture, as one would for a largely academic audience. All he had with him were some notes and a few quotations. So, quite stunningly, the lectures in Calcutta, which run to over 120 pages in print, were delivered mostly extempore.⁹

He began by arguing that his use of the term Indian 'citizen' in the title, instead of 'subject' or as some critics advised 'slave', was deliberate. A slave had neither rights nor duties, just forcefully imposed obligations. A subject had duties towards the sovereign, and accordingly received some rights, but none against the sovereign per se. A citizen in contrast had rights against the excesses of the sovereign, but also concomitant duties which could only be understood in relation to the rights. Under British rule, Indians had limited rights and even more limited recourse of access to those rights, he conceded. But the path to extending the rights was not through the denial of their existence, but through their constant assertion. In other words, even though the term 'citizen' was a rhetorical excess of sorts – Indians were certainly not citizens in the sense of British or even dominion citizens –citizenship was nevertheless an ideal that must be defined in advance and pursued relentlessly. If he had called Indians 'subjects', what would be the point of talking about rights?

Relatedly, the adoption of full rights could not be pursued without an understanding of duties, and how the two – rights and duties – existed together. The conventional view was that duties and rights were in a transactional relationship, that is, the state owed rights to the citizen, while the citizen owed duties to the state. However, he argued, there were instances where the two fused into one. The right to vote, for instance, was as much a duty: an individual ought to vote for the betterment of the people in general and not for purely individual or sectional interests. A person who did not exercise their given right to vote morally forfeited their right to criticize the government, because voting was as much a duty as a right.

The responsibility for providing and protecting citizenship rights rested on the three organs of the state, the executive, the legislature and the judiciary. He was scathing in his audit of their work in India. Among the three, he viewed with alarm the executive's tendency to rule through fiat. Even though in the past few years several repressive laws had been repealed, including the Rowlatt Acts, the executive retained dangerous powers to arraign and incarcerate citizens without following the due process of law. The legislature, which was ideally a check on the executive, was in its infancy in India. It was hampered not just by its lack of powers but also the lack of political education among the members themselves. Compared to these two institutions, the judiciary was measurably less arbitrary. In India, he argued, law was indeed the shield of the citizen, which had been strengthened by the introduction of *habeas corpus*.

The right to resist the state was inherently a moral right, but not a legal right. The battle must be fought to turn the moral right into a legal right; that was where politics must focus. The effort must be to broaden the ambit of the law, rather than to demolish it. A common problem with anarchic violence and civil disobedience was that while they were effective in engineering a total breakdown of law and order, they had no vision for 'what next'. What was the guarantee that the breakdown of law would not eventually lead to the return of traditional, regressive, authoritarian forms of rule? Hence, while each individual had the right and indeed a duty to resist the state, the wrong must be viewed beyond its immediate harm to the person or a section of people; one must also consider the result of the reaction, and whether it 'will still be on the credit side of the account or leave the community worse than when you meddled'.[10]

As a liberal, he was no statist, for he believed in standing up to the state not merely for the defence of one's own rights but also for one's enemy's rights. However, he differentiated a state from a community, and saw the former as inherently more secular and progressive. The state was brought into existence through 'the expressed or implied consent of the community for the management of its public affairs'. The best kind of state was one where this consent was the widest ranging; in the largest democracy the state was most coextensive with the collective community. But the community itself did not rely on consent, and accordingly had no conception of rights. Our rights are only given to us in the context of the state, which is why the loyalties of a citizen to factions within the collective, or to an abstract conception of the individual, could not exceed the loyalty to the state.

Sastri's liberalism and view towards the Indian state was far from simplistic. He would perhaps agree that the Indian state was entirely derivative, a poor copy of the one in Britain. It had no moral purpose, so to say, that catered to its Indian subjects. It was not designed to be benign to Indians, much less to be accountable to them. Rather, much of its fidelity to law came from its need to appear liberal to the public in the metropole. But even if it was a colonial mimicry of a liberal state, it had to vicariously apply the logics of liberal statecraft. So even as the colonial state was oppressive and discriminating, such acts could only be rationalized through recourses to the arguments of emergency and exception. Once the Indian government had been set on a path of reforms, with responsible government as its aim, governance by executive orders could be legitimized only so long as the Indian government could justify to the British public that such measures were brought forth by exceptional conditions. Sastri argued that the more the situation was normalized in the colony and the less the state was threatened through unconstitutional means, the more difficult it became for the colonial state to withhold rights from individuals.

His liberalism is neither Kantian, nor laissez faire. In other words, it does not consider the state's purpose as raising the moral worth of the individual, nor does it view it with assertive disdain. Sastri's liberalism is ardently manoeuvred to its colonial form, where liberalism operated through the deceit of normality.

While Sastri discoursed on the essence of a liberal response in the times of non-cooperation, another derivative of the British liberal state practised a form of politics which was total anathema to him: South Africa. His attention and practice of liberalism would soon shift to working towards a compromise with that country.

### III

Jan Smuts had been voted out in 1924, and replaced by J.B.M. Hertzog. Hertzog and his National Party were emphatically to the political right of Smuts. The Minister of Interior, Education and Health was Daniel F. Malan, a former Dutch Reformed Church minister, who was if anything even more uncompromising in his white supremacist politics than Hertzog, and would eventually become the first apartheid Prime Minister in 1948.

On 23 July 1925, Malan introduced the Areas Reservation and Immigration and Registration (Further Provisions) Bill in the South African parliament. The bill, colloquially called the Asiatic Bill, envisioned the compulsory segregation of Indians for trading and residential purposes, and considerably tightened the immigration laws particularly aimed at the wives and children of those already in the Union. It also imposed new restrictions on Indians in acquiring ownership and leases. The Indian population was, Malan said, 'an alien element' in the country and his government would accept no solution unless it resulted in its 'considerable reduction'.[11] The aim, spelled out clearly as a government policy for what was until then a conventional talking point of white politicians, was to reduce the Indian population to the barest minimum through repatriation.

A series of laws passed in the previous five years, mainly at the provincial and municipal levels in Natal and Transvaal, had already considerably diminished political, social and property rights of the Indian community.[12] In his response to the bill, Smuts warned that it would 'cast a stigma on the Asiatics', earning South Africa 'the hatred of the whole of Asia from one side to the other'.[13] He was typically sly, considering Malan's bill was modelled on the Class Areas Act of 1923, introduced by Smuts' minister Patrick Duncan, another famous South African liberal. If at all, Hertzog's party, as a newspaper noted, 'had stolen the thunder from its dispossessed opponents, and sought thereby to impress the world with its own omniscience'.[14]

Expectedly, Malan's bill received wide support from most of the European population and the three major parties in South Africa,[15] and caused a furore in India. Leaders of all political hues from Gandhi to Jinnah to Motilal Nehru to Sastri condemned it. Deva Prasad Sarvadhikary placed a resolution in the Legislative Council appealing to the Indian government to take immediate steps to protect South African Indians. In the council debate, others called for retaliatory steps, such as stopping the export of coal, and sought the British government's intervention.[16] To end the indignities suffered by South African Indians, Umar Hayat Khan offered a permanent solution: bring back all Indians from South Africa and provide them with land to settle in India, he suggested.[17] A delegation of the South African Indian Congress (SAIC), led by a prominent leader of the coloured community, Abdullah Abdurahman, visited India to urge the Indian government to intervene.

To the Indian leaders, Reading's government advised caution and argued that an extremist stance might worsen matters for South African Indians. But in his letters to Secretary of State Birkenhead, Reading was anxious, and demanded urgent measures from the British government. He argued that inaction from the British and Indian governments in the previous years had encouraged South Africa to pursue more oppressive measures against South African Indians. South Africa treated its Indians worse than even those whites who had been enemies during the war. Gandhi continued to remind his audiences that the British Empire had fought a three-year war in South Africa when some whites were similarly deprived of their rights in the Transvaal. But the British government would not even stir for Indians. Reading warned that such pleas had created a strong impression among Indians that they were included in the empire as inferiors, with no advantage or privilege, and that it was better to be born outside of the empire.[18]

The India Office shrugged off Reading's frantic pleas for help, and remonstrated that he was being 'unduly harsh' on the imperial government. Louis Kershaw, the Assistant Under-Secretary of State, wrote that Britain had given 'every moral support to Indian claims' but any pressures on South Africa would mean 'secession pure and simple'. He added, 'the one issue on which the Boers and British [in South Africa], Unionists and Nationalists, are united is "No surrender to Indian claims"', which 'successive Viceroys and their councils are very slow to realise'. South Africa 'would rather lose the whole of their Natal Indian coal trade than concede an inch of Indian claims'.[19]

Reading's helpless appeals and Kershaw's stoic response were symptomatic of the way Britain now handled affairs between the dominions and India. It was terrified of alienating dominions over the race question. 'Secession' had swelled into a paranoia, and caution had overstepped into paralysis. But Britain could also not afford to alienate India by appearing to be unsympathetic.[20] If any form of intervention by the British government that might 'cause the Dominion Legislature to stiffen its attitude by way of asserting Dominion independence' was ruled out, a direct approach by the Indian government was encouraged. Indeed, the India Office suggested that the Union government might actually appreciate a direct approach as an assertion of dominion autonomy. Since it was impossible to evade the logical inference of such a move, an India Office internal memo rolled its apathy into policy and flung it towards Reading's government as a congratulatory message: 'it is a fitting consequence of India's new status that she should negotiate with South Africa direct in the matter of Imperial concern between her and South Africa'.[21] The British government had kicked its problems down to the India government as a splendid bounty of opportunity.

## IV

Following this advice, Reading approached the South African government through the Governor General, Lord Athlone, for a round table conference.[22] South Africa swiftly dismissed any such possibility unless India had specific proposals on developing a repatriation scheme. The Indian government followed up with a cleverly worded pitch. It proposed sending a fact-finding deputation to collect information about the economic position of Indians and their general condition. This would enable India to consider ways in which it could help with the settlement of the Indian question in South Africa. The Indian government had shrewdly evaded any mention of 'repatriation', while indicating a willingness to settle the issue. Hertzog's government relented, and India wasted no time in assembling and dispatching a delegation to South Africa.[23] George F. Paddison, the Labour member in the Madras government, was appointed as leader, and Reza Ali and Deva Prasad Sarvadhikary were drafted as non-official Indian members. Bajpai, who had risen to become the deputy secretary in the Department of Health, Education and Lands, accompanied the delegation as its secretary.

While the deputation was in South Africa, the Indian government, using the good offices of Athlone, was able to convince Hertzog and Malan to allow the deputation to present their evidence to a select committee of the Union parliament on the Asiatic Bill. In the select committee, the Indian deputation showed that even a modest repatriation scheme would be immensely expensive. Repatriating about 12,000 South African Indians over four years – a reduction of 7.5 per cent – would cost the exchequer about £1 million. They added that such high costs were, however, no guarantee of the scheme's success. In 1924, Hertzog's government had incentivized repatriation by doubling the individual as well as family bonuses granted as part of the voluntary repatriation scheme. Despite this, the repatriation numbers fell further by 40 per cent.[24] This was because the social and economic conditions of most repatriates had worsened after they went to India, and as these experiences filtered back, there was greater reluctance to benefit from the repatriation scheme.[25]

Furthermore, the voluntary repatriation scheme, the Indian deputation told the select committee, was hardly attractive to its primary targets, the Indian trading class, who were alleged to be in competition with the Europeans. The bonuses could only induce those who were on the verge of destitution or who were unable to find jobs, not the relatively economically better-off class of traders. In any case, the deputation's findings showed no empirical evidence to support the accusation that Indian traders competed against white traders. Repatriation was therefore a misplaced solution to the South African government's concerns.[26]

These submissions evidently had a positive effect on the select committee. Barring Malan who had the author's partiality to the bill; all other members were sympathetic to the deputation's case. When Malan placed his resolution within the committee to confirm the principles of the bill, it received a rather lukewarm response. As a result, he hesitated to put it to a vote. This opened a space for informal consultations. With some prodding from Athlone, Paddison and Bajpai were invited for two rounds of informal meetings with Hertzog and Malan, where the latter duo finally agreed to a round table conference with India and put on hold the Asiatic Bill until the conference.[27] South Africa's agreeing to the conference was a good start; even a great achievement under the circumstances.[28]

As the Paddison deputation was returning from South Africa, a new Viceroy arrived in India in early April 1926. Edward Wood (of the Wood–Winterton proposal on Kenya), now Lord Irwin, replaced Reading.

The two governments officially entered into talks about organizing a round table conference, and soon agreed to hold it in Cape Town.[29] Irwin's main concern regarding the conference was the membership of India's delegation and, equally importantly, its leader. The leaders and the members, he noted, must have opposite qualities. The leader should seem conciliatory and magnanimous, should not appear to be a hard negotiator or someone interested in scoring points. The latter part should be left to the delegation members. The leader, in addition, should be someone who was acceptable to both Indians and South Africans, someone with experience of handling Indian issues but no direct connections to the imperial government, as the latter would be frowned upon by South Africans.[30] He preferred the leader to be an Englishman, who would, he surmised, impress South African opinion better than any Indian. He approached his predecessor, Reading, and subsequently Lord Ronaldshay, the former Governor of Bengal, to lead the delegation, but both declined.[31]

Unable to find an agreeable Englishman to lead, Irwin now reversed his earlier opinion and asked his staff to suggest Indian names. The upside of an Indian-led delegation would be its enhanced credibility in the eyes of Indians in India and South Africa and, consequently, easier public acceptance of any resulting agreement. This change was most likely influenced by Charles Andrews who, although deeply distrusted by the India Office, shared an unusually close relationship with Irwin. Irwin was the son of Lord Halifax, the recognized leader of the Anglo-Catholics in England. Often labelled the 'Holy Fox', Irwin exuded austere piety, a quality that he shared with Andrews.[32] Sastri once compared Andrews to the Indian mythological character *Narada*, someone who had easy access across the political spectrum.[33]

Lord Satyendra Sinha was Irwin's first suggestion. But Sinha, apart from being in ill health, had come to embrace strange beliefs, one of which was that the only way to treat Indians in South Africa was to shoot them.[34] The India Office vetoed Sinha. Irwin then proposed Mohammad Habibullah, the member in charge of the Department of Education, Health and Lands.

Habibullah obviously knew the matter well, for it fell under his department. But, for Irwin, that was not the only advantage. In a remark laced with racial contempt, Irwin noted that Habibullah was also 'a Muhammadan, and suitable Muhammadans do not grow on every mulberry bush'.[35] Irwin did not have much respect for Habibullah's intellect either. He wrote: 'He is a straightforward gentleman and would do his best. Unluckily, he is not endowed with many brains and I could only think of choosing him if I could get the deputation

I have in my mind to support him.'³⁶ But if Habibullah was given a strong delegation, the one Irwin said he already had in mind, he could prove to be an ideal leader.

Irwin proposed a five-member delegation to support Habibullah, covering a spectrum of interests. G.L. Corbett and George Paddison, both officials who had created favourable impressions in South Africa on their earlier official visits, were drafted as officials on the delegation. Darcy Lindsay, a member of the Emigration Committee, would be the British non-official. This left space for two Indian non-officials. Irwin was keen to have a Parsi Bombay businessman in the delegation and chose Phiroze Sethna. For the final member, Irwin proposed to draw Sastri out of his retirement. Why Sastri, asked Birkenhead. Sastri 'no longer count[ed] for much in India', he demurred.³⁷

## V

A sympathetic assessment in *Indian Opinion* concluded in December 1925 that as a political leader Sastri had been uniquely misunderstood in his time. His eminence as a speaker and thinker and his love for his country were unquestionable. But his best days were already behind him. In political parlance, he was a 'back-number' who could only now wait for future historians to rescue his legacy from the muddle of contemporary emotions.³⁸ Sastri shared the writer's opinion. He had started to look at his career in the rear-view mirror, at times glossing it with self-aware pomposity:

> I am believed to have been disabled from active life. Much is excused to a man no longer in the competitive ring. Whatever people once thought office hasn't come to me, nor any ordinary title. [Privy Councillorship] is a windfall from beyond and doesn't hurt any aspirant. Forgive this little bit of egoism.³⁹

His health had ebbed and flowed ever since he came back from London in 1923. Long periods of rest were followed by some activity. After resigning from his council seat, he cut back on his public engagements and went into semi-retirement. He used the time to write; in fact, this turned to be one of his most productive writing periods. He contributed regularly to the Servant of India Society newsletter and busied himself in writing a biography of his mentor, Gokhale. Unfortunately, in May 1926, a fire broke out in the society's Arya Bhushan Press and Sastri's manuscript of Gokhale's biography was destroyed.

His views on South Africa were hardly unknown. To him, South Africa was the epitome of an illiberal state within the British Commonwealth, an archetype of what the Commonwealth ought never to be. He had little faith in any negotiations with South Africa. After Duncan had introduced the Class Areas Bill, Sastri had demanded extreme steps from the government of India. In early 1924, he had asked the Viceroy and his Executive Council to resign in protest, for that was the only way in which His Majesty's government could be called upon to spring into action. If the British government still failed to act, the Indian government could rightfully demand to be raised to the full status of a self-governing dominion and examine the possibility of taking the issue to the League of Nations. India would then appeal to the world's public opinion, 'seeing as the "lesser league of nations" [purposefully using Smuts' preferred description of the Commonwealth] has confessed its impotence to deal with such internal squabbles', he had argued.[40]

He made a rare public appearance on 15 January 1926 at Adyar, the headquarters of the Theosophical Society in Madras. The meeting had been organized to felicitate Sastri and a visiting Australian senator Matthew Reid for their work towards the recent granting of civic equality to Indian residents in Australia. Reflecting on his Australia visit in the (southern) winter of 1922, Sastri now felt more hopeful of attempting to persuade South Africans. The change in Australia showed that:

> [Indians must continue] to educate our South African fellow-citizens, so that they may understand fully what this Empire stands for, and if that the Empire did not realise it, it would mean nothing to us in India, but, on the other hand, would bring in a disaster which will not only overwhelm the Empire, but probably overwhelm the rest of the world as well.[41]

The speech indicated Sastri's return to a more conciliatory stance. Ever since Kenya, he had been a strong advocate of boycott and retaliation. The belated success of his Australia visit surely provided a strong rationale for this change of stance. But the liberal in him had also bowed to the innate and unceasing desire for expediency. A SAIC delegation was in India and an Indian government delegation was in South Africa; both were pushing for negotiations and Sastri endorsed these efforts.

With Sastri's confrontational days seemingly behind him, Irwin proposed to Birkenhead that Sastri's inclusion was the most desirable from the Indian point of view.[42] Sastri was that rare figure who could carry the support of Gandhi as well as the Indian government. He was also the most experienced of all Indians in diplomatic skills, and knew when to press a point assertively and when to concede.[43] He also knew the South African issue better than most. Birkenhead conceded. And Irwin was immediately proven right: Gandhi approved the delegation mostly because Sastri was on it.[44] However, South Africa could still raise objections to Sastri's inclusion. Smuts had twice refused to invite him in the past and in the preceding years Sastri had earned an international reputation of being one of the staunchest opponents of racism in South Africa.

## VI

While Irwin finalized the delegation, Hertzog marched off to London to attend his first imperial conference. The Afrikaner leader, who unlike Smuts had no love for the empire, resolved to assert South Africa's constitutional 'independence' at the conference. He pushed for a declaration of dominion equality with Britain, which resulted in the Balfour Declaration of 1926. The compromise formula arrived at in London declared all dominions as 'autonomous communities' which were not subordinate to each other in domestic and external affairs, although they declared their allegiance to the crown.[45] For someone who had built a lifelong reputation on being a fervent critic of Britain, Hertzog's conciliatory approach at the conference was a revelation. He shed his image of being the parochial South African nationalist to Smuts' cosmopolitan liberal. He was hailed and feted in both Britain and South Africa as an imperial statesman and, fortuitously for India, this coincided with the upcoming visit of the Indian delegation.

On the side-lines of the conference in London, Hertzog invited Bajpai for two informal meetings. Bajpai ran the list of Indian delegates past Hertzog, who raised no objections to Sastri's name. Bajpai was surprised at the liberality of Hertzog's views. The South African premier, quite uncharacteristically, complained about the anti-Asian elements in South Africa. If only he did not have electoral considerations to think of, he would treat Indians in South Africa on the same footing as Europeans.[46] Nevertheless, if India showed genuine desire to help in the matter of repatriation, Hertzog promised to prevail upon Malan to postpone, or even altogether withdraw, his bill.[47]

With a green light from Hertzog, the Indian delegation set off from Bombay on the SS *Karapura* on 24 November 1926. Sastri, still in ill health, was accompanied by a young secretary from the Servants of India Society, P. Kodanda Rao.[48] The delegation spent a good part of the journey studying and discussing a set of documents they were supplied with, including a 78-page brief of instructions.[49] From a negotiation point of view, there were two policy proposals at play: repatriation and segregation. The first was advanced to reduce the Indian population. As an 'alien' population, Malan viewed repatriation as the primary solution to the Indian issue. But since it was physically impossible to remove 173,959 South African Indians (since 1914, South Africa had managed to repatriate only about 20,000 Indians),[50] those who remained in the country could be kept in conditions which did not impinge upon the continuation of European life, or 'western standards', to use the official term. Whites resented Indians for lowering 'western standards' through their way of life, as well as taking away mid-level, semi-skilled jobs, mostly in trade, which would otherwise go to 'poor whites'. Segregationist policies were thus meant to maintain 'western standards' by benefiting whites at the expense of Indians.

From his meetings with Hertzog, Bajpai had surmised that the South African delegation would focus primarily on seeking India's help with repatriation, and compromise on segregation laws. A contradictory message came from Andrews, who had travelled in advance to South Africa. Andrews argued that South Africa saw getting India's consent on segregation as a priority, and would be willing to scale back on repatriation. Repatriation was mostly a decoy to push India to accept segregation, he argued. The delegation chose to trust Bajpai over Andrews, quite correctly as it turned out.

Until now, the South African Indian repatriation had been voluntary. A scheme of 'voluntary repatriation' had been settled in the Gandhi–Smuts agreement of 1914, which Gandhi called the 'Magna Carta of Indian liberty'. The South African government had ever since encouraged Indians to repatriate through financial help, but the numbers had ebbed and flowed. A key reason was the lack of facilities on the Indian side to provide for the settlement of the 'returning' Indians. They often found themselves economically much worse off than they were in South Africa. However, the term 'repatriation' itself, even if voluntary, contained several associations which raised red flags. 'Repatriation' stamped South African Indians to be 'aliens', or non-South Africans: that is, immigrants. They had no political rights but only privileges that could be snatched away at will. Further, the South African government had no welfare responsibilities towards them and as soon as Indians were 'repatriated', they automatically lost any rights of domicile in South Africa.

In the strategy meetings of the Indian delegation, Sastri pushed for a terminological change. Instead of 'voluntary repatriation', he preferred a term Corbett had suggested, 'assisted emigration'.[51] Sastri recalled that in his 1912 visit to South Africa, Gokhale had insisted that in any negotiations with South Africa, under no condition must the self-respect of India and South African Indians be sacrificed. The term 'repatriation' was offensive to this self-respect. Non-South African European residents retained domicile rights if they returned to their own land, but not Indians. Sastri asserted that this was a mark of inferiority.

Assisted emigration recognized the South African Indians, three quarters of whom were local-born, as 'South Africans' first. The term also placed welfare responsibilities upon the South African state. Furthermore, Sastri insisted on demanding the right of domicile for the emigrants for three years after their departure, the same as other Europeans in South Africa. They could return within this period on the condition that they reimburse the total expense made on them by the South African government. Sastri acknowledged that the high cost of return would make it almost impossible for most, but it allowed for the principle of return and affirmed their 'South Africanness'. The term 'assisted emigration' also had an added diplomatic advantage. 'Voluntary repatriation' could only be made to the home country, India, where, as we will see in the next chapter, South African Indians were reluctant to go. Emigration opened the possibility of finding other places in the empire for Indians to migrate to. The Indian delegation agreed with Sastri and decided to push for 'assisted emigration' in negotiations.

On segregation, the Indian delegation could not press for replacing the problematic term 'western standard of life'. In their agreement with the Paddison deputation, South Africa had conditioned it to be the primary basis for talks. But its meaning could be altered in the details: in other words, it could be made to imply a class-based distinction, instead of a race-based distinction. In general terms, the 'western standard of life' implied the standard of life enjoyed by the white community in South Africa. But in concrete terms, it referred to a life of higher educational and economic status. And racial segregation worked entirely to undermine the latter meaning of the term. Indeed, the more ghettoized a community became through segregation, the fewer opportunities they had of becoming economically prosperous and educationally advanced. Segregation, in fact, admitted and ensured that a community could never be raised to 'western standards'. Hence, if a large population of a country was never to be raised to western standards, it would become impossible for even the minority to maintain these standards for long.

The Indian delegation aimed to argue that the primary duty of the South African government was to raise Indians to such 'western standards' by fulfilling its welfare functions towards them, providing for education, health and non-racial laws governing employment, residential and commercial activities. The more the social and economic benefits were distributed across the racial barriers, the less would be any need for segregation. It was understood that not everyone could be 'uplifted'; even welfare measures were often not enough for those who were too poor. This class of people could be encouraged to repatriate through sufficient incentives, such as free passage and an adequate bonus for them to be able to settle in a new life.[52]

In essence, the Indian strategy aimed at pushing South Africa to make greater commitments towards Indians in South Africa, scrap schemes of segregation and agree to South Africa's demand for repatriation as long as the country agreed to treat it as emigration.

## VII

A large crowd of South African Indians cheered as a special train from Lourenco Marques (present-day Maputo) crawled into the Cape Town station on 16 December 1926.[53] It carried the Habibullah-led Indian delegation. Bajpai, who had arrived separately three days earlier from London on the same ship as Hertzog, was present. And, significantly, so was Malan, who came with his wife to receive the delegation. Scarcely visible were any signs that just two days previously he had threatened to resign from the Hertzog Cabinet over a controversial bill.[54]

The conference started the very next day with an opening address from Hertzog. Basking in all-round applause for his role in the Balfour Declaration, he played the statesman and called upon both delegations to jettison the bargaining spirit and discuss 'broad principles with a wide and just outlook and on the principles of friendliness of one nation towards the other'.[55] He announced that if the two sides could mutually agree to some definitive steps, the South African government would put aside the Asiatic Bill to set a tone of 'friendliness and goodwill'.[56] Later that evening, the core leadership of the two parties met at Hertzog's official residence, Groote Schuur, and agreed upon a common agenda; the first item on the list was the scheme of repatriation.

On 18 December, as the conference resumed, under Malan's chairmanship,[57] Tommy Boydell, the South African Minister for Labour, insisted on prioritizing segregation over repatriation on the agenda. Malan responded that segregation was a secondary issue to repatriation. A sense of vindicated assurance ran through the Indian delegation, who had strategized for this very scenario, disregarding Andrews' advice for Bajpai's. Happily for the Indian delegation, 'as the Conference progressed, segregation continued to recede until it could scarcely be mentioned by a Union delegate with the disapproval of his colleagues'.[58]

In his opening statement, Malan sought India's help in advertising the advantages of repatriation to South African Indians, and devising mechanisms to make the repatriates feel welcome in India. In reply, Habibullah promised cooperation on the scheme and made specific administrative proposals. He urged discarding the practice of using recruiters in South Africa for repatriation. They exaggerated the prospects of emigration to India and in the long run were counterproductive to increasing the rate of emigration. Instead, he advocated the creation of a specialized agency in South Africa which would provide official details about the number of emigrants and their settlement preferences. In parallel, India would also designate specialized staff to handle emigrants on the Indian side who would assist the emigrants in finding employment opportunities as well as in using their bonuses and savings efficiently. He also suggested increasing the bonus to help the emigrants find better settlement opportunities.

Besides these administrative issues, the more difficult problem, Habibullah asserted, was of sentiment. Voluntary repatriation gave Indians the feeling that they were undesirables, and that the South African government was intent on getting rid of them. To solve this, he sprang the term 'assisted emigration' and suggested that the emigrants retain their domicile for three years.

Malan's response to these proposals came on 23 December. He agreed to the administrative suggestions and, to the Indian delegation's delight, also to term the scheme as 'assisted emigration'. However, he invited more discussions on the conditions for surrender of domicile. Sastri intervened to make a passionate plea for the three-year domicile clause. How would the South African delegates feel, he asked at one point, if they were pressed to leave their country with a bonus of £5.[59] Corbett, who was keeping Athlone fully informed on the daily progress, commented that Sastri spoke 'most effectively and convincingly'.[60] Although no decision was yet taken, the Indian side emerged confident that the Union government was likely to agree. The specifics of assisted emigration were thrashed out in a sub-committee, which agreed on almost all points over a series of meetings.

The provisions about 'western standards' were taken up in subsequent meetings of the main conference. A sub-committee was formed to discuss the fine print of the progressive 'uplift' for Indians, a point the Indian delegation had conceded. By 11 January 1927, the two sides had come to an agreement in which the Indian delegation had gained considerably more than they had initially set out to achieve. In the main, the Union government had agreed to a three-year domicile even after emigration, which was exactly the same as for the European population. It also decided not to proceed with the Asiatic Bill and its several segregationist provisions.

While the Indian delegation agreed to the principle of the 'maintenance of western standards of life', Malan committed South Africa to 'the principle that it is the duty of every civilized government to devise ways and means and take all possible steps for upliftment of every section of their permanent population to the full extent of their capacity and opportunities'. This specific formulation in Malan's speech was drafted almost wholly by Sastri. It is seemingly inane, if rhetorical, but beneath its layer of simplicity lay the work of a crafty diplomat; a statement that could very well claim to underscore a paradigmatic shift in India's diaspora diplomacy.

Malan's statement recognized South African Indians as part of South Africa's 'permanent population': they were no longer 'aliens', although neither were they citizens. However, leaving their status open-ended allowed for a further negotiation of rights. Moreover, this recognition committed the South African state to its welfare responsibility towards every community. Education, housing and sanitation were the responsibility of the Union towards every community, including Indians, irrespective of their status of citizenship. Relatedly, the fulfilment of this welfare responsibility towards every community was what made each state 'civilized'. As works by scholars such as Gerrit Gong and others have shown,[61] a country's recognition as a legitimate part of the international system depended on their recognition as 'civilized' and living up to the 'standards of civilization'. In most cases, whiteness was the primary criterion (although whiteness itself was contested from within, leading to categorical innovations such as 'honorary whites' for the Japanese and debased whites for other communities such as the Irish and the Afrikaners). By making 'civilized' status incumbent upon the fulfilment of welfare responsibilities towards every internal community, Sastri's formulation had turned the rationale of civilized status on its head. Even a white state had to earn its civilized status through the provision of welfare. It had also played on the anxieties of the Afrikaner claim to whiteness as such. Welfarism, in particular towards non-white populations, was also a ticket to whiteness for Afrikaners.

Attentive to the implications of the formulation, Malan had been careful to add a rider which acknowledged that at times welfarist measures may be perceived 'considerably in advance of public opinion'. Antagonizing white opinion through hasty steps may in turn cause irreparable harm to South African Indians.[62] Consequently, rather than automatically extend educational, housing and sanitary facilities to Indians, the joint agreement outlined some steps. The South

African government would facilitate the formation of an educational commission in Natal, and initiate inquiries into housing and sanitation conditions of Indians. For the latter, it would consider setting up advisory committees with Indian representatives. These steps would pave a more realistic and gradual pathway towards the 'upliftment' of Indians to 'western standards'.

Habibullah's delegation had set out to establish broad principles. So although the recommendations (in education and health) were more promissory than concrete, the delegation was largely satisfied with the overall result. Crucially, both sides also agreed that an official representative of the Indian government, an Agent, would be invited by the Union government. This was an old proposal, made first by Lord Sinha at the Imperial War Conference in 1918, that had only now been accepted by South Africans.

Other important demands of South African Indians such as the restoration of the franchise in Natal were seen as crossing South African red lines, and hence were not raised. The delegation reasoned that they could only be granted after Europeans' antagonistic feelings towards Indians had abated, towards which the agreement would be a step. Moderate voices such as A.I. Kajee, the SAIC secretary, also assured the Indian delegation that they were only looking to maximize their demands with political franchise and then retreat 'all along the line'.[63]

The conference wound up on 12 January with the joint agreement, called the Cape Town Agreement, secretly stowed away until the upcoming local elections in South Africa were over. Considering the historically tense relations between the two countries, the agreement was a remarkable bilateral achievement. Throughout the conference Malan, who could often seem dogmatic, had shown willingness to reconsider his positions, to the extent that he was severely criticized by members of his own party. Coming in the immediate aftermath of the Balfour Declaration, the agreement, the first ever Commonwealth bilateral agreement without Britain's involvement, gestured towards new beginnings of Commonwealth diplomacy. For India, too, it had an unparalleled significance: the dominion-like colony had signed its maiden bilateral agreement as an autonomous international entity. More gratifyingly, it was negotiated and signed by a delegation led by an Indian.

## VIII

On the evening of the joint agreement, the Indian community organized a farewell reception for the Indian delegation. Since the

**8: The delegates to the Cape Town Conference in 1927**

'The seven men of Moidart' who negotiated the Cape Town Agreement from the Indian side included, seated, G. Corbett (second from left), Habibullah (centre-left), Sastri (extreme right), and standing, middle row, Bajpai (extreme left), Sethna (fourth from left), G. Paddison (fourth from right) and Darcy Lindsay (third from right). D.F. Malan (centre-right, seated) led the South African delegation.

contents of the agreement were secret, the delegation could neither confirm nor deny anything at the reception. Both sides had issued a general statement, and Corbett issued strict instructions to every delegation member against revealing anything. Habibullah spoke a few formal words without any hints about the agreement. Both his audience and the press contingent were disappointed and cries were raised for Sastri to speak. Just as Sastri was exiting the door, Habibullah hailed him to say a few words. Sastri had opposed keeping the agreement secret so preferred to leave with a tantalizing sentence: 'We leave Cape Town pleased with our labours, and if Indians in South Africa will play the game, the future is full of hope.'[64] Wild cheers followed for it implied that the conference was a success. Corbett was livid at Sastri's 'indiscretion', and complained to Habibullah that this could put the agreement in jeopardy. Corbett and Bajpai attempted damage control by seeking assurances from the local press that they would not publish these remarks. All except one newspaper, the *Cape Times*, obliged.[65]

The 'seven men of Moidart'[66] travelled from Cape Town to Johannesburg via Durban and Pietermaritzburg. Given the 'indiscretion', they declined invitations to all public functions, except mayoral receptions and receptions made in their honour by the Indian community. On 15 January, they were ushered into a venue which they assumed was a reception but turned out to be a town hall meeting of several thousands in Pietermaritzburg. Stumped, the delegation members consulted and decided that Habibullah and Sastri would speak briefly, so as not to disappoint the large audience. Habibullah, in perfect bureaucratic speak, 'successfully said nothing at all at considerable length'. Sastri, initially very reluctant to speak, when pushed by the audience delivered 'a delightful address'. To Corbett's utter horror, he 'repeated and emphasised' what he had said in Cape Town.[67] Sastri said:

> A new era is dawning on the relations between South Africa and India. Although, as I have said before, you may easily expect too much, it is a bare truth to say that our negotiations will bear some fruit of which we need not be ashamed and for which you may be grateful.[68]

This time, Sastri did not even regret the 'indiscretion', and cuttingly remarked: 'We in the non-official world cannot pretend to have mastered that art [of saying nothing in many words], when we say anything, we mean it, and when we mean anything, we say it.'[69]

Even Corbett was grudgingly appreciative of the fact that 'the effect of his speech on his immediate audience, European as well as Indian, was … good'.[70] Despite Corbett's frantic sweating, neither Athlone nor Hertzog nor Malan raised any objections to Sastri's speeches. The delegation departed from Johannesburg on 18 January and sailed from Lourenço Marques the next day, completing a month-long eventful and successful tour.

## IX

The Cape Town agreement was made public on 21 February. Before the announcement, however, Sastri counselled Irwin to obtain Gandhi's approval. No one was more respected by Indians on both sides of the Indian Ocean, Sastri argued, and Irwin agreed. The Viceroy asked Sastri to do it himself. Sastri set off to chase down Gandhi, who was on a tour of Central Provinces and Berar. He caught up with the Mahatma in a train carriage at Bhusaval, a small town near Jalgaon. To ensure privacy, Gandhi and Sastri moved to a first-class carriage on the moving train, where the latter gave a full summary of the conference, and produced the confidential document of the agreement. Gandhi read the document and immediately approved. He lauded the Indian delegation for achieving more than what was expected. Soon after it was made public, he endorsed the agreement in *Young India* as an 'honourable compromise' and 'the best that could be possible'.[71]

The reception of the agreement in South Africa was somewhat mixed. Several South African Indians had higher expectations, ranging from 'trivial pinpricks to the parliamentary franchise'.[72] Those who expected the restoration of the franchise were notably disappointed.[73]

In the Indian Council of State, the agreement was lauded by all members of the opposition. The 83-year-old veteran Dinshaw Wacha moved a resolution in support calling it 'a minor Locarno'.[74] Another leader, G.S. Khaparde, equated the Commonwealth to a joint Hindu family which had been reunited by the agreement.[75] Polak wrote from London: 'we have left the regions of negation for negotiation, and our worst difficulty has been removed'.[76] Attentive to its diplomatic salience, Sarojini Naidu called it 'a memorable performance'.[77] For once, despite the bitterness between the British Indian government and the nationalist movement on the one hand, and the nationalists and the liberals on the other, this was one issue on which India presented a united front. Not surprisingly, the India Office was more concerned than jubilant about how to view the agreement. The Under-Secretary of State's uneasiness appeared in a note: '[t]he Comparative success of the Indian delegation where HM's Government had so often failed to secure anything for India will be a fresh argument for Swaraj!'[78]

Andrews underscored the Africa-wide value of the agreement, for the Indian diaspora as well as Africans. The Cape Town Conference was 'a golden opportunity to get all the dominions on India's side'.[79] In Kenya in particular, white settlers would be alarmed at losing the support of other white settler states, especially South Africa. This would herald 'a settlement all-round the semi-circle of these new white nations, surrounding Asia, from British Columbia on the one side to Kenya on the other'.[80] Another author pointed out in the *Manchester Guardian* that the settlement in South Africa may indeed provide a template to settle issues between white settler populations and African populations across Africa.[81]

The agreement in itself meant little, however; it was in its implementation that the real worth would lie. Andrews emphasized that who India sent out as the Agent was key to its success. His own hopes increasingly rested upon one person, whom he noted that even Afrikaners treated 'not with cold politeness but warm honest friendship'. It was a rare gesture accorded to someone from across the colour line. This was Sastri.[82]

9

# A Trustee of India's Honour

I

On the morning of 28 May 1927, Sastri arrived in the summer capital Shimla for an appointment with Lord Irwin in his official residence. Architecturally inspired by the English Renaissance, the Viceregal House (now the Indian Institute for Advanced Studies) is reminiscent of Scottish castles with its grey stone exterior. It sits atop Observatory Hill, a watershed that cleaves the Indian subcontinent into two. On its one side waters fall into the Arabian sea and on the other into the Bay of Bengal. Each summer since 1888, when the Viceroy retreated with his government's entourage from the sweltering heat of Delhi to the hills of Shimla, figuratively, India's governmental and geological centres merged. Sastri had arrived in Shimla to officially take charge as India's first Agent to South Africa. While he had served earlier in government delegations in a non-official capacity, this was his first appointment as a full-time official of the Indian government.

Two days later, John Tyson, an Indian Civil Service officer, joined as his official secretary. A First World War veteran, Tyson had entered the ICS in 1920 and shot into the public limelight recently on account of his progressive judgements as the officiating chief presidency magistrate in Calcutta. The young magistrate was brought to the notice of the Home member in the Viceroy's Council, Alexander Muddiman. When asked if he would go to South Africa, Tyson jumped at the opportunity to escape a provincial life and immediately set off for Shimla.[1]

The third official member of the delegation was the Office Superintendent, Claude Stanley Ricketts. At the time employed at the Viceroy's Office, Ricketts had also served in the Paddison and Habibullah delegations. He was a qualified stenographer, approvingly noted as an asset in the notoriously thrifty colonial administration because it would save one extra person's salary.² Sastri brought along a fourth, non-official member to the group, P. Kodanda Rao. Rao resumed his duty as Sastri's private secretary, just as he had done during the Cape Town Agreement.

Large public meetings to bid farewell to Sastri were organized in Poona and Bombay. The Bombay meeting, held at Cowasji Jehangir Hall, was quite unusual and unique. Presided over by Sarojini Naidu, then president of the South African Indian Congress (SAIC), it brought together leaders from across the political spectrum, from non-cooperators to the European association, to wish Sastri bon voyage. Messages from the governors of Bombay and Madras, the rulers of the princely states of Alwar and Bikaner, and officials and leaders including Habibullah, Gandhi, Jinnah and Sivaswamy Iyer, among others, were read aloud.³ Purshottamdas Thakurdas noted the rare universal approval Sastri's appointment had received. M.R. Jayakar called him 'the custodian of India's honour', while Phiroze Sethna referred to him as 'one of the greatest Indians' alive. Sethna compared Sastri's appointment to James Bryce's ambassadorship to America two decades before. The intellectual prowess of both, he argued, allowed them to understand the other country better than its inhabitants. On the afternoon of 8 June, as the 7,000-tonne passenger vessel, the SS *Karoa*, prepared to leave Alexandra Dock in Bombay, a large crowd of Indians gathered to see off the delegation.⁴

This was without question the most significant, and the most difficult, task of Sastri's career yet. '[B]y temperament and training', as a contemporary noted, he was 'an ambassador and a reconciler'.⁵ However, the life of an official barely excited him. He humorously told a crowd of officials in Shimla that now that he was an official he expected to grow wings like the gods and inculcate 'sublime indifference to humanity'.⁶ But, turning sombre, he noted to the same gathering that the Indian problem in South Africa was 'tragic in its potentiality'. However, its peaceful resolution would open a vista of possibilities for addressing racial conflicts globally. The Cape Town Agreement was unique because the two governments had decided to address a racial issue through an intergovernmental dialogue. To be able to contribute to that effort was both a stiff challenge and a remarkable opportunity, he confessed.⁷

Sastri the statesman was the agreement's creator. But now Sastri the Agent had to transform into its creature, trapped very much within the confines of its limited mandate. No one really knew what to expect out of this mission, and that included the two governments. The title 'Agent' itself was vague. South Africans asked the Indian government to clarify whether Sastri should be treated as a diplomat, or merely as an Indian representative on a special mission to work towards the upliftment of the Indian community in cooperation with the South African government. The latter was not a diplomatic function. Furthermore, in the hierarchy-enshrining rituals of state protocol, where did the Agent fit in the order of precedence?

The Agent was a diplomatic position, the Indian government replied. Given the importance of the Agent's mission in South Africa, it was far too important a post to be reduced to a consul (who were appointed to foreign countries and generally to seaports or specific places). Only the position of the High Commissioner was comparable. However, there was no precedence yet of a High Commissioner being appointed to another dominion.[8] Caught in a rare bureaucratic absence of precedence, both sides agreed to go by Sastri's personal stature.[9] The South African government agreed to accord him the same privileges as a Privy Councillor.[10]

Sastri was to be, to put it in Tyson's terms, 'virtually an ambassador to a hostile nation'.[11] He added: 'our mission is so delicate and "diplomatic" and unprecedented that it is very difficult to embody in writing any precise instructions at all'.[12] An 11-page memo, drafted by the Education, Health and Lands (EHL) Department, was cautiously generic in its instructions.[13] Broadly, the Agent's remit was defined by two primary functions: to work in close collaboration with the Union government in implementing the Cape Town Agreement, and to act as a liaison between the South African Indian community and the Union government, without interfering in the workings of the latter.[14] But, the EHL memo emphasized, Sastri's main task was cultivating an amicable relationship between the two settler communities. 'You will endeavour to create a circle of European friends, through whom you may mould European opinion generally to view the Indian question with greater sympathy', advised the EHL Department.[15]

## II

The first person to publicly suggest Sastri's name was Gandhi.[16] No one was better suited than Sastri to help the South African Indians, the Mahatma wrote. His suggestion was promptly endorsed by the SAIC. Following this, Irwin offered Sastri the post. But he immediately declined. Sastri told the Viceroy that he wanted to be in India for the Royal Commission that was expected to arrive there in 1927 to review the working of the Montford reforms (later the Simon Commission). The main cause of his reluctance, however, was his distaste for administrative work, which he would be required to perform in a formal capacity. Scarcely a popular figure for his moderate views, Sastri was also worried that his departure, like his dominion tour, would invite unpleasant denigration from his country folk. Given his poor health, he was unenthused at the prospect of dying in exile.[17]

Gandhi made another earnest plea; this time in a letter written from his sick-bed.[18] In Sastri's words, this was a letter to 'settle one's fate', one whose sentiment he could not ignore.[19] Gandhi's public endorsement of him as 'a trustee of India's honour'[20] soothed his concerns about criticisms from the nationalist press.[21] In addition, the Viceroy assured him that the Royal Commission would not be appointed that year, so Sastri would be able to return by the time it arrived in India.

Sastri agreed, but on two conditions. First, he would only stay for a year and, second, an ICS-level secretary would accompany him to help with the administrative matters. Tyson's was the resulting appointment. The Bengal official was sceptical about Sastri's resolve to stay, and hoped to keep Sastri in South Africa for at least nine months by performing most of the administrative tasks. The mission, he wrote privately to a friend, 'would be unpopular and I do not know how long Sastri will want to stick it out'.[22] Muddiman explained Tyson's job to him, rather bluntly: to compensate for Sastri's skin colour and to help Sastri 'with the Europeans in Natal and with the Jo'burg Jews!' Tyson had to be ready 'at all times to placate (with a cocktail or an automatic pistol) any outraged British colonist or infuriated Transvaal Boer to whom Mr. Sastri's opinions, clothes, habits or colour may prove offensive'.[23]

The decision came with hard personal choices for Sastri. Once he had agreed to become a government official, he could not continue to lead the Servants of India Society. He resigned from its presidency and his place was taken by G.K. Devadhar.[24] Having steered the Society since his mentor's demise in 1915, this was indisputably an emotional decision for him. But still perhaps not as difficult as leaving his wife, Lakshmi, at home. It was made more arduous because Lakshmi had initially been excited at the prospect of going to South Africa. Gandhi himself had pleaded that she accompany him. But Sastri persuaded her against taking the journey. Sastri as well as Kodanda Rao are rather evasive about the exact reasons, but they hint towards three broad concerns. First, the diplomatic necessities of frequent hosting as the Agent's wife were likely to overwhelm the introverted Lakshmi.[25] Second, the Agent's work would require a lot of travel, and in a racially segregated South Africa this would create several difficulties of finding appropriate means of travel and lodging. Finally, Sastri was also concerned that given the racial hatred in South Africa, the couple might find themselves in life-threatening situations.[26] As we will see later, he was not wrong.

## III

The first stop on the SS *Karoa*'s itinerary was Mombasa. Once the ship docked at the port city after ten days of travel, Sastri's party experienced a taste of what was to come. Despite being an Indian government representative and a Privy Councillor, hotel accommodation was denied to Sastri (and Kodanda Rao).[27] None of the white government officials were ready to meet him. The tenor of the white opposition to and racism against Indians, Tyson noted in his diary, was even stronger than in South Africa. Sastri's stance on the Kenya question had no doubt contributed to his notoriety among the Kenyan whites, settlers and officials alike.

Things improved as the SS *Karoa* moved further south to Zanzibar, Dar-es-Salaam and then Beira. At each of these stops, Sastri was given warm receptions by European officials as well as the local Indians.[28] In Lourenço Marques (now Maputo), he was received by Harry N. Venn, the Australian-born South African commissioner for Asiatic affairs. Venn's appointment, just like Sastri's, was a consequence of the Cape Town Agreement. His presence in Lourenço Marques echoed the importance Hertzog's government gave to Sastri's mission. Impressed by Sastri's performance at the Cape Town Conference, the Union government had enthusiastically received the news of his appointment. Venn was to accompany Sastri's party to Pretoria by a special wagon reserved for Cabinet ministers in South Africa.[29]

In a country where Indians had always been treated as second-class citizens, the government's recognition of Sastri's position, not just as a representative of another government but as a prominent leader of the British Commonwealth, had an important symbolic import. As Andrews emphasized, for the first time the Union government was ready to give an Indian representative a status equal to Europeans.[30] In diplomacy, where rituals are recorded with a puritanical gaze, Sastri's elevation above other foreign European diplomats certainly carried enormous significance.[31] Even white supremacists acknowledged it grudgingly. Oswald Pirow, a National Party leader and later a Nazi sympathizer, wrote in *Ons Vaderland*: 'We have now given the coolie a highly civilized and intelligent leader, who will have to be received by every white man on an equal footing.'[32]

Exactly a month after Sastri officially took up the post in Shimla, he arrived in Pretoria. Early morning on 28 June, he was received at the Pretoria Central Station by local Indians and H. Pring, the under-secretary for the Interior Department. A small contingent of Africans, led by Chief Sikhuni of the Pedis, were also present to receive him. The Governor General, several ministers and even Jan Smuts sent welcome telegrams.[33]

The South African government had booked accommodation for the Indian party at the Grand Hotel, which stood on the south-eastern corner of the city's historic centre, Church Square. The hotel, once one of the finest in the country, was noticeably past its prime; Tyson described it as 'the best of the bad lot'.[34] Sastri and Kodanda Rao were possibly its first non-white lodgers in its history of more than three decades. Pretoria's supposedly liberal cousin, Johannesburg, was however more prudish about racial transgressions. Johannesburg hotels found ingenious excuses to deny Sastri a stay. He had to set himself up in the lodgings of the Theosophical Society when he visited the city.

Further, the Grand Hotel may have opened its doors for Sastri (and Kodanda Rao), but they were still firmly shut for others of his race. As other Indians would still not be welcome in the hotel, Hertzog's government asked the visiting party to lease a house for the ease of receiving Indian guests. In Pretoria, Indians were legally barred from buying property. They could only lease it for less than a month at a time. In such a segregated space, being asked by the government to lease a house long term for Indian occupants was indeed a significant gesture. Soon, a house was procured close to the Prime Minister's house in Pretoria, and another was rented in mid-October for six months in Cape Town's up-market Rondebosch locality.[35]

A cynical eye may accord only an incidental significance to these developments. But these strongly suggest South Africa's own reconciliation with its newly found international status following the Balfour Declaration, as much as they reflect Sastri's ability to straddle racial barriers. The country was now required to abide by international norms and protocol despite domestic opposition. The more South Africa asserted its autonomy from the British Empire, claiming sovereignty in the domestic sphere, the more it was required to hive off its domestic from the international, and acknowledge and accept the equality of other sovereigns. Increasingly, then, a distinction had to be drawn between Sastri as a non-white individual and Sastri as an international diplomat. The fact that the South African government also went out of its way could perhaps be attributed to the eagerness with which the Hertzog government wanted to 'resolve' the Indian question. Obviously, the principle works more in theory than in practice.[36]

## IV

For much of the segregated history of South Africa, Indians were spread mostly across three of its four provinces: Transvaal, Natal and the Cape Province. In 1925, Natal alone housed 87.5 per cent of the total Indian population. About 7.5 per cent Indians resided in Transvaal, and 5 per cent in the Cape Province. The fourth province in the Union, the Orange Free State, prohibited Indians from living there. They could only receive special permission to work in European households. Consequently, the Indian population in the province was negligible (about 200).[37]

Transvaal welcomed Sastri with warm yet sceptical countenance.[38] A well-attended welcome banquet of about 700 guests, more than half of whom were Europeans, was organized in his honour by the Transvaal Indians. Sections of the Transvaal Indians were on the whole opposed to the Cape Town Agreement, and were at loggerheads with the Natal-dominated SAIC. Prominent Europeans wondered why someone as distinguished as Sastri was sent merely as an Agent by the Indian government. Leslie Blackwell, the local South African Party MLA, wondered if there was an intention to push for franchise and other political rights.[39] Sastri expected strong opposition from Transvaal settlers, both Europeans and Indians, in the coming days.

His first two weeks in the country were spent in meeting and familiarizing himself with government leaders and influential political figures. Most profitable of such acquaintances was Patrick Duncan, Smuts' deputy in the parliament. The two leaders were to cultivate a warm relationship, quite in contrast to Sastri's strained and difficult relationship with Smuts himself. Richard Feetham, Duncan's old associate from their days of Milner's Kindergarten and now a Supreme Court judge, was known to Sastri from the time they spent together in the Southborough Committee in 1919. The Feethams became Sastri's closest European friends in the country. Over the course of his 19-month stay, Sastri spent many an evening socially hobnobbing with these and other crucial connections, and accordingly cultivated strong inside connections across all shades of the European political spectrum.

The Cape Town Agreement, as discussed in the previous chapter, had two important sections: Assisted Emigration and the Upliftment of Indians. The Union government's concern was manifestly more in assisted emigration while the Indian interest was in the upliftment scheme. So, while the Union government had left no stone unturned to implement the first part of the scheme regarding 'Assisted Emigration' (more on this later), little had been done for the upliftment clause until Sastri's arrival. Since most of the Indian population was concentrated in Natal, the main issues related to the upliftment section, primarily education and housing, were matters concerning mostly Natal.

In this notoriously English province, the administrator and his council belonged to the Smuts-led South African Party. Hertzog's National Party, which ruled at the centre, faced stringent opposition in the province and its executive. The agreement was deeply unpopular in Natal, largely because it called upon provincial coffers to provide for the 'upliftment' of Indians, in particular regarding education and housing. Indeed, soon after the agreement was announced, the Natal Provincial Council had passed a resolution deploring the fact that the province was not consulted.[40] Malan told Sastri in their first meeting on 11 July that he had little influence in Natal. The Provincial Council had paid no attention to his instructions to set up an Education Commission. Hence, Malan apprised Sastri, the upliftment of Indians in this province depended almost entirely on how much Sastri was able to convince white, predominantly English, opinion in favour of the agreement.[41]

Sastri arrived in Durban, Natal's heart, on 14 July. Again, none of the hotels could be booked for him, always on the pretext that they were full (although Tyson was allowed in and Ricketts had stayed back in Pretoria). He was instead hosted by an Indian businessman, E.M. Paruk, in his little-used house in the European part of the town. Sastri's initial reception among the European Natal leaders was lukewarm.[42]

However, in a province steeped in imperial nostalgia, enthusiastic introductions from Governor General Athlone, and Sastri's credentials as Privy Councillor brought him considerable social capital. For one thing, it automatically elevated him to the main table at all social gatherings.[43] In the highly racialized Durban English social circles, where imperial sentiment perhaps counted as much as the racial one, Sastri's high imperial status elicited the bewildered enthusiasm of his European hosts.[44] An illustration will explain the point better.

In one of his early meetings in Durban, Sastri called on Charles Smith, a sugar baron and a very influential provincial leader from Smuts' South African Party. Overbearing and patronizing, Smith looked uninterested in whatever Sastri might say and instead preferred to harangue him on how Natal Indians were a happy lot. Unable to reign in Smith's tongue, Sastri let it slip in a moment of brief interlude that he had dined at His Majesty's table. Suddenly, Smith was all ears;

the Agent could now speak uninterrupted. After Sastri had spoken, the sugar baron railed against his own party folk who had attempted to dissuade him from meeting and taking part in any of the ceremonies that honoured a man of Sastri's stature. He invited the Indian Agent for dinner at his house, and spoke enthusiastically at a banquet honouring Sastri, much to the dismay of his own party crowd.[45]

Soon, Sastri was invited to deliver public lectures to European audiences. His political speeches to the whites in Natal almost always contained three elements. He would first provide information about the Cape Town Agreement; then he would emphasize its novelty in terms of finding a new way of approaching the question of racial relations in global politics; and, finally, he would appeal to the broader ideals of the British Commonwealth, urging the local population, to rise to the established principles of the Anglo-Saxon world.[46]

In making such appeals, however, he reassured the European public that he would not go beyond 'the four corners' of the agreement. Although he was, as he acknowledged to his audiences in Natal, 'a political agitator of some standing',[47] he conceded the European 'right to determine the public policy' and maintain their civilization.[48] In other words, he firmly refused to align himself with the demand for political rights for Indians in the Union.

The two core principles of the Cape Town Agreement, he argued, had accommodated the sensitivities of both settler populations. The 'assisted emigration' clause recognized the fears of the European part of the population, and accordingly the need for reduction of the Indian population in the Union. Hence, he acknowledged the political primacy of the white component of the population. The 'upliftment' clause recognized that the living conditions of Indians were considerably poorer than those of the white population. And it called upon the state – the Union as well as the provincial governments – to fulfil its welfare function, in particular of providing for health, education and sanitation.

He also agreed with the government's view that upliftment was dependent on the success of assisted emigration, that is, it is only when the population of Indians was reduced that the state would have enough finances to contribute to their upliftment. But, taken together, the assisted emigration and upliftment clauses also rejected a racial and communitarian approach to social welfare. As he said in his remarks to the Education Committee in Natal:

> Interpreted broadly, [the agreement implies] that the communal way of looking at these questions should be

dropped; that is to say, that in considering what should be done for a community you must not ask: Who are they, which community do they belong to, what is their complexion, and so forth? But you must consider their capacity to develop by measures of upliftment, and whatever they can turn to their advantage must be afforded to them. ... In considering how much education an individual should receive, the question should not be asked: What community does he belong to, where does he come from, how much tax does he pay, but what is his capacity? How much education is he capable of receiving and turning to his advantage and to the advantage of the community?[49]

This reframing of the agreement as prioritizing an individual's capacity for development over a community project had strong echoes of the credo of the *Servants of India Society* which mandated that '[m]uch of the work of the Society must be directed towards building a higher type of character and capacity than is generally available at present'.[50] Furthermore, prioritizing the individual over the community placed a liberal spin on the issue of rights that was likely to find more acceptance among the English in Natal.

The agreement, Sastri would often emphasize, was novel not only because of its diplomatic uniqueness within the British Commonwealth, but also because it served as an example of a nuanced way of resolving conflicts that emerged from deep racial divisions. Signed in the true spirit of compromise, the agreement allowed the representatives of the two governments to take a broader view of the issues. If successful, this could become a precedent for negotiating across the colour line, especially within the British Commonwealth.

Contingency and precedent aside, he reminded his English public in Natal of the high ideals of the British Commonwealth which made it superior to every other European form of political organization. The ideal of equality before law and justice was the British Commonwealth's unique contribution to the world. He scarcely hid his great admiration for the British Empire, even to the extent of saying: 'we in India know no other flag. We have only got the Union Jack'.[51]

Speaking to a gathering of over 2,000 Europeans, mostly of British origin, he stated that the empire 'cannot live on air. "It lives in the blood of the British people"'. Each British settler constituted 'the vehicle of the British spirit' and for that spirit to survive, for the British empire to survive, each British settler must embody and carry forth those ideals. 'If each one of us betrays it where then will the Empire be?', he asked. The discrimination against Indians authorized by law in South Africa was unquestionably incompatible with the British ideals of 'common fair play ... elementary rights of citizenship, the means of earning an honest living and ... enjoying the fruits of labour'. He urged them to do away with these injustices in order to realize the true greatness of the empire.[52]

Delivered in Sastri's characteristic style, and almost always impromptu, the charm of his voice and the studied sincerity of his bearing captivated his audiences. After a speech in Maritzburg, a newspaper correspondent called it 'almost the finest speech ever made in the City Hall'.[53]

Skilfully, he would also tailor his speeches according to the demographic component of his audience. When his public was predominantly Afrikaner, as in Newcastle and Greytown, or in towns with an Anglo-Boer War history such as Ladysmith and Dundee, he avoided invoking the empire sentiment.[54] In smaller Transvaal towns with strong Afrikaner presence, he would instead appeal to the spirit of the Gandhi–Smuts Agreement, liberally refer to Kruger's accommodative approach towards the Indians, and invoke the principles of justice and fair play. In contrast to his English audiences, to whom he emphasized equality as the spiritual foundation of the Commonwealth, he would cleverly shift to the tropes and ideas about mutual respect and the pain of humiliation with the Afrikaners. Equality carried little purchase with his Afrikaner audiences when 'no equality in Church and State' was the core principle of Afrikaner supremacism. But the themes of respect and humiliation resonated more easily, considering their importance in the Afrikaners' own tortured relationship with the British.[55]

He would also make connections between caste and race in order to empathize with racialism but repudiate racism. He emphasized that as a Brahmin he could understand the need for racial purity. He did not advocate for 'race mixture'; Brahmins in India for better or worse had kept their race pure. However, the choice to remain 'pure' was exactly that: a choice about sexual relations made by the community from within. On its own, it had little or no relation with political, social and economic intermixture. Going further, a self-imposed sexual exclusion was entirely different from political, social and economic discrimination. Indeed, the lesson from India was that this rather innocuous desire for racial purity when it degenerated into racial discrimination stifled the growth and vitality of societies for centuries: 'no nation should try and imitate the evil course which we trod'.[56]

Caste was 'a slavery of the soul', and Brahmins were the 'whites' of India. Caste was a demon that needed to be exorcized, and the greatest

**9: Sastri with the Governor General, Lord Athlone**

The Governor General, Lord Athlone (here at a function in Cape Town), had been extremely helpful to Sastri in the latter's dealings with the South African government as well as with the provincial administration in Natal. When he asked the Indian leader to extend his stay in South Africa for six months, Sastri could not refuse.

achievement of British rule in India was that through its institutions it had attempted to stamp out this inhuman practice. People of British stock in South Africa, who prided themselves on its institutions, he suggested to his audiences in Natal, could not do otherwise.[57]

Importantly, these denunciations of caste and race discrimination typify what M.S.S. Pandian sees as a predictable response of a reform-oriented Brahmin. The private domain of sexual relations and cultural rituals is presented as a benign, even positive, identity-reinforcing realm. The discriminatory ramifications of these practices are offered not as inevitable consequences of an exclusivist agenda, but rather as insidious machinations of a separate, autonomous political realm. In this way, the personal is hived off from the political. The brahmin embraces modernity by limiting its exercise to the public domain, and recasting the power permeated in intimate relations as merely non-political, private practice.[58]

## V

Education sat at the top of Sastri's priorities, for reasons both personal and contextual. He was a teacher by profession and felt very strongly about the importance of education in the progress of a society. Accordingly, his focus on upliftment remained largely on education, although housing and sanitation were also core issues. The condition of education for Indians in Natal was miserable. Less than one third of Indian children of school-going age were enrolled in the segregated schooling system of Natal. Only 53 schools were open for almost 10,000 Indian school-going children across the province, most of them in urban centres. For an almost equal number of European students, there were 192 schools.

Natal's education system permitted two kinds of schools: government-run schools and government-aided schools. The latter were usually missionary schools supported by the government, and were plagued by financial difficulties, poor infrastructure and organizational crises. Playgrounds, students' accommodation, or indeed funds for extra-curricular activities were rarely available. Teachers' salaries could be as low as 30 cents a month. In contrast, government schools were discernibly better managed and resourced. A large number of Indian schools were government-aided (44 out of 53), whereas most European schools were government-run (160 out of 192).

The rate of attrition among Indian students also tended to be very high. For instance, in 1927, out of 9,934 enrolled students, only 66 were in High School. Such low numbers tapered the pool of qualified students for teacher training. According to the government's own figures, 91 out of 176 teachers in the government-aided school were unqualified. The whole education system was trapped in a circle of incompetency: poor education standards led to a paucity of qualified teachers, and without qualified teachers the education standards remained poor. Citing the lack of qualified teachers, the government shirked its responsibility of opening more schools.[59] The principal of Fort Hare, the only higher education college available to Indians, found Indian students to be 'generally weaker in their preparation than any other single group that comes to Fort Hare'.[60] Overall, the quality of education for Indians was in desperate need of an overhaul.

An education commission was mandated by the agreement to look into these concerns. The Natal administration, as we have noted, was opposed to spending its own funds on a matter that the Union government had decided on without their consent. The Provincial Council was, as Tyson described it, 'a most uninspiring body of men … an ignorant and intensely narrow and parochially minded lot of men with the colour prejudice ingrained in them'.[61] Quietly and persuasively, he conducted backroom meetings with several influential members, including the members of the council, to convince them to set up a commission. In this he was greatly helped by the Governor General. Athlone, who remained consistently helpful to Sastri throughout his tenure, personally intervened to influence the administrator, George Plowman, who in turn arranged for Sastri to address the Provincial Council.[62] Sastri made a considerable impression on the council.[63]

In addition, Sastri also wanted the Indian community to take initiatives towards improving education. It would signal to the administration their readiness for self-help. He proposed an Education Fund, created through donations by the Indian community, for building a teacher training-cum-high school. Such a school would address two core needs of Natal Indians: good teachers and a fully functional high school.[64] Durban's only high school for Indians, on Carlisle Street, was woefully inadequate in both equipment and accommodation. It had no laboratory, library or playground.[65] Sastri expected to raise £20,000 for a school building through a tour of Natal. And hoped that the municipality would provide land for this initiative.[66]

In August and early September 1927, Sastri toured Natal, especially in the anti-Indian North Natal sugar belt which employed a large Indian indentured labour force. In towns like Stanger, Tongaat, Lady Smith, New Castle, Dannhauser, Dundee, Colenso, Estcourt, Grey Town and Escombe, his reception by Europeans and Indians was mostly cordial. He attended several receptions and banquets, making as many as five speeches in a day.[67] Often in these locations, his receptions were the first ever opportunities to bring together Indians and Europeans at lunches and dinners.[68]

The response to his appeal for funds was more enthusiastic among the indentured Indians than the more affluent traders. The latter, Sastri felt, held dismissive opinions towards education. In particular, he encountered dogged resistance to the idea of girls' education. Even boys, he was often told, were raised to serve as apprentices in their fathers' businesses and thus needed, at best, middle school education for these tasks.[69] Nevertheless, he persisted, eventually raising £18,000 through his appeals, £2,000 short of the £20,000 required.

Sastri's moves were keenly followed by the European press. *Natal Mercury*, the Durban-based newspaper, and decidedly anti-Indian in its views, cautioned its readers against Sastri's tactic of placing upliftment over emigration. Emigration, the *Mercury* insisted, was the only viable solution. Natal did not have the money to put towards the education costs of Indians, especially when the percentage of Indians in schools was still higher in Natal than in India. Instead it demanded more scrutiny of the unsanitary living conditions of Indians. If at all, the *Mercury* editorialized, a commission was required over public health, not education.

Such calls for a public health commission were aimed at segregation. The white public expected that a public health commission that looked into sanitation would recommend dismantling houses in overcrowded Indian locations inside the city and moving them outside the town. Indians preferred overcrowding to segregation, as eviction from inner cities to outer areas would ruin Indian businesses in the city.[70]

Sastri's efforts were rewarded on 22 September 1927, his 59th birthday, when the Education Commission Enquiry was formally announced. The council had also approved Sastri's suggestion to invite two education experts from India to participate in the commission. Kailas P. Kichlu, deputy director of public instruction in the United Provinces, and Corrie Gordon, an Edinburgh-born teacher of method from Sastri's *alma mater* Saidapet Teacher Training College, were soon dispatched from India. However, the commission was packed with uninspiring South African names; three in particular were notoriously anti-Indian: Frank H. Achutt, John A. Lidgett and F.C. Hollander. Sastri convinced Plowman, who by now had become fairly sympathetic to the Indian demands, to preside over the commission.[71] Nevertheless, the appointment of the commission was a major win; *Natal Mercury* called it a 'birthday present to Sastri'. Sastri in turn dedicated it to his birthday twin, Mohammad Habibullah.[72]

## VI

It was, however, a long time before the commission had its first sitting. Expected to start before Christmas in 1927, it only started its work on 2 April 1928. The delay was caused by change in the personnel in the

**10: With the Education Committee**

'A most uninspiring body of men' is how Tyson characterized the Education Committee. Here Sastri is with them, and the two Indian experts. Front row (L–R): A.L. Pretorius, V.S.S. Sastri, J. Dyson (chairperson), F.C Hollander, K.P. Kichlu; Standing: F.H. Achutt, F.W. Fell, C. Gordon, C.F. Clarkson, C.A.B. Peck.

provincial administration. Plowman had resigned and was replaced by Gordon Watson, who appointed a new chairperson, J. Dyson.

On the opening day of the commission's sitting in Pietermaritzburg, the director of education, Hugh Bryan, gave a detailed and grim account of the state of education for Indians.[73] Natal had not even used the subsidy given to it by the Union government for Indian education. Instead, these funds were routinely channelled towards other expenses.[74] In 1925–26, less than half of the subsidy was spent on Indian students, although this increased to marginally less than three quarters in 1926–27.[75] Between 1925 and 1927, as Kichlu was to write in his own report to the commission, £27,215 had been misdirected in this manner. This was in contrast to European and Coloured education, on which the provincial government had spent £168,914 and £22,966, respectively, from its own funds, in addition to the Union government's subsidies.[76]

Sastri was examined the next day. A committee member, Frank H. Achutt, contended that subsidy towards Indian education would overburden the European population of Natal who paid income tax.[77] Sastri responded that every part of the population, including

Indians, contributed to the general revenue of the province and the Union through indirect taxes. Since the Union subsidy on education for Indians drew entirely from general revenue, the argument about burdening Natal Europeans with taxes was superfluous. If at all, not only were Indians not getting education benefits for the taxes they were paying, but they were also monetarily contributing to the education of Europeans.

While Indians did not pay income tax, he reminded Achutt that they also did not have any rights of franchise. The provincial as well as municipal franchise had recently been withdrawn from Indians. Without going into the merits of whether Indian disenfranchisement was just, he reasoned that even if one were to justify the taking away of political rights of a whole community, a state cannot compartmentalize the social well-being of its population. Education, health, sanitation, housing and justice were social rights that the state ought to grant everyone equally.[78] 'You don't say that the Jews pay on the whole so much in taxation, and therefore they shall have so many schools', he added.[79]

The proceedings of the committee on the whole were hostile to Indians. Sastri commented that the administration had taken every possible measure to make sure that the commission appeared anti-Indian to the public.[80] The members were ignorant, unwilling to be informed and prejudiced.[81] Achutt wanted the two Indian experts to respond to Katherine Mayo's accusations about the backwardness of Indians in her recently published scandalous book, *Mother India*, but was turned down by other members.[82] Another member, John A. Lidgett, asked how Indians expected to bring down the Indian population when their birth rate (4,000–5,000 per year) was higher than the proposed emigration rate (3,000 people). 'There is such a thing as a death rate', Tyson, who was sitting in the room, blurted.[83] Several European depositions were nasty and full of anti-Indian diatribe.[84]

Sastri confided in Habibullah, disappointedly, that he did not expect the committee to provide any money for Indian education except the Union government subsidy. He was, however, willing to take a broader view of things:

> Occasionally, I give way to a feeling of remorse when I think of the great expense to which the Government of India has been put on account of the prolonged deputation of Kichlu and Miss Gordan; but the proper way of assessing their work is not to look at the exact gain in pounds, shillings and pence to the cause of Indian education here but to the moral effect produced on the European community

and the fresh hope given to the Indian community. The change that has come over the Natal Executive not only in respect of the education question, but of the Indian problem generally, is remarkable.[85]

As he expected, the committee did not provide any separate funds in its final report. However, the report on the whole was sympathetic to many of the Indian demands. It acknowledged that education facilities for Indians were inadequate, and the grants-in-aid were insufficient. The committee recommended extending the grants throughout the province together with opening more government schools in the larger centres of Indian population. While opposed to any rises in taxation on either the Europeans or the Indians, the committee advocated that Natal should fully utilize the Union subsidy for Indian education and appeal to the Union government for higher subsidies in lieu of the expected increase in the number of Indian students. It also accepted Sastri's gift of a training college-cum-high school.[86]

Back in India, Irwin took a most enthusiastic view of the report. He wrote: '[i]t seems to me a very remarkable event and a kind of thing that would surely have been inconceivable two or three years ago'.[87] The *Indian Opinion* called the report 'not beyond our expectations', noting in a back-handed way that the expectations were already quite low. *Natal Witness*, a Martitzburg paper and Indian-friendly in its views, was scathing of the committee, calling the report a 'sorry and shame-faced document', especially in light of the gross disparities that Kichlu's report had shown.[88] Watson, however, congratulated Sastri for bringing a considerable change in the committee's thinking, commenting that even Achutt had been 'Sastricized'.[89]

For the proposed training college-cum-high school, Sastri was keen to get teachers from India, and had offered this to the Natal Education Department.[90] But he found his scheme opposed by Charles Loram, the acting superintendent of education.[91] With a doctorate from Columbia, Loram had written his PhD thesis on *The Education of the South African Native*, where he advocated the Tuskegee model of industrial education for Africans in South Africa. He was a member of the Phelps–Stokes Commission in 1921 and 1924 (and later left South Africa in 1931 to join the Yale faculty). His paternalistic education philosophy had two core assumptions. First, whites would forever rule South Africa, thus African education must endeavour to shape Africans into becoming, metaphorically, the 'junior partners in the firm'. Second, a pastoral way of life was the primary character of Africans, and the contribution of Africans to the country would be maximized if they contributed to the rural economy.[92] Seeing education in these racialized binaries, he was of the view that only European teachers should be teaching in all non-European schools, and hence opposed Sastri's suggestion of recruiting teachers from India.

Sastri believed Loram to be 'pronounced anti-Indian though he [did not] admit the fact'.[93] Loram, however, seems to have retained a far more positive appreciation for Sastri, at least in hindsight. He compared Sastri to Booker T. Washington, 'one with large universality, a heart big enough for all the world', and credited him as one of the two non-Europeans to influence his life; the other being the Ghanaian-born educationalist, James Aggrey.[94]

Sastri was anxious to avoid Loram's equation of the Indian education problem with African education.[95] In this, Sastri's view was informed by his own racism as well as his compulsion of being primarily a representative of Indians. Culturally and educationally, he believed that Indians were more advanced than Africans. Hence, their problems were fundamentally different. However, he argued that the African struggle in South Africa was also different from the Indian one. The latter were supported by the Indian government, and already had an existing framework which was diplomatically agreed. Linking the two struggles would slow the Indian progress towards equality and also compromise the 'upliftment' clause of the agreement.[96] He dissuaded South African Indians from identifying with African struggles in general. In any case, Sastri's desire was fulfilled when, upon the opening of the school two years later, its first batch of teachers arrived from India.

For the school, Sastri had originally requested from the town council a vacant six-acre plot on Centenary Road which was adjacent to the municipal (Indian) playground. Earlier reserved for poor whites' housing, the site was abandoned after it was declared unsuitable for a residential area.[97] It was, however, within 100 yards of three Indian schools – a boys' primary, a girls' primary and a boys' high school – which could serve as practice schools for the trainee teachers and as feeders for the high school.[98] Sastri was allotted only two acres. Upon inspection, Tyson noted: 'Afraid that Corporation have "sold us a pup"; the site is mostly drains, underground cables and overhead wires! Amazing that the Department concerned knew nothing about it.'[99] Sastri appealed to the Borough Council several times to allot two more acres. Every time his request was put to vote and turned down by a small margin.[100]

Tyson noted in his diary that 24 August 1928 was 'a red-letter day for Indian education in the Union'.[101] Watson laid the foundation stone of the school. Hermann Kallenbach, Gandhi's friend, and his partner, Alexander Kennedy, were appointed as the architects, which would have the school building, the principal's house and a hostel for 40 students.[102] The school was officially opened in 1929. Sastri was by now back in India, but 52 donors to the school fund signed to name it, quite appropriately, 'Sastri College'.[103]

Sastri College is perhaps the most enduring legacy of Sastri in South Africa; it is 'a visible monument to Mr. Sastri's term in office', as Tyson commented on the foundation day. The college, still functioning, remained the centrepiece of Indian education in South Africa for several decades and provided quality education to generations of South African Indians. The number of schools admitting Indians quickly rose from 53 in 1927 to 78 in 1931.[104] Sastri's focus on education may seem pedantic from the distance of over a century, but it was, in his view, a crucial lever of Indian 'upliftment', both social and eventually political.

10

# We Have No Sastri

I

As soon as the Cape Town Agreement was announced, the South African government wasted little time in pushing for the assisted emigration scheme. A piece of legislation, called Act 37 of 1927, to implement the agreement's undertakings on assisted emigration was introduced in the Union parliament and passed without opposition a week after Sastri's arrival. The government also raised bonus rates for emigrants, which led to an appreciable rise in the numbers early on. Compared to 1,358 Indians who emigrated in 1925, the numbers for 1927 and 1928 rose to 2,975 and 3,477, respectively.

Assisted emigration was stringently opposed by many Indians, especially in the Transvaal. Their criticisms were mainly around three concerns. First, the emigration was not really voluntary. It allowed the Union government to create conditions, through racial laws and public pressure, which would drive out Indians from their jobs, reduce their means of livelihood and therefore force them to leave. Second, it was widely feared that the emigrants would be worse off in India than in South Africa. Third, the scheme considered the Indian as a foreigner in South Africa, even when a large percentage of them were South Africa-born.[1]

The South African government also noted a key operational flaw in the scheme. The European opposition against Indians in Natal and Transvaal was largely based on the assumption that Indians competed with Europeans in trade. In contrast, agricultural labourers, employed mostly in the sugar-cane industry, were paid a pittance, and were valued by Europeans. Through travel bonuses and assistance with finding jobs in India, the emigration scheme incentivized those who were closer to subsistence levels rather than the comparatively affluent trading class.[2] It targeted the wrong demographic, as far as the Europeans were concerned.

In his various speeches to South African Indians, Sastri acknowledged that the assisted emigration scheme was hardly an ideal solution, especially for the poor. With the government rolling out welfare schemes for the 'poor whites', the employment opportunities for poor Indians were limited and they were forced to emigrate. But such welfarist policies towards 'poor whites' would remain regardless of the agreement, Sastri argued. The agreement at least provided a financially sustainable way for the poor Indians to leave the country.[3] Considering that the only other alternative the Union government contemplated was segregation, the scheme was the better of the two bad choices.[4]

Were emigrant Indians worse off in India? Sastri argued that there was no conclusive data yet to support this.[5] Consequently, Bhawani Dayal Sanyasi, a Johannesburg-born social activist, undertook a tour to India to ascertain the condition of South African Indians.[6] He found their conditions so dire that not a single emigrant he met wanted to remain in India. Several had been socially ostracized upon their return because they had lost caste. Living in India was especially alienating for South Africa-born Indians, for whom South Africa, not India, was the homeland. Even though the Indian government had found them employment, the emigrants earned much less than they had made in South Africa.[7] In the majority of the cases, such jobs were rejected for being too low-paid. In principle, they retained their domicile in South Africa for three years, but the high costs of return made it virtually impossible. They were required to repay the bonus for each family member as well as the total cost of travel. In the case of one family, for instance, the total amount to be returned was £457. By 1930, only 1 per cent of all emigrants were able to return to South Africa.[8] However, Sanyasi's report, co-written with Banarasidas Chaturvedi, was only published after Sastri's departure in 1931. While in India, Sanyasi ended up serving a one-year prison term for participating in Gandhi's civil disobedience movement.

On the criticism of the treatment of the South African Indian as a 'foreigner' under the agreement, Sastri disagreed. He found this spin positively mischievous on the part of those Transvaal Indians who had supported Gandhi–Smuts Agreement of 1914. Indeed, Gandhi's agreement used the term 'voluntary repatriation', which affirmed the South African Indian as being a foreign element. He emphasized that the status of 'emigrant' was a considerable improvement over the 'repatriate' with no right of return in Gandhi's agreement with Smuts.

## II

A key provision of Act 37 was a section that amended the immigration laws of the country. According to Section 5 of this Act, immigration officers, pending the Minister of Interior's approval, could cancel registrations of individuals in case they were found to be in possession of fraudulent certificates. Any appeal against such cancellations could only be made to the appeals board of the ministry. This clause superseded a previous judgement of the Transvaal Supreme Court which had allowed individuals to appeal to the court against cancellations. This left the fate of Indians entirely in the hands of partisan and often racist white bureaucrats.

The court had also made a distinction between two kinds of fraudulent certificates: those which a person obtained on their own and those where such a certificate was obtained by another person, such as in the case of a minor. Section 5 did away with the distinction, thus making even former minors liable for a mistake that they did not commit.[9]

Finally, Section 5 also declared those who had entered through illicit means but had not obtained any document of domicile (mainly in Natal and the Cape where such certificates were not required) as 'prohibited immigrants', thereby extending the scope of law also to those without any certificates.

The Indian community, particularly in the Transvaal where as many as two thirds of Indians were likely to be affected, protested strongly against these provisions. A retrospective imposition, they contended, would be an infringement of a right (given by the Transvaal Supreme Court) as well as going against the spirit of the Cape Town Agreement. Prior to Sastri's arrival, the SAIC, along with Andrews, had appealed to Malan, who had agreed to scrap the retrospective imposition but declined to do so through an amendment in the parliament. He reasoned that any amendment would be difficult to pass in the parliament, given the anti-Indian sentiment of the European population. However, he was willing to provide retrospective amnesty in writing on the condition that the Indian community would promise not to encourage fraudulent entry. Malan also made a statement to the same effect in the parliament later. He offered Indians what was called the Condonation Scheme.

Andrews consulted Smuts and Duncan, who agreed that a written promise by Malan would be binding on successive governments. They also counselled that a failure of any amendment in the parliament would preclude the government from any further voluntary action in support of Indians. Consequently, the SAIC accepted the minister's offer.

However, this caused a major rift within the SAIC. The Transvaal British Indian Association (TBIA), an affiliate of the SAIC, blamed the SAIC for not pressing the matter of amending the legislation enough. The association opposed Malan's insistence on the SAIC's assurance about discouraging future fraudulent entry. Accusing the SAIC of being dominated by Natal Indians, who were not as affected by the issue, the TBIA asserted its claim as the sole voice of the Transvaal Indians. In a mass meeting on 8 May 1927, the TBIA severed its connection with the SAIC and opposed the Condonation Scheme.[10]

Sastri's arrival in South Africa at this juncture had kindled hopes of reconciliation. In his opening speeches in Pretoria and Johannesburg in late June and early July 1927, Sastri appealed to Transvaal leaders to resolve their differences in order to speak with one voice to the South African government. Political opinion in India ranging from Gandhi to the Indian government, he informed them, insisted on a united front. He reminded them of the seriousness of the Indian government in support of their cause by emphasizing that even though it did not recognize the Indian National Congress in India, the Indian government had recognized its South African affiliate, the SAIC.[11]

His intervention initially raised hopes of a truce. Many of these squabbles and conflicts, Sastri wrote to Habibullah, were personal rather than political. Upon Sastri's request, the TBIA agreed to assure Malan on not encouraging fraudulent entries. The organizational split had, however, now created another difficulty: who had the authority to commit on behalf of the Indian community? Would the SAIC, as a representative body of South African Indians, be the chief agency, or would the provincial bodies in Transvaal, the Cape and Natal give individual assent, especially as the TBIA had branched off? Malan was unlikely to accept separate guarantees, and therefore unity was essential.

But things turned sour in a meeting on 9 October 1927, when a delegation of nine Transvaal Indians called on Sastri. They insisted on discussing 'local grievances only', signalling that Sastri should refrain from meddling in the politics between the two bodies. They believed Sastri to be pro-SAIC. Sastri was displeased. His tone in a public meeting on 12 November was sterner as he implored the TBIA to show unity with SAIC on the Condonation Scheme.[12]

Some leaders of the TBIA such as M.I. Patel and N.A. Camay threatened to denounce Sastri to the Indian government.[13] P.S. Aiyar, the founder of the strongly anti-SAIC *African Chronicle* and at the time associated with the Free Press and *The Hindu*, wrote anti-Sastri pieces for the Indian press. Aiyar's writings greatly perturbed Sastri, as he thought that Aiyar deliberately peppered them with a good dose of lies.[14] He lamented to Habibullah that the TBIA leadership was adamant to 'pose as martyrs or the victims of a faithless government', rather than working towards an amicable solution.[15] He confessed that the Machiavellian in him had considered supporting a proposal from Natal Indians to start a counter-organization in the Transvaal, but gave up after considering the consequences of him being seen as partisan.

'A tendency to schism', responded Habibullah, 'seems to be the bane of our race',[16] and assured Sastri of the government's full support against this slandering and for Sastri's efforts towards reconciliation.[17] Gandhi too sent a letter of support, urging Sastri not to be distressed by Aiyar's propaganda. In a rare display of immodesty, the Mahatma assured him that 'no real stir will be made in India on the S. African question unless I stir'.[18]

However, as things progressed, the hoped-for reconciliation was achieved with another split, this time within the TBIA. On 18 December 1927, a large faction of the TBIA, supporting re-affiliation with the SAIC, held a mass meeting and reconstituted itself as the Transvaal Indian Congress (TIC). Two weeks later, at the Annual Conference of the SAIC held in the mineral town of Kimberley, the TIC officially joined the SAIC.

Over 100 Congress representatives had gathered in Kimberley, housed and fed by a local businessman, Ahmed Mahomed, between 2 and 5 January 1928. Here, the SAIC addressed the concerns about the dominance of Natal in intra-organizational matters. It welcomed an equal number of 30 delegates from each province and appointed a delegation to meet the minister consisting of two delegates each from Natal, the Cape and Transvaal. The headquarters of the SAIC were also moved from Natal to the Transvaal.[19] The Kimberley Conference also welcomed for the first time eight Indians from Rhodesia as 'fraternal delegates'. Also for the first time, the South African government sent its representatives and the Indian government was represented by Sastri, giving the organization an official sanction of both countries.[20]

The show of unity in Kimberley was not without its detractors. On 28 December 1927, those who were opposed to the new Transvaal body as well as those who in general were opposed to the Cape Town Agreement came together to form another organization, the South African Indian Federation (SAIF). Aiyar was instrumental in its formation. The SAIF's founding document repudiated the Cape Town Agreement for being 'of no practical advantage' to South African Indians. Instead, the SAIF promised to work for obtaining for Indians a status equal to the Coloureds in South Africa.[21] The leftover TBIA affiliated with the SAIF and repudiated their 'misguided compatriots – a few Patidars and Tamils, and a sprinkling of Muslims' who were 'lured into a trap' by the SAIC.[22] Both the TBIA and SAIF remained a minority in South African Indian politics, however, even though their views were propagated through two newspapers: the *African Chronicle* and *Indian Views*.

Even though the two main warring factions had come together, the difficulties of condonation did not end. The Immigration Department insisted on knowing how exactly the SAIC planned to prevent fraudulent entrants. A known practice in the Transvaal and the Cape was of tampering the registration certificates of those who had already emigrated and re-using them for the new entrants. The department had insisted on the emigres returning their registration certificates which was no longer possible because under the agreement they could retain their domicile for three years. Consequently, the department now decided to ask all resident Indians to register with their old certificates, which would be cancelled and replaced with new certificates.

Any idea of forceful registration was repugnant to Indians in the Transvaal and Cape Town, especially in light of the history of Gandhi-led passive resistance campaigns against compulsory registration.[23] Further, as per Malan's assurance, those found with false certificates would be charged first, and then condoned. Often the gap between a policy and its local implementation could be precarious. Local officials were notoriously prejudiced against Indians, and thus more likely to prosecute Indians for these offences. In fact, in several cases, Sastri had to personally intervene when local officials proved difficult.[24] This made Indians reluctant to register.

A more controversial issue was that the Transvaal Indians claimed that the Gandhi–Smuts Agreement had already condoned all those who had entered until then. In other words, they reasoned that since those with fraudulent certificates until 1913 had already been pardoned, they should not need to individually re-apply. Not only was re-application insulting, but also the new regulations prevented those who were condoned from bringing their families. This meant that those among the previously condoned who had not yet brought their families to South Africa would no longer be able to do so. This unfairly discriminated against them vis-à-vis those whose families were already in South Africa.[25]

Until now, in his negotiations with Malan, Sastri had managed to secure important concessions. Minor sons of those condoned under the current scheme were also given registration certificates. If the protection certificates under the Condonation Scheme were challenged and barred in a court of law, Malan promised to bring an amendment to the legislation to make them legal.[26] Sastri now took up the matter of discrepancy regarding families with Malan's department. The department contradicted these claims about a condonation scheme in the Gandhi–Smuts Agreement and showed him official documents. The language of the agreement between Gandhi and Smuts was vague and merely advised immigration officers that Indians who could prove themselves to have been residing in the Union before 1 August 1910 should not be disturbed. It was expected, however, that those who entered illegally would take steps to regularize their status. Accordingly, individuals had to apply to legalize their status and around 400 Indians had gained such certificates. A separate condonation scheme was announced in 1915 but withdrawn in 1916. In other words, the 1913 blanket condonation, which Transvaal Indians seemed primed to fight for, was a myth.

Sastri confronted the Transvaal leadership of the SAIC with official documents. They admitted to having misled Sastri on the facts. Miffed, Sastri complained of bad faith.[27] It was unethical, he wrote to Habibullah, for those who had entered illegally and procured fraudulent certificates to insist that the government should not require them to get legal documents, especially when the government had agreed to consider their circumstances and condone them. The detractors also provided no alternative to the Condonation Scheme, thereby empowering the government to lawfully deport the illegal entrants. Tyson wrote in his diary:

> [The Transvaalers'] attitude towards the Minister's scheme is to 'look a gift horse in the mouth' and to claim as a right what is offered as a gift – to claim that and much more. They are going entirely the wrong way about these things and are a sore trial to Mr. Sastri, greatly trying even his patience … it is impossible beyond a certain point to take up the cudgels for people whose whole presence here (I am speaking of these illegal migrants) is the result of fraud … we have very few friends there among the Indian community.[28]

Meanwhile, the SAIC executive wrote to Gandhi, asking him to clarify whether he had indeed obtained protection for all entrants with fraudulent certificates. Gandhi sent back a terse and cryptic response: 'settlement covered by correspondence … strongly advise pulling full case before Sastriji and then accept his guidance'.[29]

Sastri fretted that Gandhi had opened another front with the use of the word 'settlement' and what that meant. But he was also relieved that the Mahatma had shown full faith in his leadership. Tired of repeatedly going over the same argument with the Transvaal Indians, Sastri wrote bitterly:

> I shall be a happy man when this wretched business is over, for it is the experience which I would not go through again for all the world. If the men of the Transvaal were in Mr. Gandhi's time at all like what they are now, he has indeed performed miracles with them. He cannot help smiling at my complaints.[30]

Sastri made yet another appeal directly to Malan,[31] who declined to consider the 1913 line but partially relented by granting that those who had obtained condonation certificates under any earlier scheme would not need it again.[32] They would also retain their right to bring their family. On Sastri's request, Malan's department also issued instructions to local offices not to harass the applicants.[33] Sastri had pushed Malan as far as he could.

The public meetings on condonation were contentious and wore Sastri down even more. On 27 May 1928, at a large gathering with the Transvaal Indians, Sastri spoke for an hour and half. An even longer, and more confrontational, meeting followed a few days later in Cape Town. His speech and the question and answers session took over three hours (as everything had to be translated into Hindustani) and representatives from the SAIF got into severe arguments with the local leadership of the SAIC. He wrote to Habibullah that he was 'threatened, bullied and cajoled', and heard 'brave talk of passive resistance, of readiness to be deported rather than surrender the fruits of the 1914 settlement'.[34] He addressed another meeting of Indians in the Midlands, Natal, with about 750 attendees on 1 July. This meeting, although not as stormy as the one in Cape Town, was still considerably charged. It didn't help that Sorab Rustumji, the chair, took an off-hand attitude towards critics, and only an occasional intervention from Sastri calmed things down.[35]

By early July 1928, even the position of the Union government had begun to harden. What did not help was that seven Indians were caught trying to make an illegal entry on 6 July, which caused a furore. Such incidents compromised Sastri's ability to negotiate further with the government. The Condonation Scheme was gazetted on 29 July 1928, and the last date for application was 30 September 1928.

The numbers of applications were worryingly low in the late winter of July and August 1928. To encourage more people to apply, Sastri addressed various meetings in Durban and Transvaal in August and September.[36] Meanwhile, the SAIF continued to undermine his efforts. It organized a conference in Cape Town in September where the Agent and the SAIC were roundly condemned.[37] The pace of applications increased measurably in the last ten days however. Overall, 1,616 applications were made, bringing the issue to a close.

## III

Although Sastri's mandate concerned mainly the two issues of assisted emigration and upliftment, from time to time he was also called upon to intervene on other issues concerning Indians. The Liquor Bill was one such issue which almost put the agreement in jeopardy.

The Liquor Bill had first been introduced in 1925. One of the clauses of this bill, Clause 107, barred employment for Africans and Indians in any profession concerning manufacturing, processing, sale and serving of liquor. About 3,000 Indians, employed mainly as waiters, were likely to lose their jobs as a consequence. Indians expected the clause to be withdrawn after the Cape Town Agreement since it contravened its spirit. But the Union government reintroduced these provisions, albeit as Clause 104, in September 1927.

The politics of drafting the bill, however, was entwined in the tensions brewing within the Union government. Tielman Roos, the Minister for Justice and the person in charge of the bill, was locked in what was seen as a battle of succession with Malan within the National Party. As bitter rivals, Roos and Malan had been on opposing sides in a controversy over the Flag Bill. Roos was intent on sabotaging the Cape Town Agreement, seen as Malan's baby, and saw Clause 104 as an opportunity. Malan, as Sastri quickly realized, was not ready to put his personal capital at stake and bluntly told a SAIC delegation that such measures were never meant to be excluded by the Cape Town Agreement.[38] Even the *Natal Mercury* disputed Malan's reasoning. Calling the Liquor Bill 'unjust', the paper argued that the Union government would in effect be 'wrecking the one diplomatic success it has achieved during its term of office'.[39] Tyson was convinced that Sastri would ask the Indian government to recall him if the bill was passed.[40] The SAIC sent distress cables to the Indian government appealing for its intervention.[41]

Just before the bill came up for discussions in the parliament in February 1928, Sastri found himself 'in the thick of ... indescribable machinations, plottings and intrigues' as he negotiated across party lines to secure votes against the bill. He had travelled to Cape Town and held several meetings with key leaders, the likes of Malan, Duncan, Colonel Creswell, Thomas Smartt and Morris Alexander.[42] Tylor wrote in his diary: 'nearly everyone has a view, always very strongly held, either for or against cl. 104, and as a matter when it comes before the House is to be treated as non-party we find ourselves ranged with, or "up against", all sorts of queer people'.[43]

To break the deadlock, Sastri sought a direct interview with Roos and met him on 7 February. Somewhat miraculously, in a 'very friendly interview',[44] Roos agreed to drop the clause, emphasizing that he was ready to do this not because it clashed with the agreement but because it would keep a good atmosphere for the emigration scheme. The explanation was not entirely to Sastri's liking, but he was willing to let it slide for the greater good.[45] Soon thereafter, Roos announced the withdrawal of the clause (however, the limitations on Africans remained) much to the relief of the Indian community.

Another issue that came up during his tenure was the matter of trade licensing in the Transvaal. Indians were routinely refused trade licences by the prejudiced, all-white licensing board. Their only recourse was an appeal to the court, with the rider that their case had to reasonably suggest that the refusal was only on the basis of colour. A Transvaal Provincial Council member named Schonken introduced an ordinance to take away this right to appeal to the court, on the plea that this was a 'provincial matter' within the legislative domain of the Provincial Council. His ordinance would leave the Transvaal Indians without any chance of appeal and justice. It also contravened the agreement where the Union government had promised to consider entrenching the Indian right to appeal to courts if existing trade licensing were to be revised.

This being a provincial matter, the Union government did not have the right to intervene. If put to a vote, the ordinance would easily pass; no European member would vote against it although the council was led by the National Party. It would then impose a difficult choice on the Union government and the Governor General. A passed resolution would go to Athlone for assent, who could choose to protect the agreement by vetoing the bill and antagonize National Party supporters. Or he could maintain the tradition of non-intervention in provincial affairs and put the agreement in jeopardy. To avert such a situation, Sastri lobbied Hertzog to prevent the ordinance from being introduced in the council. Hertzog reassured Sastri privately. A few days later Schonken got involved in a criminal case. His forced absence also lapsed his motion, and the matter was quietly dropped.[46]

Sastri's incessant lobbying efforts and personal influence had contributed to these successes. But they had also demonstrated that the agreement could be easily sabotaged by political and personal interests within South African politics. It was important, he felt, to assert the non-party character of the agreement and its anniversary on 21 February was an opportune moment.

With his staff, Sastri organized a banquet to celebrate the anniversary. To make the participation as wide as possible, he had originally considered inviting all the members of the Union parliament along with the Governor General.[47] But the Liquor Bill controversy had derailed those efforts. By the time the clause was withdrawn, there was little time left to organize a big affair. So a select group of 34 members of parliament from the major parties were sent invitations; 27 of them accepted.

Hertzog readily agreed, and so did Malan and Roos. Sastri was also keen to invite his nemesis and the main opposition leader, Smuts. Given the history they shared, Smuts had not only kept his distance from Sastri, but also targeted the agreement in his political rallies. On the afternoon of 13 February 1928, Duncan dragged Sastri into Smuts' office in the parliament building for an unplanned rendezvous. Smuts was cordial but indicated a previous engagement to get out of attending the banquet. However, he agreed to his party members accepting invitations. The old diplomatic foes spent an hour together, discussing mostly the Simon Commission; and as was fitting for their only close meeting in South Africa, much of it was spent sparring on whether Indians should boycott the Simon Commission. Sastri favoured the boycott, Smuts opposed it, and all Sastri had to say about Smuts was: '[h]e talks like an Anglo-Indian'.[48]

On 21 February, the anniversary banquet at Mt Nelson Hotel in Cape Town was well attended.[49] Hertzog, Malan and Duncan gave impressive speeches, in particular lauding Sastri's work in making the agreement a success.[50] Hertzog acknowledged that the agreement had allowed the Afrikaners 'who are made out to be the most stubborn in their prejudices' appreciate the 'viewpoint of India'.[51] Malan put it thus:

> One result of the Agreement ... is that South Africa has discovered India, and India has discovered South Africa. India does not look today upon South Africa ... as a country where common justice was absent, and we ourselves look on India to play today as a country where there is understanding of our problems, and to a great extent a sympathy with

us in our different problems, resulting in assistance being rendered to us as far as possible.[52]

This is probably the farthest the two South African leaders would come to acknowledge the racism in their country. Duncan, making Sastri's favourite speech of the evening, was even more effusive on the agreement: 'The Agreement has brought about a method of approaching these questions by friendly discussion, and coming, if possible, to an agreement rather than being left to coercion. It is an example set for the world. It is bound to have far-reaching effects the world over.'[53] In two years' time, the South African government would go on to denounce India and its approach towards the agreement, but for now the words sounded like manna. Smuts, who had remained uneasily quiet until then, would also go on to attack the agreement later in the year. In a speech in October 1928, with elections in sight, he criticized the Hertzog government for the agreement which 'gave Indians firmer ground under foot than they had ever before'.[54] In a backhanded compliment, he called Sastri 'the most honoured man in South Africa' who has 'proved too clever for the Government of Hertzog'.[55] Hertzog, in turn, accused Smuts of 'fanning into flame the embers of racial feeling' in trying to 'canvas for votes'.[56] It was quite an unusual turn in South African politics where Hertzog was complaining about Smuts stoking racial hatred against Indians. Sastri protested to Duncan that Smuts was unnecessarily dragging the agreement into a political fight. Duncan reassured him that it would not become an election issue. Smuts did not raise the issue again, due largely to Duncan's quiet persuasion.[57]

## IV

Sastri's involvement with affairs in the Transvaal brought him into close contact with the province's academic-turned-administrator, Jan Hofmeyr. Both liberals shared political beliefs but also connected cerebrally. Similar to his earlier Natal-wide tour, Hofmeyr proposed to Sastri a tour in the Transvaal in order to create greater sympathy for the Indian cause. Accepting this suggestion, Sastri toured the province in September 1928, travelling to Krugersdorp, Heidelberg, Potchefstroom, Klerksdorp, Ventersdorp and Springs.[58] This was the heartland of Afrikanerdom and the hotbed of anti-Indian feeling. However, by now South Africans had warmed up to Sastri's presence and frequent references to his oratorical wizardry in newspapers helped. His meetings were well attended and usually cordial, except at Klerksdorp, where things turned somewhat ugly.

Sastri was due to speak in Klerksdorp on 15 September 1928. The banquet in his honour in a local hotel was attended 'by 138 Europeans', a newspaper emphasized, including the mayor, the resident commissioner and the police commissioner. There was one notable absentee, however: the deputy mayor, Morgan Evans. A dentist by profession, Evans was also a founding member of the anti-Asiatic League in West Transvaal. The previous evening, he had organized a protest meeting to boycott Sastri, where he issued a 'dodger', calling any concessions to 'coolies' (a term of derision for Indians) a grave danger to the national interests of Afrikaner youth.

After the banquet, Sastri and his audience moved to the Railway Institute Hall for his talk. The hall had already been broken into, and some front seats were occupied by Evans and his supporters, who booed and hooted. They heckled and interrupted Sastri as he spoke. About ten minutes into his speech, the lights went out, a match was lit and in no time a gas bomb was flung towards the platform. Fumes and the ensuing melee made it impossible to contain the audience in the room. The police were quick to vacate the venue. A woman and a child were carried to the hospital and some women fainted, but others were safe.

The gathering resumed outside the venue, as those assembled implored Sastri to continue his speech. Unharmed and seemingly unperturbed, Sastri recommenced: 'Ladies and Gentlemen, as I was saying before the venue of the meeting was altered from indoor to the open air!' His wit was intact, and so was the audience's as they burst into laughter. Sastri made an eloquent case for the rights of Indians in South Africa.

After the eventful evening, Sastri retired to his hotel room and slept soundly, unaware of commotion outside his room. Two men, it turned out, had barged into the hotel with a tin of petrol, intending to burn it down. Once again, the police were vigilant and apprehended the two men before they acted.[59]

Messages of concern poured in from all parts of South Africa and India, including from Athlone, Hertzog, Malan, Irwin and Gandhi. Hertzog in particular was in 'towering rage' when he heard about the incident,[60] and called it 'one of the most deplorable incidents that ever occurred in South Africa'.[61] The *Natal Advertiser* summed up the outrage more perspicaciously:

> Martyrdom is the food that unpopularity thrives on. Rotten eggs and stink bombs do not hinder the Indian cause. They help it. The hooligans of Klerksdorp did not

win on Saturday. Mr. Sastri won. Today, metaphorically if not actually, South Africa with its sovereign status and its excessive national self-consciousness is busy apologizing to India for the savagery and intolerance of its own white inhabitants towards a cultured and dignified gentleman who, before now, has adorned the most exclusive diplomatic and social circles of Europe. This is the pass to which our people have been brought by their own fellows! This is the sort of figure South Africa is being made to cut in the eyes of the world! This is the fruit of that sturdy plant of European self-consciousness that wants always to keep the n****r in his place, and the Indian in his, and to see that both places are always at an untouchable distance from the perfumed elegance of a sahib race![62]

## V

A good part of Sastri's 19 months in South Africa was consumed by travelling around the country. In 1928, he spent in total a month in transit alone. Crossing the length and breadth of the country, he delivered lectures on political, philosophical and theological issues at several universities and clubs, in Johannesburg, Pretoria, Cape Town, Stellenbosch, Durban, Pietermaritzburg, Potchefstroom, Kimberley, Rustenburg and Alice (Fort Hare). His range of topics included Hindu philosophy, Gandhi, Gokhale, caste, Christianity, missions in India, the idea of public service, women in India, world peace, Sanskrit literature, non-violence and the labour movement in India. On the whole, they created a sterling impression on his Indian and European audiences alike.

Even his critics acknowledged that through the sheer force of his personality, he was able to straddle the colour line easily, and his tenure was diplomatically a period where the governments of India and South Africa at least broadly agreed on the common principles driving their relationship.

Sastri's tenure was not entirely uncontroversial, however. We have noted previously the strong criticisms and opposition he encountered in the Transvaal, especially from the SAIF. His insistence on the British Commonwealth as an ideal polity drew strong denunciation from several Indians. Manilal Gandhi, the editor of *Indian Opinion* complained to his father that Sastri 'crossed the limits' in praising the empire.[63] The president of East African Indian National Congress, S. Achriar, called Sastri 'Britain's advertising agent', panning the 'typical old school Madrassi brahmin' for being 'cowardly' and 'servile'.[64] *Indian Views* found his pronouncements on the empire 'nauseating'.[65]

Sastri's response was that he had remained consistent in his views on the empire and that 'people must make allowance for the difference in latitude and longitude'.[66] Gandhi would agree, and counselled his son:

> If we judge Sastriji by the standard of satyagraha, we would do him injustice. If we look to the service which he renders to the nation, though in Government service, we shall see that he has no equal. If, then, he were to plunge into the field of satyagraha, he would probably have no equal there too. It is my belief that no one else would give as much satisfaction, through his uprightness, as Sastriji does. In my view, he sincerely follows his conscience in everything he does.[67]

His racial politics was also suspect. In public, he never made any patronizing remarks towards Africans, but in his private communications he would often mention that Indians were more advanced than Africans when it came to standards of civilization. He actively discouraged Natal Indians to link the issue of Indian education with Africans, driven in part also by pragmatic concerns. He also advised against Indians joining efforts at non-European unity. His argument was that the Indian government, which he represented, obviously could not speak for Africans and hence joining Indian and African interests would compromise India's interventions. Moreover, the lack of funding for education for Indians in Natal was an issue specifically about Indians, since the provincial government on the whole had fully utilized educational subsidies for the rest of its non-European population. Furthermore, the South African government at times disingenuously interpreted the 'upliftment clause'. Indians understood it to be 'upliftment' to the European level, while another point of view, privately expressed by members of the Union Cabinet, including Malan, was upliftment to the Coloured level.[68] The separation of Indian demands from non-European demands, in Sastri's view, was also to ensure that the government did not cheat them on the promises made under the agreement. But an acknowledgement of difference is not the same as an assertion of superiority. Sastri surely leaned towards the latter, as we saw in the previous chapter in his response to Charles Loram.

He also made little effort to interact with Africans. He was squarely focused on changing the opinion of the European population, as was his mandate, and his public diplomacy was reflective of this. During his time, there is only one record of him addressing a predominantly African gathering, at Fort Hare. A cursory look through *Abanya Bantu* for 1927 and 1928 shows no mention of Sastri. It is likely that Sastri interacted with black intelligentsia in Kimberley (he certainly met the two stalwarts, John T. Jabavu and Sol Plaatje, in Kimberley) but there is very little to suggest he made any efforts to interact with Africans. There is not a single letter in his collections written to any South African black leader. However, there are records of his attending meetings organized by South African Coloureds, where he even went on to espouse the cause of the unity of non-Europeans.[69]

But he also received criticism from some local Indians when he did try to stray across the racial line. Habib Motan, a SAIF member, wrote an insulting letter to Sastri after the latter visited Fort Hare. It was 'humiliating to India's national honour and civilization', Motan lashed out, that 'our Agent General is trying to bring us down to such a low level [of Africans and Coloureds]'.[70] Motan's letter stirred even the poet Rabindranath Tagore, who wrote: 'Such a colour prejudice from an Indian who has himself suffered from colour prejudice of the Europeans is to me revolting to the extreme. It is neither in accord with the Indian sentiment nor with the Indian national honour and civilization.'[71]

## VI

By mid-July 1928, Sastri had made up his mind to leave South Africa, although both Irwin and Habibullah strongly implored him to reconsider. Earlier in the year, he had agreed to their request to extend his stay by six months beyond the one year he had originally agreed. Athlone, who had been exceedingly helpful to him, had personally insisted that he stay, and he could not refuse. His health had also improved considerably. The South African weather had been remarkably healing for his troubled heart. He was able to walk four to five miles without tiring. His family and friends, including Polak, Venkatarama Sastri and Bajpai, insisted he stay longer, as did the SAIC.[72] But by July, the bitterness of the Condonation Scheme had made him determined to return.[73]

Based on his experience, however, he listed a few qualities for the next incumbent to Habibullah. His successor, he argued, should be a non-official, who was thoroughly secular, intellectually forceful and a good speaker.[74] The Agent's main task in South Africa was to convince Europeans about an agreement that their own government had signed. This work required a political passion for service of the country rather than a dispassionate, machine-like efficiency of a bureaucrat. Further, Hindu–Muslim bitterness, which had crept into politics in India, must not be allowed to enter South African Indian politics through the Agent. The Agent must be thoroughly secular in outlook.

The qualities he wanted in his successor also elucidate how he saw his own role as the Agent. For him, the Agent was constantly under the European gaze. Acting as the 'official speaker of the Indian community',[75] the Agent's primary function was, as Andrews argued, to shatter the image of the Indian as 'coolie'.[76] The *Cape Times* editorialized on his departure:

> Before Sastri came to South Africa, the popular idea of the Indian leader was of a glib, plausible, not too honest person, with slightly ludicrous ways and an inflated idea of his own importance. The mere sight of Mr. Sastri, dignified and imperturbable among a hustling crowd at some official function, has withered that idea in the minds of numberless South Africans. … And the thought has come into the mind of many South Africans, when they have seen him for the first time, that, if he is typical of the best of India, their ideas about India and her people must be sadly wrong.[77]

However, such paeans to Sastri on 'embodying the best of India' are also revealing of another subtext: the Agent as being the arch-civilizer. His inordinate focus on education and 'upliftment' of local Indians in his work could partly be attributed to the nature of his mandate, but it also comes out of a keen desire to 'civilize' the overseas Indian. To convince the whites of the justness of their demands, local Indians had to do their own bit at 'civilizing' themselves. The Agent ought to be, in a double-play on the word, an agent of such change, through his personal bearing as well as his political conduct.

Therefore, the Agent should be able to straddle the racial divide, and be invited to European spaces and gatherings. Whether in a university, a public meeting or political circles, the Agent must be admitted without question into the highest circles, Sastri reasoned. His stress on 'entry' through what could be called performative Brahminness, with an emphasis on displaying culture, learning and purity of individual conduct and bearing, against the common image of a social outcaste 'coolie', endorsed a form of politics which had long-term ramifications. As Uma Dhupelia-Mesthrie's pioneering work has shown, while in the first years of the Agency this emphasis on entry may have had a significant symbolic import, the excitement wore off soon when Sastri's successors repeatedly emphasized their own elevation as a sign of the uplift of the community and in the process undercut any political struggles for tangible rights.[78] Further, from Sastri onwards, the Agents aligned themselves with the commercial Indian elite, and kept studied distance from political groups comprising 'colonial-born' Indians, the descendants of indentured labourers.

Sastri's diplomacy thus came at the cost of weakening movements for political rights. Performative Brahminness guards against pollution of all kinds, most of all messy subaltern politics. Sastri's successors followed his template and prevented South African Indians from going on passive resistance campaigns, and asking for political rights.[79] In early 1930s, Manilal Gandhi, writing in *Indian Opinion*, complained that the Agency had 'killed the manhood' of the Indian community, making the South African Indian Congress 'weak and helpless' as the Agent stood between the South African government and the Indian population.[80]

Sastri's suggestion for his successor was his Servants of Society colleague R.P. Paranjpe. But the Indian government decided on Kurma V. Reddi. Sastri was not overly enthused with the selection. Reddi, as we can recall from our discussions on the Joint Select Committee on the Montford Reforms in 1919, came from the Justice Party whose politics was quite opposed to Sastri's person as well as his politics. The Justice Party also took an overtly pro-government stance on most issues. Reddi, the *Mahratta* noted, was 'out-and-out a Government man', and the *Leader* opined that 'a worse selection' could not have been made.[81] Notably, both these papers, and the *Indian Social Reformer* and *Bombay Chronicle*, often severely critical of Sastri while in India, were unanimous in praise for Sastri's work in South Africa.[82]

The Agent's last few months in South Africa were spent in travelling. In late September 1928, he went on a ten-day tour of the Victoria Falls, and addressed meetings in Bulawayo, Livingstone and Salisbury (now Harare).[83] In December 1928 and January 1929, several farewells were organized for him in different cities. In Cape Town, several people, including the Malans, came to the station to bid him goodbye. In Johannesburg, the South African mining royalty, the Oppenheimers, received him at the station, and hosted him in their house for the duration of his stay. Hertzog organized a farewell for Sastri at Pretoria Club. From there he left for Kimberley, where again he was very warmly received, and his farewell was well attended by people of all races. Even the African stalwart John T. Jabavu made an appearance.

In the farewell messages, government ministers including the Prime Minister, public figures, newspaper editorials and prominent associations paid rich tributes to his work. Hailing him as 'the apostle of reconciliation', various commentators noted that while he may have been able to clinch some material victories concerning the upliftment of Indians, his real contribution lay in demolishing the idea of the Indian as a 'coolie'.[84] The claim, as noted, is certainly more about symbolism than effective change, but it did reverberate strongly. The liberal intellectual, Howard Pim, put it succinctly: 'there never has been a mission in this country, in which the personality of the envoy has had the greater effect'.[85] The bishop of the cathedral in Johannesburg where Sastri gave a lecture on 'Christianity as a Non-Christian sees it' said: 'As I watched him on the pulpit, pleading for the brotherhood that Christ had advocated, his face shining with the radiance of altruism, I felt that Christ himself was speaking. I felt that I should kneel and worship.'[86]

The veteran journalist Vere Stent wrote a farewell letter in *Pretoria News*:

> Reading your speeches, knowing you personally, I find myself wishing that we, in South Africa could boast of a House of Assembly, the members of which approached you if only to some small degree in patriotism, altruism and intellect. In all this Union, we have only one man approaching you in intellect and love of the country, another who comes near in honesty – even in politics – and a steadfast determination not to do wrong, even though no good comes of it, and one who imposes upon himself your ascetic regime. We have no Sastri.[87]

But this veneer also hid a starker truth: that his tenure only managed to postpone the inevitable. The limited period of this diplomatic romance between two countries which remained at loggerheads for most of the twentieth century was achieved partly because Sastri's less than two years produced on average the highest numbers of yearly emigrants to India. Rumours that the South African government would stop the bonus for emigrants after he left were already rife, albeit without any truth in them. The consensus on the agreement had already begun to wane. General elections were due for 1929, and the South African political parties had upped the anti-Indian rhetoric.[88] Despite Sastri's protests, Smuts' South African Party's programme mentioned going back to permanent repatriation.[89] The month Sastri left was also the

**11: The Agency**

Sastri with Kodanda Rao and John Tyson. Kodanda Rao had accompanied Sastri as his private secretary from the Servants of India Society, while Tyson was plucked out of Bengal and sent to assist Sastri with administrative matters. Kodanda Rao later wrote the first biography of Sastri, while Tyson too was attempting to write a book on Sastri's South Africa work, but could never finish it.

last instance in which more than 300 emigrants boarded a vessel for India. By the time he returned to the country in 1932 as part of the Indian delegation for a round table conference, the assisted emigration scheme to India was seen as a failure.

## VII

To honour Sastri's South Africa work, the Indian government proposed his name for the KCSI (King Commander of the Order to the Star of India) and sought his consent. A few years before, after his dominions tour, the Viceroy had deliberately deleted his name from the list. This time Sastri refused to take the honour. He decided to follow Gokhale, who had also similarly declined.[90] He was 'more honoured with the honour refused than with it accepted', Gokhale had written then.[91] Sastri now concurred.

On 28 January 1929, the Agency, consisting of Ricketts, Tyson, Kodanda Rao and Sastri, had a quiet breakfast at Currie Road and proceeded to the quay in Durban. The SS *Karoa* awaited them, and so did a huge crowd that included several friends and well-wishers. The captain delayed the sailing time by an hour to enable people to greet and see off Sastri. At 9 am, as the last ropes were being cast off, the crowd gave three cheers. A garlanded Sastri came out on the deck, raised his turban in his hand, and said his final words: 'For the last time, ladies and gentlemen, goodbye!'. Tyson allowed his ICS steel frame to emotionally crumble a bit, writing: 'So the old man has gone, and Africa is the poorer, as most men will admit. I also am infinitely the poorer ... Things cannot be the same here now that he has gone ... it is a sad business, this parting!'[92]

11

# Conclusion: An Amiable Usurper

## I

The business of a biographer is, C.L.R. James reminds us, to keep in mind that 'great men [and women] make history, but only such history as it is possible for them to make'. A biographer's task is 'to portray the limits of those necessities and the realization, complete or partial, of all possibilities'.[1] A biographer in essence is almost always a historian of the limits on the individual.

Our narrative of Sastri's diplomatic life ends here, but before we turn to conclude with the key themes, we have the small matter of 17 years to talk about. Our narrative ends in January 1929 and Sastri lived until April 1946. It is only fair that we at least offer a synoptic view of the rest of his life.

Sastri returned from South Africa to be taken off to East Africa by Irwin in May 1929. The Commission on Closer Union of the East African Commission, also known as the Hilton Young Commission, had recently submitted its report to the British government. The majority report rejected the demand for a more federated and self-governing polity that the whites had demanded.[2] A federal union, along the lines of South Africa, would have given them greater political distance from London and more autonomy to form a white supremacist state. The report took a more pro-African and pro-Indian stance, recommending a common franchise and common electoral roll for all races, with a rider that the consent of whites must be requisitioned before a common roll was adopted. It recommended a closer union between the three territories of Kenya, Uganda and Tanganyika but only for the purposes of coordinating native policy. However, Leo

**12: The family**

Upon his arrival back in India, Sastri preferred to return to his family home rather than live in the Servants of Indian Society house in Pune. Here, his wife Lakshmi is to his left and his daughter Rukmini to his right. His son, Sankaran, and daughter-in-law, Sita, stand behind them. Sastri's grandchildren, Srinivasan, Parvathi, Alamelu and Seshu, sit in front.

Amery, the Secretary of State for Colonies, unabashedly sympathetic to the interests of Kenyan whites, discarded the recommendations of this commission and as compensation sent a permanent under-secretary, Samuel Wilson, to ascertain local reactions.

To minimize the damage of Amery's actions for Indians in East Africa, Irwin proposed to send Sastri to help/assist with their case. Amery conditioned that Sastri would not raise the issue of the common roll.³ Sastri refused to go with his hands tied behind his back. Very reluctantly, Amery relented.⁴

Arriving in Mombasa in 1929, Sastri brimmed with confidence from his work in South Africa. He conducted several meetings with prominent white leaders, including Delamere, to urge them to agree to a common roll, albeit with an understanding that even with a common roll the European majority in the legislature would be preserved. Meanwhile, playing the mediator, he counselled Kenyan Indians to work towards seeking the consent of the white community. Privately, he also recommended entering councils on communal franchise under protest, and jettisoning non-cooperation. This understandably earned him the wrath of a section of the Indian community. And not much love from whites either; he was subjected to personal insults from both sides.

In any case, his mission itself was cloaked in dishonesty by Amery. While Amery had given the Viceroy and Sastri to understand that Sastri was free to discuss the common roll, to Wilson his instructions were very clear: not to raise the common roll issue. Wilson's narrow official outlook 'untouched at any point by idealism' irked Sastri.⁵ He left East Africa 'in a spirit of gloom' with no prospect of any agreeable settlement.⁶ In his report, Sastri was frank and critical about the pro-white sympathies of Wilson and the Governor, Edward Grigg.⁷ He was eventually persuaded to remove certain bitter remarks about them.⁸ His report was published in March 1930.

By the time Sastri returned from East Africa, Labour had stormed back into power in England, so he was hopeful of a more sympathetic hearing in London. He was deputed to give evidence before the Joint Select Committee of parliament where he took a firmer position on the common roll. No longer did he insist on securing the consent of whites. The committee, to his utter dismay, rejected the common roll. The Kenya issue continued to undermine his faith in the empire.

The internal reforms in India remained his major preoccupation over the next few years. He participated very actively in the first two round table conferences held between 1930 and 1932 in London for political reforms in India, under the auspices of Ramsay MacDonald's prime ministership. Sastri played a crucial role in arranging for Irwin and Gandhi to meet, which led to the latter agreeing to participate in the second conference. At these conferences, the aim of dominion status was replaced by the idea of an Indian federation, comprised of British India and princely states. Initially, Sastri saw the proposed federation as a ploy to delay and dilute the demand for dominion status for British India. But after appeals by his liberal colleagues such as Sapru and M.R. Jayakar, he accepted it.⁹

From London, as soon as the second round table conference came to an end, Sastri was deputed to travel to South Africa for another conference. South Africa had reinstated the Asiatic Bill, largely because the number of Indian emigrants had dwindled after Sastri's departure from the country. The uplift principle was dependent on assisted emigration, and as the emigrants plummeted so did the South African government's commitment to the Cape Town Agreement. It was difficult, as Sastri admitted to Kodanda Rao, to pull the same trick twice.[10] At the conference, Sastri and his colleagues were able to convince South Africa to look into schemes of Indian emigration to other countries, such as British Guiana, Brazil, Tanganyika and Portuguese East Africa. A committee set up for this purpose produced a report in 1934 but the proposal was never followed up.[11]

Meanwhile, Sastri's health continued to deteriorate. Periods of strenuous activity were interspersed with long periods of rest, in which he continued to write and speak.[12] He declined an offer for the presidency of the Council of State. He was made Companion of Honour and given the Freedom of the City of Edinburgh. In 1932, H.A.L Fisher asked him to take the prestigious Rhodes Lectureship, which involved giving three lectures and spending some months in Oxford. Sastri requested postponement for a year on account of Laxmi's and his own deteriorating health, but eventually declined the following year on the advice of his physician.[13]

In June 1934, his wife, Lakshmi, passed away. Lakshmi has appeared very little in our narrative, and partly this is because her presence is fleeting in documents by, on and about Sastri. A biography is a prisoner of the documented life and, regrettably, Laxmi's life, like that of many women of fortitude and strong will, remains unexplored in this, yet another, biographical effort at Sastri. However, by all accounts, it was a loving relationship, encumbered by the bounds of tradition and patriarchy. Sastri's own letters to Laxmi, which would perhaps provide a more holistic assessment of their relations, cannot be located and are most probably lost.

Raja Annamalai Chettiar invited Sastri to return to his first love, education. He served as Vice Chancellor of Annamalai University from 1935 to 1940. In 1937, on Bajpai's request on behalf of the Indian government, he undertook a tour of Malaya to ascertain the condition of the Indian labourers. His report recommended continuing with non-recruited assisted emigration and the restoration of standard wages, after they had been reduced on account of the economic slump.

Between 1935 and his death, Sastri delivered numerous lectures. His series of lectures on Gokhale and Pherozeshah Mehta were published as books.¹⁴ Likewise, thumbnail sketches of his lectures and writings on other individuals were also published through the efforts of T.N. Jagadisan.¹⁵ These longish biographical sketches are consistently perspicacious but also delightfully playful in the art of analysing others, often layering the autobiographical with the biographical. It is only a pity that his own autobiography, written in the form of a series of short articles for the Tamil newspaper *Swadesamitran* in 1941, is rather plain, although very informative for a biographer.

Another enjoyable group of lectures and writings, ranging from personal reading preferences to political ideas about citizenship and world peace, appeared as *The Other Harmony*.¹⁶ He delivered 30 lectures on the *Ramayana* in 1944 in Madras, which, upon Gandhi's request, were curated into a book.¹⁷ The lectures treated Rama not as a god but as a human with decided failings and as someone who yearned to live by his *dharma*. These writings are rich resources on Sastri's breadth of knowledge and politics. Incredibly, he delivered these lectures, too, with a few jottings. Except in two instances, one on the Kenya issue at the invitation of Ali Imam in 1923 and another on Dinshaw Wacha's passing in 1940, his speeches were delivered with minimal notes.

After he returned from South Africa in 1929, Sastri was asked to resume his presidency of the Servants of India Society. However, he recused himself of the responsibility. His fragile health made him reluctant to perform the daily leadership responsibilities as well as travel to and spend longer periods in Poona. In the 1930s, he attended fewer and fewer of the society's events. By the early 1940s, he actively considered leaving it. He was pained at two decisions of the society, which caused him to offer his resignation. The first instance was the society's instruction to forbid its members from participating in any of the government's war committees. The decision was taken after Sastri had already joined the War Committee in Madras. Once the direction was passed by the society, he stopped attending the committee's meetings, but refused to resign on the principle that he could not step back from a position for the sake of public theatricality. The second, a more agonizing episode for Sastri, was in January 1943 when the society lent its support to the partition idea; Sastri sent his resignation (which was eventually not accepted). He remained to the very end of his time staunchly opposed to partition.¹⁸ In October 1945, Sastri issued a joint appeal, along with P.A. Wadia, K. Natarajan and Jahangir Petit. They argued that the principle of self-determination used for breaking up political entities was in contravention to all the lessons of the past. In an ever-shrinking world in which small political entities were becoming anachronistic, the deliberate breaking up of a well-knit unit into conflicting and rival powers went against the lessons of history and the currents of passing time.[19]

In the late 1920s, under younger leaders such as Nehru, the Congress moved from demanding dominion status to seeking full independence. Sastri was circumspect about the latter, even as late as the early 1940s when the Congress pushed full throttle for independence. Practically, he argued, dominion status was the same as independence; in fact the right to secede was implicit in it (as Ireland did in the 1930s). Under the circumstances, dominion status was both more likely as well as more profitable for India. While Sastri was certainly quite divorced from the aspirations of the country at the time, it is worth thinking how far he was from the reality of politics as such. After all, the 'Indian Independence Act of 1947' only granted dominion status to India and Pakistan, and post-independence India decided to continue its association as a Commonwealth member, albeit as a republic.

In these years, as in the past, Sastri remained a trenchant critic of the tactics of the Congress. He firmly opposed the Quit India Movement because of its anticipated violence and anarchy. He remained a reviled figure for the Congress' younger generation. A Congress fortnightly newsletter in 1936 wrote wryly:

> The Rt. Hon. Sir V.S. Srinivasa Sastri has decided to do many things. He would object to the Federal constitution, give the Indian states a place under the paramountcy of British India, enforce elementary education on a national scale, ruthlessly abolish all religious organizations 'that people would have to assemble under one banner' and introduce Hindustani as the national language of India. These are only a few items of his programme subject to a very modest condition that he should be appointed a dictator.[20]

Nehru, in particular, was very critical of Sastri, and in his *Autobiography* made several unkind references to him. Some of Nehru's comments were ill-informed, and at one point Gandhi offered to intervene, but Sastri politely declined. In private, Sastri thought of Nehru as 'a spoilt youth' whom Gandhi had destined for greatness but would 'collapse like a child's balloon' after Gandhi.[21]

## II

Sastri's first editorial in the *Servant of India* starts with Ranade's definition of the Indian liberal:

> The spirit of Liberalism implies a freedom from race and creed prejudices and a steady devotion to all that seeks to do justice between man and man, giving to the rulers the loyalty that is due to the law they are bound to administer, but securing at the same time to the people the equality which is their right under the law. Moderation implies the conditions of never vainly aspiring after the impossible or after too remote ideals, but striving each day to take the next step in the order of natural growth by doing the work that lies nearest to our hands in a spirit of compromise and fairness.[22]

Liberals do not make attractive polemicists: no wonder the term 'liberal' is often in contemporary times invoked as a term of derision. Revolutions, of the left or the right, are teeming with radical possibilities. The brimming romance of a political order careening towards utopia elevates politics into a moral battle between good and evil. Revolutionaries are seen as principled articulators of morality in politics, even if, as Ashis Nandy reminds us, the dream worlds of utopia often find their historical end in wretched dystopias. In contrast, liberals are by default believers in the politics of manoeuvre; for them, negotiation is politics. They value predictability and incrementalism in political conduct. As constant negotiators who prioritize compromise over steadfast adherence to moral certitudes, they often enter our history books as scheming and craven individuals.

Sastri was an unrepentant votary of reason who placed his faith in the moving force of a rational argument. His sense of morality was Kantian, that is, the belief that morals could only emerge from an unreserved application of reason. He would accede to the value of principles: they were one's truths, they were the ideals that stirred the march of history. But a blind, dogmatic adherence to these principles was to forget the social, contingent nature of reality. 'The empire of truth', as he once argued, 'is totalitarian; it tolerates no reservations; it cannot allow exceptions.'[23] He would rather err on the side of doubt than of truth; 'there is more faith in honest doubt than in half the creeds'.[24]

The Marxist credo that the oppressed have nothing but their chains to lose would be an anathema for Sastri. For him, as far as British India was concerned, losing constitutional politics was measurably worse, for it was the best defence against arbitrary British rule. Arbitrary rule is fundamentally a rule through exception, and the more institutions are strengthened, the more constitutional procedures are routinized, the less rationale the state, even a colonial state, has to appear arbitrary.

For a liberal, negotiation is not the curtailment, but the creation of possibilities. Sastri saw the revolutionary as someone who refused to engage rationally with matters at hand and sacrificed substantive politics for its sublime theatricality.

His understanding of politics, as with liberals in general, was entirely based on a fundamental distrust of mass politics. Much like the Anglophile liberals of the time, people and politics were seen in opposing binaries of irrational/emotional versus rational. The 'brutish mass', to use J.S. Mill's phrase, was irrational and volatile, and hence could only be represented and ruled by a qualified elite. He remained in his political articulation a proponent of what was called 'civilizational franchise', that is, franchise for those who could be shown to have leisure and, therefore, understanding of politics. Remaining mostly at the margins of popular movements, usually at the receiving end of their bitter criticisms, he preferred to view them with deep, elitist cynicism.[25]

His opposition to Gandhi's non-cooperation and civil disobedience came from this fundamental distrust of the masses. But equally, as he pointed out, Gandhi's non-cooperation was wrought by the circularity of its own argument. Its success relied on cooperation from the government in desisting from using violence. If the government resorted to violence, only the very disciplined, like Gandhi himself, would be able to refrain from responding with violence. A circle of violence, and consequently the end of non-cooperation, was inevitable in the very method of Gandhi's application.

For him, politics was always conducted within the confines of what was reasonable and possible. A cynic by inclination but an optimist by profession, he turned to rational discourse as the placeholder that limited the range of his cynicism and manoeuvred the space of possibility. In a vacuum of plausible alternatives, politics was overtaken by theatrics at best, anarchy at worst; a tendency of both revolutionaries and Gandhians, he would argue. Revolutionaries and anarchists sought to dismantle the institutions and start anew. With all the brooding excess of internal strife in India, of caste, of religion, of region, he did not think there was a political *tabula rasa* India could afford to create. The only alternative on the horizon was one of traditional rule, which was not merely lodged in India's historic past but was also ever-present in the other half of India, the princely states. This option was not worth salivating over. He had a fundamental dread of the past returning as India's future.

Sastri's political liberalism has a streak of conservative bite like that of Burke's and Mill's appeal for liberty, but speaking from the position of the emaciated he does not have the option of being puritan in his beliefs or articulation. Instead, he operates in what Jurgen Habermas calls a mode of 'communicative rationality'. His is an appeal for claiming a space for reasoned argument for those who have been cast out. To dialogue or not, for him, is not an option for the dispossessed. To speak is to assert oneself; but to dialogue, and dialogue continuously, is to reclaim one's voice. In politics, he could compromise to the extent that the ideal, or the principle, was not entirely lost; so long as one could navigate the crevices along the way and find alternative, more possible ways of reaching the principle. To insist on the fulfilment of the principle in the very first act, in the very moment of engagement, was to kill politics altogether. He would emphasize placing one's faith in reason; exactly the opposite of Gandhi, who placed his reason entirely at the service of faith.

Gandhi, the great 'anarch', in being the exact opposite of Sastri, also helps us unlock the answers about the political praxis of Sastri-ism. It is in this capacity to combine the two opposites, faith and reason, that Gandhi and Sastri speak to, about and past each other. Sastri was a virulent critic of Gandhi, but also, as the Mahatma acknowledged, someone who understood Gandhi's politics better than most. And this is why both Sastri and Gandhi, despite being on the opposite ends of politics, retained so much love – and that is indeed the right word – for each other.

Gandhi's own adherence to truth was totalitarian, a point that the Congress leaders often mistook for a strategic choice. Sastri would later equate Gandhi with Lord Rama precisely for this reason: both Gandhi and Rama made several mistakes, which either baffled their worshippers or pushed them to rationalize their idols' actions through recourse to specious arguments. But these mistakes were a natural part of the observance of *dharma*, of taking an absolutist position with regard to principles (Rama asking Sita for a purity test is one instance). Their observance of *dharma* did not make their wrongs right; it merely made them understandable. As the Cambridge liberal Isiah Berlin would later argue: liberalism entailed not an absolute adherence to principles, but managing diverging principles to emerge at a position of least harm. Sastri's liberal code prevented him from taking absolute positions, Gandhi's spiritual anarchism was loaded with no other options.

## III

On the limits of what is possible, what is often missed in our presentist writings on history is that India's independence from Britain was unimaginable up until the late 1920s, or some would argue even into the early 1940s. Except to the radical revolutionaries, the idea seemed outlandish. Despite the success of the Russian Revolution and the Irish Free State, the sheer scale of violence expected in a country of 300 million was inconceivable. In the late 1920s, when the Congress changed its slogan to complete independence at the insistence of its younger leaders like Nehru, it was more of an aspiration rather than a reality. It was largely the Second World War that forced the issue.

The accusation that liberals were very limited in their demands, of only wanting dominion status, must also then be placed at the feet of Gandhi and most of the Congress until the late 1920s. The cry for complete independence, no matter how enervating it was for the nationalist sentiment, remained for the most part of the 1930s a rhetorical call, which, from a liberal point of view, hindered rather than pushed further reforms. For the liberals, the Montagu–Chelmsford reforms not only provided India a semblance of internal voice, but also firmly placed the country on the path of incremental autonomy of which the 1935 Government of India Act was a successor. In any case, the *Swarajists* in the 1920s and the Congress in the mid-1930s accepted the reforms in due course. Indeed, the broad structural features of the post-independence Indian Constitution were retained from the 1935 act.

Dominion status, which was Sastri's demand even in the 1940s, was not starkly different from what Nehru eventually agreed to: India remained part of the Commonwealth even after becoming a republic. The dominions and India had little substantive differences of status, except in the matter of the titular head of state. A key rationale for Sastri in retaining dominion status, at least as a transitional arrangement, was the lack of an independent armed force. Sastri believed that India still needed Britain's military umbrella, because the leadership of India's military was still largely British. The transfer of power ensured that the military transition was drawn out, and Nehru certainly showed that India did not need Britain's military protection, although for a substantive period after independence India remained dependent on Britain for military supplies. If Sastri had been alive to see this, he would have endorsed the transition.

Another worry was the partition. Sastri's life-long aversion to grotesque violence in the pursuance of political freedom was key to his vehement opposition to partition. And it was clear that independence could not be achieved without it. In general, he opposed the movement towards national and, in India's case, sectional self-determination as a relic of the past order. Historical progress was shaping towards greater federations, he argued, not ethnic nation state, a view that Nehru would endorse and advance in his own writings and speeches.

In fact, although Nehru despised Sastri's politics, the post-1946 Nehru is remarkably similar to the pre-1946 Sastri: Brahmin liberal intellectuals, suave English-language orators, secular thinkers with a deep appreciation of the spiritual and cultural significance of the Hindu religion, critical of the liberal international order but with a reformative rather than a revolutionary intent, and proponents of the Commonwealth and Westminster institutions. Both also display a sublimated sense of Indian race pride, which pushed them to be highly critical of white racism but masked their own implicit racism against Africans through invocations of civilizational advance.

Liberals obviously get their fair share of criticisms for being the 'advertising agents of the British', a criticism directed specifically at Sastri. They are no angels, of course. Their politics is elitist and largely evasive of any substantive moves towards caste, class or gender equality. This criticism would also apply to most of the nationalists, including Gandhi. But a long view of history allows us to appreciate the incremental way in which some of the most significant changes in India's political history came about. On the eve of independence, India not only had a wide pool of politicians and administrators but also a strong constitutional tradition developed over the previous three decades. This was despite the fact the nationalist political party remained either outside the remit of constitutional politics, or at times suspended politics completely. Many, like Sastri, continued to practise politics from within and contribute to the development of political institutions. To treat reform and revolution as moral choices, the latter to be celebrated at the cost of former, does disservice to both our history as well as to the present.[26]

Most controversially, Sastri was an unapologetic Anglophile, although his regard for British politics waxed and waned. His faith in the British Commonwealth remained, despite the several setbacks, quite firm even to the end of his days. His regard for British institutions of democracy and justice was unbounded, for reasons not just political but also profoundly personal. His own life was in some ways an ode to the British system. Rising from abject poverty, he became one of India's best-known leaders, mostly because of his education in an English system. Coming from a family of priests, he saw from close quarters the ways in which traditional education impeded the growth of an individual and the society. His own progress could be credited to a large degree to his education (caste and gender privilege is of course the very condition of its possibility), which continued even after he finished college. His repute as a scholar was despite the shortness of his formal education. As Gandhi once wrote to Natesan: 'few are as well read as [Sastri] and ... the books he had not read are not worth reading'.[27]

His own traditional upbringing had instilled in him a benign disregard for their non-modernist ways. But he could only rebel like a liberal, through subtle acts of negotiation, never in gushes of wild action. Barring his decision of joining Gokhale's society in 1906 and his radical disapproval of the British Empire in 1923, there are hardly any instances in his life of radical departures from his positions, ideas and methods. He applied the same principle to his politics. Ray T. Smith explains the intertwined nature of his personal and political choices:

> A habit of purposeful moderation, temperamentally congenial but also deliberately cultivated, can be seen as an essential feature of his whole 'style of life' in Max Weber's sense. In other words, Sastri was committed to a calm, reflective, tolerant, and accommodating manner intended to put opponents at ease (politically but also socially) and to encourage compromise in the practical realization of their principles. We can trace this to the combined effect of the innate disposition, class interests generated by his education and profession, 'status' concerns involving his access to British circles, and personal values like his loyalty to his 'master', Gokhale. For all these reasons moderation became an avowed principle for Sastri, intrinsic to his ideology.[28]

His inability to commit fully to radical departures is also true of his personal life. He supported social causes, such as education, women's rights and inter-caste marriages, but remained wary of applying them fully to his own household. This is quite symptomatic of his reform-oriented Brahminism, where the modern self is overtly displayed in the political realm, and tradition is confined to but firmly guarded in the personal domain. For instance, he opposed caste prejudice, but according to Kodanda Rao only once did he admit a dalit to live in his house. It was in May 1915 when Gandhi came to Madras with the son of a passive register in South Africa who was a dalit. Gandhi had first asked to stay at Natesan's, whose mother would not allow it. Natesan asked Sastri, who readily agreed. Sastri held a personal prejudice against inter-caste marriage, although he supported it politically.[29]

His fetishization by Indians and foreigners alike of being a great orator does often miss the nuanced articulation of his speeches. Incredibly, even though I have not been able to find any recordings of his voice, his speech transcripts are remarkably aural, as if one can hear him speaking. His arguments never hide behind thick prose and have a word-perfect symmetry, as if a change in a syllable could collapse the argument.

Even when his speeches are laced with rhetoric, they are not jarring or ostentatious. His body movements while delivering those speeches were minimal, he did not gesticulate violently or scratch his head: 'there is too much restraint in the man – the restraint imposed by an innate dignity which is always alert', noted an admirer.[30] The focus of the listener as of the reader is entirely on the words. The moment those words emerged from his throat, as most testimonies remind us, they were tinged by his musical voice. However, despite the absence of the voice in print, the melody of the words is unmissable. Even as one reads the speeches, the words do not lose their lustre because the distractions are minimal. It is the pure force of argument that confronts the listener/reader.

## IV

Sastri, as the title of the book says, was India's first diplomat. The claim was not made in a technical sense, although one can make a good case for why he deserves that title officially. He attended the first ever Imperial Conference in 1921 as an Indian representative,[31] along with a representative of a princely state. He was the first Indian to be sent in the capacity of a plenipotentiary to the Washington Conference. His dominion tour was India's first ever public diplomacy tour. The Cape Town Conference was another first, the first ever bilateral conference without Britain in the British Commonwealth, and consequently it produced the first such bilateral agreement. He was the first Indian Agent to go on a diplomatic post to another dominion. Perhaps no other Indian leader or civil servant in the inter-war period, except for his secretary on many of these tours, Bajpai, could boast of a more extensive and diverse diplomatic experience.

However, the origins of Indian diplomacy and the realm of possibility for the Indian diplomat need to be understood in the specific circumstances of the period. The Indian diplomat was a representative of new India: an aspiring dominion firmly on the path of responsible government. The cultured, mild, well-mannered, English-speaking Indian was meant to showcase the advances of British colonialism in shaping the character of the Indian. This figure was also what the main representative of India to the outside world until now, the pejoratively called 'coolie', was not. The new India had cut its links with indenture (literally, with its abolishment in 1918). Sastri's own caste credentials, as we have seen in the book, were entangled with his diplomacy in a way that was perceptual and performative. His conduct and manner were perceived to represent his caste. But he was the exception; in the imperial frontiers the normal was the 'coolie'. This exceptionalism, as noted in the book, was simultaneously empowering and weakening for his diplomacy.

Consequently, even when Indian diplomacy was mostly about ensuring the rights of Indians abroad, the micro-relations between the diplomat and the diaspora were suffused with undertones of the former being a *petit* civilizer. In what is called performative Brahminism in this book, Sastri emphasized the importance of entry into high echelons of the white society through inculcation of a cultured life.

But these relations were also being played out in a larger imperial setting. In the 1920s, the decade covered in the book, our protagonist saw Britain as the bulwark against the rising tide of colour in the dominions. The First World War had strengthened dominion patriotism and its corollary, white nationalism. Indeed, this was a period in which the concretization of a transnational white solidarity was done in ways that were seemingly more organized and virulent than earlier. As the dominions wrested more powers from Britain, they fenced off their borders against 'Asiatic hordes'. As an Indian diplomat, Sastri entered the picture when immigration restrictions were already an empire-wide reality. His mandate was reduced to ensuring that those Indians who were already within the dominions were granted equal rights, and preventing other territories such as in East Africa from turning into exclusive white spaces.

As Britain divested itself of its responsibility toward its Indian subjects, it placed the onus for negotiating the rights of Indians on the Indian government. This was an adversity, marking the death of imperial citizenship dreams, but also an opportunity for India to assert its status as a dominion-like colony. Sastri's diplomatic inventiveness, as shown in the book, was asserted in the context of the fateful circumstance of the increasingly racialized nature of sovereignty in the British Empire. This vicarious form of sovereignty may have deprived Indian diplomats like Sastri of their strongest argument of 'imperial citizenship', but Sastri also recalibrated the principle of imperial citizenship into the principle of a state's responsibility of civic welfare.

Our view of liberal internationalism as a system of progressive ideas and institutions fails to deal with its granular aspects, which were neither always benign nor always negotiated in a straightforward manner. Diplomats like Sastri were entrepreneurial in manoeuvring the several contradictions of liberal internationalism, making compromises on how far they could negotiate their rights, but also informing key ideas of the time by systematically moulding them from within. Which is why asserting Sastri as key to the making of liberal internationalism is important. Western leaders, backed by the power of their respective states, had easier access to rule-making. Those like Sastri who negotiated these rules in their everyday aspect and despite the hostility of the system worked them to their own advantage had no option but to be entrepreneurial.

As a liberal, Sastri was suited for a role as a diplomat. He was well aware that he was negotiating from a position of weakness. If diplomacy is about give and take, he rarely had anything to give. But still, he was able to effectively marshal the power of the argument to engineer what we could call a diplomacy of dissection. He was, somewhat successfully, able to dissect the seeming uniformity between ideas and their practices. A constant theme of his speeches, and how his communicative rationality operated, was the articulation of a conceptual fracture. And when asserting these, he made four kinds of moves.

The first fracture was between the ideas of British Commonwealth and their racial reality. The British Commonwealth had been popularized as an idea during his time, the credit for that largely goes to the Round Table (especially Curtis) and Jan Smuts. What Sastri did masterfully was point to the inconsistencies of the ideal of the British Commonwealth and its racialized practice. The liberal theoreticians and practitioners of the Commonwealth idea were either evasive on the issue (like Smuts) or dealt with it in a specious manner (like Curtis). Sastri responded to both by a sustained rational, rather than just rhetorical, critique of their arguments. He was able to articulate a vision for the British Commonwealth that might not have been profoundly original, but was strikingly nuanced as well as novel in the setting of an imperial conference. To the extent that his distinction between the two ideals of the Commonwealth, British and Boer, respectively, were also invoked in the post-Second World War era, and decisively shaped its politics in the sense that a white Commonwealth was replaced by a coloured Commonwealth,[32] his authorial claims on conceptualizing the British Commonwealth are as strong as those of Curtis and Smuts.

The second of these was his dissecting of an issue into its principle and its practice, and highlighting different temporal pathways. The solution he would offer, as in the case of the 1921 Conference, was to assert the inviolability of the principle but concede that that the practice was often not in sync with the principle. The latter proposition allowed the other side to agree to the principle as the desired end, not an immediate need. This fracturing opened two possibilities: (a) of India offering to assist in the fulfilment of the practice, and (b) the necessity of continuing negotiations. This strategy also avoided the spectre of virtue signalling and moral one-upmanship, destructive of any practice of rational negotiations.

The third way in which he was to drive a wedge into a conceptual whole was to differentiate between political equality and civic equality. While political equality was always the desired end, civic equality did not always have to wait for political equality to be achieved. Political equality, while desirable, was also less likely to be attained in the immediate future in the white dominions such as Canada and South Africa. Further, it would be impossible to convince the dominion leaders to grant full political rights to Indians when Indians in India were deprived of them. Consequently, in South Africa he took a more piecemeal approach to rights, laying immediate focus on civil rights and welfare responsibilities.[33]

Finally, in response to the emergence of a transnational whiteness, which categorized non-white races in a blanket fashion, Sastri articulated a race/civilization divide. While opposing the racism of white supremacy, the logic of Sastri, and most other Indian leaders of the time including Gandhi, was not inherently anti-discriminatory. For instance, in many ways they held similar views to Europeans about Africans. Sastri's complaint was against the treatment of Indians in the same manner as Africans. India, on account of its long civilizational heritage and not least the long period of tutelage under the British, had achieved a form of civilizational equality with Europeans, he argued. If one accepted that India's political development had reached the stage where it was considered eligible for dominion status in some years, to treat Indians in the same manner as Africans was not merely an affront to Indians but also to British colonialism. So it was not the exclusion that he critiqued but race as the basis of exclusion that he fundamentally opposed. As long as civilization was used as a criterion of exclusion, he did not mind. These are scarcely the arguments of a progressive anti-colonial thinker; although, more often than not, anti-colonial thinkers could be problematic. Race prejudices are ingrained in the thinking of many, including Sastri.

Knowing that diplomacy can only take place within the convivial but transactional frame of rationality, these four fractures, put together, allowed for the possibility of a diplomatic dialogue. They also allowed Sastri a space for tactical manoeuvre.

But what was its use? His critics reminded him that the rights overseas Indians could receive depended on the rights Indians had in India, so was his diplomacy not a mere distraction from the real struggles at home. He would disagree. Japan had internal sovereignty and was indeed a powerful nation, but could it secure the rights of its overseas people? In other words, to wait for full independence to speak for the rights of overseas Indians gave a false sense of security. It was imperative to speak, because the ill-treatment of Indians abroad was not just a matter of the rights of Indians but also a question of India's self-respect (or *izzat*).

## V

In January 1946, Sastri was admitted to the Madras General Hospital. His health had deteriorated considerably. He gave himself less than two months to live.[34] T.N. Jagadisan, a close confidant of Sastri, cabled to inform Gandhi of Sastri's worsening condition. Gandhi travelled to Madras with 'only Sastri in mind',[35] and spent his time on the train in writing a foreword to a collection of Sastri's writings on Gokhale. Sastri was a 'fellow disciple … what a disciple and yet an amiable usurper!'[36]

On 22 January, as Gandhi entered Sastri's hospital room accompanied by his South Africa-based son Manilal and his close associates, the siblings Pyarelal and Susila, Sastri rose up on his bed with excitement. Choked with emotion, Sastri asked to hug his 'little brother'. Gandhi held his hands and tenderly lay him down on the bed, urging him not to strain his heart with excitement.

In the preceding years, Sastri had become restless about the prospects for world peace. He despaired that neither the government nor the Congress was capable of seeing beyond their own quarrels. He had pressed Gandhi, who needed no government's official position, to play a more global role. In several letters, he urged the Mahatma to go to the San Francisco Conference on a three-point agenda: (a) disarmament; (b) equality of political and economic opportunities for all peoples; and (c) elimination of the colour bar in the British Commonwealth and the world at large.[37]

Speaking softly and with much effort on his hospital bed, Sastri again begged Gandhi to make world peace his mission. No one else but Gandhi, he emphasized, could speak for humanity as a whole. Gandhi joked that he was not there to discuss politics; Sastri shot back in mocking self-pity: 'I see, you think I am no good for it.'[38]

Gandhi returned to the hospital eight days later.[39] Sastri's frailty disappeared the moment he saw Gandhi and the two discussed Sastri's latest revelations about *Ramayana*. Gandhi was an embodiment of Rama, 'the greatest fellow alive in the world', he told his somewhat embarrassed visitor.[40] Listening at the side, Sastri's doctor, worried about his patient's bout of excitement and uncharacteristic garrulity. He muttered in Tamil, asking Sastri to stop. Sastri turned to Gandhi and, in a sombre but satisfied tone, uttered that this was their last meeting. He wanted to ensure that he had talked enough to his 'little brother' of 30 years. Promptly dismissing this grim forecast, Gandhi promised to return. 'You are the prince of optimists', Sastri said. 'Oh yes, an irrepressible one', came the reply.[41]

The Mahatma made sure to live up to his promise. He made time to visit Sastri's house in Triplicane on 4 February while finishing other engagements. Words grew heavier in Sastri's throat: 'Brother, you have done me an exceptional honour, especially by paying this visit when you were in great hurry. You are dearer and nearer to me than my own brothers and sons and members of the family.'[42] Moments later, when Gandhi, who was observing his day of weekly silence, rose to bid goodbye, Sastri was breathless with emotion.

His last gasp of passion was, however, stirred by his other adversary from across the Indian Ocean. In the middle of March 1946, Smuts introduced an anti-Indian bill in the Union parliament, infamously termed the 'Ghetto Act', which significantly formalized segregation for Indians. Sastri sent out a message: '[N]ever was there and we trust never will be such naked and unashamed use of political power – that the new world, reborn after the terrible struggle of the past few years should witness and quietly tolerate as its monstrous progeny is a tragedy of blackest order.' Smuts had finally buried the Cape Town Agreement, which for all its faults was an 'understanding between two honourable peoples'. 'In my closing days I seem to be punished by events for an act of virtue', Sastri lamented. He called for exposing Smuts' 'sonorous hypocrisy' at the United Nations. And thus the great liberal's last words to the world were, very uncharacteristically, Gandhian: 'The Indian community is now fighting against the wall, and will be fully justified in seeking honourable suicide in preference to ignominious surrender.'[43]

On 17 April, when he looked more cheerful than usual in his days of ill-health, Sastri lost consciousness at 10:15 pm. He died 20 minutes later.[44] Two months after his death, on 18 June, the Indian government asked its representative at the newly formed United Nations to deliver a telegram to the Secretary General. India was taking Smuts to the UN.

APPENDIX A

# The 1921 Imperial Conference Resolution

The Imperial Conference while reaffirming the resolution of the Imperial War Conference of 1918 that each community of the British Commonwealth should enjoy complete control of the composition of its own population by means of restriction of immigration from any other communities, recognised that there is incongruity between the position of India as an equal member of the British Empire and the existence of disabilities upon the British Indians lawfully domiciled in some other parts of the Empire. The Imperial Conference, accordingly, is of the opinion that in the interests of the solidarity of the British Commonwealth, it is desirable that the rights of such Indians to citizenship should be recognised. The representatives of South Africa regret their inability to accept this resolution in view of the exceptional circumstances in a great part of the Union. The representatives of India, while expressing their appreciation of the acceptance of the resolution recorded above, feel themselves bound to place on record their profound concern for the position of Indians in South Africa and their hope that by negotiation between the two Governments of India and South Africa some way can be found as soon as may be to reach a more satisfactory position.

APPENDIX B

# The Cape Town Agreement of 1927

JOINT COMMUNIQUÉ ISSUED BY THE GOVERNMENT OF INDIA AND THE GOVERNMENT OF THE UNION OF SOUTH AFRICA

It was announced in April, 1926, that the Government of India and the Government of the Union of South Africa had agreed to hold a round table conference to explore all possible methods of settling the Indian question in the Union in a manner which would safeguard the maintenance of western standards of life in South Africa by just and legitimate means. The conference assembled at Cape Town on December 17th, and its session finished on January 11th. There was in these meetings a full and frank exchange of views which has resulted in a truer appreciation of mutual difficulties and a united understanding to co-operate in the solution of a common problem in a spirit of friendliness and goodwill.

Both Governments reaffirmed their recognition of the right of South Africa to use all just and legitimate means for the maintenance of western standards of life. The Union Government recognise that Indians domiciled in the Union who are prepared to conform to western standards of life should be enabled to do so. For those Indians in the Union who may desire to avail themselves of it, the Union Government will organise a scheme of assisted emigration to India or other countries where western standards are not required. Union domicile will be lost after three years' continuous absence from the Union, in agreement with the proposed revision of the law relating to domicile, which will be of general application. Emigrants under the assisted emigration scheme who desire to return to the Union within the three years will only be allowed to do so on refund to the Union Government of the cost of the assistance received by them.

The Government of India recognize their obligation to look after such emigrants on their arrival in India. The admission into the Union of the wives and minor children of Indians permanently domiciled in the Union will be regulated by paragraph 3 of resolution 21 of the Imperial Conference of 1918. In the expectation that the difficulties with which the Union has been confronted will be materially lessened by the agreement which has now happily been reached between the two Governments, and in order that the agreement may come into operation under the most favourable auspices, and have a fair trial, the Government of the Union of South Africa have decided not to proceed further with the Areas Reservation and Immigration and Registration (Further Provision) Bill.

The two Governments have agreed to watch the working of the agreement now reached and to exchange views from time to time as to any changes that experience may suggest. The Government of the Union of South Africa have requested the Government of India to appoint an agent in the Union in order to secure continuous and effective co-operation between the two Governments.

Summary of Conclusions reached by the Round Table Conference on the Indian Question in South Africa

## I. Scheme of Assisted Emigration

(1) Any Indian of 16 years or over may avail himself of the scheme. In case of a family, the decision of the father will bind the wife and minor children under 16 years.
(2) Each person of 16 years or over will receive a bonus of £20, and each child under that age a sum of £10. No maximum shall be fixed for a family. A decrepit adult who is unable to earn his living by reason of a physical disability may, at the discretion of the Union authorities, receive a pension in lieu of or in addition to the bonus. The pension will be paid through some convenient official agency in India out of a fund provided by the Union Government to such amount as they may determine. It is expected that the amount required will not exceed £500 per annum in all. In every case the bonus will be payable in India on arrival at destination or afterwards through some banking institution of repute.
(3) Free passage, including railway fares to port of embarkation in South Africa and from port of landing in India to destination inland will also be provided.
(4) Emigrants will travel to India via Bombay as well as via Madras. Emigrants landing at Bombay will be sent direct from the ship to

their destination at the expense of the Union Government. Survey and certification of ships shall be strictly supervised, and conditions on the voyage, especially in respect of sanitary arrangements, feeding and medical attendance, improved.

(5) Before a batch of emigrants leaves the Union information will be sent to some designated authority in India at least one month in advance, giving (a) a list of intending emigrants and their families, (b) their occupation in South Africa and the occupation or employment which they would require in India, and (c) the amount of cash and other resources which each possesses. On arrival in India, emigrants will be (i) advised, and so far as possible, protected against squandering their cash money or losing it to adventurers, and (ii) helped as far as possible to settle in occupation for which they are best suited by their aptitude or their resources. Any emigrant wishing to participate in emigration schemes authorized by the Government of India will be given the same facilities in India as Indian nationals.

(6) An assisted emigrant wishing to return to the Union will be allowed to do so within three years from the date of departure from South Africa. As condition precedent to re-entry, an emigrant shall refund in full to some recognized authority in India the bonus and cost of passage, including railway fares, received on his behalf and, if he has a family, on behalf of his family. A *pro rata* reduction will, however, be made (i) in respect of a member of the family who died in the interim or of a daughter who marries in India and does not return, and (ii) in other cases of unforeseen hardship at the discretion of the Minister.

(7) After expiry of three years, Union domicile will be lost in agreement with the proposed revision of the law relating to domicile which will be of general application. The period of three years will run from the date of departure from a port of the Union and expire on the last day of the third year. But to prevent the abuse of the bonus and free passage by persons who wish to pay temporary visits to India or elsewhere, no person availing himself of the benefits of the scheme will be allowed to come back to the Union within less than one year from the date of his departure. For purposes of re-entry within the time limit of three years, the unity of the family group shall be recognised, though in cases of unforeseen hardship the Minister of the Interior may allow one or more members of the family to stay behind. A son who goes with the family as a minor, attains majority outside the Union, marries here and has issue, will be allowed to return to South Africa but

only if he comes with the rest of his father's family. In such cases he will be allowed to bring his wife and child or children with him. But a daughter who marries outside the Union will acquire the domicile of her husband, and will not be admitted into the Union unless her husband is himself domiciled in the Union.

## II. Entry of Wives and Minor Children

To give effect to paragraph 3 of the Reciprocity Resolution of the Imperial Conference of 1918, which intended that an Indian should be enabled to live a happy family life in the country in which he is domiciled, the entry of wives and children shall be governed by the following principles:

(a) The Government of India should certify that each individual for whom a right of entry is claimed is the lawful wife or child, as the case may be, of the person who makes the claim.
(b) Minor children should not be permitted to enter the Union unless accompanied by the mother, if alive: Provided that –
   (i) the mother us not already resident in the Union; and
   (ii) the Minister may in special cases permit the entry of such children unaccompanied by the mother.
(c) In the event of divorce, no other wife should be permitted to enter the Union unless proof of such divorce to the satisfaction of the Minister has been submitted.
(d) The definition of wife and child as given in the Indians Relief Act (No. 22 of 1914) shall remain in force.

## III. Upliftment of Indian Community

(1) The Union Government firmly believes in and adhere to the principle that it is the duty of every civilized Government to devise ways and means and to take all possible steps for the uplifting of every section of their permanent population to the full extent of their capacity and opportunities, and accept the view that in the provision of educational and other facilities the considerable number of Indians who will remain part of the permanent population should not be allowed to lag behind other sections of the people.
(2) It is difficult for the Union Government to take action, which is considerable advance of public opinion, or to ignore difficulties arising out of the constitutional system of the Union under the

functions of Government are distributed between the Central Executive and the Provisional and minor local authorities. But the Union Government are willing:

(a) in view of the admittedly grave situation in respect of Indian education in Natal to advise the Provincial Administration to appoint a provisional commission of inquiry and to obtain the assistance of an educational expert from the Government of India for the purpose of such inquiry:

(b) to consider sympathetically the question of improving facilities for higher education by providing suitable hostel accommodation at the South African Native College at Fort Hare, and otherwise improving the attractiveness of the institution for Indians;

(c) to take special steps under the Public Health Act for an investigation into sanitary and housing conditions in and around Durban, which will include the question of:
   (i) the appointment of advisory committees of representative Indians; and
   (ii) the limitation of the sale of municipal land subject to restrictive conditions.

(3) The principle underlying the Industrial Conciliation Act (No. 11 of 1924) and the Wages Act (No. 27 of 1925) which enables all employees, including Indians, to take their places on the basis of equal pay for equal work, will be adhered to.

(4) When the time for the revision of the existing trade licensing laws arrives, the Union Government will give all due consideration to the suggestions made by the Government of India delegation that the discretionary powers of local authorities might reasonably be limited in the following ways:

(a) The grounds on which a license may be refused should be laid down by the statute.

(b) The reasons for which a licence is refused should be recorded.

(c) There should be a right to appeal in cases of first applications and transfers as well as of renewals, to the courts or to some other impartial tribunal.

# List of Archives

National Archives India, New Delhi (India)
Nehru Memorial Museum and Memorial Library, New Delhi (India)
Gokhale Institute of Politics and Economics, Pune (India)
British Library, London (United Kingdom)
National Archives, Kew (United Kingdom)
Centre for South Asian Studies, University of Cambridge (United Kingdom)
Churchill College, University of Cambridge (United Kingdom)
National Archives of South Africa, Pretoria (South Africa)
University of South Africa Archives, Pretoria (South Africa)
Johannesburg City Library (South Africa)
Wits Historical Archives, Johannesburg (South Africa)
Gandhi-Luthuli Centre, Durban (South Africa)
University of Cape Town, Cape Town (South Africa)
National Archives of Australia (Australia)
Library and Archives Canada, Ottawa (Canada)
Library of Congress, Washington (United States)

# List of Illustration Sources and Acknowledgements

1. 'Famous Brahmin leader here: Rt. Hon. S. Sastri', *Victoria Daily Times*, 12 August 1921. The original is quite damaged, so the picture produced here is from the personal collection of Alamelu Padmanabhan.
2. 'It ain't polite to interrupt'. Original cartoon by Charles Henry Sykes for *Philadelphia Evening Public Ledger*. Reproduced in *Manitoba Free Press*, 12 August 1921. Source: Library and Archives Canada.
3. 'His big brother'. Original cartoon by Edmund Waller Gale for the *Los Angeles Times*. Reproduced in *Manitoba Free Press*, 12 August 1921. Source: Library and Archives Canada and Los Angeles Times.
4. 'Sastri and Bajpai in America'. Creator: Bain News Service, publisher. Source: Library of Congress Prints and Photographs Division Washington, DC.
5. 'Sastri at the Conference on Limitation of Armaments, Washington DC.' Creator(s): Harris & Ewing, photographer. Source: Library of Congress Prints and Photographs Division Washington, DC.
6. 'Sastri in Australia, 1922'. Source: *Sastriana: The Mother-in-Law*, Servants of India Society, Madras, 1962.
7. 'Equal in rank but inferior in status'. Creator: The 'Doodle'. Source: *Indian Review*, Vol. 25, No. 5, May 1924.
8. 'Representatives of the Government of India and the Union of South Africa, with Officials, at the First Round Table Conference at Cape Town, December 1926'. Source: The Bramdaw Archives.
9. 'Governor General and Agent General', *Natal Witness*, 21 February 1928. Source: Johannesburg City Library and the Bramdaw Archives.
10. 'A Historic Committee'. Source: The Bramdaw Archives.
11. Kodanda Rao, V.S.S. Sastri and John Tyson. Source: Ragini Tharoor Srinivasan.
12. The family. Source: Ragini Tharoor Srinivasan.

# Notes

## Chapter 1

1. 'Sastri, Celebrated Indian leader is here from Antipodes', *Victoria Daily Times*, 12 August 1922, pp 1, 24; 'A distinguished visitor', *Victoria Daily Times*, 12 August 1922, p 4
2. 'Sastri, Celebrated Indian leader'; 'A distinguished visitor'.
3. By then into its third year, the Greco-Turkish war had seen both sides resorting to indiscriminate killing of civilians. At this point in the war, the Turkish troops under Mustapha Kemal had gained significant advantage and were in the process of pushing out Greeks from Anatolia. Britain stood gingerly at Greece's side, provoking the Greeks to fight through promises of support without actually helping directly. In the process, the Treaty of Sevres had become redundant, as Turkey also concluded separate treaties with France (and Russia).
4. A kirpan is a dagger that Sikhs carry as an article of faith.
5. Both the cartoons are also reproductions from American newspapers. The first appeared in *Evening Philadelphia Ledger* on 5 June 1922 (p 10) and the second in the *Los Angeles Times* on 30 March 1922 (p 26).
6. 'The Turkish question', *Manitoba Free Press*, 12 August 1922, p 11.
7. Leo Pasvolsky, 'The scorching flames of open rebellion spring up in India', *New York Tribune*, 19 March 1922, p 23. British intelligence authorities kept a constant check on the Afghan amir for his efforts to undermine British India militarily, see Weekly Report of the Director, Central Intelligence, Shimla, 12 May 1919, Home Political, B, 1919 JUN 494–497, Repository II, National Archives of India, Delhi (henceforth NAI).
8. See Viceroy to the Secretary of State, Telegram P No 95, 26 January 1921, Home Political, Deposit/1921/Feb/61, NAI.
9. S.D. Waley, *Edwin Montagu: A Memoir and an Account of his Visits to India*, Delhi: Asia Publishing House, 1964, p 272.
10. Waley, *Edwin Montagu*, p 274.
11. *SS Komagata Maru*, a Japanese ship, was chartered by a Sikh, Gurdit Singh, in Hong Kong. It brought around 380 Indians to Vancouver on 23 May 1922. To subvert the principle that Indians had equal access to all parts of the British Empire as whites, Canada had passed legislation blocking the entry of anyone who came through a discontinuous journey. Since there were no ships running directly between Indian and Canadian ports, this effectively banned the entry of Indians. After almost two months of confrontation in Vancouver, which also turned violent, Komagata Maru was sent back to India. On reaching Bengal on 27 September 1922, 20 boarders

were killed in an encounter with the police as the British government attempted to transport them forcefully to Punjab. The incident has remained a deep painful memory for the Sikh community, particularly in Canada.

12. Seema Sohi, *Echoes of Mutiny: Race, Surveillance, and Indian Anticolonialism in North America*, New York: Oxford University Press, 2014.
13. On this point, also see Arnold Toynbee, *The Western Question in Greece and Turkey: A Study in the Contact of Civilizations*, London: Constable and Company, 1922.
14. H. Wilson Harris, 'Outward bound', *Daily News*, September 1921.
15. See R. Sadashiv Aiyar, 'Rt. Hon. V.S. Srinivasa Sastri: a study in personality', *Hindustan Review*, 45 (268), 1922, pp 537–546.
16. L.S. Subramania, 'The Rt. Hon. V.S. Srinivasa Sastri', *India Review*, 30 (2), 1929, pp 106–108.
17. The library is in state of neglect and disrepair, although Srinivasa Sastri Hall is better maintained. Sastri was a Vice Chancellor of Annamalai University from 1935 to 1940.
18. Iver Neumann, *At Home with the Diplomats: Inside a European Foreign Ministry*, Ithaca, NY: Cornell University Press, 2012.
19. Whether diplomatic professionalism constitutes serving the country or the government is another debate. See Peter Vale, *The Changing World and Professional Diplomacy, A Workshop Report*, Organized by Centre for Southern African Studies and the International Studies Unit, Cape Town, 12–14 January 1993.
20. In performing this function, Sastri is a typical example of how the sociologist M.S.S. Pandian characterizes Tamil Brahmins. Pandian argues that colonialism forced Tamil Brahmins to play the dual albeit contradictory roles of appearing both authentic and modern. See M.S.S. Pandian, *Brahmin and Non-Brahmin: Geneologies of Tamil Political Present*, Ranikhet: Permanent Black, 2007.
21. The word 'coolie', a derogatory term for those taken as indenture labour, was also used to refer to Indian migrants in general. However, much like negritude, 'coolitude' seeks to reclaim the histories and identities of Indian labour in their adoptive homelands. See Marina Carter and Khal Torabully, *Coolitude: An Anthology of the Indian Labour Diaspora*, London: Anthem Press, 2002.
22. In the hierarchical and hereditary caste order, shudras are at lowest ranked of the four varnas, who perform artisanal and labour functions in society.
23. Kalathmika Natarajan, 'Entangled Citizens, Undesirable Migrants: The Imprint of Empire and Afterlives of Indenture in Indian Diplomacy (1947–1962)', PhD thesis, University of Copenhagen. Also see Latha Varadarajan, *The Domestics Abroad: Diasporas in International Relations*, New York: Oxford University Press, 2010.
24. Srinivas used the term 'sanskritization' to explain the process of upward social mobility of the so-called lower castes by emulation of upper caste rituals, manners and practices. For the role of Indian agents in South Africa as 'civilizers', see Uma Mesthrie, 'From Sastri to Deshmukh: A Study of the Role of the Government of India's Representatives in South Africa', PhD thesis, University of Natal, Durban, 1987.
25. H.S.L. Polak, 'Mr. Sastri and his mission', *Hindustan Review*, 44 (274), 1922, p 8.
26. Radhika Singha, 'The Great War and a "proper" passport for the colony: border-crossing in British India, c. 1882–1922', *Indian Economic and Social History*, 50 (3), 2013, pp 289–315.
27. Subramania, 'The Rt. Hon. V.S. Srinivasa Sastri'.
28. Aiyar, 'RT Hon. V.S. Srinivasa Sastri'.

29 Frank Nickovich, *The Wilsonian Century: U.S. Foreign Policy since 1900*, Chicago: University of Chicago Press, 1999; G. John Ikenberry, 'Liberal internationalism 3.0: America and the dilemmas of liberal world order', *Perspectives on Politics*, 7 (1), 2009, pp 71–87.

30 For a sample of this thinking see Inderjit Parmar, 'The US led liberal order: Imperialism by other name?', *International Affairs*, 94 (1), 2018, pp 151–172, at 155; and Adom Getachew, *Worldmaking after Empire: The Rise and Fall of Self-determination*, Princeton, NJ: Princeton University Press, 2019. For an excellent overview and critique of liberal internationalism, see Beate Jahn, *Liberal Internationalism: Theory, History and Practice*, London: Palgrave Macmillan, 2013.

31 See Erez Manela, *The Wilsonian Moment: Self-Determination and the International Origins of Anticolonial Nationalism*, New York: Oxford University Press, 2007; Trygve Throntveit, 'The fable of fourteen points: Woodrow Wilson and national self-determination', *Diplomatic History*, 35 (1), 2011, pp 445–481; Thomas Bender, *A Nation Among Nations: America's Place in World History*, New York: Hill and Wang, 2006, pp 242–243; Rayford W. Logan, 'The operation of the mandate system in Africa', *Journal of Negro History*, 13 (4), 1928, pp 423–477; Brett Reilly, 'The myth of the Wilsonian moment', Wilson Centre Blog, 17 June 2019, www.wilsoncenter.org/blog-post/the-myth-the-wilsonian-moment, accessed 10 October 2019; Arno Mayer, *Wilson vs. Lenin: Political Origins of the New Diplomacy, 1917–1918*, New York: Meridian Books, 1967; Carolien Stolte, 'Uniting the oppressed peoples of the East: revolutionary internationalism in an Asian inflection', in Mohammad Ali Raza, Franziska Roy and Benjamin Zachariah (eds) *The Internationalist Moment: South Asia, Worlds, and World View 1917–1938*, Los Angeles: Sage, 2015, pp 47–58.

32 Daniel Gorman, *The Emergence of International Society in the 1920s*, Cambridge: Cambridge University Press, 2012; Akira Iriye, *Global Community: The Role of International Organisations in the Making of the Contemporary World*, Berkeley, CA: University of California Press, 2002; Helen McCarthy, 'The lifeblood of the League: voluntary associations and League of Nations activism in Britain', in Daniel Laqua (ed) *International Reconfigured: Transnational Ideas and Movements between the World Wars*, London: I.B. Tauris, 2011.

33 Susan Pedersen, *The Guardians: The League of Nations and the Crisis of Empire*, London: Oxford University Press, 2015.

34 Oona Hathaway and Scott Shapiro, *The Internationalists: And Their Plan to Outlaw War*, Great Britain: Penguin, 2017.

35 W.E.B. Du Bois, 'Worlds of colour', *Foreign Affairs*, 3 (3), 1925, pp 423–444.

36 See Madison Grant, *The Passing of the Great Race*, New York: Charles Schribner, 1916; Ibram X. Kendi, *Stamped from the Beginning: The Definitive History of Racist Ideas in America*, London: Bodley Head, 2016, p viii. Also see Lothrop Stoddard, *The Rising Tide of Colour against White World Supremacy*, New York: Charles Scribner, 1920.

37 In 1919, the South African government passed the Asiatic (Land and Trading Amendments) (Transvaal) Act, imposing further restrictions on Indians from owning companies. In 1919, New Zealand also passed its Immigration Restrictions Amendment Act. In British Columbia, a measure introduced in the legislative assembly to confer votes on those Asians who had served with the Canadian forces during the First World War was defeated. Under Jan Smuts, South Africa passed a slew of segregationist measures. His party lost the elections in 1924 to J.B.M.

Hertzog's National Party, which took to segregation with religious – metaphorical as well as, in some cases, literal – zeal.

38   Stoddard, *The Rising Tide of Colour*, p 281.
39   One must here question the canonization of the 'Wilsonian Moment', when as Erez Manela himself shows, it is a moment in which Wilson acts only as an absentee presence, and ask and if the phrase and its centring of Wilson does more analytical harm than good. In fact, Manela even musters a quote from Sastri where the latter had speculated that if Wilson had gone to Asia after the war, he would have been received with 'wild delirium of joy' as though 'Christ or Buddha had come back to his home'. But Manela misses that Sastri was equally clear in the same text that Wilson's message was hardly intended for the people of Asia. Sastri credited Japan, rather than America, for raising the voice of Asia at the League of Nations. See V.S. Srinivasa Sastri, 'Foreword', in Woodrow Wilson, *Woodrow Wilson's Message to Eastern Nations*, Calcutta: Association Press, 1925.
40   The limited work on this period includes: T.T. Poulose, 'India as an anomalous international person (1919–1947)', *British Yearbook of International Law* 44, 1970, p 201, Itty Abraham, *How India Became Territorial: Foreign Policy, Diaspora, Geopolitics*, Stanford, CA: Stanford University Press, 2014; Pradeep Barua, 'Strategies and doctrines of imperial defence: Britain and India, 1919–45,' *Journal of Imperial and Commonwealth History* 25 (2), 1997, pp 240–266; Sneh Mahajan, *Foreign Policy of Colonial India, 1900–1947*, New Delhi: Routledge, 2018; Vineet Thakur, *Jan Smuts and the Indian Question*, Pietermaritzburg, University of KwaZulu Natal Press, 2017; Stephen Legg, 'An international anomaly? Sovereignty, the League of Nations, and India's princely geographies', *Journal of Historical Geography*, 43, 2014, pp 96–110; Hugh Tinker, *Separate and Unequal: India and the Indians in the British Commonwealth, 1920–1950*, Queensland: University of Queensland Press, 1976.
41   This comment on V.S. Srinivasa Sastri was made by the Eastern African Indian National Congress. See 'RT Hon. Mr. Sastri: England's advertising agent', *Democrat*, 2 March 1929, FD 8, AICC Papers: I Instalment, Nehru Memorial Museum and Library, New Delhi (henceforth NMML).
42   Maganlal A. Buch, *Rise and Growth of Indian Liberalism: From Ram Mohan Roy to Gokhale*, Baroda: no publisher, 1938, p 302. For an extended discussion of how liberals have been treated, see C.A. Bayly, *Recovering Liberties: Indian Thought in the Age of Liberalism and Empire*, New Delhi: Cambridge University Press, 2012.
43   'Benarasidas Chaturvedi to Srinivasa Sastri', 23 December 1922, V.S. Srinivasa Sastri Papers, Ist Instalment (henceforth VSS Papers (1)), Correspondence: Benarasidas Chaturvedi, NMML.
44   See Suraj Yengde, 'Race, caste and what it will take to make Dalit lives matter', *The Caravan*, 3 July 2020.
45   'Mr. Sastri's appeal to Natal', *Natal Witness*, 3 August 1927, p 5.
46   See, for instance, Peter Gourevitch, 'The second-image reversed: the international sources of domestic politics', *International Organisation*, 32 (4), 1978, pp 881–912.
47   He also did not want any memorial to be raised in his honour, which may partly explain the absence of public memorials to him. See 'Written statement of Srinivasa Sastri', VSS Papers (I), Writings and Speeches, S No 47, NMML.
48   These were published as 'En Vazhkayin Amsangal' in Tamil and translated to 'Aspects of my life'. The English version is in Sastri's papers at the Nehru Memorial Museum and Library in New Delhi. See V.S. Srinivasa Sastri, 'Aspects of my life', VSS Papers (I), S No 82, NMML.

49 P. Kodanda Rao, *The Right Honourable V.S. Srinivasa Sastri: A Political Biography*, Bombay: Asia Publishing House, 1963, p xviii.
50 T.N. Jagadisan, *V.S. Srinivasa Sastri*, Publications Division, Ministry of Information and Broadcasting, Government of India, 1969.
51 See R. Sadasivan to T.N. Jagadisan, V.S. Srinivas Sastri Papers, IInd Installment (henceforth VSS Papers (II)), S No 2, f 18, NMML.
52 S.R. Bakshi, *Struggle for Independence: V.S. Srinivasa Sastri*, New Delhi: Anmol Publications, 1992; Mohan Ramann, *V.S. Srinivasa Sastri: A Study*, New Delhi: Sahitya Akademi, 2007.

# Chapter 2

1 Jagadisan, *Sastri*, pp 2–4; V.S. Srinivasa Sastri, 'A confession of faith', in *The Other Harmony: A Selection from the Writings and Speeches of the Right Hon. V.S. Srinivasa Sastrii*, ed T.N. Jagadisan, 2nd edn, Madras: S. Viswanathan, 1949, pp 2–3.
2 R. Shantha Ramaswami and K.S. Srinivasan, *V.S. Srinivasa Sastri*, Remembering our Leaders, Vol 5, New Delhi: Children's Book Trust, 2015, p 27; M.S. Raghavan, 'The Rt. Honourable Srinivasa Sastri', VSS Papers (I), Writings by Others, S No 30, f 1787.
3 Jagadisan, *Sastri*, p 5; Sastri, 'Aspects of my life', pp 3–4.
4 In the Hindu ashrama system, an individual goes through four stages of life: *Brahmacharya* (celibate, dedicated to education); *Grihastha* (married life dedicated to fostering a family); *Vanaprastha* (retirement); and *Sanyas* (complete renunciation, focused entirely on the attainment of liberation from the cycle of life and death).
5 Anon, 'Sastri – a vignette', VSS Papers (I), Writings by Others, S No 27.
6 Anon, 'Sastri – a vignette'.
7 Jagadisan, *Sastri*, p 9.
8 Jagadisan, *Sastri*, p 9.
9 He would even correct his own principal's diction, an Englishman by the name of A.A. Hall who brandished his friendships with Oxford dons to assert his authority on the language.
10 Sastri, 'Aspects of my life', pp 11–12; Jagadisan, *Sastri*, pp 9–10, Kodanda Rao, *Sastri*, p 5.
11 See www.hinduhighschool.net/lifesketches/life_sketches8.htm, accessed 12 January 2020. Also see S. Muthiah, 'Presidency's feeder', *The Hindu*, 2 February 2004.
12 Jagadisan, *Sastri*, pp 10–11; K. Balasubramania Iyer, 'My early reminiscences of Sastri', in A. Ranganathan (ed) *The Right Honourable V.S. Srinivasa Sastri Centenary Souvenir*, Madras: Servants of India Society, 1969, pp 8–11; 'Sanctity of teaching: Srinivasa Sastri on co-education', *Bombay Chronicle*, 8 June 1927, p 8.
13 S. Muthiah, 'Presidency's feeder'; Anon, 'Sastri – a vignette'; G.A. Natesan, 'The Rt. Hon. Srinivasa Sastri', *Bharat Dharma*, 24 (5), May 1946, p 5, in VSS Papers (II), Speeches and Writings by, S No 2, f 39.
14 V.S. Srinivasa Sastri, 'The schoolmaster's test', *Sastriana*, No 7, ed S.R. Venkataraman, Madras: Servants of India Society, 1968 (originally published in *Educational Review*, Feb–March 1896).
15 I am grateful to Ole Birk Laursen for bringing this detail to my attention.
16 Natesan, 'The Rt. Hon. Srinivasa Sastri'.

17. V. Sriram, 'Hundred years of a statue', *The Hindu*, 3 April 2012, www.thehindu.com/news/cities/chennai/hundred-years-of-a-statue/article3274235.ece, accessed 12 January 2020.
18. Jagadisan, *Sastri*, p 12; Natesan, 'The Rt. Hon. Srinivasa Sastri', f 39.
19. See Tridip Suhrud, *An Autobiography or the Story of my Experiments with Truth: A Table of Concordance*, New York: Routledge, 2017; see V.S. Srinivasa Sastri, 'Letters to Mahadev Desai', in T.N Jagadisan (ed) *Letters of The Rt. Hon. V.S. Srinivasa Sastri*, Madras: Rochhouse, 1944, pp 129–140.
20. Diary 1915, 30 April 1915, VSS Papers (I), NMML. Neither did he spare Winston Churchill when the latter described Louis Mountbatten as 'tribian', rather than 'triphibian'. Se, Anon, 'Review of letters of Rt. Hon. Srinivasa Sastri', *Roy's Weekly*, 6 August 1944, p 8.
21. For a discussion on the monopoly of Brahmans among the professional elite in Madras presidency, see R. Suntharalingam, *Politics and Nationalist Awakening in South India, 1852–1891*, Jaipur: Rawat Publications, 1958; Pandian, *Brahmin and Non-Brahmin*, pp 50–53.
22. Sastri, 'Aspects of my life', f 14.
23. 'The Triplicane Urban Co-operative Society Limited. Silver Jubilee 1930', http://dspace.gipe.ac.in/xmlui/bitstream/handle/10973/24290/GIPE-048762.pdf?sequence=3&isAllowed=y, accessed 26 October 2020, Dhananjayarao Gadgil Library, GIPE-PUNE, p 27.
24. R. Balaji, 'Triplicane Urban Co-op Society turns 100', *Hindu Business Line*, 9 April 2004, www.thehindubusinessline.com/todays-paper/tp-others/tp-states/article28856814.ece, accessed 13 January 2020; 'The Triplicane Urban Co-operative Society Limited', pp 27–28.
25. 'Sastri to K.S. Venkataramani, 3 May 1915', in Jagadisan (ed) *Letters of Sastri*, p 191.
26. V.S. Srinivasa Sastri, *'My Master Gokhale'*, ed T.N. Jagadisan, Madras: Model Publications, 1946, p 76.
27. A founding member of Fergusson College, Gokhale rose to become its principal but resigned in 1902 to concentrate on his political work.
28. B.R. Nanda, *Gokhale*, New Delhi: Oxford University Press, 1977.
29. He had first expressed this to his student and close confidante R.P. Paranjpe on a trip to London. See R.P. Paranjpe, *Gopal Krishna Gokhale*, Poona: Aryabhushan Press, 1916, p 65.
30. 'Puntoojism run mad with "cooperation"', *Bengalee*, 22 September 1917, in Servants of India Society Papers (henceforth SOIS Papers), Subject File 12, NMML, f 194–195.
31. Nanda, *Gokhale*, pp 169–170; Paranjpe, *Gopal Krishna Gokhale*, p 65.
32. *The Servants of India Society*, Poona: Aryabhushan Press, 1915, pp 3–4.
33. Young apprentices received 30 rupees per month, and full members 50 rupees.
34. These were: country will always be first in thoughts and service; seeking no personal advantage while serving the country; seeking advancement of all Indians without distinction of caste or creed; no part of work to be devoted to earning money; leading a pure personal life; never engaging in personal quarrel with any one; and, finally, never to do anything that was inconsistent with the objects of the society. See *The Servants of India Society*, p 6.
35. Paranjpe, *Gopal Krishna Gokhale*, p 66.
36. Selby quoted in V.S. Srinivasa Sastri, *Life of Gopal Krishna Gokhale*, Bangalore: Bangalore Printing and Publishing, 1937, p 53.

## NOTES

37. Gokhale to Krishnaswami Iyer, 31 July 1905, SOIS Papers, Subject File 23 (part 2), f 235.
38. Sastri to Gokhale, 27 December 1905, in Jagadisan (ed) *Letters of Sastri*, pp 1–2.
39. David Hardiman, *The Non-Violent Struggle for Indian Freedom, 1905–19*, Gurgaon: Penguin Viking, 2019, pp 23–24.
40. Sastri, *'My Master Gokhale'*, p 77.
41. An account of his visit to Poona is in 'My first meeting with Gokhale' (pp 69–75) in Sastri, *'My Master Gokhale'*.
42. A false rumour was spread that Krishnaswami Iyer had given Sastri 10,000 rupees to stabilize his finances while he joined the society.
43. Diary 1907, 6 January and 15 January, VSS Papers (I).
44. See his letters to Gokhale in Jagadisan (ed) *Letters of Sastri*, pp 5–15.
45. Sastri, *'My Master Gokhale'*, pp 109–110.
46. Sastri to V.K. Krishnaswami Iyer, 9 August 1908, in Jagadisan (ed) *Letters of Sastri*, pp 45–50.
47. See 'The first member's inaugural address', SOIS Papers, Subject File 4 (part 2), f 490–497.
48. Nanda, *Gokhale*, p 464; Also see Sastri's letters to Gokhale in VSS Papers (II), Correspondence: Gokhale, Gopal Krishna.
49. Sastri, 'Aspects of my life', f 98.
50. V.S. Srinivasa Sastri, *Life and Times of Sir Pherozeshah Mehta*, Madras: Madras Law Journal Press, 1945, pp 104–105.
51. V.S. Srinivasa Sastri, *Thumbnail Sketches*, ed T.N. Jagadisan, Madras: S. Visvanathan, 1946, p 191.
52. Quoted in Nanda, *Gokhale*, p 290.
53. Jagadisan, *Sastri*, p 17.
54. Sastri, *'My Master Gokhale'*, p 269 (footnote 2).
55. Sastri to Krishnaswami Iyer, 25 July 1908, in Jagadisan (ed) *Letters of Sastri*, pp 51–52.
56. Quoted in Jagadisan, *Sastri*, p 18.
57. Sastri to Natesan, 31 May 1907, in Jagadisan (ed) *Letters of Sastri*, p 188.
58. Diary 1915, 22 February, VSS Papers (I).
59. Letter to Sarojini Naidu, 23 February 1915, in *Collected Works of Mahatma Gandhi* (henceforth CWMG), Vol 14, New Delhi: Publications Division, Ministry of Information and Broadcasting, Government Of India, p 371.
60. Sastri to Krishnaswami Iyer, 22 June 1909, in Jagadisan (ed) *Letters of Sastri*, p 53; Nanda, *Gokhale*, p 462; see Sastri to Members and Permanent Assistants, May 1912, SOIS Papers, Subject File 13, f 231.
61. Nanda, *Gokhale*, p 462; 'A brief account of the work of the Servants of India Society, Poona (from June 1905 to December 1916)', Poona: Aryabhushan Press, January 1917.
62. Nanda, *Gokhale*, pp 174–175.
63. Sastri to Krishnaswami Iyer, 22 June 1909, in Jagadisan (ed) *Letters of Sastri*, p 53.
64. Sastri to Gokhale, 25 December 1911, in Jagadisan (ed) *Letters of Sastri*, p 30.
65. Sastri, *Thumbnail Sketches*, p 199.
66. Sastri, *Thumbnail Sketches*, p 199.
67. Sastri, *Thumbnail Sketches*, p 199.
68. Nanda, *Gokhale*, p 421.
69. Nanda, *Gokhale*, p 415.

70. Quoted in Ramchandra Guha, *Gandhi: The Years that Changed the World, 1915–1948*, London: Penguin, 2019, p 15.
71. Sastri, *Life of Sir Pherozeshah Mehta*, p 171.
72. Sastri to BS Ramaswami Sastri, 10 January 1915, in Jagadisan (ed) *Letters of Sastri*, p 190.
73. Sastri, *Life of Sir Pherozeshah Mehta*, p 172.
74. Sastri, *Life of Sir Pherozeshah Mehta*, p 172; Diary 1915, 27 February 1915, VSS Papers (I).
75. Other sympathizers of the Society, Madanmohan Malviya, Tej Bahadur Sapru, and Aga Khan agreed with the decision to keep Gandhi out. See H.N. Kunzru to V.S. Srinivasa Sastri, 6 March 1915, SOIS Papers, Subject File No 12, f 87–97.
76. In 1908, the Madras Session had 626 delegates (434 from Madras alone) while in 1911, only 300 delegates attended. In the next two years, the numbers declined further to about 250 members. See S.R. Mehrotra, *A History of the Indian National Congress, Vol 1, 1885–1918*, New Delhi: Vikas, 1995, p 251; 'Report of the Proceedings of the First All India Session of the Moderate Party held at Bombay in the Empire Theatre, 1–2 November 1918', Bombay: Times Press, 1919, p 136.
77. The 1914 Government of Ireland Act had promised an Irish parliament. See Mark R. Frost, 'Imperial citizenship or else: liberal ideals and the India unmaking of the empire, 1890–1919', *Journal of Imperial and Commonwealth History*, 46 (5), 2018, pp 845–873.
78. Mehrotra, *A History of the Indian National Congress*, pp 274–281.
79. See Nanda, *Gokhale*, pp 451–460.
80. See Natesan, 'Introduction', in G.A. Natesan (ed) *The Indian Demands*, Madras: G.A. Natesan, 1917, p 12.

## Chapter 3

1. Diary, 30 April 1919, VSS Papers (I); V.S. Srinivasa Sastri, 'If I live again', VSS Papers (I), S No 82, f 157–158.
2. Sastri to Ramaswami, 19 June 1919, f 39, VSS Papers (I), Subject File 5.
3. Sastri to Ramaswami, 1 May 1919, f 25–26, VSS Papers (I), Subject File 5.
4. Sastri to Ramaswami, 7 May 1919, f 27–28, VSS Papers (I), Subject File 5.
5. For Indian revolutionaries, see Arun C. Bose, *Indian Revolutionaries Abroad, 1905–1922: In the Background of International Developments*, Patna: Bharati Bhawan, 1971; Nirode K. Barooh, *Chatto: The Life and Times of an Indian Anti-Imperialist in Europe*, New Delhi: Oxford University Press, 2004; Kama Maclean, *A Revolutionary History of Interwar India: Violence, Image, Voice and Text*, London: Hurst, 2015; Kris Manjapra, *M.N. Roy: Marxism and Colonial Cosmopolitanism*, New Delhi: Routledge, 2010; Maia Ramnath, *Haj to Utopia: How the Ghadar Movement charted Global Radicalism and attempted to overthrow the British Empire*, Berkeley: University of California Press, 2011; Michele Luoro, *Comrades against Imperialism: Nehru, India and Interwar Internationalism*, Cambridge: Cambridge University Press, 2018; Ole Birk Laursen, *M.P.T. Acharya, We Are Anarchists: Essays on Anarchism, Pacifism, and the Indian Independence Movement, 1923–1953*, Chico, CA: AK Press, 2019.
6. *Servant of India*, 1 (13), 16 May 1918, p 146.
7. Quoted in Joanne Stafford Mortimer, 'Annie Besant and India 1913–1917', *Journal of Contemporary History*, 18, 1983, pp 61–78 at 76.
8. Lord Ampthill quoted in Lionel Curtis, *Dyarchy*, Oxford: Oxford University Press, 1920, p xxvii.

9. Arnold Toynbee, *Acquaintances*, New York: Oxford University Press, 1967, p 139.
10. Lionel Curtis, *The Commonwealth of Nations: An Inquiry into the Nature of Citizenship in the British Empire, and into the Mutual Relations of the Several Communities Thereof*, Part I, London: Macmillan, 1916, p 696.
11. Curtis, *Dyarchy*, p 53.
12. Curtis, *Dyarchy*, p xxi.
13. Curtis, *Dyarchy*, p xxxii.
14. Curtis, *Dyarchy*, p xxvii.
15. V.S. Srinivasa Sastri, *Self-Government for India: Under the British Flag*, Allahabad: Servants of India Society, 1916, p 7.
16. Sastri, *Self-Government*, p 7.
17. For Gokhale's 'Political will and testament', see V.S. Srinivasa Sastri, *'My Master Gokhale'*, pp 280–285.
18. Natesan, 'Introduction', p 37.
19. Sastri, *Self-Government*, pp 11–25.
20. Sastri, *Self-Government*, p 13.
21. Sastri, *Self-Government*, p 32.
22. Sastri, *Self-Government*, p 35.
23. 'Power without responsibility', *Servant of India*, 1 (3), 7 March 1918, p 28.
24. 'Power without responsibility', p 28; V.S. Srinivasa Sastri, *Congress–League Scheme: An Exposition*, Poona: Aryabhushan Press, 1917, pp 40–44.
25. 'The Reform Proposals', *Servant of India*, 1 (21), 11 July 1918, p 243.
26. 'Power without responsibility', p 28; Sastri, *Congress–League Scheme*, pp 40–44.
27. Sastri, *Self-Government*, p 40.
28. Sastri, *Self-Government*, p 46.
29. Sastri, *Self-Government*, p 47.
30. See Hansard, The House of Common Debates, Court of Enquiry, 12 July 1917, Vol 95, https://hansard.parliament.uk/commons/1917-07-12/debates/c8fdbdc8-6895-42ce-99c2-240e5a769904/CourtOfInquiry, accessed 21 February 2020.
31. Philip Woods, 'The Montagu–Chelmsford reforms (1919): a re-assessment', *South Asia: Journal of South Asian Studies*, 17 (1), 1994, pp 25–42; Shane Ryland, 'Edwin Montagu in India, 1917–1918: politics of the Montagu–Chelmsford report', *South Asia: Journal of South Asian Studies: Series 1*, 3 (1), 1973, pp 79–92.
32. See Richard Danzig, 'The announcement of August 20th, 1917', *Journal of Asian Studies*, 28 (1), 1968, pp 19–37; Valentine Chirol, *Indian Unrest*, London: Macmillan, 1910.
33. Sastri, *Congress–League Scheme*, pp 35–39.
34. Lord Sydenham, *My Working Life*, London: John Murray, 1927, pp 339–340.
35. See Indo-British Association, *The Crumbling of an Empire: September 1916–March 1922: A Chronological Statement of the Decline of British Authority in India*, London: Indo-British Association, 1923.
36. So instead of each person only voting for their caste, it was better if two or three districts were combined to form a constituency with multiple representations. Brahmin and non-Brahmin seats would, in this case, be restricted to the proportion of their population. Hence, a large constituency with five seats and 80 per cent non-Brahmins would elect four non-Brahmins and one Brahmin.
37. Sastri, *Congress–League Scheme*, p 4.
38. *The Servant of India*, 1 (13), 16 May 1918, p 150.
39. Edwin S. Montagu, *An Indian Diary*, ed Venetia Montagu, London: William Heineman, 1930, pp 9–10.

40 Montagu, *An Indian Diary*, p 8.
41 Montagu, *An Indian Diary*, p 122.
42 Montagu, *An Indian Diary*, p 236.
43 *Report on Indian Constitutional Reforms*, Calcutta: Superintendent Government Printing, 1918.
44 'The reform scheme', *New India*, 10 July 1919, p 3.
45 Annie Besant, 'The Montagu–Chelmsford proposals', *New India* (Mail edition), 8 July 1918, p 1.
46 Published in 'The reform proposals – a manifesto', *New India*, 9 July 1918, p 3.
47 'Surendranath Banerjea to Srinivasa Sastri, 18 July 1918', SOIS Papers, Subject File 14.
48 *The Servant of India*, 1 (23), 25 July 1918, p 265.
49 For an analysis of opinions, see 'Opinions on the reforms: an analysis', *New India*, 16 July 1918, p 3.
50 *Letter from the Government of India, dated 5 March 1919, and Enclosures, on the Questions Raised in the Report on Indian Constitutional Reforms*, London: His Majesty's Stationery Service, 1919, pp 2–3.
51 'A fresh start', *Servant of India*, 1 (5), 21 March 1918, p 2.
52 'A fresh start', p 2.
53 Tilak had originally advised this course of action in his 1907 speech to the Indian National Congress. He had stated: "I say I want the whole bread and that immediately. But if I cannot get the whole, don't think that I have no patience. I will take the half they give me and then try for the remainder. This is the line of thought and action in which you must train yourself." See Bal Gangadhar Tilak, 'Address to the Indian National Congress, 1907', in William T. de Bary, Stephen Hay, Royal Weiler and Andrew Yarrow, *Sources of Indian Tradition*, New York: Columbia University Press, 1958, p 722.
54 V.S. Srinvasa Sastri, 'The coming proposals: our attitude towards them', *Servant of India*, 1 (20), 4 July 1918, pp 232–235.
55 *Servant of India*, 1 (19), 27 June 1918, pp 217–218.
56 Madhan Mohan Malaviya was closer to Sastri's personal view that moderates must attend the Congress session and prevent a wholesale rejection of the scheme. See M.A. Parmanand, *Mahamana Madan Mohan Malaviya: A Historical Biography*, Allahabad: Malaviya Adhyayan Sansthan, Banaras Hindu University, p 364.
57 See Sastri, *'My Master Gokhale'*, p 92.
58 Sastri and Paranjpe, 23 July 1918, R.P. Paranjpe Papers, Correspondence: V.S. Srinivasa Sastri, f 5, NMML.
59 'A letter from London', *Servant of India*, 1 (31), 19 September 1918, p 369.
60 *Servant of India*, 1 (29), 5 September 1918, p 338.
61 'The wing and the whirlwind', *Servant of India*, 1 (26), 15 August 1918, pp 303–305.
62 'Choice of the S.I.S.', *Servant of India*, 1 (27), 22 August 1918, pp 315; 'The Congress of moderates', *Servant of India*, 1 (27), 22 August 1918, pp 314–315.
63 See Paramanand, *Malaviya*, p 367.
64 'Report of the 1918 Special Session', All India Congress Committee Papers (Ist Instalment), File 8–9/1918, NMML.
65 *Joint Select Committee on the Government of India Bill, Vol I – Report and Proceedings of the Committee*, London: His Majesty's Stationery Service, 1919, p 189.
66 *Servant of India*, 1 (12), 9 May 1918, p 134.
67 *Servant of India*, 1 (44), 19 December 1918, p 519.

68. *Report of the Proceedings of the First Session of the All-India Conference of the Moderate Party*, 1–2 November, Bombay: Times Press, 1919.
69. Paramanand, *Malaviya*, p 367.
70. *Servant of India*, 1 (44), 19 December 1918, p 509.
71. *Servant of India*, 2 (1), 6 February 1918, p 1; *Servant of India*, 1 (47), 9 January 1918; 'The Delhi Congress', *Servant of India*, 1 (46), 2 January 1919, pp 548–551.
72. V.S. Srinivasa Sastri, *Speeches and Writings of the Right Honourable V.S. Srinivasa Sastri*, Vol 1, Madras: G. Natesan, 1924, pp 161–162.
73. Sastri, *Speeches and Writings*, pp 135–140.
74. Mahatma Gandhi, *An Autobiography: The Story of My Experiments with Truth*, reprint, Ahmedabad: Navajivan Publishing House, 1948, p 560.
75. *Letter from the Government of India, Dated 5 March 1919, and Enclosures.*
76. Sastri to Ramaswami, 28 May 1919, VSS Papers (I), Subject File 5, f 32.
77. Sastri to Ramaswami, 28 May 1919, f 32; Diary 1919, 25 May 1919, VSS Papers (I).
78. 'Indians gather in force. Great assembling in London. Reformers and their outlook', *Pall Mall Gazette*, 18 August 1919, p 4.
79. Sastri to Ramaswami, 4 June 1919, VSS Papers, Subject File 5, f 35.
80. Sastri to Ramaswami, 28 May 1919, f 32.
81. In Kodanda Rao, *Sastri*, p 77. Also see 'Another Ireland: penalty of refusing India self-government', *Leeds Mercury*, 2 July 1919, p 19.
82. Sastri to Ramaswami, 3 September 1919, VSS Papers (I), Subject File 4; f 98.
83. Sastri to Vaze, 29 May 1919, VSS Papers (I), Subject File 5, f 41; Sastri to Ramaswami, 27 August 1919, VSS Papers (I), Subject File 5, f 51.
84. See Secretary of State, 'Government of India Bill', House of Commons, 5 June 1919, *Hansard*, Vol 116, https://hansard.parliament.uk/commons/1919-06-05/debates/7d9f8350-7aeb-4f39-99af-b64d90a621a1/GovernmentOfIndiaBill, accessed 3 March 2020.
85. *Joint Select Committee on the Government of India Bill.*
86. Sastri to Vaze, 28 May 1919, Sub File 5, f 33.
87. *Joint Select Committee on the Government of India Bill*, pp 292–314.
88. Towards the end he got into a testy exchange with Sydenham and Selborne. See *Joint Select Committee on the Government of India Bill*, pp 326–327.
89. See 'From an unspecified friend in Kodanda Rao', *Sastri*, p 77; Sastri to Ramaswami, 14 August 1919, VSS Papers (I), Subject File 5, f 46; Montagu, *An Indian Diary*, p 122.
90. *Joint Select Committee on the Government of India Bill*, p 250.
91. Sastri to Ramaswami, 17 August 1919, VSS Papers (I), Subject File 4; f 86.
92. Pandian, *Brahmin and Non-Brahmin*, p 68.
93. See Reddi's testimony from pp 258–276 and Rayaningar's testimony from pp 276–285 in *Joint Select Committee* report.
94. Sastri to Ramaswami, 14 August 1919, f 46.
95. Sastri to Ramaswami, 31 January 1918, Sub File 5, f 12, VSS Papers; Sastri to D.V. Gundappa, 28 August 1927, f 99; Correspondence, VSS Papers, Ist Inst.
96. Sastri to Venkatasubbiah, 27 August 1919, VSS Papers (I), Subject File 5, f 53.
97. Sastri to Ramaswami, 17 August 1919, f 86.
98. Reproduced in *Servant of India*, 2 (48), 1 January 1920, p 575.
99. Sastri to Ramaswami, 17 August 1919, f 86.
100. G.A. Natesan, 'The Rt. Hon. VS Srinivasa Sastri', VSS Papers (II), Speeches and writings about him by others, S No 2, f 47.

101 'Thirty Fourth Session of the Indian National Congress, Amritsar, December 27–30, 1919', in A.M. Zaidi (ed) *The Encyclopedia of Indian National Congress, Volume Seven: 1916–1920*, New Delhi: S. Chand, 1979, pp 454–455.

102 'The Reform Bill: Mr. Sastri's views', *Servant of India*, 2 (48), 1 January 1920, p 574.

103 'Thirty Fourth Session of the Indian National Congress', p 454.

104 'Presidential address by Pt. Motilal Nehru', pp 470–525 and 'Resolutions adopted by the Congress', in Zaidi (ed) *Encyclopedia of the Indian National Congress*, pp 526–539.

105 See *Report of the Proceedings of the First Session of the All India Conference of the Moderate Party*, Calcutta, 1 and 2 November 1918, Bombay: Times Press, 1919, p 29; and *Report of the Proceedings of the Second Session of the All India Conference of the Moderate Party*, Calcutta, 30 and 31 December 1919, Calcutta: Sanskrit Press, 1920, pp 22, 115.

## Chapter 4

1 In the 1911 census, Indians constituted 28 per cent of the total population of the town.

2 Extracts reproduced in C.F. Andrews, *Documents Relating to the New Asiatic Bill and the Alleged Breach of Faith*, Cape Town: Cape Times, 1926, p 21.

3 Quoted in Ronald Hyam, 'Smuts in context: Britain and South Africa', in *Understanding the British Empire*, Cambridge: Cambridge University Press, 2010, pp 342–360, at 346.

4 Isaria N. Kimbambo, Gregory H. Madox and Salvatory S. Nyanto, *A New History of Tanzania*, Dar-es-Salam: Mkuki Na Nyota, 2017, p 18.

5 W. Keith Hancock, *Smuts: The Sanguine Years, 1870–1919*, Vol 1, Cambridge: Cambridge University Press, 1962, pp 556–557.

6 As a retaliatory measure the government declared that no South African company would be given mining concessions in Burma. See Hugh Tinker, *Separate and Unequal: India and the Indians in the British Commonwealth, 1920–1950*, London: Oxford University Press, 1971, p 32.

7 'Indians in South Africa: deputation to the Secretary of State', in *The Indian Annual Register 1920*, Vol 2, ed H.N. Mitra, New Delhi: Gyan Publishing House, 2000, pp 333–334.

8 'Indians in South Africa', p 335.

9 'A Hirtzel to Undersecretary of State, Colonial Office, Confidential and Immediate, 26 July 1919', National Archives Repository/Sentrale Argiefbewaarplek (SAB), Governor General (1905–1974) (GG), Vol 707, National Archives of South Africa, Pretoria (henceforth NASA).

10 Sastri, 'Aspects of my life', p 120; for South Africa's views on this, see SAB, GG, Vol 907.

11 Quoted in, Sastri, 'Aspects of my life', p 20.

12 See Vineet Thakur, *Postscripts on Independence*, New Delhi: Oxford University Press, 2018, pp 169–170; 'Indian Information Index, January–June 1941', Vol 8, New Delhi: Bureau of Public Information, Government of India, 1941, p 300. For an extended discussion on Bajpai's pre-independence role, see Amit Das Gupta, 'Indian civil service and Indian foreign policy', in Madhavan K. Palat (ed) *India and the World in the First Half of the Twentieth Century*, London: Routledge, 2017, pp 134–159.

[13] Bajpai to Sapru, 19 April 1921, IOR Neg 4986 – The Sapru correspondence: letters to and from Sir Tej Bahadur Sapru (1872–1949), 1st series, Reel 1 (A–G), IOR&PP, British Library, B 6, f 14–16.
[14] Bajpai to Sapru, 28 April 1921, IOR Neg 4986, B 7, f 17–19.
[15] Vajapeyeam Venkatasubbaiyah was a Servant of Society member from Madras, and also headed the Madras chapter of the society.
[16] Sastri to Suryanarayana Rao, 9 June 1921, VSS Papers (I), Subject File 5, f 76–77.
[17] 'Srinivasa Sastri: Statesman, Scholar, Ascetic', *The Week* (Brisbane), 30 June 1922, p 25.
[18] Sastri to Venkatasubbaiyah, 26 May 1921, VSS Papers (I), Subject File 5, f 73.
[19] Bajpai to Sapru, 9 June 1921, IOR Neg 4986, B 12, f 31–32.
[20] Bajpai to Sapru, 11 May 1921, IOR Neg 4986, B.9, f 26–27.
[21] Sastri to Suryanarayana Rao, 9 June 1921, f 76–77; Sastri, Diary 1921: 7 June, VSS Papers (1).
[22] Chamberlain to Hilda, 18 June 1921, in Robert Self (ed) *The Neville Chamberlain Diary Letters: Volume 2, The Reform Years, 1921–27*, London: Routledge, 2000, p 65.
[23] Bajpai to Sapru, 15 June 1921, IOR Neg 4986, B 13, f 33–34.
[24] 'The Punjab Reports', in *The Indian Annual Register 1921, Part I*, ed H.N. Mitra, 2nd edn, Calcutta: Annual Register Office, 1921, p 106.
[25] 'The Non-Cooperation Agitation', *The Indian Annual Register 1921*, p 193.
[26] Sastri to Paranjpe, 24 July 1921, RP Paranjpe Papers, Correspondence: VS Srinivasa Sastri, NMML, f 8–11.
[27] D.V. Gundappa on Sastri, VSS Papers (I), Writings by others: D.V. Gundappa.
[28] Annie Besant, 'The special congress', *Servant of India*, 3 (33), 16 September 1920, pp 389–390.
[29] W. Keith Hancock, *Smuts: The Fields of Force, 1919–1950*, Cambridge: Cambridge University Press, 1968, pp 89, 100.
[30] O. Geyser, 'Irish independence: Jan Smuts and Eamon de Valera', *Round Table*, 87 (348), 1998, pp 473–484.
[31] Jean Van der Poel (ed), *Selections from Smuts Papers, Vol V, September 1919–November 1934*, Cambridge: Cambridge University Press, 1973, pp 83–107.
[32] Van der Poel, *Selections from Smuts Papers*, p 99.
[33] Sastri to Ramaswami, 16 June 1921, VSS Papers (I), Subject File 5, f 81,
[34] Bajpai to Montagu, MSS Eur 238/3, 1921, IOR&PP, BL, p. 189; Sastri to Ramaswami, 16 June 1921, VSS Papers (I), Subject File 5, f 81.
[35] Sastri to Ramaswami, 16 June 1921, f 81.
[36] Sastri to Sankaran, 7 July 1921, VSS Papers (I), Subject File 5, f 80.
[37] Sastri to Ramaswami, 30 June 1921, VSS Papers (I), Subject File 5, f 82.
[38] Secretary of State to Viceroy, 20 June 1921, IOR/L/E7/1242, F No 2547, IOR&PP.
[39] Quoted in Bajpai to Montagu, MSS Eur 238/3, p 189.
[40] E – Second Meeting, Imperial Conference 1921, SAB, A1, A1/35, NASA, 1921, p 9.
[41] E – Second Meeting, pp 9–10.
[42] E – Second Meeting, p 17.
[43] 'Government of India memorandum on India in the dominions', in *The Indian Annual Register 1922*, Vol 2, ed H.N. Mitra, Calcutta: Annual Register Office, 1923, pp 212–216.

44 E – Nineteenth Meeting, The Imperial Conference 1921, SAB, A1, A1/35, NASA, p 6.
45 Sastri, Diary 1921: 21 June.
46 Bajpai to Montagu, MSS Eur 238/3, p 189.
47 Bajpai to Montagu, MSS Eur 238/3, p 192.
48 Sastri to Sankaran, 7 July 1919, f 80–81.
49 Sastri to Sankaran, 7 July 1921, f 80–81.
50 This had in particular been a consistent theme of Charles Andrews' writings in 1920–21, which influenced young radicals like Jawaharlal Nehru. See Charles Andrews, *How India Can Be Free*, Madras: Cambridge University Press, 1921; Charles Andrews, *Indian Independence: The Immediate Need*, Madras: S. Ganesan, 1921; Charles Andrews, *The Indian Problem*, Madras: G. Natesan, 1921, Charles Andrews, *The Claim for Independence: Within or without the British Empire*, Madras: S. Ganesan, 1921; also see S.R. Mehrotra, 'Gandhi and the British Commonwealth', *India Quarterly*, 17 (1), 1961, pp 44–57.
51 E – Nineteenth Meeting, p 6.
52 E – Nineteenth Meeting, p 7.
53 Sastri to Sankaran, 10 July 1921, in Jagadisan (ed) *Letters of Srinivasa Sastri*, pp 216–217.
54 Bajpai to Sapru, 14 July 1921, IOR Neg 4986, f 9–10; 'Srinivasa Sastri: statesman, scholar, ascetic. India's distinguished delegate', *Argus* (Melbourne), 10 June 1922, p 6.
55 Bajpai to Montagu, MSS Eur 238/3, p 192.
56 E (SC) – Fourth Meeting, The Imperial Conference 1921, SAB, A1, A1/35, NASA, p 3.
57 E (SC) – Fourth Meeting, p 3.
58 E (SC) – Fourth Meeting, p 8.
59 E (SC) – Fourth Meeting, p 8.
60 E (SC) – Fourth Meeting, p 9.
61 Marilyn Lake and Henry Reynolds, *Drawing the Colour Line: White Men's Countries and the International Challenge of Racial Equality*, Cambridge: Cambridge University Press, 2008, p 302.
62 E (SC) – Fourth Meeting, p 10.
63 Van der Poel, *Selections from Smuts Papers, V*, p 152.
64 E (SC) – Fourth Meeting, p 11.
65 E (SC) – Fourth Meeting, p 13.
66 Bajpai to Montagu, MSS Eur 238/3, p 193.
67 Sastri, Diary 1921: 15 July.
68 Bajpai to Montagu, Mss Eur 238/3, p 193. For Montagu–Churchill discussions see Winston Churchill Papers, CHAR/17/7, f 61; 76–81, 95–102, 104–105, 112–115, Churchill College Library, Cambridge University.
69 Sastri to Vaman Rao, 28 July 1921, f 87; Sastri to Sankaran, 21 July 1921, f 86, both in VSS Papers (I), Subject File 5.
70 Sastri to Vaze, 21 July 1921, f 84; Sastri to Sankaran, 21 July 1921, f 86, both in VSS Papers (I), Subject File 5.
71 Quoted in Bajpai to Montagu, MSS Eur 238/3, p 195.
72 Bajpai to Montagu, MSS Eur 238/3, p 197.
73 Sastri, Diary 1921: 2 August 1921.
74 Sastri to Ramaswami, 4 August 1921, VSS Papers (I), Subject File 5, f 89.
75 'Indian rights of citizenship: a step forward', *The Times*, 9 August 1921, p 7.

[76] 'Racial equality or arrogance?', *Bombay Chronicle*, 13 August 1921.
[77] Montagu to Churchill, 21 July 1921, CHAR/17/7, f 102.
[78] 'Rt. Hon. Srinivasa Sastri. Visit to New Zealand. Orator and statesman', *The Press*, 20 April 1922, p 11.
[79] Sastri to Ramaswami, 30 June 1921, VSS Papers (I), Subject File 5, f 79.
[80] 'Empire parliaments. Dominion premiers at the House of Lords', *Otago Daily Times*, 5 September 1921.
[81] Sastri, 'The Guildhall speech', in Natesan (ed) *Speeches and Writings*, p 189.
[82] 'Our London letter', *The Tribune*, 23 June 1921, p 2.
[83] For criticism of the speech, see Taher S. Mahomed, 'The Indian situation', *Bombay Chronicle*, 9 August 1921, p 9.
[84] Sastri, Diary 1921: 25 May; Sastri, 'Aspects of my life', pp 53–54; Bajpai to Sapru, 26 May 1921, IOR Neg 4986, B 10, f 28–29.
[85] Bajpai to Sapru, 26 May 1921, f 28–29.
[86] Sastri, Diary 1921: 5 June; Sastri to Venkatasubbaiyah, 26 May 1921, f 73; Sastri to Ramaswami, 26 May 1921, VSS Papers (I), Subject File 5, f 74; Sastri's address in Shakespeare Hut, 25 May, Weekly Report of the Director, Intelligence Bureau, Home Department, Government of India, Simla, 29 June 1921, Home Department, Political B, Proceedings June 1921, No 287, National Archives, New Delhi, p 2.
[87] Sastri, Diary 1921: 27 July.
[88] H. Wilson Harris, *Geneva 1921: An Account of the Second Assembly of the League of Nations*, London: Daily News and League of Nations Union, 1921, p 3.
[89] Sastri to Ramaswami, 7 September 1921, VSS Papers (I), Subject File 5, f 96.
[90] Sastri to Ramaswami, 7 September 1921, f 96.
[91] Sastri to Ramaswami, 7 September 1921, f 96.
[92] 'What the League is doing. Notable speeches', *The Times*, 20 September 1921, p 9; Bajpai to Sapru, 16 September 1921, IOR Neg 4986, B 21, f 51–52.
[93] Sastri to Ramaswami, 7 September 1921, f 96.
[94] Bajpai to Sapru, 16 September 1921, IOR Neg 4986, f 51–53.
[95] H. Wilson Harris quoted in Kodanda Rao, *Sastri*, p 109.
[96] Sastri, 'Speech at the League of Nations', in Natesan (ed) *Speeches and Writings*, p 195.
[97] Sastri, 'Speech at the League of Nations', p 196.
[98] Sastri, 'Speech at the League of Nations', p 198.
[99] Sastri, 'Speech at the League of Nations', p 204.
[100] Sastri, 'Aspects of my life', pp 43–44.
[101] Bajpai to Sapru, 16 September 1921, IOR Neg 4986, B 21, f 51–52.
[102] Wilson Harris, 'Outward bound'.
[103] See Aiyar, 'Rt. Hon. V.S. Srinivasa Sastri', pp 537–546.
[104] 'What the League is doing. Notable speeches', p 9.
[105] Advisory Committee on Traffic in Opium 1921, Report of Dr. Wellington Koo, C 191 (a) M 133, 1921, XI, League of Nations; *Report of the Delegates of India to the Second Session of the Assembly of the League of Nations*, Delhi: Superintendent Government Printing, 1922, p 125.
[106] Bajpai to Sapru, 16 September 1921, IOR Neg 4986, B 21, f 51–53.
[107] *Report of the Delegates of India*, p 38.
[108] Sastri to Sankaran, 16 September 1921, VSS Papers (I), Subject File 5, f 99.
[109] *Report of the Delegates of India*, pp 36–37.
[110] Sastri to Vaman Rao, 22 September 1921, VSS Papers (I), Subject File 5, f 96.
[111] *Report of the Delegates of India*, p 38.

112. In a final compromise, Sastri agreed to an appended statement of China (and Siam) to the sub-committee's report. *Report of the Delegates of India*, pp 125–127.
113. Bajpai to Sapru, 22 September 1921, IOR Neg 4986, B 22, f 53–54.
114. Sastri, 'Aspects of my life', p 46.
115. Bajpai to Sapru, 6 October 1921, IOR Neg 4986, B 27, f 57–58.

# Chapter 5

1. See 'The delegation to Washington', *Manchester Guardian*, 23 September 1921, L/E/7/1230, IOR&PP.
2. See Michael Graham, 'The Pacific dominions and the Washington Conference, 1921–1922', *Diplomacy and Statecraft*, 4 (3), 1993, pp 60–101 at 69.
3. South Africa had no interest in the Pacific, hence asked Balfour to represent the country.
4. Some Montagu letters, in Jagadisan (ed) *Letters of Srinivasa Sastri*, pp 55–56.
5. Sastri to Rukmini, 27 October 1921, in Jagadisan (ed) *Letters of Srinivasa Sastri*, pp 17–172.
6. Judith Woods, 'Edward, Prince of Wales's tour of India, October 1921–March 1922', *Court Historian*, 5 (3), 2000, pp 217–221.
7. Sastri, 'Aspects of my life', pp 28–29; Sastri to Ramaswami, 17 November 1921, VSS Papers (I), Subject File 5, f 114.
8. See Report on the political situation in India during the month of November 1921, Home Department, Political Branch, File no 18, NAI.
9. Sastri to Ramaswami, 5 October 1921, VSS Papers (I), Subject File 5, f 99.
10. Sastri to Ramaswami, 20 October 1921, f 109 and Sastri to Ramaswami, 12 October 1921, f 107, both in VSS Papers (I), Subject File 5.
11. Sastri to Rukmini, 27 October 1921, p 171.
12. Bajpai to Walton, 2 November 1921, MSS EUR D 545/1, IOR&PP.
13. Sastri to Sankar, 3 November 1921, VSS Papers (I), Subject File 5, f 111.
14. Sastri to Ramaswami, 2 November 1921, VSS Papers (I), Subject File 5.
15. Bajpai to Walton, 2 November 1921.
16. Sastri to Ramaswami, 11 November 1921, VSS Papers (I), Subject File 5, f 113.
17. 'Wells and Edison fear greed and bias will menace parley', *Washington Times*, 6 November 1921, p 1.
18. Sastri to Ramaswami, 11 November 1921, f 113.
19. 'Harding's tribute to unknown hero', *Standard Union*, 11 November 1921, p 1; 'Unknown soldier sleeps at Arlington', *Baltimore Sun*, 11 November 1921, p 1.
20. H.G. Wells, 'German and Russian war dead will be mourned by all', *Baltimore Sun*, 11 November 1921, p 1.
21. Diary 1921: 11 November.
22. Mark Sullivan, *The Great Adventure at Washington: The Story of the Conference*, New York: Doubleday Page and Company, 1922, pp 1–2.
23. This included the president, the four members of the American delegation and four naval experts.
24. Charles Repington, *After the War; London–Paris–Rome–Athens–Prague–Vienna–Budapest–Bucharest–Berlin–Sofia–Coblenz–New York–Washington; a Diary*, Boston: Houghton Mifflin, 1922, p 432; Thomas Bailey, *A Diplomatic History of American People*, 10th edn, New Jersey: Prentice Hall, 1980, p 640.
25. Repington, *After the War*, p 433.
26. Ring Lardner quoted in Sullivan, *The Great Adventure at Washington*, p 67.

## NOTES

27 Sastri to Ramaswami, 17 November 1921, VSS Papers (I), Subject File 5, f 114,
28 V.S. Srinivasa Sastri, 'Impressions of America', *Servant of India*, 5 (13), 27 April 1922, pp 150–151.
29 See British Empire Delegation Conference: Minutes 48–73, CAB – 30/1A, Cabinet Papers, The National Archives, London.
30 Enclosure 1: The Right Hon. V.S.S. Sastri to Secretary of State for India, I&O 2641/1921, L/E/7/1245, IOR&PP.
31 Wickham Steed, 'Sees momentous events at next plenary session: British editor here raps Prophets of Failure for Parley', *Washington Herald*, 1 December 1921, p 3.
32 Quoted in Sullivan, *The Great Adventure at Washington*, p 58.
33 Quoted in Sullivan, *The Great Adventure at Washington*, p 52.
34 Sullivan, *The Great Adventure at Washington*, p 53.
35 Sullivan, *The Great Adventure at Washington*, pp 63–64.
36 Minutes of Meetings, AC 1–10, p 31, CAB 30/9.
37 Sullivan, *The Great Adventure at Washington*, pp 83–84.
38 Air power was also discussed, but it was still considered a technology of the future, hence any consensus was unlikely.
39 In addition, Japan replaced one specific ship, the *Mutsu*, with another, the *Settsu*. America agreed to Japan's demands on the condition that Hawaii was exempted, and that all other powers which had signed the Quadruple Treaty would also accept the status quo. Report by G.S. Bajpai, 22 December 1921, I&O 23/1922, L/E/7/1245, IOR&PP; and Sadao Asada, 'From Washington to London: the Imperial Japanese Navy and the politics of naval limitation, 1921–1930', *Diplomacy and Statecraft*, 4 (3), 1993, pp 147–191 at 154.
40 Sullvan, *The Great Adventure at Washington*, p 157.
41 Minutes of Meetings, AC 1–10, pp 78–86, CAB 30/9.
42 Report by G.S. Bajpai, 22 December 1921.
43 Minutes of Meetings, AC 1–10, pp 78–86, CAB 30/9.
44 As the *New York Herald* called the submarine. See Sullivan, *The Great Adventure at Washington*, p 168.
45 Memorandum by the Standing Sub-Committee: The Washington Conference on Limitations of Armaments, Secret 280-B, October 1921, p 5, CAB 30/1A.
46 Fourteenth Conference of British Empire Delegation, Held at the British Embassy, Washington, on Monday, 19 December 1921, CAB 30-1A.
47 Report by G.S. Bajpai, 12 January 1922, I&O 23/1922, L/E/7/1245.
48 Enclosure 1: The Right Hon. V.S.S. Sastri to Secretary of State for India, I&O 2641/1921, L/E/7/1245, pp 5–6.
49 These were the words of Japan's Navy Minister, Kato Tomosaburo. See Asada, 'From Washington to London', p 149.
50 Frederick McCormick, *The Menace of Japan*, Boston: Little, Brown, and Company, 1917; Walter Pitkin, *Must We Fight Japan?* New York: The Century Company, 1921; Sidney Osborns, *The New Japanese Peril*, New York: Macmillan, 1921; Jesse F. Steiner, *Japanese Invasion: A Study in the Psychology of Interracial Contacts*, Chicago: A.C. McClurg, 1917.
51 Thomas A. Bailey, *A Diplomatic History of American People*, p 638; Sadao Asada, *Culture Shock and Japanese–American Relations*, Columbia: University of Missouri Press, 2007, p 36.
52 T. Fraser, 'India in Anglo-Japanese relations during the First World War', *History*, 63 (209), 1978, pp 366–382.

53 Enclosure 1: The Right Hon. V.S.S. Sastri to Secretary of State for India; Report by G.S. Bajpai, 7 December 1921, I&O 23/1922, L/E/7/1245.
54 'India's part in conference to be that of an onlooker', *Evening Star* (Washington), 8 November 1921, p 4.
55 'Behind the scenes at the nation's capital', *Philadelphia Inquirer*, 21 November 1921, p 10.
56 Edwin C. Hill, 'Emancipation of races once ignored is strikingly shown in world gathering in the US capital – delegates expect to complete work before Christmas', *New York Herald*, 1 December 1921, p 3.
57 Hill, 'Emancipation of races', p 3.
58 Hill, 'Emancipation of races', p 3.
59 Arthur S. Draper, 'Britain sends a family party?', *New York Tribune*, 6 November 1921, p 27.
60 H.G. Wells, 'Urge consideration for India's problem', *Philadelphia Inquirer*, 8 December 1921, p 4.
61 'Sastri to Rukmini, 27 October 1921', in Jagadisan (ed) *Letters of Srinivasa Sastri*, p 171.
62 'India strong for peace, says Sastri', *Washington Herald*, 9 November 1921, p 4; 'Britain would limit armament to point of nation's safety', *Philadelphia Enquirer*, 2 November 1921, p 3.
63 'Japan. Confidential: racial discrimination and immigration, 10 October', I&O 2334/1921, L/E/7/1239, IOR&PP, pp 1, 22.
64 Louis Kershaw, Note on 15 October 1921, I&P 2267/1921, L/E/7/1234, IOR&PP; also F.W. Duke, Note on 14 November 1921, I&P 2267/1921, L/E/7/1234, IOR&PP.
65 'Prince Sastri to talk on Oriental affairs', *Washington Times*, 22 January 1922, p 3; 'Foreign envoys will meet Red Cross leaders: arms delegates accept invitations to gathering at Shubert–Garrick theater', *Washington Times*, 12 November 1921, p 12.
66 David L. Blumenfeld, 'Washington now "wetter" than European capitals; and envoys shoot craps!', *Brooklyn Daily Times*, 1 January 1922, p 18.
67 'Dark propaganda clouds hover over arms parley', *Washington Herald*, 9 December 1921, p 2.
68 William K. Hutchison, envoy of India likens Gandhi to Roosevelt', *Washington Times*, 27 November 1921, p 5.
69 'Says India will speak as co-equal partner in 10 years', *Baltimore Sun*, 14 December 1921, p 9; also 'Predicts India will win autonomy', *New York Times*, 14 December 1921, p 12; 'India really in the conference', *Brooklyn Daily Eagle*, 15 December 1921, p 6; 'Speaks to club on India: can be saved only by dominion government, Sastri says', *Washington Post*, 31 January 1922, p 12.
70 'Conditions in India described', *Caledion-Record* (Vermont), 14 September 1922, pp 1, 4; 'Likens Gandhi to Christ', *Los Angeles Times*, 29 July 1922, p 29; P.W. Wilson, '"The things that are Caesar's"', *New York Times*, 9 April 1922, p 62.
71 'Predicts India will win autonomy', p 12.
72 'Gandhi urges back to nature, lives along the lines he teaches', *Evening Star* (Washington), 20 March 1922, p 17.
73 'Predicts India will win autonomy', p 12.
74 See in particular the coverage of Bombay Chronicle, in *Report on Native Papers for the Week Ending 5 November 1921*, jstor.org/stable/10.2307/saoa.crl.25637246, 21

March 2020, p 1289; *Report on Native Papers for the Week Ending 19 November 1921*, jstor.org/stable/10.2307/saoa.crl.25637248, 21 March 2020, pp 1359–1360.
75. 'British rule in India has a harsh critic', *Altooba Tribune* (Pennsylvania), 22 December, p 1; 'British rule criticized by a speaker from India', *New York Tribune*, 22 December 1921, p 2.
76. See Bose, *Indian Revolutionaries Abroad*; Ramnath, *Haj to Utopia*.
77. Taraknath Das, 'India and the conference', *San Francisco Examiner*, 2 November 1921, p 26.
78. Taraknath Das, *Is Japan a Menace to Asia?*, Shanghai: Author, 1917.
79. Das, *Is Japan a Menace to Asia?*, p 55.
80. Das, *Is Japan a Menace to Asia?*, p 79.
81. ' "Republicans" of India plan boycott on Japanese goods as well British imports', *Democrat and Chronicle*, 1 November 1921, p 1; 'India boycotts Japanese goods to fight Britain', *Washington Times*, 6 November 1921, p 7.
82. Das, 'India and the conference'.
83. Taraknath Das, Sailendranath Ghose, Sarat Mukherji, Nani Gopal Bose and Haridas Gayadeen, 'A protest against the torture of war prisoners in India, 7 December 1921', *South Asian American Digital Archive*, www.saada.org/item/20130131-1285, accessed 16 November 2019.
84. Sastri to Ramaswami, 24 November 1921, VSS Papers (I), Subject File 5, f 115–116.
85. 'Indian delegate is heckled here', *New York Times*, 29 January 1922, p 25.
86. For a good discussion on the constant maneuvers of strategy that both sides engaged in see, D.A. Low, 'The government of India and the first non-cooperation movement', *Journal of Asian Studies*, 25 (2), 1966, pp 241–259.
87. D.G. Tendulkar, *Mahatma: Life of Mohandas Karamchand Gandhi*, Vol 2 (1920–29), New Delhi: Publications Division, Ministry of Information and Broadcasting, Government of India, p 104.
88. G.L. Corbett to J.C. Walton, 25 November 1921, I&O 2620/1921, L/E/7/1239, IOR&PP.
89. Sastri to Ramaswami, 30 December 1921, VSS Papers (I), Subject File 5, f 118.
90. Quoted in 'A distinguished visitor', *Evening Post*, 11 July 1922, p 6.
91. Bajpai to Sapru, 17 November 1921, IOR Neg 4986, B 21, f 61–62.
92. Bajpai to Sapru, 17 November 1921, B 21, f 61–62.
93. M. Jeffrey Brenner, *Structure of Decision: Indian Foreign Policy Bureaucracy*, New Delhi: South Asian Publishers, 1983, p 79.

# Chapter 6

1. 'Mr. Sastri's view: effects of N.C.O., the British attitude', *Times of India*, 18 February 1922, p 9.
2. Waley, *Edwin Montagu*, p 269.
3. Sastri to Ramaswami, 23 February 1922, VSS Papers (I), Subject File 5, f 119–120.
4. Sastri, Diary 1921: 11 August; Sastri, 'Aspects of my life', p 30.
5. For his views on Montagu, see V.S. Srinivasa Sastri, 'Montagu memorial lecture', Bombay: Committee of the Montagu Memorial Fund, 1925, p 28.
6. 'Further constitutional advance: Mr. Sastri's speech', *Servant of India*, 5 (15), 11 May 1922, pp 178–179.
7. Reading to Peel, 22 June 1922, MS EUR 238/5, f 70, IOR&PP.
8. 'West's clash with the East', *Daily Mail*, 15 May 1922, p 10.

9. 'India's place in the empire: Mr. Sastri's speech', *Servant of India*, 5 (16), 18 May 1922, pp 189–191 at 191. Later in his memoirs, Sastri argued that even though he stood by what he said, his conduct was inappropriate for the occasion. See Sastri, 'If I live again', VSS Papers (I), Speeches/Writings by Him, S No 82, f 162–163.
10. A. Aravauda Aiyagar, 'Our Indian visitor: the Rt. Hon. V.S. Srinivasa Sastri, a character sketch', *Daily News* (Perth), 1 June 1922, p 3 (this article was reproduced from *New India*, 5 April 1922).
11. Aiyagar, 'Our Indian visitor', p. 3.
12. *The Indian Sociologist: An Organ of Freedom, and of Political, Social and Religious Reform*, 13 (1), August 1922, p 2, in Syud Hossain Papers, Periodicals, S No 3, NMML.
13. Whip, 'From the desk', *Hindustan Review*, 44 (264), September 1921, p 7.
14. 'Notes of the day', *Bombay Chronicle*, 13 October 1921.
15. Sastri to G.A. Natesan, 8 March 1922, VSS Papers (II), Correspondence: G.A. Natesan.
16. 'The servant in a temper', *Indian Social Reformer*, 33 (34), 23 April 1922, pp 579–580.
17. Bajpai to Sapru, 31 May 1922, IOR Neg 4986, Reel 1 (A–G), IOR&PP.
18. G.S. Bajpai, 'Report to the Secretary of State', MSS EUR 238/3, p 197.
19. Secretary of State to Viceroy, 20 June 1921, F No 2547, IOR/L/E7/1242.
20. Bajpai, 'Report to the Secretary of State', p 197.
21. Sastri was also expected to go to Fiji alongside the dominion tour which he later cancelled, preferring to return on a short break to India instead.
22. Sastri to Montagu, 29 August 1921 and 19 September 1921, F No 2547, IOR/L/E7/1242.
23. Sastri to Montagu, 29 August 1921, F No 2547, IOR/L/E7/1242.
24. 'Question of Mr. Sastri's deputation in Canada, New Zealand and Australia to consult with governments of these countries as to the translation into practice of the imperial conference resolution on Indians in the empire', 3 February 1922, IOR/L/E/7/1242, F No 2547.
25. On the SS *Ormonde*: www.ssmaritime.com/RMS-Ormonde.htm, accessed 22 June 2018.
26. 'Brief of instructions for the Right Honourable Srinivasa Sastri', F No 2547, IOR/L/E/7/1242.
27. Sastri to Rukmini, 13 March 1922, VSS Papers (II), Correspondence: Rukmini.
28. Lake and Reynolds, *Drawing the Colour Line*, p 2.
29. Further, the brief of instructions to Sastri asked him to obtain more information on: the attitude of Australia towards Anglo-Indian immigrants and the possibility of permitting some Asiatic immigrants into the tropical regions of Australia.
30. A.D. Ellis, 'Srinivasa Sastri: a racial ambassador; visit to Australia', *Argus* (Melbourne), 27 May 1922, p 6.
31. Ellis, 'Srinivasa Sastri', p 6.
32. Ellis, 'Srinivasa Sastri', p 6.
33. 'The Right Hon. V.S. Sastri: a distinguished indian. Visit to Adelaide', *Chronicle* (Adelaide), 10 June 1922, p 42.
34. 'Mr. Sastri arrives. A striking personality', *Advertiser* (Adelaide), 7 June 1922, p 9.
35. V.S. Srininasa Sastri, 'Report by the Right Hon'ble V.S. Srinivasa Sastri, P.C., regarding his deputation to the dominions of Australia, New Zealand and Canada', Simla: Government Central Press, 1923, p 7.
36. V.S. Srinivasa Sastri, 'Speech at Perth', in Natesan (ed) *Speeches and Writings*, p 257.
37. Sastri, 'Speech at Perth', p 258.
38. Sastri, 'Speech at Perth', pp 258–259.
39. Sastri, 'Speech at Perth', pp 254–265.

40. Sastri, 'Speech at Perth', p 267; 'Indians in Australia. Mr. Sastri pleads their case', in 'Dr. Sastri visit to Australia', WA 22/348, A1, 1923/7187, National Archives of Australia (henceforth NAA).
41. 'Grievances: points to visitor', in A1, 1923/7187, WA 22/348, A1, 1923/7187, NAA; Bajpai to J. Hullah, 3 June 1922, in Sapru Correspondence, 2nd Series, Reel 1, B6.
42. 'India's delegate. Mr. Sastri's visit. Stirring speeches', *West Australian* (Perth), 3 June 1922, p 8.
43. 'Mr. Sastri's visit. To the editor', *West Australian* (Perth), 13 June 1922, p 10.
44. 'Mr. Sastri', *Advertiser* (Adelaide), 8 June 1922, p 12.
45. 'Mr. Sastri's visit', *Queenslander* (Brisbane), 1 July 1922, p 9.
46. 'Full Status', *Evening Star*, 12 July 1922, p 3.
47. 'Full status', p 3.
48. A.G. Stephens, 'Indians in Australia. The Rt. Hon. Srinivasa Sastri', *Northern Champion* (NSW), 29 July 1922, p 2.
49. Stephens, 'Indians in Australia', p 2; also see 'A distinguished visitor', *Manawatu Daily Times*, 13 July 1922, p 4.
50. 'Servant of India', *New Zealand Herald*, 16 May 1922, p 5.
51. 'Notes of the day. Mr. Srinivasa Sastri's visit', *Daily Mail* (Brisbane), 5 June 1922, p 6.
52. For debates on this in Australian newspapers, see Matthew Cranston, 'Tropical Australia', *Register* (Adelaide), 7 January 1922; 'Coloured labour: for the Northern Territory', *The Journal* (Adelaide), 10 January 1922, p 3 (comments from: F.W. Birrell, John. H. Packard and Matthew Cranston); Matthew Cranston, 'White Australia and coloured labour', *Register* (Adelaide), 10 February 1922, p 3; 'White Australia and coloured labour', *Register* (Adelaide), 27 March 1922, p 5; Matthew Cranston, 'White Australia and coloured labour', *Register* (Adelaide), 7 June 1922, p 9; Matthew Cranston, 'White Australia and coloured labour', *Register* (Adelaide), 7 June 1922; Matthew Cranston, 'White Australia and coloured labour', *Register* (Adelaide), 16 June 1922, p 4; Arch McDonald, 'Mr. Sastri and White Australia', 26 June 1922, p 9.
53. Matthew Cranston, 'White Australia and coloured labour', *Register* (Adelaide), 16 June 1922, p 4.
54. V.S. Srinivasa Sastri, 'Confidential report by the Rt. Hon'ble V.S. Srinivasa Sastri, P.C. regarding his deputation to the dominions', Simla: Government Central Press, 1923, p 5.
55. 'Srinivasa Sastri welcomed to Melbourne; interesting interview, patience and resignation India's national character', *Ballarat Star* (Victoria), 12 June 1922, p 3.
56. 'Indians' status. Appeal for equality. Mr. Sastri in Melbourne', *Brisbane Courier*, 13 June 1922, p 10; 'Equality for Indians. Mr. Sastri's appeal', *Daily News* (Perth), 13 June 1922, p 5.
57. 'Labour and Mr. Sastri', *Daily Telegraph* (Sydney), 22 June 1922, p 8; also Sastri, 'Confidential report', p 4.
58. 'Srinivasa Sastri. In Sydney today. Claims of Indians', *Daily Telegraph* (Sydney), 14 June 1922, p 6.; 'India's aims. Mr. Sastri at Trades Hall. Officials ask questions', *Argus* (Melbourne), 14 June 1922, p 11.
59. 'What is the Sastri move?', *Daily Standard* (Brisbane), 21 June 1922, p 4.
60. 'What is the Sastri move?', p 4.
61. 'Indians and the empire', *New Zealand Herald*, 19 July 1922, p 8; 'Mr. Sastri's mission', *Evening Star*, 11 July 1922, p 4.

62. 'Mr. Sastri', *Advertiser* (Adelaide), 8 June 1922, p 12.
63. A.G. Stephens, 'Indians in Australia', p 2.
64. 'What's Sastri's game? Indian tiger on the prowl, in Australia with sheathed claws. An enemy invited by W.M. Hughes', *Smith's Weekly* (Sydney), 17 June 1922, in A1, 1923/7187, 22/10271, NAA.
65. 'G.S. Bajpai to J.C. Walton, 7 June 1922', MSS Eur D. 545/1, IORPP, BL.
66. Sastri, 'Report', pp 12–13.
67. 'Sastri's mission. Australia's position. Letter from Mr. Hughes', *Brisbane Courier* (Queensland), 16 September 1922, p 7.
68. Sastri, 'Report', p. 4.
69. Dorothy Evelyn Walker, 'Srinivasa Sastri and his dominion tour of 1922, MA Thesis, University of London, 1976', MSS EUR Photo EUR 299, IOR&PP, p 26. Also see Margaret Allen, '"I am a British subject": Indians in Australia claiming their rights, 1880–1940', *History Australia*, 15 (3), 2018, pp 499–518.
70. Walker, 'Srinivasa Sastri', p 26.
71. Sastri, 'Report', p. 8.
72. B.N. Sarma, 'Appendix, 3 May 1922, pp 8–9', in 'Brief of Instructions for the Right Honourable Srinivasa Sastri', IOR/L/E/7/1242, F No 2547.
73. Sastri, 'Confidential report', pp 5–6.
74. 'Mr. Sastry's report on his deputation', *Indian Social Reformer*, XXXII (28), 10 March 1922, p 443.
75. Brij Lal, 'East Indians in British Columbia, 1904–1914: An Historical Study in Growth and Integration', Master's thesis, University of British Columbia, 1979.
76. Bruce Hutchinson, *The Incredible Canadian: A Candid Portrait of Mackenzie King; His Works, His Times, and His Nation*, New York: Longmans, Green and Co, 1953.
77. 'White Australia. Mr. Sastri's visit to Canada', *The Australian* (Perth), 17 November 1922, p 3.
78. Sastri to Ramaswami, 15 August 1922, VSS Papers (I), Subject File 5, f 124.
79. Sastri, 'Confidential report', p 6; Joseph Pope to MacKenzie King, 14 August 1922, f 67591–67598, MG26-J1. Volume/box number: 80, C-2248, Library and Archives Canada, Ottawa (Henceforth, LAC). Pope also thought that Sastri was playing a little bluff, for Sastri was too wise to engage in such a childish act. See Pope to Mackenzie King, 19 August 1922, f 67607–67610, C-2248.
80. Pope to Mackenzie King, 19 August 1922, f 67607–67610, C-2248, LAC.
81. Sastri to Ramaswami, 19 August 1922, VSS Papers (I), f 125, Subject File 5; Sastri, 'Confidential report', p 6.
82. 'Status of Indians. Mr. Sastri in British Columbia', *The Press*, 23 August 1922, p 7.
83. Sastri, 'Confidential report', pp 6–7; Sastri to Ramaswami, 15 August 1922, f 124.
84. Sastri to Ramaswami, 15 August 1922, f 124.
85. Sastri, 'Confidential report', p 7.
86. Sastri, 'Confidential report', p 7.
87. 'Race and creed no barrier, says Sastri', *Vancouver Sun*, 17 August 1922, p 1.
88. Walker, 'Srinivasa Sastri', p 27.
89. Sastri, 'Speech at the Reform Club, Montreal, 1922', in Natesan (ed) *Writings and Speeches*, p 300; 'Sastri in Canada', *Brisbane Courier*, 12 September 1922, p 7.
90. 'The higher imperialism', *Vancouver Sun*, 25 August 1922, p 4.
91. Sastri, 'Speech at the Reform Club, Montreal, 1922', pp 300–304.
92. Ladner to Meighen, 19 September 1922, MG26-I. Volume/box number: 98, C-3455, f 056205-056206, LAC.
93. Bajpai to J.S. Walton, 17 September 1922; Sastri, 'Confidential report', p 8.

94 For these discussions, see Meighen Correspondence, C-3455, f056187-056217, LAC.
95 Sastri, 'Confidential report', p 7.
96 Sastri, 'Confidential report', p 7.
97 Sastri, 'Speech at the Canadian Club, 1922', in Sastri, *Writings and Speeches*, pp 315–318, p at 317.
98 Sastri, 'Report', p 12.
99 Bajpai to J.S. Walton, 17 September 1922, F No 2547, IOR/L/E7/1242.
100 Kodanda Rao, *Sastri*, p 126.
101 Peel to Reading, 3 October 1923, MSS 238/6, IOR&PP.
102 H.S.L. Polak, 'Mr. Sastri and his mission', pp 194–196.
103 'Notes and news', *Indian Opinion*, 34 (20), 25 August 1922, p 197.
104 'Notes and news', p 197.
105 Banarasi Das Chaturvedi to Srinivasa Sastri, 6 October 1922, VSS Papers (I), Correspondence: Banarasi Das Chaturvedi; Polak, 'Mr. Sastri and his mission'.
106 M.K. Gandhi, 'The Simla visit', *The Tribune*, 1 June 1921, p 5.
107 Reproduced as Benarasi Das Chaturvedi, 'Mr. Sastri's tour', *Servant of India*, 5 (17), 25 May 1922, p 203.
108 H.S.L. Polak, 'Equal status: the next step', *Servant of India*, 5 (16), 18 May 1922, pp 184–185.
109 'The world's public opinion', *Servant of India*, 5 (11), 13 April 1922, p 122.
110 'Mr. Sastry's report on his deputation', *Indian Social Reformer*, 32 (28), 10 March 1922, pp 443–445.
111 'The Indians. Claim for equal status. Mr. Srinivasa Sastri speaks of his tour of the dominions', *Tweed Daily* (Murwillumbah), 16 December 1922, p 5; 'India and empire. Mr. Sastri's mission', *Telegraph* (Brisbane), 27 December 1922, p 2.
112 'A remarkable statement. Sastri's anti-British attitude', *Brisbane Courier*, 14 September 1922, p 5.
113 Austen Chamberlain to Winston Churchill, 11 October 1922, Churchill Papers, CHAR 2/125/17.
114 Reading to Peel, 20 September 1921, MSS EUR 238/5, IOR&PP.
115 Kodanda Rao, *The Right Honourable*, p 143.

## Chapter 7

1 'A new massacre of S. Bartholomew in Kenya? Threats of white savages', *New India*, 3 April 1923, in IOR/L/PO/6 (ii), f 150.
2 William M. Ross, *Kenya from Within: A Short Political History*, London: George Allen, 1922, p 362; Christopher P. Youe, 'The threat of settler rebellion and the imperial predicament: the denial of Indian rights in Kenya, 1923', *Canadian Journal of History*, 12 (3), 1968, pp 347–360 at 349.
3 C.J.D. Duder, 'The settler response to the Indian crisis of 1923 in Kenya: brigadier general Philip Wheatley and "direct action"', *Journal of Imperial and Commonwealth History*, 17 (3), 1989, pp 349–373 at 360.
4 Ross, *Kenya from Within*, p 367; 'Kenya', in S.A. Waiz (ed) *Indians Abroad*, 2nd edn, Bombay: Imperial Indian Citizenship Association, 1927, p 12.
5 Ross, *Kenya from Within*, p 373; 'The racial trouble in Kenya', *The Times*, 23 January 1923, in IOR, L/PO/1/6 (iii).
6 See Youe, 'The threat of settler rebellion', p 350.
7 See in 'Indians in Kenya: Memorandum by the Secretary of State for the Colonies', 14 February 1923, CAB/24/158, National Archives, London.

8. Ross, *Kenya from Within*, pp 375–376.
9. See Duder, 'The settler response', pp 362–363.
10. Duder, 'The settler response', pp 360–361, and Ross, *Kenya from Within*, pp 375–376.
11. Duder suggests that this was not considered to be practical. Instead, it was expected that strict rationing would push the Indians out of the Highlands.
12. For a brilliant discussion on the role of British Indian army veterans like Wheatley in the 1923 settler rebellion, see Duder, 'The settler response', pp 355–356.
13. Ross, *Kenya from Within*, pp 365–366.
14. Ross, *Kenya from Within*, p 370, Waiz, *Indians Abroad*, p 12.
15. Waiz, *Indians Abroad*, p 17.
16. Letter reproduced in Waiz, *Indians Abroad*, pp 19–20.
17. Sana Aiyar, *Indians in Kenya: The Politics of Diaspora*, Cambridge, MA: Harvard University Press, 2015, p 25.
18. Ernst L. Bentley and Frederick Lugard, *British East Africa and Uganda: A Historical Record compiled from Captain Lugard's and Other Reports*, London: Chapman and Hall, 1892, p 25.
19. See Aiyar, *Indians in Kenya*, pp 26–27.
20. Aiyar, *Indians in Kenya*, p 27.
21. Bentley and Lugard, *British East Africa and Uganda*, p 25.
22. Elspeth Huxley, *White Man's Country: Lord Delamere and the Making of Kenya, Volume I – 1870–1914*, London: Macmillan, 1935, p 33.
23. Kennedy, *Islands of White: Settler Society and Culture in Kenya and Rhodesia, 1890–1939*, Durham, NC: Duke University Press, 1987, pp 2–8.
24. Levi I. Izuakor, 'Kenya: demographic constraints on the growth of European settlement, 1900–1956', *Africa: Rivista trimestrale di studi e documentazione dell'Istituto Italiano per l'Africa e l'Oriente*, 42 (3), 1987, pp 400–416 at 404.
25. A.J.P. Taylor, *English History, 1914–45*, Penguin: Harmondsworth, 1976, p 151.
26. Huxley, *White Man's Country*, pp 107–109.
27. M.P.K. Sorrenson, *Origins of European Settlement in Kenya*, Oxford: Oxford University Press, 1968, p 230. Also see Brian M. Du Toit, *The Boers in East Africa: Ethnicity and Identity*, Westport, CT: Bergin and Garvey, 1998.
28. W. McGregor Ross, Director of Public Works (1905–1923), quoted in Izuakor, 'Kenya', p 406.
29. See C.J.D. Duder, '"Men of the officer class": the participants in the 1919 Soldier Settler Settlement Scheme in Kenya', *African Affairs*, 92 (366), 1993, pp 69–87 at 70.
30. Kennedy, *Islands of White*, pp 2–8.
31. Quoted in Aiyar, *Indians in Kenya*, p 36.
32. Further, there were 2,431 Goans and 10,102 Arabs. See 'Annual Report of the Social and Economic Progress of the People of the Kenya Colony and Protectorate, 1931', Colonial Reports – Annual, No 1606, London: His Majesty's Stationery Service, 1923, p 6, http://libsysdigi.library.illinois.edu/ilharvest/Africana/Books2011-05/5530244/5530244_1931/5530244_1931_opt.pdf, accessed 25 July 2019.
33. Robert G. Gregory, *India and East Africa: A History of Race Relations within the British Empire, 1890–1939*, New York: Oxford University Press, 1971, pp 182–183.
34. Waiz, *Indians Abroad*, p 4.
35. Waiz, *Indians Abroad*, p 5.

## NOTES

36. William K. Hancock, *Survey of the British Commonwealth, 1918–39*, Vol 1, London: Oxford University Press, 1977, pp 212–213.
37. Robert J. Blyth, *The Empire of the Raj: Eastern Africa and the Middle East, 1858–1947*, Basingstoke: Palgrave Macmillan, 2003, pp 95–96.
38. Theodore Morison, 'A colony for India', circulated by Edwin Montagu to the War Cabinet, CAB/24/58/32, National Archives, London.
39. Aga Khan, *The Memories of Aga Khan: World Enough and Time*, New York: Simon and Schuster, 1954, p 35.
40. Morison, 'A colony for India'.
41. Aga Khan, *Memories*, p 132.
42. Aga Khan, *Memories*, p 127.
43. Morison, 'A colony for India'.
44. Aga Khan, *Memories*, p 127.
45. Aga Khan, *Memories*, p 127.
46. Aga Khan, *Memories*, pp 128–129.
47. Aga Khan, *Memories*, p 130.
48. See, D.M. Desai, 'Indians in Kenya (British East Africa)', *Indian Review*, 24 (5), May 1923, pp 354–358.
49. Blyth, *The Empire of the Raj*, p 120.
50. Whip, 'From the desk', p 5.
51. Gregory, *India and East Africa*, p 178.
52. Gregory, *India and East Africa*, pp 191–192, 195.
53. Montagu, 'Grievance of Indians in Kenya: memo', CAB 24/114/39.
54. Winston Churchill, *My African Journey*, Toronto: William Briggs, 1909, pp 49–50.
55. Lionel Curtis quoted in Deborah Lavin, *From Empire to International Commonwealth: A Biography of Lionel Curtis*, Oxford: Clarendon Press, 1995, p 121.
56. Sastri to Ramaswami, 23 August 1921, VSS Papers (I), Sub File 5, f 95.
57. See, 'Lord Delamere's Memorandum on the case against the claims of Indians in Kenya', in Waiz, *Indians Abroad*, pp 21–31.
58. Mr. Churchill's Speech at the Kenya and Uganda Dinner, 28 January 1922. This is Appendix IV in CAB 24/158, National Archives, London.
59. Gregory, *India and East Africa*, 214–215.
60. 'Some Montagu letters', in Jagadian (ed) *Letters of Srinivasa Sastri*, p 57; Sastri to Natesan, 1 September 1921, VSS Papers (II), Correspondence: G.A. Natesan.
61. 'From Washington to Montagu, 1 Feb. 1922', CAB/24/132/87.
62. Sastri to Ramaswami, 23 February 1922, VSS Papers (I), Sub File 5, f 119–120.
63. Gregory, *India and East Africa*, p 215.
64. Gregory, *India and East Africa*, pp 219–220.
65. Devonshire, 'Memorandum by the Secretary of State for the Colonies', 14 February 1923, CAB/24/158, f 3.
66. Duder, 'The settler response', p 363.
67. Sastri, 'Resolution in the Council of State', in *The Kenya Problem*, p 10.
68. Sastri, 'Resolution in the Council of State', p 5.
69. Kodanda Rao, *Sastri*, p 146; 'Monday's proceedings: Indians' rights in Kenya', *Times of India*, 7 March 1923, p 12.
70. Sastri to Rukmini, 22 April 1923, in Jagadian (ed) *Letters of Srinivasa Sastri*, p 181.
71. Gorman, *The Emergence of International Society*, p 123.
72. 'A letter from London', *Servant of India*, 6 (12), 19 April 1923, p 140.
73. Elspeth Huxley, *White Man's Country: Lord Delamere and the Making of Kenya, Volume 2 – 1914–1931*, London: Macmillan, 1935, p 144.

74 'Revision of Kenya Constitution: Mr. Andrews returns, need for fresh consultations in India', *Times of India*, 30 June 1926, p 11; Huxley, *White Man's Country*, Vol 2, pp 144–145.
75 The Kenya Woman's Committee, 'The Indian question in Kenya: the woman's point of view', IOR/L/PO/6 (ii), IOR&PP, f 104.
76 The Kenya Woman's Committee, 'The Indian question in Kenya', f 105.
77 'An African 1776?', *The Outlook*, in IOR, L/PO/I/6 (iii) – East Africa: Kenya, IOR&PP, BL. Also 'Montaguism after Montagu', *Northern Whig* (Belfast), 23 January 1923, in IOR, L/PO/I/6 (iii) – East Africa: Kenya, IOR&PP, BL.
78 Sastri, 'Kenya deputation's statement', in *The Kenya Problem*, p 54. Also see Charles F. Andrews, 'The abolition of colour bar', *Indian Review*, 24 (12), December 1923, pp 725–729; Memorandum from Tej Bahadur Sapru to Lord Reading, November 1928, IOR Neg 4986, Reel 4, IOR&PP, BL.
79 See *Servant of India*, 9 (12), 19 April 1923, p 134.
80 Sastri, 'Kenya Deputation's statement', in *The Kenya Problem*, p 54.
81 Sastri to Natesan, 22 May 1923, in Jagadisan (ed) *Letters of Srinivasa Sastri*, p 234.
82 Sastri to Natesan, 22 May 1923, p 234.
83 See Sastri's letter to *The Times* reproduced in V.S. Srinivasa Sastri, 'Indians in Kenya', *Servant of India*, 6 (24), 12 July 1923, p 287.
84 Anonymous, 'How we treat natives in Kenya: champions or oppressors', *Manchester Guardian*, 28 April 1923, p 12.
85 Norman Leys, 'Letter to the editor: the Kenya problem', *Manchester Guardian*, 26 April 1923, p 6.
86 'The administration of Kenya', *Servant of India*, 6 (23), 5 July 1923, p 274.
87 Alexander C. May, 'The Round Table, 1910–1966', PhD thesis, University of Oxford, 1995, p 289.
88 Although published anonymously as was the practice of this journal, one of the two authors was its editor, John Dove. Anon [John Dove and Rice], 'Kenya', *Round Table*, 13 (51), 1923, pp 507–529 at 526.
89 Dove and Rice, 'Kenya', p 527.
90 Sastri to Natesan, 22 May 1923, pp 234–235.
91 Sastri to Natesan, 22 May 1923, pp 234–235.
92 Sastri to Ramaswami, 10 May 1923, in Jagadisan (ed) *Letters of Srinivasa Sastri*, p 230–231.
93 Sastri to Ramaswami, 10 May 1923, p 232.
94 Sastrt, 'Kenya Deputation's statement', in *The Kenya Problem*, p 59.
95 Sastri, 'Some interviews', in *The Kenya Problem*, pp 18–19.
96 Sastri, 'Some interviews', p 19.
97 Sastri, 'Some interviews', pp 20–21.
98 See 'Surprise move in Kenya', *Manchester Guardian*, 31 May 1923, p 8. On the role of missionaries, see Brian G. MacIntosh, 'Kenya 1923: the political crisis and the missionary dilemma', *TransAfrican Journal of History*, 1 (1), 1971, pp 103–129.
99 'A letter from London', *Servant of India*, 6 (18), 31 May 1923, pp 213–214.
100 On this, see MacIntosh, 'Kenya 1923'; John Harris 'The Kenya question: four deputations, the positions defined', *Manchester Guardian*, 26 April 1923, p 16.
101 'Annual meeting of the society', *Anti-Slavery Reporter and Aboriginies' Friend*, 13 (2), July 1923, p 57.
102 'Annual meeting of the society', p 58.
103 'Annual meeting of the society', p 58.
104 'Annual meeting of the society', p 61.

[105] 'Annual meeting of the society', p 61.
[106] 'Annual meeting of the society', p 59.
[107] 'Annual meeting of the society', p 59.
[108] 'Annual meeting of the society', p 60.
[109] H.S.L. Polak, 'Mr. Sastri's health', *Servant of India*, 6 (26), 19 July 1923, p 299. See Sastri's medical report in VSS Papers (II), Subject File 9, NMML.
[110] Sastri to Ramaswami, 10 May 1923, p 230.
[111] 'The biggest meeting in England', *Servant of India*, 6 (25), 19 July 1923, p 299.
[112] 'Dominion status for India: Mr. Sastri and the Indian question', *Manchester Guardian*, 27 June 1923, p 8.
[113] 'Dominion status for India: Mr. Sastri and the Kenya question', p 8.
[114] Sastri, 'Queen's Hall meeting', in *The Kenya Problem*, pp 28–29.
[115] Sastri, 'Queen's Hall meeting', p 26.
[116] Sastri, 'Queen's Hall meeting', p 28.
[117] *Servant of India*, 6 (17), 24 May 1923, pp 193–194.
[118] 'Kenya colony: appeal by European community with regard to the Indian East African policy', SAB, GG/164, 3/3165, National Archives, Pretoria.
[119] Marjorie Ruth Dilley, *British Policy in Kenya Colony*, London: Frank Cass, 1966, p 155.
[120] See E.F. Lane to H.W. Smyth, 26 February 1923, SAB, PM-1/2/242, PM64/20, National Archives, Pretoria; also see NTS-2003, 6/280; GG-912, 15/1165; PM-1/2/241, PM64/19; GG-913, 15/1220; GG-2287, 11/49; GG-164, 3/3165; GG-910, 15/1086, all in National Archives, Pretoria.
[121] Telegram from Viceroy, 8 May 1923, IOR/L/PO/6 (ii), f 160–161.
[122] Telegram from Viceroy, 8 May 1923, f 160–161, 'Indians in Kenya: General Smuts's position', *Morning Post*, 7 May 1923.
[123] Telegram to Viceroy, 15 May 1923, IOR/L/PO/6 (ii), f 159.
[124] Telegram from the Governor General of South Africa to the Secretary of State for the Colonies, 10 July 1923, IOR/L/PO/6 (ii), f 112.
[125] Telegram from the Secretary of State for the Colonies to the Governor General of the Union of South Africa, 14 July 1923, CAB/24/161/25.
[126] Sastri to Natesan, 12 July 1923, VSS Papers (I), Correspondence: Natesan, NMML.
[127] Huxley, *White Man's Country*, Vol 2, p 156.
[128] Sastri, 'Kenya deputation's statement', in *The Kenya Problem*, p 62.
[129] Sastri, 'Kenya deputation's statement', p 64.
[130] Sastri, 'Kenya deputation's statement', p 64.
[131] See 'Indians in South Africa: Gen. Smuts on the racial problem', *The Register* (Adelaide), 26 July 1923, p 9.
[132] Hancock, *Survey of the British Commonwealth*, p 224.
[133] Sastri, 'At the Hotel Cecil', in *The Kenya Problem*, p 41.
[134] Huxley, *White Man's Country*, Vol 2, p 163.
[135] 'A letter from London', *Servant of India*, 6 (30), 23 August 1923, p 358.
[136] Telegram from Viceroy, 16 July 1923, f 127–130 and Telegram from Viceroy, 17 July 1923, f 131, IOR/L/PO/6 (ii).
[137] Sastri, 'Interview with Reuter', in *The Kenya Problem*, p 30.
[138] Charles Andrews, 'The Kenya Lowlands', *Indian Review*, 26 (4), April 1925, pp 268–272 at 269.
[139] Sastri, 'At the Hotel Cecil', p 38.
[140] 'Mr. Sastri's denunciation: a deep affront to India', *Manchester Guardian*, 27 July 1923, p 10.

141. Sastri, 'Kenya deputation's statement', p 61.
142. Sastri, 'An appeal to the public', in *The Kenya Problem*, pp 70, 72. Also see 'Kenya decision: Sir Imam's speech, sacrifice of justice to fear', *Times of India*, 21 August 1923, p 7.
143. Sastri, 'An appeal to the public', p 68.
144. On Sastri's opposition to the exhibition, see Deborah L. Hughes, 'Kenya, India and the British Empire Exhibition of 1924', *Race & Class*, 47 (4), 2006, pp 66–85.
145. Sastri, 'A statement', in *The Kenya Problem*, p 33.
146. Sastri, 'Interview with *Manchester Guardian*', in *The Kenya Problem*, pp 48–49.
147. Sastri, 'A statement', p 34.
148. Sastri, 'An appeal to the public', pp 66–67.
149. Hughes, 'Kenya, India and the British Empire Exhibition of 1924', p 77.
150. See Sastri to Peel, 6 August 1923, IOR, L/PO/1/6 (i).
151. See Sastri, 'Indians and Kenya: imperial equality, Mr. Sastri's views', *Times of India*, 27 August 1923, p 11.
152. Sastri to Hope Simpson, 10 April 1923, in Jagadisan (ed) *Letters of Srinivasa Sastri*, p 245, footnote 1.
153. Memorandum from Tej Bahadur Sapru to Lord Reading, November 1928, in Sapru Correspondence: II Series Reel 4 (P–R), IOR Neg 4986, IOR&PP, BL.
154. 'The proposed Kenya settlement', *Manchester Guardian*, 25 July 1923, p 6.
155. 'A letter from London: English opinion on Kenya', *Servant of India*, 6 (30), 23 August 1923, p 357.
156. 'Duke of Devonshire on Kenya settlement', *Manchester Guardian*, 27 July 1923, p 12.
157. 'Labour hostile to Kenya decisions: sharp passages Col. Wedgwood challenges an opponent', *Manchester Guardian*, 26 July 1923, p 10.
158. Memorandum from Tej Bahadur Sapru to Lord Reading, November 1928, IOR Neg 4986.
159. Sivaswamy Iyer to Sastri, 21 August 1923, VSS Papers (II), Correspondence, P.S. Sivaswamy Aiyar, NMML.
160. Hughes, 'Kenya, India and the British Empire Exhibition of 1924', p 78.
161. Bajpai to Sastri, 2 September 1923, VSS Papers (I), Correspondence: G.S. Bajpai, NMML.
162. Bajpai to Sastri, 2 September 1923.
163. Benarasi Das Chaturvedi, 'The Red Letter day in the History of Greater India', *Indian Overseas*, 5th letter, 29 August 1923, VSS Papers (I), Correspondence: Benarasi Das Chaturvedi.
164. 'Reprisal bill passes Simla Assembly', *Manchester Guardian*, 28 July 1923, p 10.
165. An organized cessation of work as a protest measure.
166. 'Kenya protest *hartal*: partial success in native quarters', *Manchester Guardian*, 28 August 1923, p 8.
167. 'Indian nationalists and Kenya', *Manchester Guardian*, 20 September 1923, p 8.
168. See Vineet Thakur, *Jan Smuts and the Indian Question*, Pietermaritzburg: UKZN Press, 2017, pp 42–46.
169. See, 'Statement by Tej Bahadur Sapru', *The Imperial Conference: Appendices to the Summary of Proceedings*, London: His Majesty's Stationery Office, 1923.
170. 'Statement by Tej Bahadur Sapru', p 85.
171. Sastri to Vaze, 4 November 1923 and Sastri to Vaze, 6 November 1923, in VSS Papers (I), Correspondence: S.G. Vaze.
172. Sastri to Vaze, 5 November 1923, VSS Papers (I), Correspondence: S.G. Vaze.

173 Sastri, 'Africa or India?', in *The Kenya Problem*, p 96.
174 Sastri, 'Africa or India?', pp 96–97.
175 Sastri, 'Africa or India?', p 110.
176 H.N. Kunzru speaking in the United Provinces Legislative Council on 27 October made a similar assessment. See 'Boycott of the "white" Empire Exhibition'. *Servant of India*, 6 (43), 22 November 1923, pp 514–515.
177 Andrews' statement in: 'The Kenya betrayal', *Indian Review*, 24 (9), September 1923, p 567. In the Bhagat Singh Thind case, the American Supreme Court had ruled that Indians were not 'free white persons' and hence not eligible for naturalized citizenship. Earlier judgements in lower courts had held Indians under the white category, and thus eligible for naturalization.
178 Andrews, 'The abolition of colour bar', p 729.
179 'A letter from Mrs. Polak', *Servant of India*, 6 (45), 6 December 1923, p 539.

## Chapter 8

1 Kodanda Rao, *Sastri*, pp 178–190; Sitaramayya, *History of the Indian National Congress*, pp 313–520.
2 V.S. Srinivasa Sastri, 'Our plan for Swaraj', *Servant of India*, 6 (3), 15 February 1923, pp 27–29.
3 See Sastri's letters to A.V. Pathwardhan and D.V. Gundappa, in Jagadisan (ed) *Letters of Sastri*, pp 257–264.
4 Sastri to Sarojini Naidu, 30 April 1924, in Jagadisan (ed) *Letters of Sastri*, pp 254–257.
5 See Jagadisan, *Sastri*, pp 83–84.
6 Kodanda Rao, *Sastri*, pp 192–193.
7 Kodanda Rao, *Sastri*, pp 192–193.
8 V.S. Srinivasa Sastri, *The Rights and Duties of the Indian Citizen*, Calcutta: Calcutta University Press, 1927. Madras lectures were reproduced in V.S. Srinivasa Sastri, 'Kamala lectures', *Speeches and Writings of The Right Honourable V.S. Srinivasa Sastri*, Vol 1, Madras: South Indian National Association, 1969, pp 78–143.
9 Kodanda Rao, *Sastri*, p 192.
10 Sastri, 'Kamala lectures', p 134.
11 For details, see Position of Indians in South Africa – statement submitted to His Excellency the Viceroy of the South African Deputation, Pro No 80, in I Proceedings Overseas – A, March 1926 (Nos 1–88), IOR/L/E/7/1411, IOR&PP.
12 For more on specific bills, see Position of Indians in South Africa.
13 'Indians overseas: Gen. Smuts on colour bar', *Indian Review*, 26 (4), April 1925, pp 311–312.
14 Natal Advertiser, 'The men who sit on the safety valve', *Natal Advertiser*, 27 July 1925, Pro No 12, in I Proceedings Overseas – A, March 1926 (Nos 1–88), IOR/L/E/7/1411.
15 See J.E. Corbett, 'A study of the Cape Town Agreement', MA Thesis, University of Cape Town, Cape Town,1947, pp 49–52.
16 Telegram, Viceroy, Department of Education, Health and Lands, to Secretary of State, 11 September 1925, Tel No 4239, IOR/L/PO/1/22 (ii), f 204–206, IOR&PP, BL.
17 Extract from Official Report of the Council of State Debates, 10 September 1925, E&O 5512/75, IOR/L/E/7/1411.
18 See letters from Reading to Birkenhead on 3 September 1925, 11 September 1925, 28 October 1925, 24 December 1925, 8 January 1926, in IOR/L/PO/1/22 (ii).

19. Note from Sir L. Kershaw, 25 September 1925, IOR/L/PO/I/22 (ii), f 171–174; Telegram from Viceroy, 19 December 1925, Tel 5920, IOR/L/PO/I/22 (ii), f 175–177.
20. See Note by the Secretary of State to Sir Arthur Hitzel, 20 February 1926, E&O 620/1926, IOR/L/E/7/1411.
21. Scope of the Asiatic Bill. Annexure C: Constitutional position, E&O 597/1926, IOR/L/E/7/1411.
22. A round table conference between India and South Africa had been first proposed by Sarojini Naidu on a tour of South Africa in mid-1924. Six months later when the Secretary of State for Colonies in the short-lived Labour government, James Thomas, visited South Africa in December 1924, he made a similar suggestion for a conference between India, South Africa and Britain. By the time the India government approached the Colonial Office via the India Office, Leo Amery had taken over. Amery, a Milner acolyte and long-time friend of South Africa, refused to intervene. See 'Indians overseas', *Indian Review*, 26 (5), May 1925, pp 379–381; and Telegram from the Governor General, South Africa, Pretoria, 24 September 1925, Pro No 17, Proceedings Overseas – A, March 1926 (Nos 1–88), IOR/L/E/7/1411; Irwin to Birkenhead, 3 September 1925, IOR/L/PO/I/22 (ii), f 197–201.
23. Telegram from the Governor General, South Africa, to Viceroy, Delhi, 10 November 1925, in Proceedings Overseas – A, March 1926 (Nos 1–88), IOR/L/E/7/1411.
24. The scheme for voluntary repatriation with free passage to India was first introduced after the Gandhi–Smuts Agreement of 1914. In 1920, the Smuts government introduced a bonus of £5 pound per person and £25 maximum for a family to repatriate. But after an initial increase, the numbers declined. In 1924, the bonus was further raised to £10 for an individual and a maximum of £50 for a family, but the numbers had shockingly fallen to 1,063. The respective numbers for 1921, 1922 and 1923 were 2,927, 2,324 and 2,716. See Note by J.C. Watson: Indians in South Africa: The Asiatic Bill, E&O, 1388/26, IOR/L/E/7/1411.
25. For this, see Bhawani Dayal Sanyasi and Benarasidas Chaturvedi, *A Report on the Emigrants Repatriated to India under the Assisted Emigration Scheme from South Africa and on the Problem of Returned Emigrants from all Colonies*, Bihar: Pravasi Bhavan, 15 May 1931. Also see Uma Mesthrie, 'Reducing the Indian population to a "manageable compass": a study of the South African Assisted Emigration Scheme of 1927', *Natalia* 15, 1985, pp 36–56.
26. Confidential memorandum submitted by the Government of India deputation to South Africa, IOR/L/E/7/1411, IOR&PP, BL.
27. However, Malan insisted that if the bill were ever to become a law, it would be applied retrospectively, that is from 1 August 1925, when it was first introduced. See Viceroy, Department of Education, Health and Lands, to Secretary of State for India, 9 April 1926, Tel No 1799, IOR/L/PO/I/22 (i), f 15–19; Viceroy, Department of Education, Health and Lands, to Secretary of State for India, 10 April 1926, Tel No 1816, IOR/L/PO/I/22 (i), f 20; Viceroy, Department of Education, Health and Lands, to Secretary of State for India, 10 April 1926, Tel No 1808, IOR/L/PO/I/22 (i), f 21–22.
28. For an extended analysis of the work of the Paddison deputation, see Vineet Thakur and Sasikumar S. Sundaram, 'India, South Africa and the Cape Town Agreement: a diplomatic history', *Indian Politics and Policy*, 2 (2), 2019, pp 3–26.

## NOTES

29  Governor General, Cape Town, to Viceroy, Shimla, 15 May 1926, E&O 5614/926, IOR/L/E/7/1411; Telegram from Viceroy, 30 June 1926, f 459–460.
30  Telegram from Viceroy, 2 August 1926, IOR/L/PO/I/22 (ii), f 452–454.
31  Telegram from Secretary of State to the Viceroy, 30 August 1926.
32  Hugh Tinker, *The Ordeal of Love*, New Delhi: Oxford University Press, 1979, pp 219–220.
33  Sastri, 'If I were to live again', f 167.
34  Note by Sir A. Hirtzel, 20 August 1926, IOR/L/PO/I/22 (ii), f 435.
35  Irwin to Birkenhead, 26 August 1926, IOR/L/PO/I/22 (ii), f 430.
36  Irwin to Birkenhead, 26 August 1926, f 430.
37  Birkenhead to Irwin, 14 September 1926, IOR/L/PO/I/22 (ii), f 427.
38  Anon, 'Random thoughts: Sastri – the man', *Indian Opinion*, 49 (23), 4 December 1925, p 314.
39  Sastri to Gundappa, 5 April 1926, VSS Papers (II), Correspondence: D.V. Gundappa, f 75.
40  V.S. Srinivasa Sastri, 'Official resignations', *Servant of India*, 7 (10), 10 April 1924, pp 112–113.
41  'Australia and South Africa: Mr. Sastri's speech', *Servant of India*, 8 (51), 21 January 1926, pp 608–609.
42  Telegram from Viceroy, 21 September 1926, IOR/L/PO/I/22 (ii), f 425–426.
43  Telegram from Viceroy, 15 September 1926, IOR/L/PO/I/22 (ii), f 429.
44  C.F. Andrews to the Viceroy, 17 October 1926, IOR/L/PO/I/22 (ii), f 296–302.
45  H. Duncan Hall, 'The genesis of the Balfour Declaration of 1926', *Journal of Commonwealth & Comparative Politics*, 1 (3), 1962, pp 169–193.
46  The notes of Bajpai's two meetings on 3 and 18 November 1926 are in E&O 7551/26, IOR/L/E/7/1411.
47  Note for first meeting with General Hertzog by G.S. Bajpai, 3 November 1927, E&O 7551/26.
48  Sastri to Rukmini, 29 November 1926, VSS Papers (II), Correspondence: Rukmini, f 10–13.
49  *Brief of Instructions Issued to the Delegates of the Government of India to the Conference with the Representatives of the Government of the Union of South Africa on the Indian Problem in the Union*, Simla: Government of India Press, 1926.
50  Total expenditure on repatriates was £39,534; and bonuses and grants from 1922 to June 1926 amounted to £104,252. See 'Indians in South Africa. Census deductions', *The Times*, 22 March 1927, in E&O 2063/1927.
51  The origins of 'assisted emigration' go back to the early nineteenth century when, through the Ripon Regulations, the British government allocated funds to send emigrants to the Australian colonies. See Philip Harling, 'Assisted emigration and the moral dilemmas of the mid-Victorian imperial state', *Historical Journal*, 59 (4), 2016, pp 1027–1049.
52  For these points see *Brief of Instructions Issued to the Delegates of the Government of India*; Confidential memorandum submitted by the Government of India deputation.
53  'Indian delegation's arrival. Great welcome to the city', *Cape Times*, 23 December 1927.
54  Lindie Kroots, *D.F. Malan and the Rise of Afrikaner Nationalism*, Cape Town: Tafelberg, 2014, p 229.
55  'Memorandum by the Government of India, Delegation to South Africa', E&O 1601/27, IOR/ L/E/7/1411, f 5.
56  Memorandum, f 9.

57 Hertzog preferred to spend the Christmas holidays on his farm in Transvaal than attend the whole conference.
58 Memorandum, f 9. Also see G.L. Corbett to Lord Athlone, 24 December 1926, Asiatics: Conference on Indian question – Confidential reports furnished to His Excellency Mr. G.I. Corbett, SAB GG 916, 15/1377, NASA.
59 Kodanda Rao, *Sastri*, p 222.
60 Corbett to Athlone, 24 December 1926.
61 Gerrit Gong, *The Standard of Civilization in International Society*, Oxford: Clarendon Press, 1984.
62 Statement of Union Delegation on Item B, Asiatics: Conference on Indian Question, SAB GG 916, 15/1377.
63 Memorandum, f 45.
64 Kodanda Rao, *Sastri*, p 223; also see C.F. Andrews, 'The conference and after', *Indian Opinion*, 4 (25), 28 January 1927, p 29.
65 'Light on the Indian conference. Statement by member of delegation', *Cape Times*, 12 January 1927, p 9.
66 As Sastri's later secretary, John Tyson, called them. See Tyson to Duncan, 16 June 1927, MSS EUR/E/341/16, IOR&PP, BL.
67 Corbett to Athlone, 24 January 1927, SAB GG 916, 15/1377.
68 V.S. Srinivasa Sastri, 'A new era', in *Sastri Speaks*, ed S.R. Naidoo and Dhanee Bramdaw, Pietermaritzburg: Natal Press, 1931, pp 5–6.
69 Sastri, 'A new era', p 4.
70 Corbett to Athlone, 24 January 1927; Also see, 'Our distinguished visitors', *Indian Opinion*, 3 (25), 28 January 1927.
71 Gandhi, 'An honourable compromise', *Young India*, 24 February 1927, in *Collected Works of Mahatma Gandhi* (henceforth CWMG), Vol 38, pp 160–162. Also see 'Round table conference conclusions', *Indian Opinion*, 25 (8), 25 February 1927, pp 55–58; 'An honourable compromise', *Indian Opinion*, 25 (9), 4 March 1927, p 64; 'Indo-Union Agreement: well received by all parties in India', *Indian Opinion*, 25 (13), 1 April 1927, pp 91–92.
72 Memorandum, f 45.
73 Tinker, *The Ordeal of Love*, pp 223–224.
74 'Motion re. appreciation of the results achieved by the Government of India delegation to South Africa', *Council of State Debates*, 23 February 1927, p 268, E&O 2384/1927, IOR/L/E/7/1411.
75 'Motion re. appreciation', p 275.
76 'Solving South Africa's Indian problem', E&O 2063/1927, IOR/L/E/7/1411.
77 '"A marvelous performance" Mrs. Sarojini Naidu on the Indian agreement', *Indian Opinion*, 25 (15), 8 April 1927, pp 105–106.
78 Note by Arthur Hirtzel, 20 January 1927, IOR/L/PO/1/22 (ii).
79 Andrews to the Viceroy, 12 October 1926, IOR/L/PO/1/22 (ii), f 304–308.
80 Andrews to the Viceroy, 12 October 1926, f 304–308.
81 'A new era in Africa? The Union–Indian agreement', *Manchester Guardian*, 2 March 1927.
82 Tinker, *The Ordeal of Love*, p 224.

## Chapter 9
1 John Tyson to Folk, 31 May 1927, in MSS EUR/E/341/16, Papers of Sir John Tyson, IOR&PP, BL.

## NOTES

2. G.S. Bajpai to Undersecretary of State for India, 5 July 1928, E&O 4885/1928, IOR/L/PS/8/290, IOR&PP, BL, f 334–336.
3. 'Mr. Sastri sails for South Africa', *Times of India*, 9 June 1927, p 11; 'Bristling with dangers and difficulties', *Times of India*, 7 June 1927, p 10; 'Au revoir Sastri', *The Bombay Chronicle*, 8 June 1927, p 7.
4. 'Mr. Sastri sails for S. Africa: messages from leaders', *Times of India*, 9 June 1927, p 11.
5. C.P. Ramaswami Aiyer quoted in 'Mr. Sastri sails for S. Africa: messages from leaders'.
6. 'Mr. Sastri on his mission to South Africa: smooth working on agreement', *Times of India*, 31 May 1927, p 10.
7. Kodanda Rao to Patwardhan, 2 July 1927, P. Kodanda Rao Papers, Subject File 2 (Part 1), f 56–62.
8. India had appointed a High Commissioner to the United Kingdom in 1919.
9. Technically, the High Commissioners and the Privy Councillors were placed at the same level in the order of precedence. When Sastri's successor, Kumra Reddi, joined, the same privileges were extended to him.
10. See 'Position of the Right Hon'ble V.S. Srinivasa Sastri P.C., Agent of the Government of India in South Africa for the purpose of diplomatic etiquette', Education, Health and Lands Department, Overseas A, Proceedings, November 1927, Nos 117–125, NAI; 'India: question with regard to status of Mr. Sastri raised by consular body in Pretoria', SAB, GG-917, 15/1408, NSA.
11. Tyson to Duncan Best, 16 June 1927, MSS EUR/E/341/16.
12. Tyson to his Mother, 13 June 1927, MSS EUR/E341/16.
13. 'Instructions for the guidance of the Right Hon'ble V.S. Srinivasa Sastri P.C. in South Africa during his tenure of office as Agent', Education Departments, Overseas Branch, F No 38, June 1927, National Archives, New Delhi.
14. Viceroy, Shimla, to Governor General, Pretoria, Telegram P No 1009-S, 18 May 1927, E&O 4772/24, IOR/L/PS/8/290, IOR&PP, f 349–350.
15. 'Instructions for the guidance'.
16. Gandhi 'An honorable compromise', pp 160–162.
17. Kodanda Rao, *Sastri*, p 231.
18. Gandhi to Srinivasa Sastri, 6 April 1927, in *CWMG-e*, Vol 38, p 261.
19. Kodanda Rao, *Sastri*, p 231.
20. Mahatma Gandhi, 'Sastri as first ambassador', *Young India*, 24 April 1927, in *CWMG-e*, Vol 38, pp 320–322.
21. Kodanda Rao, *Sastri*, p 233.
22. Tyson to Folk, 13 June 1927, MSS EUR E341/16.
23. Taylor to Duncan Best, 16 June 1927, MSS EUR/E341/16.
24. *The Servants of India Society: The Report of Work, 1927–1928*, Poona: Aryabhushan Press, 1928, p 1.
25. Sastri's hesitation in making his reasons clear also makes one suspect that he did not want to admit publicly that the purity of the Brahman family household could not be maintained in a job that would require frequently hosting people outside of his caste. We know from Kodanda Rao's account that, for the most part, he was strict in his observance of purity within the house.
26. Sastri, 'Aspects of my life', pp 89–90.
27. Tyson to Folk, 13 June 1927.
28. J.D. Tyson, 'Abstract diary of Mr. Sastri's term of office in South Africa', 17–25 June 1927, in 'Material for a study of Srinivasa Sastri's term as agent of the government of

India in South Africa, comprising a review of his speeches and extracts from Tyson's diaries 1927–29', Papers of Sir John Tyson, MSS EUR/E/341/48, IOR&PP, BL. Also Tyson to Folk, 21 June 1927, MSS EUR/E/341/16.

29 Tyson, 'Abstract diary', 27 June 1927.
30 Kodanda Rao to Patwardhan, 2 July 1927, P. Kodanda Rao Papers, Subject File 2 (Part 1), f 56–62.
31 John Tyson, 'Mr. Sastri's reception and treatment in the Union', MSS EUR/E/341/48.
32 Quoted in 'Dr. Pirow and the Indians', *Indian Views*, 8 July 1927, p 3.
33 'Mr. Sastri at Pretoria: appeal to the Indian community', *Times of India*, 27 July 1927, p 14.
34 Tyson to Folk, 4 July 1927, MSS EUR/E/41/16.
35 John Tyson, 'Srinivasa Sastri in South Africa: some contemporary material for review of his work as the first agent of the government of India in South Africa, 1927–29', MSS EUR/E/341/48.
36 Kodanda Rao to Patwardhan, 2 July 1927.
37 For a history of the South African Indian question, see Mesthrie, 'From Sastri to Deshmukh'; Bridglal Pachai, *The International Aspects of the South African Indian Question 1860–1971*, Cape Town: Struik, 1971; Essop Pahad, 'The Development of Indian Political Movements in South Africa, 1924–46', DPhil thesis, University of Sussex, 1972; P. Aiyar, *The Tyranny of Colour*, Durban: E.P. and Commercial Printing Company, 1942.
38 Tyson, 'Srinivasa Sastri in South Africa'.
39 Kodanda Rao to Vaze, 16 July 1927, in P. Kodanda Rao, Subject File No 1, f 110–113.
40 Sastri, 'Agent's report 1927', in *Sastri Speaks*, ed Naidoo and Bramdaw, pp 252–253.
41 Kodanda Rao to Vaze, 16 July 1927, f 110–113; Sastri to Habibullah, 17 July 1927, f 114–116, in P. Kodanda Rao Papers, Subject File No 1.
42 Notes on the conversation between Mr. Hollander and Mr. Sastri, Durban, 19 July 1927, VSS Papers (I), Subject File 12, f 4–6; Tyson to Folk, 23 July 1927, MSS EUR/E/41/16.
43 At local gatherings for visiting imperial statesmen, such as for Lord Amery in September 1927, only the host could rank higher than Sastri at the main table.
44 See Tyson to Folk, 4 September 1927, MSS EUR/E/41/16.
45 Notes on the conversation between Sir Charles Smith and Mr. Sastri on 15 July 1927, Durban, P. Kodanda Rao Papers, Sub File 1, f 104a–105.
46 Many of Sastri's speeches in South Africa are reproduced in *Sastri Speaks*. However, Tyson prepared summaries of almost all of Sastri's speeches (in which Tyson was present). They are in MSS EUR/E/41/48.
47 V.S. Srinivasa Sastri, 'Within the four corners of the agreement', in *Sastri Speaks*, pp 45–50.
48 Sastri, 'Supremacy of the white race', in *Sastri Speaks*, p 90.
49 Sastri, 'Indian education', in *Sastri Speaks*, p 220.
50 *The Servants of India Society*, Poona: Aryabhusahan Press, 1915, p 3.
51 Sastri, 'The wider point of view', in *Sastri Speaks*, p 59.
52 Sastri, 'South Africa, India and the British Empire', in *Sastri Speaks*, p 77.
53 'Mr. Sastri's appeal to Natal,' *Natal Witness*, 3 August 1927, p 5.
54 Tyson, 'Srinivasa Sastri in South Africa', MSS EUR/E/341/48.
55 Tyson, 'Srinivasa Sastri in South Africa'.

56. See 'Mr. Sastri's appeal to Natal', *Natal Witness*, 3 August 1927, p 5; 'Mr. Sastri's views on Christianity', *Cape Times*, 12 November 1928, p 10.
57. 'Mr. Sastri's views on Christianity', p 10.
58. Pandian, *Brahmin and Non-Brahmin*.
59. See 'N.I. Congress on education: statement submitted to the commission', *Indian Opinion*, 26 (15), 20 April 1928, pp 106–109; and 'Education Inquiry Commission', *Indian Opinion*, 26 (14), 13 April 1928, pp 97–98.
60. Quoted in 'N.I. Congress on education'.
61. Taylor to Folk, 11 September 1927, MSS EUR/E/41/16.
62. On Sastri's notes on his various meetings with Athlone, Hollander, and Plowman, P. Kodanda Papers, Subject File 1; Tyson to Folk, 15 August 1927, MSS EUR/E/41/16.
63. 'Notes and news', *Indian Opinion*, 26 (37), 21 September 1928: 278; Kodanda Rao to Patwardhan, 31 July 1927, P. Kodanda Rao Papers, Subject File 2 (Part I), f 15–17.
64. 'Indian training college, proposed site on Centenary Road', *Natal Mercury*, 9 November 1927.
65. Sastri, 'Memorandum and evidence Indian education', in *Sastri Speaks*, pp 218–219.
66. Kodanda Rao to Patwardhan, 26 August 1927, P. Kodanda Rao Papers, Subject File 2 (Part I), f 46–49.
67. Tyson to Folk, 20 September 1927, MSS EUR/E/41/16.
68. Sastri to Habibullah, 23 September 1927, P. Kodanda Rao Papers, Subject File 1, f 79–80.
69. Tyson, 'Abstract diary', 19 September 1927.
70. Kodanda Rao to Patwardhan, 13 August 1927, P. Kodanda Rao Papers, Subject File 2 (Part I), f 39–45.
71. Tyson, 'Srinivasa Sastri in South Africa'; Kodanda Rao to Patwardhan, 9 September 1927, P. Kodanda Rao Papers, Subject File 2 (Part I), f 18–19.
72. Sastri to Habibullah, 23 September 1927, P. Kodanda Rao Papers, Subject File 1, f 79–80. For Habibullah's response, see Habibullah to Sastri, 10 October 1927, VSS Papers (I), Correspondence: M. Habibullah.
73. 'Education Inquiry Commission', *Indian Opinion*, 26 (14), 13 April 1928, pp 97–98.
74. Sastri to Habibullah, 20 April 1928, P. Kodanda Rao Papers, Subject File 1, f 29–33.
75. 'Natal witness on Indian education', *Indian Opinion*, 26 (14), 13 April 1928, pp 99–100.
76. 'Truth about Indian education', *Indian Opinion*, 26 (17), 4 May 1928, pp 154. Also see Frene Ginwala, 'Education feature from Frene Ginwala's thesis', www.sahistory.org.za/archive/education-feature-frene-ginwalas-thesis, accessed 27 February 2019.
77. Sastri, 'Memorandum', in *Sastri Speaks*, pp 217–230. Also see 'Education Inquiry Commission: further evidences', *Indian Opinion*, 26 (15), 20 April 1928, pp 111–114.
78. Sastri, 'Memorandum', pp 227–229.
79. Sastri, 'Memorandum', p 228.
80. Sastri to Habibullah, 9 March 1928, VSS Papers (I), Subject File 12, f 43–44.
81. Kodanda Rao to Patwardhan, 11 March 1928, P. Kodanda Rao Papers, Subject File 2 (Part 1), f. 53; Sastri to Habibullah, 20 April 1928, P. Kodanda Rao Papers, Subject File 1, f 29–33.
82. Sastri to Habibullah, 20 April 1928, P. Kodanda Rao Papers, Subject File 1, f 29–33.

83. Tyson, 'Abstract diary', 3 April 1928.
84. Tyson, 'Abstract diary', 17 April 1928.
85. Sastri to Habibullah, 6 April 1928, P. Kodanda Rao Papers, Subject File 1, f 43–46.
86. Sastri, 'Agent's report 1928', in *Sastri Speaks*, pp 285–289.
87. Irwin to Sastri, 2 June 1928, VSS Sastri, Ist Installment, Correspondence: Irwin, f 10–12.
88. '"A pretty poor bit of work" – "Natal witness" on Education Committee's report', *Indian Opinion*, 26 (21), 1928, pp 159–160.
89. Kodanda Rao to Patwardhan, 22 April 1928, P. Kodanda Rao Papers, Subject File 2 (Part 1), f 82–83.
90. Sastri to Habibullah, 7 May 1928, P. Kodanda Rao Papers Subject File 1, f 25–27.
91. The previous occupant of this post, Hugh Bryan, had been supportive of Sastri's views, but left to take up the vice chancellorship of the University of South Africa.
92. R. Hunt Davis, Jr, 'Charles T. Loram and an American model for African education in South Africa', *African Studies Review*, 19 (2), 1976, pp 87–99.
93. Sastri to Habibullah, 30 June 1928, P. Kodanda Rao Papers, Subject File 1, f 11–12.
94. CT Loram to Srinivasa Sastri, 6 January 1936, VSS Papers (I), Correspondence: CT Loram.
95. Sastri to Habibullah, 30 June 1928.
96. Tyson, 'Abstract diary', 25 June 1928.
97. Sastri to Habibullah, 15 November 1927, P. Kodanda Rao Papers, Subject File 1, f 72–74; Kodanda Rao to Patwardhan, 5 November 1927, P. Kodanda Rao Papers, Subject File 2 (Part 1), f 24–25; 'Indian training college. Proposed site in Centenary Road', *Natal Mercury*, 9 November 1927.
98. Sastri, 'Agent's report 1927', in *Sastri Speaks*, pp 240–241.
99. Tyson, 'Srinivasa Sastri in South Africa'.
100. Sastri, 'Agent's report 1928', in *Sastri Speaks*, p 278.
101. Tyson, 'Abstract diary', 24 August 1928.
102. Tyson, 'Abstract diary', 18 July 1928; Sastri, 'Instance of self-help', in *Sastri Speaks*, p 119.
103. Memorandum presented to the Hon. S.J. Marais Steyn, Minister of Indian Affairs, Re: Sastri College, in Sastri College Papers, Gandhi–Luthuli Documentation Centre, University of KwaZulu Natal, Durban.
104. See Ginwala, 'Education feature from Frene Ginwala's thesis'.

# Chapter 10

1. Sastri, 'Agent's report 1927', in *Sastri Speaks*, p 248.
2. The Union government realized this, and looked to explore other avenues with Sastri, such as extending emigration to Kenya. Notes of Mr. Sastri's interview with Dr. Malan, on the 11 July, 1927 at, VSS Papers (I), Subject File 12, f 13–15.
3. See Sastri, 'Agent's report 1928', in *Sastri Speaks*, pp 264–265.
4. Sastri, 'Agent's report 1927', pp 248–249.
5. Sastri, 'Agent's report 1928', p 248.
6. Prem Narain Agarwal, *Bhawani Dayal Sanyasi: A Public Worker of South Africa*, Etawah, India: Indian Colonial Association, 1939.
7. Sanyasi and Chaturvedi, *A Report on the Emigrants Repatriated to India*; Uma Dhupelia-Mesthrie, 'South Africa to India: narratives of a century of repatriation (1871–1975)', Paper presented at Centre for African Studies, Leiden University, 12 September 2019.

# NOTES

8. See Sanyasi and Chaturvedi, 'A report', p 58. The Indian government also appointed a committee to enquire into the working of the special office in Madras dealing with the assisted emigrants. See 'Report submitted to the Government of India by Hon'ble Mr. G.A. Natesan and Mr. J. Gray on the working of the special organization in Madras or dealing with emigrants returning from South Africa under the scheme of assisted emigration'. The report is appended in the Sanyasi and Chaturvedi report.
9. Sastri, 'Agent's report 1927', pp 243–244; Sastri, 'Agent's report 1928', in *Sastri Speaks*, pp 267–268.
10. Sastri, 'Agent's report 1927', pp 244–245.
11. Sastri, 'The task of the peacemaker', in *Sastri Speaks*, pp 34–35.
12. Tyson, 'Abstract diary', 9 October 1927.
13. Kodanda Rao to Patwardhan, 14 January 1928, P. Konadana Rao Papers, Subject File 1, f 60.
14. Kodanda Rao to Patwardhan, 30 November 1927, P. Konadana Rao Papers, Subject File 2 (Part 1), f 25–27; Sastri to Habibullah, 20 August 1927, P. Konadana Rao Papers, Subject File 1, f 89–91.
15. Sastri to Habibullah, 28 August 1927, P. Kodanda Rao Papers, Subject File 1, f 89–91.
16. Habibullah to Sastri, 29 August 1927, VSS Papers (I), Correspondence: M. Habibullah.
17. See, Habibullah to Sastri, 27 September 1927, VSS Papers (I), Correspondence: M. Habibullah.
18. Gandhi to Sastri, 22 September 1922, in Jagadisan (ed) *Letters of Srinivasa Sastri*, p 167.
19. Sastri, 'Agent's report 1927', pp 244–245.
20. 'South African Indian Congress – eighth session at Kimberley, a successful conference', *Indian Opinion*, 26 (2), 13 January 1928, pp 1–2.
21. Sastri, 'Agent's report 1927', p 245.
22. 'Transvaal British Indian Association. Emphatic protest against S.A.I Congress misrepresentations', *Indian Views*, 16 March 1929, p 5.
23. Kodanda Rao to Patwardhan, 13 August 1927, P. Konadana Rao Papers, Subject File 2 (Part 1), f 39–45.
24. Kodanda Rao to Patwardhan, 31 July 1927, P. Konadana Rao Papers, Subject File 2 (Part 1), f 15–17; Sastri to Habibullah, 28 August 1927; Sastri to Habibullah, 16 December 1927, P. Konadana Rao Papers, Subject File 1, f 64–66.
25. Others, like John L. Roberts, took a maximalist position and insisted that Indians as citizens of the British Commonwealth had the same rights as the English, so could not be called illegal. See 'Sunday's mass meeting: Mr. Sastri's stirring speech to take condonation', *Indian Opinion*, 26 (32), 17 August 1928, pp 237–238.
26. Sastri to Habibullah, 20 May 1928, P. Kodanda Rao Papers, Subject File 1, f 21–23; Letter from D.F. Malan to V.S. Srinivasa Sastri, 16 May 1928, *CWMG-e*, Vol 42, p 473.
27. 'Condonation of illegal entrants', Subject File 1, f 34–39. Also see Memorandum: Condonation of the illegal entry of Asiatics, Subject File 1, pp 40–41; Sastri to Habibullah, 6 April 1928, Subject File 1, f 43–46, all in P. Kodanda Rao Papers.
28. Tyson, 'Abstract diary', 30 April 1928.
29. Cable to South African Indian Congress, 29 May 1928, in *CWMG-e*, Vol 42, p 58.
30. Sastri to Habibullah, 1 June 1928, P. Kodanda Rao Papers, Subject File 1, f 17–19.

[31] See Letter from V.S. Srinivasa Sastri to D.F. Malan, 14 May 1928, in *CWMG-e*, Vol 42, pp 472–473.
[32] Malan to Sastri, 16 May 1928, p 473.
[33] Sastri, 'Agent's report 1928', p 270.
[34] Sastri to Habibullah, 1 June 1928, f 17–19.
[35] Tyson, 'Abstract diary', 1 July 1928.
[36] See 'Sunday's mass meeting: Mr. Sastri's stirring speech to take condonation'; 'Condonation scheme explained in Maritzburg: Mr Sastri's exhortation', *Indian Opinion*, 26 (33), 24 August 1928, pp 245–246; 'Mr. Sastri's eloquent appeal to Transvaal Indians', *Indian Opinion*, 26 (36), 14 September 1928, p 270.
[37] See 'Cape Conference', *Indian Opinion*, 26 (36), 14 September 1928, p 267–268; 'Cape Indian Provincial Conference', *Indian Opinion*, 26 (36), 14 September 1928, p 272; 'TBIA meeting at Pretoria – terminated in disorder', *Indian Opinion*, 26 (31), 10 August 1928, pp 233–234.
[38] Sastri to Habibullah, 24 February 1928, VSS Papers (1), Subject File no 12, f 38–41.
[39] Article reproduced in *Indian Opinion*, 26 (3), 20 January 1928, p 1.
[40] Tyson, 'Abstract diary', 6 February 1928. Also Tyson to Folk, 7 February 1928, MSS EUR/E/341/17.
[41] 'Cables to India', *Indian Opinion*, 26 (5), 3 February 1928, p 36.
[42] Tyson, 'Abstract diary', 6 February 1928.
[43] Tyson, 'Abstract diary', 6 February 1928.
[44] Tyson, 'Abstract diary', 7 February 1928.
[45] Tyson, 'Abstract diary', 7 February 1928.
[46] Tyson, 'Abstract diary', 14 May 1928.
[47] Sastri to Habibullah, 23 September 1927, P. Kodanda Rao Papers, Subject File 1, f 79–80.
[48] Sastri to Ramaswami, 24 February 1928, in Jagadisan (ed) *Letter of Srinivasa Sastri*, p 172; Diary 1928: 13 February.
[49] Roos pulled out at the last moment (and so did the Labour minister, Colonel Creswell), but otherwise the top leadership of both the government and the opposition (except Smuts) was present.
[50] Tyson, 'Abstract diary', 21 February 1928.
[51] Sastri, 'Anniversary of the Indo-Union Agreement', in *Sastri Speaks*, p 212.
[52] Sastri, 'Anniversary of the Indo-Union Agreement', pp 213–214.
[53] Sastri, 'Anniversary of the Indo-Union Agreement', pp 213–216.
[54] Quoted in Kodanda Rao, *Sastri*, p 249.
[55] Quoted in Kodanda Rao, *Sastri*, p 250.
[56] Hertzog to Sastri, 25 October 1928, VSS Papers (II), Correspondence: JBM Hertzog.
[57] See Sastri to Duncan, 19 October 1928, BC 294, D1/32/2; Duncan to Sastri, 23 October 1928, BC 294, D1/32/3; Sastri to Duncan, 25 October 1928, BC 294, D1/32/4; Sastri to Duncan, 6 November 1928, BC 294, D1/32/5; Sastri to Duncan, 9 May 1929, BC 294, D1/32/6, in Patrick Duncan Papers, University of Cape Town.
[58] Sastri to Habibullah, 6 April 1928, P. Kodanda Rao Papers, Subject File 1, f 43–46.
[59] 'Violent disorder at Sastri meeting. Klerksdorp hooligans throw "gas bomb"', *Rand Daily Mail*, 17 September 1928, p 7; Tyson, 'Abstract diary', 15 September 1928.
[60] Tyson to Folk, 23 September 1928, MSS EUR E/341/17.
[61] 'The Klerksdorp incident', *Indian Opinion*, 26 (38), 28 September 1928, p 289.

## NOTES

62. 'Press Comment on Klerksdorp outrage', *Indian Opinion*, 26 (37), 21 September 1928, p 282.
63. Gandhi to Sastri, 20 October 1927, in Jagadisan (ed) *Letters of Srinivasa Sastri*, p 80.
64. For a more scathing and personal criticism of Sastri, see 'Rt. Hon. Mr. Sastri: England's Advertising Agent', *Democrat*, 2 March 1929, FD 8, AICC Papers: Ist Instalment.
65. 'Beauties of the British Empire: India takes Mr. Sastri to task', *Indian Views*, 9 December 1927, p 4.
66. Gandhi to Sastri, 20 October 1927, p 80.
67. Gandhi to Maninal and Sushila, 12 August 1928, *CWMG-e*, Vol 42, p 356.
68. Sastri to Habibullah, 9 March 1928, VSS Papers (I), Subject File 12, f 48–49; Konadana Rao to Patwardhan, 11 March 1928, P. Kodanda Rao Papers, Subject File 1, f 53; also, Habibullah to Sastri, 12 March 1928, VSS Papers (I), Correspondence: M. Habibullah.
69. 'If Sastri were a free man', *Indian Opinion*, 26 (9), 1928, pp 71–72.
70. See Kodanda Rao to Patwardhan, 30 November 1927, P. Kodanda Rao Papers, Subject File 2 (Part 1), f 25–27; Copy of Mr. Habib Motan's letter to Mr. Sastri, 19 November 1927, P. Kodanda Rao Papers, Subject File 1, f 108–110.
71. See 'Dr. Tagore on Indians in South Africa', *Indian Opinion*, 26 (14), 13 April 1928, p 102.
72. Kodanda Rao to Patwardhan, 28 January 1928, P. Kodanda Rao Papers, Subject File 2 (Part 1), f 53.
73. Tyson, 'Abstract diary' 17 July 1928.
74. Sastri to Irwin, 15 July 1928, VSS Papers (I), Correspondence: Lord Irwin. In India, several names were being considered, including that of Bajpai and Maharaj Singh. See Tyson to Folk, 22 August 1928; and Tyson to Birch Reynardson, 14 October 1928: MSS EUR/E/341/17.
75. Sastri to Irwin, 15 July 1928, VSS Papers (I), Correspondence: Lord Irwin.
76. Kodanda Rao to Patwardhan, 2 July 1927.
77. 'Mr. Sastri', *Cape Times*, 3 January 1929, p 10.
78. Mesthrie, 'From Sastri to Deshmukh'.
79. See Mesthrie, 'From Sastri to Deshmukh', pp 143–145.
80. Mesthrie, 'From Sastri to Deshmukh', p 170; *Indian Opinion*, 24 November, 1 December 1933, 2 February, 17 August 1934 editorials.
81. Quoted in 'Mr. Sastri's successor', *Indian Opinion*, 27 (1), 4 January 1929, pp 5–6.
82. See 'Mr. Sastri's successor', pp 5–6.
83. Tyson, 'Abstract diary', entries from 25 September to 3 October 1928.
84. 'The dean moves vote of thanks', *Indian Opinion*, 26 (37), 21 September 1928, p 277.
85. 'Johannesburg's banquet to Mr. Sastri: Mr. Howard Pim', *Indian Opinion*, 27 (3), 18 January 1929, p 24.
86. 'Sastri the man: tribute by Miss Gordon', VSS Papers (II), Speeches and Writings on Sastri by others, S No 2, f 10.
87. Vere Stent, 'A farewell apostrophe to Mr. Sastri' article reproduced in *Indian Opinion*, 27 (4), 25 January 1929, p 38.
88. Indeed, the election campaigning for these elections was dominated by the rhetoric of 'swart gevaar' or 'black peril'.
89. 'Can repatriation be permanent?', *Natal Witness*, 29 January 1929, p 7.
90. Sastri, 'Aspects of my life', p 90.
91. Sastri to Gokhale, 9 July 1914, in Jagadisan (ed) *Letters of Srinivasa Sastri*, p 35.

92. Tyson to Folk, 28 January 1928, MSS Eur 341/17. This was in contrast to Tyson's impression of his new boss, Reddi, whom he felt was 'conceited' and 'jealous of [Sastri's] great success'.

## Chapter 11

1. C.L.R. James, 'Preface to the first edition', *The Black Jacobins*, 2nd edn rev, New York: Vintage Books, 1989, p x.
2. Gregory, *India and East Africa*, pp 305–306.
3. On discussions about Sastri's mission, see IOR/L/PO/1/39, IOR&PP.
4. Kodanda Rao, *Sastri*, pp 273–274; Gregory, *India and East Africa*, pp 323–330.
5. Sastri quoted in Gregory, *India and East Africa*, p 329.
6. Gregory, *India and East Africa*, p 338.
7. For Sastri's original report, see, E&O 6841/1929, and for published report, E&O 1898/1930, both in IOR/L/PO/1/39, IOR&PP.
8. Gregory, *India and East Africa*, pp 338–339.
9. For an excellent resource on these conferences, see Stephen Legg's project 'Conferencing the international', www.nottingham.ac.uk/research/groups/interwarconf/home.aspx, accessed 25 March 2021.
10. Uma Mesthrie, 'From Sastri to Deshmukh', p 134.
11. See, Mesthrie, 'From Sastri to Deshmukh', p 180; Mesthrie, 'Reducing the Indian population to a "manageable compass"'; Dhanee Bramdaw, *Out of the Stable*, Pietermaritzburg: Natal Witness, 1935, pp 16–18.
12. Kodanda Rao, *Sastri*, pp 338–339.
13. Sastri, 'If I live again', f 176.
14. V.S. Srinivasa Sastri, *Life of Gopal Krishna Gokhale*, Bangalore: Bangalore Printing and Publishing, 1937.
15. Sastri, *Pherozeshah Mehta*; Sastri, *Thumbnail Sketches*.
16. V.S. Srinivasa Sastri, *The Other Harmony*, ed T.N. Jagadisan, Madras: S. Viswanathan, 1945.
17. V.S. Srinivasa Sastri, *Lectures on the Ramayana*, Madras: S. Viswanathan, 1949.
18. Kodanda Rao, *Sastri*, pp 388–394.
19. Copy of Joint Statement by V.S. Srinivasa Sastri, P.A. Wadia, K. Natarajan and Jehangir Petit on the implications of the two-nation theory, VSS Papers (I), Speeches and Writings by Sastri, S No 59.
20. *Indian Struggle: A Periodical Survey of Indian Developments*, Number 1, 1936, 10 November 1936, AICC Papers (Ist Instalment), FD 39/1936.
21. Sastri to P. Sivaswamy Iyer, 30 June 1942, in *Sastriana*, No 26, ed S.R. Venkataraman, Madras: Servants of India Society, 1983, p 22.
22. 'The Servant of India', *Servant of India*, 1 (1), 19 February 1928, p 5.
23. Sastri, 'Values in life', in *The Other Harmony*, p 121.
24. Sastri, 'A confession of faith', in *The Other Harmony*, p 5.
25. For a defence of the Brahman leadership as the preservers of order and peace in anti-colonial politics and a lament on its passing after the First World War, see: G. Annaji Rao, 'Passing of the Brahmana', *New India*, 25 July 1919.
26. On Sastri's style of politics see, Ray T. Smith, 'V.S. Srinivasa Sastri and the moderate style in Indian politics', *Journal of South Asian Studies*, 2 (1), pp 81–100; Ragini Tharoor Srinivasan, 'Moderating revolution: V.S. Srinivasa Sastri, Toussaint Louverture, and the civility of reform', *The Comparatist*, 41, 2017, pp 133–152.

27. Gandhi to Natesan, 12 January 1946, in *CWMG*, Vol 82, p 407.
28. Smith, 'V.S. Srinivasa Sastri', p 83.
29. G.A. Natesan, 'The Rt. Hon. Srinivasa Sastri', f 39; also see, Kodanda Rao, *Sastri*, pp 386–387. Sastri was a vocal supporter of women's suffrage, although as part of the Southborough Committee he agreed with others in not recommending a women's vote because there was not enough demand for it.
30. Subramania, 'The Rt. Hon. V.S. Srinivasa Sastri', pp 106–108.
31. The conferences during the war in 1917 and 1918 were 'Imperial War Conferences'.
32. See Hugh Tinker, 'Colour and colonization', *Round Table*, 60 (240), pp 405–406.
33. His approach in Australia and New Zealand was exactly the opposite. There he focused more on political rights, since they were more achievable.
34. Gandhi to Sastri, 4 January 1946, *CWMG*, Vol 82, p 341.
35. Gandhi to C. Rajagopalachari, 16 January 1946, *CWMG*, Vol 82, p 431.
36. Foreword to *'My Master Gokhale'*, 20 January 1946, *CWMG*, Vol 83, p 1.
37. See Sastri's letters to Gandhi on 2 June 1944, 17 June 1944 and 25 June 1944, in VSS Papers (I), Correspondence with M.K. Gandhi, f 57–64.
38. Talk with V.S. Srinivasa Sastri, 22 January 1946, *CWMG*, 83, pp 15–16.
39. He was accompanied by C. Rajagopalachari, Thakkar Bappa, Amrit Kaur, Agatha Harrison and Jagadisan, in addition to Pyarelal and Sushila.
40. Talk with V.S. Srinivasa Sastri, 30 January 1946, *CWMG*, Vol 83, p 62.
41. Talk with V.S. Srinivasa Sastri, 30 January 1946, p 64.
42. Talk with V.S. Srinivasa Sastri, 4 February 1946, *CWMG*, 83, pp 87–88.
43. 'Srinivasa Sastri indicts anti-Indian drive: naked and unashamed use of power by Smuts', *Bombay Chronicle*, 24 March 1946, p 16.
44. Jagadisan, *Sastri*, p 183.

# Index

## A

*Abanya Bantu* 210
Abdurahman, Abdullah 159
accommodation difficulties 55, 64, 180, 182
Acharya, M.P.T. 22, 30
Achriar, S. 208
Achutt, Frank H. 189, 190, 192
Ackworth, W 64
aerial bombings 54
Afghanistan 4
Africa 127, 133, 137, 141, 142, 144, 174, 180, 192
 Africans, views held of 78, 124, 129, 136, 193, 209–10, 227, 232
*African Chronicle* 198, 200
Afrikaners 61, 126, 170, 185, 206
Aga Khan 124, 128–30
Agent to South Africa 6, 171–5, 211–12
agitation 27, 39, 87
*agraharam* 57
agricultural labourers 195
aircraft carriers 93
Aiyangar, S. Kasturi Ranga 49
Aiyar, P.S. 198, 199
Ali, Mohammad 4
Ali, Reza 160
America *see* United States of America
Amery, Leo 218, 219
Amritsar 54, 67, 134
anarchists 22, 54, 68
Andrews, Charles 13, 105, 136, 140, 150, 174, 197
Anglo-Irish Treaty 99
Anglo-Japanese Alliance 71–9, 94, 100
Anglophile 227
Annamalai University 220
anti-Asian immigration 115–17
Anti-Asiatic League 207
anti-Indians 115
anti-Japanese hysteria 94
 *see also* Japan
anti-Semiticism 4, 105
Anti-Slavery Society 140
apartheid 14, 158
appeals, court 204
apprentices 189
Appu Sastri, Rao Bahadur 20
aristocrats 126
Arlington Memorial Amphitheater 89
armaments 101
Armenian Christians 2
armies 92, 146
arms control 11
Arthur, Rev. J.W. 135, 140
ashrams 33
Asians 11, 77, 115
Asiatic Bill 158, 159, 161, 168, 220
Asiatics Land Trading (Transvaal) Act 62
assisted emigration 166–7, 181–2, 183, 195, 213
Athlone, Lord 160, 188, 204, 210
Australia 6, 76, 77, 85, 94, 107–14, 164
*Autobiography* 119
autonomy 2, 48, 120

## B

Bajpai, Girija S. 13, 104, 105, 107, 160, 166, 210
 at the Imperial Conference 64–5, 74, 79, 83
'baking' 101
Baldwin, Stephen 133
Balfour, Arthur 39, 80, 91, 93, 94
Balfour Declaration 165, 168, 171, 180
Ballantyne, Charles 75, 77
*Baltimore Sun* 89
banana and sugar industries 109, 113
Banerjea, Surendranath 27, 49, 50, 55, 57, 60, 63
Bardoli 102
Barlow, Glyn 23
Barwell, Henry 110
battleships 123–4
Bellegarde, Louis-Dantès 6, 82

Benaras Congress 27
Bengal 26–7, 42, 100, 154
*Bengalee* 49
Bennett, Thomas 147
Berlin, Isiah 225
Besant, Annie 34–5, 48, 53, 56, 68, 153, 154, 155
*Bhagavat Gita* 34
bilateral agreement 6, 171
biography 16, 217
Birkenhead, Lord 79, 154, 164
birth rates 191
black intelligentsia 210
Blackwell, Leslie 181
Blyth, Robert 130
Boer War 61, 126
Bolsheviks 4, 38
Bombay 24, 47, 51, 102, 176
*Bombay Chronicle, The* 78, 107, 212
bombs 207
Bonnerjee, W.C. 52
bonuses 161, 168, 169, 195, 196, 213
Bose, Nani Gopal 101
Botha, Louis 62
boycotting 27, 67, 100, 102, 146, 147, 148, 164, 205
Boydell, Tommy 168
Brahmins 8, 23, 120, 185, 211, 212, 227, 230
 political power of 36, 46, 47
Brand, Robert 44
Briand, Aristide 90, 92
Britain 11, 46, 90, 93, 94
 British policy and Kenya 124, 128, 131, 134
 British policy towards Turkey 4, 67
 British reaction to Asiatic Bill 160
 British treatment of prisoners 101
British Columbia 108, 115–18, 119
British Commonwealth 69, 141, 144, 171, 226
 ideals of the 73–4, 109, 120, 183–5, 208, 231
British Empire 5, 11, 39–40, 91, 93
Bryan, H. 190
'Builders of Modern India' 16
Bullhoek massacre 69
businesses 189
 *see also* sugar industry; trade and traders

C

Calcutta 27–8, 60, 102, 155
Camay, N.A. 198
Canada 1, 5, 6, 70, 77, 85, 94, 115–19
Cape Colony 61
Cape Province 69, 181
*Cape Times* 172, 211

Cape Town Agreement 6, 162–71, 177, 179, 181, 195, 203
caste 9, 14, 38, 57, 120–1, 185, 196, 224
*Catholic Herald of India* 119
Cavendish, Victor C.W. *see* Devonshire, Duke of
Cecil, Robert 81
Central Investigation Department (CID) 54
Chamberlain, Neville 121
character, developing 184
Charan, Ambika 24
Chaturvedi, Benerasidas 14, 147
Chauri Choura 102
Chelmsford, Lord 13, 48, 64, 131
Chennai *see* Madras
Chief Sikhuni 180
China 77, 81, 82, 91, 94, 95, 100, 121
Chintamani, C.Y. 32, 55
Chirol, Valentine 37, 147
Cholmondeley, Hugh *see* Delamere, Lord
Christianity 34, 68, 213
*Chronicle* 109
Churchill, Winston 67, 74, 75, 76, 105, 140
 and Kenyan Indians 131, 132, 133, 139
citizenship 15, 69, 77, 111, 144, 156, 230
civil disobedience 4, 102, 156
civilization 129
civilizing mission 5, 7, 47
Civil Service exams 22
*Civitas Dei* 41
Class Areas Bill 164
coal 159, 160
Cobb, E.Powys 123
colonial and international status 15
colonialism 7, 66
*Colony for Africa, A* 128
colony in East Africa, proposals for 128–30
coloured Commonwealth 231
'colourless' *see* white people
colour line 11, 145, 150, 204
colour policy (South Africa) 81
common franchise 217
*Commonweal* 35
Commonwealth of Nations 40
communal franchise 144, 219
communal representation 57
communicative rationality 225
community harmony 25, 68
Companion of Honour 220
compulsory registration 200
Condonation Scheme 197–8, 200–2, 210
Congress-League Scheme 43, 46, 48, 50
Congress Party 50, 141
Conservative Party (Canada) 117, 118

Conservative Party (UK) 51, 53, 132, 134, 135, 154
constitutional politics 14, 35, 42, 43, 68, 146, 223, 227
contribution to WWI 109, 114, 128, 141, 149
'coolies' 8, 179, 211, 213, 230
cooperation 10, 24
Corbett, G.L. 64, 66, 85, 103, 163, 169, 172, 173
Coryndon, Robert 123–4, 133, 134, 135
Council of State 67, 174
coup, threatened 123, 124
criminal bills 54
Criminal Law (Emergency Powers) Bill 53
Criminal Law Amendment Bill 53
criticism of Sastri 112, 119–21, 198, 208, 212, 221
Crown Colonies and immigration policies 139
Curtis, Lionel 40, 41, 42, 44, 130, 138
Curzon, Lord 4, 27, 46

### D

Das, Chitranjan 153
Das, Taraknath 100, 101, 154
De Bon, Admiral 93
Declaration of Rights 52
Delamere, Lord 123, 126, 135, 140, 143, 145, 219
delegations 53, 55–60, 140
  to London about Indian constitution 154
  to London about Kenya 135
  to South Africa 63, 160, 165, 168
Delhi 47, 53
Desai, Manilal Ambalal 136
detention, indefinite 53
Devadhar, G.K. 178
de Valera, Eamon 69, 72
Devonshire, Duke of 133–4, 138, 143–4
diplomatic representation 7–9, 103, 179, 212, 229, 230, 231
disarmament 85, 88, 90, 92, 97
discrimination 61, 62, 64, 74, 113, 140, 200
disenfanchisement 15
display culture and learning 211
*Dnyanaprakash* 29
domicile, right of 167, 169, 196
dominion status 97, 108, 221, 226
dominion tour 107
Dove, John 138
Draper, Arthur S. 97
Dual Policy 128
Du Bois, W.E.B. 11

Duke, William 42
Duncan, Patrick 159, 181, 205, 206
Durban 7, 61, 182
Dwarkadas, J. 135, 144
dyarchy 42, 45, 48, 49
Dyer, General Reginald 67
Dyson, J. 190

### E

East Africa 61, 76, 124, 127, 129, 217–18
  E.A. Indian Congress 131, 208
*East African Chronicle* 136
*East African Standard* 124
East Asian origins 121
East European nations 10
'economic competitors, undesirable' 145
economic position of Indians 160
Edison, Thomas 88
education 11, 44, 167, 170, 182, 183, 227
  in Natal 171, 187–90, 192
  and Sastri 23, 25, 29, 36, 39, 44, 58
*Education of the South African Native* 192
*Education Review, The* 23
Egypt 40
Eliot, Charles 125
elites 33, 227
Ellis, A.D. 109
emigrate, forced to 195–6
  *see also* assisted emigration
emotional restraint 20
*Empire* 49
Empire Exhibition 146, 148, 149
Empire Parliamentary Dinner 78
employment 109, 113, 125, 137, 145, 166, 195, 196
English language 8, 9, 22, 91, 110, 121
enlightenment 25
equality 43, 71, 111, 120, 130, 137, 139, 142, 232
equality and justice 73, 78, 109, 184, 185
Essex Hall, London 56
ethnic caricatures 3
eugenicism 11
Evans, Morgan 207
*Evening Star* 111
eviction from cities 189
evolution and race 41
extremists 34, 35, 43, 48

### F

Fabian Society 153, 154
failure 214
families 158, 200, 202
famine relief 29
Far-Eastern Question 94
Feetham, Richard 181

feudal class 126
fire 102, 207
fiscal control 58
fiscal liberty 48
Fisher, H.A.L. 103
'fitness to rule' 44, 45
Five Powers Treaty 93–5
Flag Bill 203
forceful registration 200
foreign policy 52
Foucault, Michel 7
Four Powers Treaty 94
fragmentation 154
France 3, 67, 88, 90, 92, 93
franchise 43, 108, 116, 119, 130, 138, 144, 171, 219
fraudulent certificates/entry 197–8, 200
Freedom of the City of Edinburgh 220
Freedom of the City of London 79
freehold grants 126
free passage 168
Free Press 198
friendships 23, 181
Friends of Freedom for India (FFI) 100
funds, raising 29, 188

## G

gagging order 115
Gale, Edmund Waller 3
game-hunting 126
Gandhi, M. 14, 23, 49, 60, 121, 136, 177, 201, 225
  and Cape Town Agreement 173
  imprisoned/released 106, 153
  non-cooperation movement 4, 54, 67, 68, 102, 154
  philosophy of 32–4, 62, 100
  support of Sastri 119, 209, 233–4
Gandhi, Manilal 212
Gandhi-Smuts agreement 166, 196, 200, 201
Gayadeen, Haridas 101
Geddes, Auckland 101
Geneva 80
Gentlemen's Agreements 11
Germany 38, 39, 92, 93, 94
  Germanic Africa 61, 81, 125, 128
Ghadar Party 115
*Ghadrites* 38
'Ghetto Act' 234
Ghose, Aurobindo 27, 28, 30, 34
Ghose, Salindranath 100–1
Gokhale, Gopal Krishna 24–6, 27, 28, 30, 31, 50
Gong, Gerrit 170
Gordon, Corrie 189
Gorman, Daniel 10

Gouin, Lomer 117
Government of India Bill 1919 56, 58–9
Grand Hotel, Pretoria 180
Grant, Madison 11
Greaves, Robert 155
Greco-Turkish War 2, 3
Greece 3
Grigg, Edward 70, 138, 219
Gujranwala 54
Gupta, Krishna 55
Gupte, D. 55

## H

Habermas, Jurgen 225
Habibullah, M. 13, 162, 169, 172, 191, 201, 202, 210
Haldane, Richard 73, 154
Hancock, Keith 144
Harding, Warren G. 85, 88
Hardinge, Lord 136, 147
Harris, John 140
*Hartals* 147
health 24
health/illness 155, 163, 167, 210
Hearst, William 94
Hertzog, J.B.M. 158, 166, 168, 204, 206, 207, 212
  and the Balfour Declaration 165
Hilton Young Commission 217–18
Hindu 20, 22, 38
*Hindu, The* 22, 38, 49, 51, 198
Hindu-Muslim bitterness 21, 28, 211
*Hindustan* 29, 49, 68
*Hitaeveda* 29
Hitler, Adolf 11
Hofmeyr, Jan 206
Hollander, F.C. 189
Holy Places 4
Home Rule Movement 34, 39, 46
'honorary white' 14
House of Lords 51, 53
housing 170, 171, 182
Hughes, Charles Evans 90–3
Hughes, William 70, 75, 76, 77, 110, 112–14
Hunter Committee 67
Hussain, Syed 79, 100
hut and poll tax 137
Huxley, Elspeth 125

## I

Ilbert Bill 1884 134
illegal immigrants 201, 202
Imam, Syed Hasan 52
immigration 109, 120, 132, 138, 144, 145, 197, 200
  and Crown Colonies 139

# INDEX

to South Africa 62, 76, 132
Imperial British East Africa Company (IBEIC) 124
Imperial Conferences 6, 64, 68, 70–9, 146, 148–9
'Imperial Envoy' 119
Imperial Legislative Council 29
Imperial War Conference 62
indentured labour 61, 188
independence 139, 221
*Independent* 79
India 5, 12–16, 43, 83, 174
  education in 44–5
  independence 221, 226–7
  Indian National Congress 10, 14, 24–6, 34, 35, 43, 59, 153, 221
  rights of Indians abroad 63, 66, 70, 72, 77, 111
  views held of Indians 118, 127–8, 135
  *see also* Agent to South Africa; Kenyan Indians; South African Indians
*India* 29
*India in Transition* 128
*Indian Opinion* 192, 208, 212
*Indian Overseas* 147
*Indian Patriot* 49
*Indian Review, The* 23
*Indian Social Reformer* 120, 212
*Indian Views* 200
India Office 66, 103, 139, 159, 174
*India Review* 6
indigenous peoples 114, 125
individual and community 184
individual conduct 211
Indo-European Association 47, 50
industrial education 192
inequality 148
  *see also* equality
'inferior race' 42
institution-builder 23
intellectuals 23
international actor 98, 120
international conferences 85
international institutions 10
International Missionary Council 140
Ireland 38, 69, 72, 103, 226
  example of 34, 47, 52, 75, 99, 123
'irreducible minimums' 132
Irwin, Lord 13, 161, 162, 173, 175, 192, 210, 217
*Is Japan a Menace to Asia?* 100
Islamization 2
Ismaili community 124
Italy 3, 90, 92, 93
Iyer, V. Krishnaswami 23, 27, 30, 32, 35

## J

Jabavu, John T. 212
Jagadisan, T.N. 16, 221, 233
Jallianwala Bagh 54
Japan 11, 14, 39, 75, 77, 118, 120, 121
  fear of 85, 88, 94, 98, 100, 114
  Five Powers Treaty 90, 91, 95
*Japanese Invasion* 94
Jayakar, M.R. 32
Jeevanjee, Alibhai Mulla 128, 136
Jewish people 4, 105, 191
Jinnah 49, 53, 56–7, 59, 159, 176
Johannesburg 180
Johnston, Harry 125
Jones, H.G. 135, 140
judiciary 156
*Justice* 36
justice, recourse to 53
justice and welfare 41
Justice Party 36, 47, 57, 212

## K

Kajee, A.I. 171
Kamala Lectures 155
Kamat, B.S. 55, 135
Kantian morality 223
Kato, Vice Admiral 92
Kavirondo 139
Kelkar, N.C. 38
Kellogg-Briand Pact 1928 11
Kemal, Mustapha 2
Kennedy, Dane 125
Kenya 6, 12, 105, 123–30, 131, 218
  Kenyan Africans 139
  Kenyan Highlands 130, 132, 133, 144
  Kenyan Indians 11, 14, 136–44, 145–50, 219
  White Paper 144–5
Kerr, Philip 138
Kershaw, Louis 139, 159, 160
*Kesari* 48, 50
*khadi* 154
Khilafat movement 4, 67, 68
Kichlu, Kailas P. 189, 190, 192
Kikuyu 139
Kimberley Conference 199
King, W.L. Mackenzie 115, 118
Klerksdorp 207
Komagata Maru incident 5, 115, 116
Kodanda Rao, P. 16, 165, 176, 214
Koo, Wellington 82
Korea 100
Kunzru, H.N. 37, 55
Kutch, Maharao of 66, 75, 79

## L

labour 116, 120, 125, 137, 166, 188

Labour Party (Australia) 111, 113
Labour Party (UK) 147, 153, 154, 219
Ladner, Leon 117
Lake, Marilyn 108
land given to whites 126
landownership denied 137
Law College 20
*Leader, The* 49, 59, 119, 212
League of Nations 6, 10, 62, 71, 80–3
lectures 183, 208, 220, 221
Lee, Lord 93
legacy 7
Legislative Assembly 36, 37, 67, 132, 147
legislature 46
Leys, Norman 137
Liberal Party (Canada) 117
Liberal Party (India) 14, 106, 147, 149
Liberal Party (UK) 153
liberal politics 9, 24, 49, 60, 206, 223–5, 227
  ideas of liberalism 155–8
  liberal internationalism 10, 12, 231
library building 29
Lidgett, John A. 189, 191
life-threatening situations 101–2, 179, 206–7
Lindsay, Darcy 163
Liquor Bill 1925 203–4
Lloyd George, D. 46, 61, 70, 72, 74, 77, 91–2, 133
London, delegations to 53, 55–60, 65
Loram, Charles 192–3
*Los Angeles Times* 2
Lourenço Marques 179
low-incomes 196
*Lusitania* 93
luxurious living 65–6

## M

MacDonald, Ramsay 142, 153, 154, 219
MacKelvie, John A. 118
Madhava Rao, V.P. 38
Madras 19, 22, 23, 36, 51, 233
*Madras Times, The* 23
*Mahratta* 50
Malan, Daniel F. 158, 166, 168–71, 182, 197, 205
Malaviya, Madan Mohan 51, 53, 59
Malaya 220
*Manchester Guardian* 137, 139, 147, 174
mandates issue 113–14
*Manitoba Free Press* 2, 3
manual labour, dignity of 33
Marxist doctrine 223
massacres 2, 54, 69
Massey, William 70, 75, 77, 110, 114
mass movements 60, 68, 224
Masterton-Smith, James 138

Mayo, Katherine 191
McCormick, Frederick 94
medicinal use of opium 82
Mehta, Pherozeshah 22, 27, 30, 35
Meighen, Arthur 70, 107, 117
*Menace of Japan, The* 94
merchant-politicians 136
Meston, James 56
Meyer, William 42, 63, 80
military considerations 39, 123, 133
Mill, J.S. 224
Milner, Alfred 131, 132
miners, striking 62
mining rights 110
Mitter, Benode 55
'model Indian' 120
moderates 2, 24, 43, 50
*moksha* 25
Montagu, Edwin 4, 6, 63, 105, 106, 128, 131, 132
  and policy in India 45–7
  working with 58–9
Montagu-Chelmsford Reforms *see* Montford reforms
Montford reforms 48–55, 58–60, 130, 153, 177, 212
*Montreal Gazette* 117
Moonje, B.S. 50
Moplah 68, 101
moral high ground 147
moral rights 156
Morison, Theodore 128–30
Morley-Minto Reforms 29
*Morning Post* 47, 51, 146
Motan, Habib 210
*Mother Nation* 191
Mukherji, Sarat 101
Murray, Gilbert 81
Muslims 4, 5, 27, 35, 43, 67, 99
*Must We Fight Japan?* 94

## N

Naidu, Sarojini 39, 176
Nair, T.M. 36, 47
Nairobi 123
Nandi 139
Nandy, Ashis 223
Naoroji, Dadabhai 28
Natal 61, 171, 181, 182, 199
*Natal Advertiser* 207
*Natal Mercury* 189, 203
*Natal Witness* 192
Natarajan, Kalathmika 8
Natesan, G.A. 23
National Conference, Delhi 142
nationalists 105, 106, 110, 119, 130, 137, 139

National Liberal Federation 5, 60
National Party 158, 179, 182, 203
nation building 25
native diplomat 7–8
'native interests,' speaking for 135
naval downsizing 90, 92, 93
negotiation and compromise 49–50, 228, 231
Nehru, Jawaharlal *Autobiography* 119
Nehru, Motilal 119, 159, 221, 226, 227
Neumann, Iver 7
new constitution in Kenya 127
New Guinea 113
*New India* 35, 48, 51
*New Japanese Peril, The* 94
New Zealand 6, 70, 85, 94, 109–14, 113, 119
*New Zealand Herald* 110
Nile 125
Non-Brahmin Movement 36
non-cooperation movement 4, 102, 146, 224
Northey, Edward 126

O

Observatory Hill 175
O'Dwyer, Michael 67
old age pensions 109, 110, 113
Oldham, J.H. 140
Oliver, John 116
Olivier, Sydney 153
*Ons Vaderland* 179
opium trade 80–3
oppression, ruthless 54
  *see also* repressive measures
Orange Free State 61, 181
oratory 8, 29, 36, 56, 78, 99, 103, 121, 227
Osborne, Sidney 94
Ottoman Empire 4
outcastes 57
*Outlook, The* 136
overcrowding 189
Overseas Association 136
ownership restrictions 158
Oxford 4

P

Pacific affairs 85
Pacific Coast of the US 115
Pacific dominions 11
Paddison, G.F. 160, 163
Pal, Bipin Chandra 27, 28
Pandian, M.S.S. 186
*Panjabee* 49
Paranjpe, R.P. 50
parents 19
Paris Peace Conference 52, 75

Parliament Dinner on Kenya 140
Parsi community 102
partition 221, 226
'passenger Indians' 61
*Passing of the Great Race, The* 11
passive resistance 33
pastoral life 192
Patel, M.I. 198
Patel, Vithalbhai 37, 52, 56
peace 6, 10, 11, 97, 221, 233
Pedi 180
Peel, Lord 13, 133, 139, 147
Pentland, Lord 35
people's power 39
perpetual bondage 137
Phelps-Stokes Commission 193
Pim, Howard 213
*Pioneer* 49
Pirow, Oswald 179
Pitkin, Walter 94
plague 29
Plowman, George 188
Polak, H.S.L. 13, 55, 59, 65, 119, 132, 174
Polak, Millie 150
political education 33
political landscape 38
political reforms 5, 36, 39, 47, 67, 106, 219–20
Pope, Joseph 1, 115
popular politics 39, 60, 224
Portugese settlers 123
post-war tensions 121
Prasad, Rajendra 32
'Present Political Situation in India' 79
presidency, dispute over the 29–30
Pretoria 180
*Pretoria News* 213
princely states 13, 35, 38
Prince of Wales Empire Tour 86, 102, 105
Pring, H. 180
prison and prisoners 53, 59, 101, 106, 153, 196
Privy Councillor 8, 105, 146, 177
progressive changes 67
propaganda in England 50–1
public health commission 189
public life, spiritualized 25
public pressure 195
'public school boy's colony' 126
Punjab 54, 59, 64, 67, 99

Q

Queen's Hall 142, 143
Queensland 108
quota systems 138

## R

race and evolution 41, 185, 232
racial discrimination 11, 38, 140, 144, 145, 150, 185, 195
racial equality 1, 6, 8, 48, 74, 75
racial purity 14, 185
racial segregation *see* segregation
racism 2, 61, 78, 108, 227
  and Sastri 193, 209–10, 232
radicals 4, 24, 27, 30, 34, 50, 60, 107, 115
Rai, Lal Lajpat 27, 28, 34, 68
Railway Committee 64
*Ramayana* 221, 234
Ranade, M.G. 25
Ranade Memorial 29
Rao, Ramachandra 49, 55, 57, 59
rational argument 223
Reading, Lord 4, 13, 105, 106, 121, 124, 154
  and the Asiatic Bill (SA) 159, 160
reappraisal of Sastri 163
rebellion 68, 123, 132, 133
reception of Sastri 99, 112, 136, 188
recession 11
Reddi, Kurma Venkata 57, 212
registration certificates 197, 200, 201
Reid, Matthew 164
'religion of whiteness' 108
religious persecution 2
repatriation 73, 124, 158, 160, 161, 166–9, 213
Repington, Charles 90
repressive measures 53, 54, 102, 134, 154, 159
'reserves' 126
resettlement plan 125
'responsible government' 46
retaliation 146–7
*Reuters* 137
revolutionaries 38, 54, 100, 123, 223, 226
Reynolds, Henry 108
Ricketts, Claude Stanley 175, 214
Rift Valley 125
rights 43, 73, 156, 191, 232
*Rights and Duties of Indian Citizens* 155
riots 102
  *see also* rebellion
Ripon, Lord 134
*Rising Tide of Colour, The* 11
rituals, observance of 19
Roberts, Charles 147
Robertson, Benjamin 63
Roos, Tielman 203, 204, 205
Round Table Movement 40, 69, 138
Rowlatt, Sydney 53–5
Roy, P.C. 55
Royal Air Force 62
Royal Commission 177, 178
Russia 4, 94, 226

## S

sacramental bond 40, 130
'sacred union' 11
Sadler, Michael 56
Salem 21–2
Samarth, N.M. 55, 58
Samoa 113
sanitation 171, 183, 189
Sanskrit scriptures 19
*sanyas* 25
Sanyasi, Bhawani Dayal 196
Sapru, Tej Bahadur 13, 52, 63, 138, 147, 148–9
Sarma, B.N. 36, 147
Sarraut, Albert 92
Sarvadhikary, Deva Prasad 159, 160
Sastri
  in Australia and New Zealand 107–14
  in Canada 115–19
  early life, family 19–24, 37, 87, 103, 178, 220, 227
  and the Imperial Conference 64, 68, 71–9
  and Kenyan Indians 136–44, 145–50, 218–19
  and the League of Nations 79–83
  in London 53–9, 219–20
  in Washington 89–94, 95–100
Sastri College, Durban 7, 193–4
Sastri Hall, Annamalai University 7
Satyamurti, S. 38
scholar-statesman 6, 228
Schonken, 204
Schuur, Groote 168
Scott, C.P. 62
Scott, Francis 141
seas, domination of the 39
Sedition Committee 53
segregation 11, 62, 127, 131, 144, 158, 166, 167
Selborne, Lord 56
self-determination 10, 52, 154
self-discipline 25
self-government 35, 41, 46, 52, 69, 127, 131, 139
serfdom 137
*Servants of India* 49, 51
Servants of India Society 24, 25–6, 31–2, 43, 178
Sethna, Phiroze 163, 176
Seton, Malcolm 143
sex 136, 185–6
Shakespeare Hut 79

Shaw, George Bernard 88, 153
Shimla 175
ships 90
shooting, mass 69
Sikhs 3, 5, 116
Simon Commission 205
Sinha, Lord 56, 67, 105, 171
Sircar, Nilratan 155
Sivaswamy Iyer, P. 60
'slaves of the nation' 57
slave trade 125
Smith, Charles 182
Smuts, Jan 16, 61, 142, 144, 205, 206, 234
  and the Bullhoek massacre 69
  and the Imperial Conferences 71, 72, 74–8, 148–9
  and Kenya 134, 143
social causes 228
social Darwinism 125
social life 67, 181
social mobility 14
social rights 191
South Africa 6, 14, 40, 61, 76, 81, 148, 220
  Asiatic Bill 158–65
  Cape Town Agreement 165–70
  'Ghetto Act' 234
  Indian population 111
  and Kenya 126, 143
  South African League 62
  South African Party 182, 213
South African Indians 61, 69, 171, 174, 177, 181–7
  and the Asiatic Bill (SA) 158–65
  and assisted emigration 195–6
  Cape Town Agreement 165–70
  Congress and Federation 159, 197–9, 208, 212
  and education 187–94
South West Africa 61, 81, 114
sovereignty 12, 128, 180, 230
speeches 56, 59, 66–7, 71, 78–9, 82, 115, 145, 155
  in Australia and New Zealand 109–10
  on Kenyan issue 141–2, 149
  in South Africa 183, 185, 202–3, 207
'spinning franchise' 154
Srinivas, M.N. 8
Srinivastra Hall, Chennai 7
SS *Kaiser-e-Hind* 64
SS *Karapura* 165
SS *Karoa* 176, 179, 215
SS *Makura* 115
SS *Manora* 37, 55
SS *Olympic* 85
SS *Ormonde* 108

*Statesman* 49
Steed, William 91
Steiner, F. 94
Stent, Vera 213
Stephens, A.G. 110, 112
Stoddard, Lothrop 11
St Stephen's College, Delhi 149
submarines 92–3
Suez 125
sugar industry 109, 113, 182, 188, 195
Sullivan, Mark 91
'Surat split' 29–30
surveillance 54, 55
*Swadesamitran* 16, 49, 221
'swamping, fear of' 62
Swaraj Party 14
*Swarijists* 153
Sydenham, Lord 47, 49, 51, 56
Sykes, Charles Henry 2
sympathy for Indian rights 108

T

Taft, William 88
Tagore, Rabindranath 210
Tamil Brahmins 14, 16
Tanganyika 62, 114
taxes 97, 99, 137, 190–1
Taylor, A.J.P. 126
teacher training 188, 192–4
teaching 19, 21
Theosophical Society 142, 164, 180
Tilak, Bal Gangadhar 24, 28, 30, 37, 38, 48, 56, 60
  exiled 31, 34
*Times, The* 77, 82, 91, 135
*Times of India, The* 49, 124, 147
torture 101
Toynbee, Arthur 40
trade and traders 95, 120, 124, 145, 158, 161, 166
trade licensing 62, 204
transnational white solidarity 230
Transvaal 61, 62, 181, 195, 196, 204
Transvaal Indian Association (TBIA) 198, 199
Treaty of Sevres 4
*Tribune* 49, 52
Triplicane Co-operative Society 24
Triplicane Literary Society 23
Turkey 2, 4, 5, 67, 99
Tyson, John 175, 178, 193–4, 203, 214, 215

U

Ugandan Railway 124, 125
Union of South Africa *see* South Africa
United Nations 234

United States of America 11, 12, 39, 52, 88, 93, 103
universal equality 78
University of Leeds 56
Unknown Soldier, The (Washington) 88–9
upliftment 25, 167, 169–71, 181–2, 209, 213, 220

**V**

Valangaiman 19
*Vancouver Sun* 116–17
Varma, B.S. 136
Venn, Harry N. 179
Viceroy, the 143, 147, 160, 164, 175, 214, 219
Viceroys Executive Council 48, 56, 65, 67, 219
*Victoria Daily Times* 1
Vijayaraghavachari, C. 21–2, 36, 49
violence 68, 102, 154, 224, 226
Virjee, Hussinbhai S 136
voluntary repatriation *see* repatriation
voting 156

**W**

Wacha, Dinshaw 49, 50, 174
wages 220
waiters 203
Wales 62
war committees 221
war veterans, votes for 116
Washington Conference 6, 85, 89–94, 95–100
Washington Four Powers' Treaty 15
*Washington Times, The* 88
Watson, Gordon 190, 192, 193
Webb, Sidney 153
Wedderburn, William 35

Wedgwood, Josiah 147
welfare functions 167, 170, 183
Wells, H.G. 88, 97
West African colonies 128
*West Australian* 110
Western Australia 108
'western standard of life' 167, 169–70, 171
Wheatley, Philip 123, 124
White Paper, Kenya 144–5, 147, 150
white people 11, 40, 74, 120, 140, 218, 230
and the British Commonwealth 69
in Kenya 123, 124, 125, 127, 132, 133, 139
white dominions 12, 42, 76, 110–16, 136, 166
whiteness and civilization 108, 170
white supremacists 115, 135, 142, 158
Wigram, Colonel K. 85
Wilson, Woodrow 10, 12, 52, 88, 219
Wilson Harris, H. 82
Wilson's Fourteen Points 100
Winterton, Lord 139, 143, 147
Wood, Edward *see* Irwin, Lord
Wood, Lord 133
Wood-Winterton Agreement 133–4, 136
working-class settlers 126, 137
world economy 11
world peace *see* peace; sugar industry
World War I 6, 10, 38, 43, 61, 127, 128
contribution to 39, 54, 109, 114, 128, 141, 149
World War II 226
writings 221

**Y**

YMCA London 79
*Young India* 63, 174

www.ingramcontent.com/pod-product-compliance
Lightning Source LLC
Chambersburg PA
CBHW071150070526
44584CB00019B/2735